Human Dignity in Contemporary Ethics

HUMAN DIGNITY IN CONTEMPORARY ETHICS

David G. Kirchhoffer

<teneo> //press
AMHERST, NEW YORK

Copyright 2013 David G. Kirchhoffer

All rights reserved
Printed in the United States of America

No part of this publication may be reproduced, stored in or introduced into a retrieval system, or transmitted, in any form, or by any means (electronic, mechanical, photocopying, recording, or otherwise), without the prior permission of the publisher.

Requests for permission should be directed to:
permissions@teneopress.com, or mailed to:
Teneo Press
100 Corporate Parkway, Suite 128
Amherst, NY 14226

This book has been registered with Library of Congress

ISBN 978-1-934844-96-0 (alk. paper)

For my parents, Joan and Nesbitt

Table of Contents

List of Tables ix

List of Figures xi

Foreword xiii

Preface xv

Acknowledgements xxi

Introduction 1

Chapter 1: Questioning Dignity 47

Chapter 2: Questioning 'Questioning Dignity' 123

Chapter 3: The Component Dimensions of Human Dignity Model 205

Chapter 4: A Descriptive Category and a Normative Criterion 255

Chapter 5: God and Human Dignity 295

Chapter 6: Conclusion 309

Bibliography 323

Index 351

LIST OF TABLES

Table 1: The component dimensions of human dignity model 3

Table 2: The component dimensions of human dignity model 208

List of Figures

Figure 1: Time and the moral event 13

Figure 2: Time and the human person's desire for dignity as self-worth 14

Foreword

Human dignity is a key concept in both secular and theological ethics. But, all too often, its meaning is taken for granted. Hence the necessity of a critical reflection on its meaning and status.

In this most insightful book, David Kirchhoffer asks how is it possible to use human dignity as a normative criterion, when one knows, from empirical research, that there is no such thing as the 'fact' of an inherent and inviolable dignity of the human person, and when one also knows that references to dignity are often an ideological disguise of a much less beautiful reality? This question could have resulted in a unilateral hermeneutics of suspicion. Yet, despite his critical a priori, the author succeeds in avoiding such an ideological pitfall by way of criticizing the methodological assumptions that underpin recent calls for the dismissal of the concept of dignity. This leads to an alternative and positive approach, in which the author proposes a multidimensional understanding of human dignity.

Balancing between deconstruction and reconstruction, Kirchhoffer offers an original and gripping reassessment of the concept of human dignity as a non-univocal and multi-dimensional concept that cannot be reduced to any single characteristic of humanness such as autonomy, moral goodness or biological life. Moreover, he distinguishes important fields of meaning: on the one hand, the tension between realised and not yet realised dignity (the tension between the already and not yet) and, on the other hand, four component dimensions of dignity—existential, cognitive-affective, behavioural and social.

In a chapter that can be considered a masterpiece of fundamental ethical reasoning, Kirchhoffer addresses the necessary tension between the descriptive and the normative aspects of human dignity in light of two cases taken from the work of James Gilligan and Ronald Dworkin. This is followed by a chapter in which the four component dimensions of human dignity serve as a framework for reassessing the meaning of "being created in the image of God." The book ends with a concise concluding chapter in which Kirchhoffer revisits the main criticisms levelled at the problematic contemporary use of the concept of human dignity, a reflection in which he introduces nuances leading to the conclusion that it remains meaningful to refer to human dignity.

This book is written with a great sense of nuance and the reasoning is averse to oversimplification and univocity, always taking into account the tension and paradoxes inherent in the concept of human dignity. The whole is extraordinarily consistent, insightful and lucid.

This work offers a way out of the impasse created by the hermeneutics of suspicion vis-à-vis human dignity. Conscious of the uncritical use of the concept, Kirchhoffer succeeds in articulating the possibilities of again giving meaning to human dignity beyond the suspicion. With this book, he urges moral theologians and moral philosophers alike to make a more nuanced use of the concept of human dignity and in so doing has enriched, up-dated and made more precise the framework of interpretation proposed by Louis Janssens. He has, thus, shown himself to be both an eminent representative and critic of the Louvain personalist school.

Johan Verstraeten

Preface

On March 7, 2009, the body of Father Lionel Sham was found dumped in a field on the outskirts of Johannesburg. Father Sham was 66. He was known for his generosity, and, indeed, as someone who embodied the spirit of Christian love. He had spent much of his life as a Roman Catholic priest in the Archdiocese of Johannesburg working with troubled youth. But on this occasion, his concern for the welfare of such young people would be his undoing. He opened his door to his alleged killers, whom he apparently knew.

Father Sham was someone who believed in the goodness of every person, the worthiness of every person, the dignity of every person. He lived out this belief in acts of kindness, love, and concern for others. He died for this belief, and because of it.

The idea of the dignity of the human person is enshrined in numerous documents, including the South African Constitution. Section 10 of its Bill of Rights states, "Everyone has inherent dignity and the right to have their dignity respected and protected." And yet, when faced with tragedies like the murder of Father Sham, tragedies that take place on a daily basis all over the world, when people like Father Sham are murdered while still believing in the inherent dignity of every human being, should this not give us cause to question what this dignity is that our constitutions protect? What does the concept of human dignity mean, and what are its implications for our ethical discourse and for our moral behaviour? As Arthur Chaskalson, Chief Justice of South Africa from 2001to 2005, asks, "Why do [these things] continue to happen, if respect for human dignity is indeed a universal social good?"[1] If the meaning of the dignity of the human person is ambiguous, then can we continue to use the term as a foundational concept in ethical discourse, or does it spell "The End of 'Human Dignity' in Ethics?"[2]

It was with such questions in mind that I began the research that led to this book. I was suspicious of the concept of human dignity and the way that it is being used in contemporary ethical discourse. I discovered that I was not alone in this regard. Several authors have recently raised questions as to the efficacy of human dignity as an ethical concept. The power of suspicion is precisely that it leads one to ask important questions. Suspicion alone, however, may not always provide meaningful answers. Thus, though born of suspicion, this book ultimately defends the concept of human dignity against the dismissal that such suspicion at first seems to suggest.

I aim to show that human dignity is still a meaningful ethical concept. Indeed, I maintain that it is so meaningful that it can help us to unravel and make sense of events like the murder of Father Sham. Human dignity, in other words, is an ethical concept that, properly understood, can help us to take seriously the existential meaning of behaviour across the moral spectrum, from the violence of the killer, to the generosity and self-sacrificing love of his victim.

I shall demonstrate that the concept of human dignity is best understood as a multidimensional concept that addresses various aspects of the human person him- or herself. It is a concept that should not be reduced to one or other feature of human beings, such as autonomy, moral goodness, or biological life; instead it should take all of these and more into account.

When human dignity is understood this way, then it serves an important descriptive function in ethics, i.e., it can help us to explain and understand why particular moral problems are moral problems, and why a person may have chosen to pursue a particular course of moral behaviour. Furthermore, I will show that a proper, multidimensional understanding of the concept of human dignity is also valuable for morally evaluating such behaviour. Thus, human dignity, properly understood, helps not only to understand human moral behaviour, but also to critique such behaviour.

The book begins with an extended introduction in which the primary thesis and associated research claim are explained in some detail. Key terms are also defined. The introduction ends with a description of the overall methodological approach, which combines a hermeneutic of suspicion with a hermeneutic of generosity. This is followed by five chapters and a sixth concluding chapter that demonstrate the validity of the research claim.

In the first chapter, the aforementioned suspicion regarding the value of the concept of human dignity is taken seriously. The chapter lays out the criticisms of the concept of human dignity to which the research claim is a response.

The second chapter reconsiders the first. It acknowledges that there are problems with the way in which the concept of human dignity is sometimes used in contemporary discourse. Nevertheless, it argues that this should not necessarily lead to the conclusion that the concept is useless and should be discarded. The chapter criticises the underlying methodological assumptions that underpin both such a dismissal and the problematic usage of the concept of human dignity identified in the first chapter. In light of these methodological criticisms, I put forward alternative assumptions that can serve as the basis for a multidimensional understanding of human dignity that is indeed useful for contemporary ethics and that overcomes the criticisms levelled in Chapter 1.

The third chapter works out a multidimensional understanding of the concept of human dignity, based on the alternative assumptions detailed in the previous chapter. This multidimensional understanding is illustrated in the form of a model: the Component Dimensions of Human Dignity model. The idea is that the model itself can serve as a useful hermeneutical tool when discussing issues of human dignity in ethics.

The fourth chapter considers two case studies to demonstrate how a proper multidimensional understanding of human dignity, exemplified in the aforementioned model, is useful both in describing what and why people do what they do, and in morally evaluating their decisions and behaviour.

The fifth chapter turns to the question of human dignity and God. My aim is to develop an understanding of human dignity that is useful to both believers and non-believers alike. Nevertheless, because of the important role that the concept of human dignity has also come to play in Roman Catholic theological ethics, especially since the Second Vatican Council, this chapter shows that the multidimensional understanding of human dignity developed in this book can still be reconciled with religious faith and the idea that human beings are created in the image of God, though such a belief is neither necessary for, nor constitutive of human dignity.

The final chapter revisits the criticisms highlighted in the first chapter and, by way of conclusion, summarises how the research undertaken and the model developed offer a meaningful response to these criticisms such that human dignity is indeed a valuable concept for contemporary ethics.

In the end, I hope to show how the concept of human dignity, properly understood, can help us to see that people like Father Sham do not live and die in vain.

Endnotes

1. Chaskalson, "Human Dignity as a Constitutional Value," 137.
2. Wils, "The End of 'Human Dignity' in Ethics?," 39–54.

Acknowledgements

As with any work of this kind, there are a large number of people deserving of my thanks.

Professor Edith Raidt, the first president of St Augustine College of South Africa, played a significant role at a key moment in my life in encouraging me to pursue an academic career. It was in part due to her sage advice that I decided to read for a master's degree at St Augustine's.

At St Augustine's, Jan Jans was instrumental in concretising my interest in ethics, and Gerard Walmsley sparked my interest in human dignity in his excellent course on the subject. It was in Professor Walmsley's course that many of the questions addressed in the present book first began to take shape.

Special thanks must go to Johan Verstraeten for his comments, guidance and support for this project. He was one of the people who first inspired me to pursue postgraduate studies at the Katholieke Universiteit Leuven.

My thanks also go to Joseph Selling, Didier Pollefeyt, Jan Jans, Stephen J. Pope, and Ellen Van Stichel, for the time they invested in reading my work and in offering critical feedback. Without them, this work would not have been what it is today.

This research would not have been possible without the financial assistance provided by the Faculty of Theology of the Katholieke Universiteit Leuven. I thank those involved in approving this financial assistance.

I would also like to thank my many friends, colleagues and teachers at the Faculty of Theology in Leuven who not only played an important role in helping me to form some of the ideas presented in this book, or helped me to overcome those moments when one feels well and truly stuck, but who also contributed to my formation as an ethicist and as a human being. One of the great privileges of studying at a faculty like Leuven is that one is exposed to so many people from different backgrounds. I am wiser and better for it.

Many of my colleagues at the Australian Catholic University have been very inspiring in seeing this work through to publication, in particular Ormond Rush and Anthony Kelly.

Thanks must go to my family for encouraging me to pursue a doctorate in Europe and a career in Australia. Leaving South Africa was a difficult decision to make at a difficult time for our family. They have been unwavering in their support.

Finally, I have read many acknowledgements and prefaces where people thank their spouses. I confess that I have often thought it sounded a bit trite. That was until I was the one trying to finish a book. Katrin, you have done so much, above and beyond what any self-respecting husband could reasonably expect. I started listing all the things you have done and the ways you have supported me over the years, but it began to get embarrassing. On more than one occasion you restored my faith in myself. But more importantly, you have restored my faith in human dignity. Thank you, for everything.

Human Dignity in Contemporary Ethics

INTRODUCTION

In recent years, questions have been raised about the concept of the dignity of the human person, with some authors concluding that human dignity is variously vacuous, useless and stupid.[1] Such conclusions may seem harsh, but the critiques that they are based on are not without merit. They force us to ask whether we may now be facing "The End of 'Human Dignity' in Ethics?"[2]

That said, however, in this book, while taking the critiques levelled at the concept of human dignity seriously, I shall seek to defend an alternative conclusion. In other words, instead of dismissing human dignity as vacuous, I shall seek to make a case for why the concept of human dignity remains valuable to ethics.

I shall primarily do so by critiquing the underlying assumptions of the critique of the concept of human dignity, particularly with regard to its hermeneutical approach, and its understandings of ethics, the human person, and the moral event. I shall then offer alternative, and arguably better, assumptions upon which a proper understanding of human dignity can be based, an understanding that is indeed of value to contemporary ethics.

This introduction presents the primary thesis regarding the value of the concept of human dignity for ethics, followed by a broader research claim and accompanying definition of terms. Thereafter, I explain the methodological approach employed in this book to substantiate this thesis and provide an overview of the structure.

Primary Thesis

In this book, I aim to defend the following thesis regarding the concept of human dignity: the dignity of the human person is a valuable, multidimensional concept for contemporary ethical discourse, because, properly understood, it can serve both as a descriptive category and a normative criterion. The concept, thus, provides the basis for a framework that can help to both understand and evaluate human moral behaviour.

This primary thesis is, of course, thick with terms that require further explanation, both in order for the thesis to become clearer, and to substantiate it over against claims that the concept of human dignity should be dismissed as a concept of any value for ethics today. Hence, in what follows, I shall elaborate on this primary thesis and provide working definitions of key terms.

Research Claim and Working Definitions of Key Terms

In order to clarify what the primary thesis mentioned above entails and to provide a more detailed picture of the research claim that I intend to defend, it is worth elaborating on key terms at the outset.

I have chosen to combine an explication of the research claim with the provision of working definitions of key terms. In other words, key terms will be given working definitions as and when they are used in the articulation of the research claim. The research claim is itself an elaboration of the primary thesis.

Since it is this research claim, and hence, the primary thesis, that I intend to substantiate in the subsequent chapters of this book, extensive explanation and argumentation to support the claim and its associated working definitions (with some exceptions) do not appear in this introduction. Such detail is left for the relevant chapter of the book. For the benefit of the reader, cross-references to the relevant chapter or section have been given where appropriate.

Because this section aims to articulate a research claim, the working definitions given below are not presented in alphabetical order, but instead in an order that follows a logical sequence in relation to the claim that this book intends to make. Capitalised First Letters are used for technical terms that are relevant to the Component Dimensions of Human Dignity model presented in Table 1. Needless to say, terms may unavoidably be used early on that may only be clarified later in the description that follows.

Before proceeding, however, an important point of clarification is necessary. In this book, no distinction will be made between the notions of 'human dignity' and the 'dignity of the human person.' The terms will thus be used interchangeably.[3]

Table 1. The component dimensions of human dignity model.

Component Dimension	Complementary Duality	
	Already	Not Yet
Existential	Have (Potential)	Acquire (Fulfilment)
Cognitive-Affective	Inherent Worth	Self-Worth
Behavioural	Moral Good	Morally Good
Social	Others' Dignity	My Dignity

The Word 'Moral' and the Moral Event
In this book, the word 'moral' is *not* meant to imply that a course of action *is* good or right, as is implied when immoral (morally bad) is contrasted with moral (morally good).[4] 'Moral' in this book is meant to describe a type of human behaviour, as well as the elements that constitute such behaviour, about which a judgement can be made regarding goodness or badness, rightness or wrongness.[5]

Such moral behaviour is found in multidimensional moral events (see 2.1.3.4 and 2.3.2.2), which occur over time and comprise, among other things, intentions, physical actions, and circumstances, all of which, as constitutive of a moral event are typically open to moral evaluation as good and bad (usually with reference to intentions), and right and wrong (usually with reference to a course of action).[6] Note that this also means that I make a distinction between acts and moral behaviour. When referring to moral behaviour I am referring to all that takes place within a moral event, i.e., the act, as well as, the reasoning behind the act, and the circumstances surrounding it. Hence, moral acts may be right or wrong, but moral behaviour, whilst containing moral acts, is, properly speaking, good or bad.

Moreover, these evaluations can be made by the actor, and hence constitute subjective moral justifications for particular behaviours, or by third parties, e.g. a court of law, which evaluate the moral legitimacy of the actor's own moral justifications usually in light of existing, supposedly objective[7] moral norms, of which laws are an example. These two levels of evaluation are important and will be described in more detail below with regard to descriptive and normative ethics. Thus, an intention can be morally good, or morally bad; an act can be morally right or morally wrong.

Note, 'good', 'bad', etc. are qualified in the previous sentence with 'morally' to emphasise that it is with reference to *moral* evaluation. 'Good', for example, can also be used in a pre-moral or even non-moral sense. Understanding these senses will help to understand what is meant in this book by 'moral'.[8] A knife is a *non*-moral good, because it can be used to bring about other good ends, like cutting up food for ease of cooking and consumption.[9] Damaging the physical integrity of another person's body is a *pre*-moral evil or pre-moral disvalue, because, among other things, it causes pain.[10] A knife (a non-moral good) can also be used to damage the physical integrity (a pre-moral evil) of another person, and depending on the intention and circumstances surrounding this physical damage one can make a moral evaluation of the moral goodness of the event as a whole.

If the knife (non-moral good) is being used by a doctor to amputate (pre-moral evil) a gangrenous leg (non-moral evil), then the event, as far as one can tell from the information provided, is morally good, and it is likely that the doctor, the patient, and most reasonable third-parties would see it this way.[11] In part, this assessment of the event as morally good, is because the doctor aims through his action to achieve a moral good, i.e., to save the life of a dying patient (the other important part is that he does so in a morally right way). The life of the patient is a pre-moral good in se. The patient's life becomes a moral good when it becomes the end of the doctor's moral reflection and behaviour. Unlike non-moral good and pre-moral good, the term moral good refers to goods, i.e., desired ends, which are "conformable to reason regulating free acts.... The useful [e.g. being alive] and pleasurable [e.g. being healthy], when they are embraced by the will according to the right order of things, and in a manner worthy of man, share in the nobility of moral good."[12] A moral good, then, is anything toward which moral behaviour is directed as an end and which contributes to or is a necessary condition for the human person's striving to live a good, meaningful life as a free, yet always related historical subject.[13]

Returning to the example: if the knife, however, is used by a person who intends to take money that does not rightfully belong to him by stabbing to death the person to whom the money in question currently belongs, then the event would most probably be evaluated as morally bad, and the killing as morally wrong, even though, subjectively, the attacker might *mistakenly* claim that he believes it was the right thing to do because the money (itself a non-moral good) rightfully belonged to him. The knife, however, is obviously neither morally good nor morally bad. It is a non-moral good. Similarly, without taking the other factors of the moral event into account, the physical change caused by the knife's cutting into flesh is only ever a pre-moral evil or disvalue.

Hence, when the primary thesis states that the concept of human dignity "provides the basis for a framework that can help to both understand and evaluate human moral behaviour," it means behaviour, freely performed by human beings, comprising various elements—e.g., intention, action, circumstances—, that is open to evaluation as morally good or bad, morally right or wrong.

Different forms of ethical reasoning, broadly grouped into deontological ethics (which tends to focus on "duty, law and obligation") and teleological ethics (which tends to focus on "ends or goals to be attained"),[14] place different emphases on the various dimensions of the moral event (actions in the case of the former; intentions or consequences in the case of the latter), sometimes to the detriment of other dimensions, in order to evaluate moral goodness and badness, rightness and wrongness. For the moment, it is not necessary to go into the pros and cons of deontological versus teleological ethics. What is important for the time being, is that the term 'moral' is used in this book to describe multidimensional, time-bound events—comprising intentions, actions, and circumstances—that involve judgements of right and wrong, good and bad.

The Vital Importance of the Distinction between a Descriptive Category and a Normative Criterion

Ethics, as a discipline having to do with the study of human moral beliefs, codes, and behaviour, can be descriptive and/or normative.[15]

Descriptive ethics describes what human beings do when they engage in moral behaviour, and why they engage in that moral behaviour. It describes the *operational* norms, justifications, reasoning, causes, and goals of human moral behaviour, at the level of both the individual and the society in which the individual is situated. Descriptive ethics *does not*, however, *evaluate* whether these operational norms, etc. are morally good or bad, or whether the resulting behaviour is morally right or wrong. It is more concerned with what the actors and their respective societies *believe* is morally good or bad, morally right or wrong. It is interested in describing what they *believe* in moral terms and how this affects their moral life. Thus, though descriptive ethics is concerned with how people *believe* they ought to behave, and in this sense describes *operational* moral norms, it says nothing about how they really *ought* to think and behave, i.e. about what moral norms they really *ought* to follow, or what moral goods they really *ought* to strive for, or what kind of moral person they really *ought* to seek to become. The latter is the job of normative ethics proper.[16]

Normative ethics addresses how people ought to behave. Normative ethics, in contrast to descriptive ethics, is concerned with 'as-objective-as-possible' argumentation and criteria that can be used to evaluate human moral behaviour as morally right or wrong, good or bad.[17] So, whereas descriptive ethics may describe the *operational* moral norm involved in a particular moral event, normative ethics seeks to evaluate not only the rightness or wrongness of the action, or the goodness or badness of the intention, but the objective legitimacy of the moral norm itself.

Consider a rather simplistic example that may help to illustrate the difference between descriptive and normative ethics, particularly with regard to their respective treatment of moral norms. A captured soldier tells his enemy where the soldier's comrades are hiding. Descriptive ethics wants to find out *why* he chose to tell the enemy the truth instead of concealing it or telling a falsehood. Upon inquiry, a descriptive-ethical analysis may conclude that the soldier told the truth because he *believed* it is always wrong to lie and that lying entails not telling the truth. Normative ethics on the other hand is more interested in whether the norm that it is always wrong to not tell the truth is in fact a legitimate norm, and whether therefore the consequent behaviour was in fact the right behaviour. If, for example, normative ethics were to show that it is *not* always wrong to intentionally conceal the truth, especially when the lives of one's comrades are jeopardised by such an action, then it might also conclude that the soldier was morally wrong to tell the truth in this case (even though he believed he was morally right, and his intentions may have been morally good). Descriptive ethics cannot make the latter judgement.

In light of this distinction between descriptive ethics and normative ethics, I have chosen to distinguish between the two functions that a proper, multidimensional understanding of human dignity serves, first, as a descriptive category and, second, as a normative criterion.

I have chosen to speak of a descriptive category to emphasise the exploratory or explanatory nature of the concept of human dignity. In other words, as a descriptive category, the concept of human dignity helps one to describe what people do, and to understand why they are doing it. Thus, one can ask three questions when considering the descriptive dimensions of a moral event: What is this person's *operative* understanding of the concept of human dignity? What are the social influences, mores, and circumstances that may have contributed to this understanding of human dignity? And how does this person's operative understanding of human dignity affect and provide subjective justification for the moral choices he or she makes, and the behavioural strategies he or she undertakes?

A normative criterion, on the other hand, helps one to evaluate the extent to which a person's moral behaviour is morally right or wrong, and his or her intentions are morally good or bad. Thus, to speak of human dignity as a normative criterion is to speak of its ability to help one to make moral evaluations of others' behaviour or to make moral decisions regarding one's own moral choices. Hence, here one can likewise ask three questions: Is this person's (or indeed one's own) operative understanding of the concept of human dignity a *proper* understanding, especially insofar as it constitutes a moral good and therefore an intended end of the person's moral behaviour? Are the social influences, mores, and circumstances that may have contributed to this understanding of human dignity, and are the person's interpretations of these mores, etc., legitimate and correct, or should they be called into question? And are the moral choices and behavioural strategies that this person's particular understanding of human dignity inspires morally right or wrong?

In order to avoid any misunderstandings, it is of vital importance that this distinction between the concept of human dignity's role as a descriptive category and as a normative criterion be understood. For example, consider the following quote, which records the justification offered by a violent criminal for his repeated physical attacks on fellow prisoners:

> Pride. Dignity. Self-esteem. And I'll kill every mother-fucker in that cell block if I have to in order to get it! My life ain't worth nothin' if I take somebody disrespectin' me and callin' me punk asshole faggot and goin' 'Ha! Ha!' at me. Life ain't worth livin' if there ain't nothin' worth dyin' for. If you ain't got pride, you got nothin'. That's all you got! I've already got my pride.[18]

I maintain that the *descriptive* properties of a proper understanding of human dignity help us to understand *why* this man has chosen to violently attack other people, even at the risk of his own life. That said, however, the description of the moral event, of the man's perceived understanding of the concept of dignity, of the social influences that support his understanding, and of his use of human dignity as a normative criterion to justify his violent behaviour as 'morally good and right', should in no way be taken as objective approval of the man's behaviour or of his understanding of the concept of human dignity. It is purely descriptive (describing both the behaviour and the moral norms that he believes justify his behaviour and make it morally right), and therefore in no way evaluative. Thus, though a proper understanding of human dignity, when used as a descriptive category, can help us describe the man's normative use of his particular understanding of human dignity, it in no way condones this use or his understanding. It can neither condone nor condemn, because it is descriptive.

In order to *evaluate* his understanding of human dignity and the moral behaviour that it inspires, we need to turn to the *normative* dimension inherent to the proper understanding of human dignity that this book is proposing. When using a proper understanding of human dignity as a normative criterion, we can assess the extent to which a person's understanding of human dignity adequately takes into account the multidimensionality inherent in a proper understanding of the concept, and whether his or her understanding and the actions it inspires adequately considers the dignity of others. This will become clearer as we proceed to further elaborate the research claim. I return to the example of the violent man to demonstrate how a proper understanding of human dignity can function as both a descriptive category and a normative criterion in Chapter 4.

I have already said that whether one uses the term 'human dignity' or 'dignity of the human person', both require an adequate anthropology. By definition, the concept of human dignity needs to take the human person adequately into account. Hence, I provide a brief working definition of the human person as understood in this book with regard to the primary thesis it seeks to defend.

The Human Person and the Desire for Dignity
Human persons, properly understood, are multidimensional. They are conscious subjects, capable of making and acting upon autonomous decisions; at the same time, through their corporeality, human beings are intimately connected to the physical world, other human subjects, and the institutions that result from this connectedness (see 2.3.2.1 for an elaboration of this anthropology).[19] This connectedness, thus, also places limits on the powers and autonomy of the human person, as well as influences how this person conceives him or herself, others, and the world, over time. The influence of relationships, and the fact that a person and their relationships change over time, means that the human person is also a *historical* being.

As conscious subjects in relationship, situated in, and subject to the passage of time, *human persons are meaning seeking and meaning giving entities*. They seek meaning and purpose in their lives in the midst of their relationships and in the face of the inevitable end of their present existence that the passage of time implies. I equate this seeking of meaning with a desire for a sense of self-worth, a desire for a sense of a life well lived (see 2.3.2.1.1). In addition, I shall demonstrate that a proper understanding of human dignity contains an element that equates dignity with a sense of self-worth. Hence, the desire for a sense of self-worth, can also be expressed as a Desire for Dignity.

Nevertheless, the historicity of the person means that how an individual person fills in this *idea* of the self-worth they seek, what for them constitutes a meaningful life, a life well lived, a life of dignity, will depend on the influences they encounter in the relationships in which they are situated and how they respond to these influences and encounters.

The term 'desire' describes the human person's directedness towards goods. Human beings share first-order desires in common with other animals, like food, sex, sleep, and so on. One might also call these first-order desires, 'needs'. When I use the word desire, I am referring not to these basic 'needs', but to so-called second-order desires. Human persons are capable of second-order desire, i.e., they are able to formulate desires about who they want to be, and what sorts of desires they want to have. These second-order desires could therefore be described as existentially significant since they help the person to order the other first-order desires, or needs, to the realisation of his or her second-order desires.[20] The desire for self-worth and the desire for dignity are second-order desires. Human persons are thus always drawn on by their desire for a sense of self-worth, their desire for dignity; this desire drives the way that a person engages in and with the relationships she finds herself in.

The person's historicity, the constant confrontation with other understandings of what a worthy understanding of self-worth should be, and the inevitability of the person's own death, mean that the desire for a sense of self-worth is never fully satisfied. Moreover, I shall argue, that since a *proper* normative understanding of self-worth requires working for the good of the dignity of others, and since the dignity of others is likely to always be under threat, so too finally attaining a complete, immutable and inviolable sense of self-worth is unlikely.

Thus, at a *descriptive* level, we could say that all human beings desire a sense of self-worth, and we can describe what *they believe* is the normative ideal to which they need to aspire in order to possess this sense of self-worth. At the same time, however, we can evaluate this description based on the normative understanding of self-worth that this book proposes in light of a *proper* understanding of the dignity of the human person; namely, true self-worth is the product of working for the moral good of the dignity of others.

Already and Not Yet
Time is a common factor in both the moral event and an adequate understanding of the human person. In the moral event, the person starts with an idea of what they desire, the moral good they seek to pursue; considers the various ways in which to attain that good; chooses a course of action that will lead to the attainment of that good; proceeds to perform the action; and, if everything goes according to plan, attains that good. All the way along, from beginning to end, circumstances play a role, in defining the good they seek, in the deliberation of the appropriate means, in the effective or ineffective performance of the action, and indeed even in the ultimate enjoyment of the good attained. For example, by the time the good is attained, the circumstances may have changed, making the good superfluous or at least insufficient.

In the working definition of the human person given above, a person's whole life can be seen as a moral event. She begins with a desire for a sense of self-worth, for the moral good of acquired dignity, i.e. a sense of self-worth. The very fact that she can desire this points to inherent capacities that will make it possible for her to pursue it, capacities of reason, free choice, and action, to name a few. The capacities combine to constitute an inherent dignity, i.e. a given potential that is a moral good in its own right, for to undermine this is to undermine any good there may be in pursuing self-worth.[21] Through formative experiences in her relationships with the world, other people, and institutions, and indeed the march of time itself, she will develop an idea of what this self-worth should look like; who, in other words, she wants to become. As a rule, in her mind, the person that she wants to become is a 'morally good' person to the extent that she believes it conforms to some or other moral norms (the mores of her society). Note, again, this is descriptive; it may not mean that her idea of the 'morally good' person is in fact morally good at an objective, normative level. She then considers and chooses behavioural strategies to that end. In order to become the idealised 'morally good' person, which will give her the sense of self-worth she desires, she must engage in 'morally good' behaviour. She must, in other words, be able to justify her behaviour as 'morally good'. Otherwise, she jeopardises her desired concept of self-worth. In the end, she has to be able to hold her head up high and *believe* that she did the right thing. At a descriptive level, these strategies, thus, always constitute moral behaviour, because they are always aimed at a moral good: her *idea of* self-worth, of a meaningful life. She engages in the behaviour, and moves, as a result, closer to or further from her desired goal, a goal which, as already pointed out, she is unlikely to ever fully attain. As in the case of the moral event, circumstances are ever present in the form of the relationships she is embedded in. Below, I have provided diagrams, first of the moral event (figure 1), and then of the life of the human person (figure 2), to show how *structurally* similar they are, and to show that in both cases, time is ever present.

Figure 1. Time and the moral event.

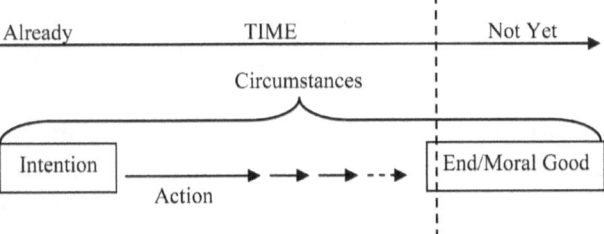

Figure 2. Time and the human person's desire for dignity as self-worth.

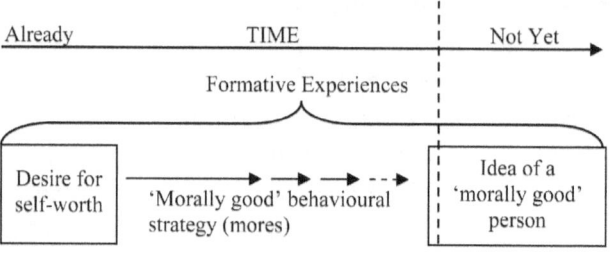

One way of explaining this 'time' component, and its relationship to the moral good of *acquired dignity,* i.e., a sense of self-worth, is to use the notion of the Already and the Not Yet. This notion of the Already and the Not Yet is borrowed from theology, but in the course of this book, I shall demonstrate that it can be applied to the concept of human dignity with or without theological overtones. The important thing about the Already and the Not Yet, in this book, is that it is a single concept, i.e., something is *both* Already *and* Not Yet. [22]

In the diagram of the moral event (figure 1), one sees how the moral event is Already *and* Not Yet. There is *already* an intention, formed in circumstances that are *already* present, to achieve an end that is *not yet* realised. There is always an aspect of the end that is never fully realised (the dotted line) and hence remains '*not yet*', perhaps because circumstances change, or because the planned actions don't go according to plan, or perhaps even because the only way to achieve the end is to engage in behaviours that are not ideally suited to the end because they oblige one to engage in so-called 'pre-moral evil' (for example, actions with double effect).[23] This is illustrated by the dashed 'action' arrows that never quite reach the desired end.

Likewise, in the diagram of the human person's life as a pursuit of the moral good of dignity as a sense of self-worth, the Not Yet is always present by virtue of its absence. As I shall demonstrate, when we use a *proper understanding of human dignity* as a *normative criterion*, then, the fullness of one's dignity as self-worth can only be attained if and when everyone can attain the same fullness, can live with the same dignity. Only if one acts for the moral good of both one's own dignity and the dignity of others, can one truly be considered morally good, and hence have a truly positive self-image. Since we live in a world in which that has never been the case, and is certainly still *not yet* the case, it is true to say that the Not Yet, is always present (see 3.4.5).

Therefore, since the notion of the Already and the Not Yet is integral to both the moral event and the human person's moral life, I argue that, since the concept of human dignity addresses both the moral event and the human person, this notion of the Already and the Not Yet is what holds the various dimensions of human dignity together to form a single, multi-dimensional framework that can serve both a descriptive and a normative function in ethics (see 3.4.1).

Moreover, *the Not Yet* pole, hints at the unattainability of the fullness of the 'ought', of the fullness of the normative ideal of human dignity that we *should* aspire to. This is a result of human limitation that is a consequence of the connectedness and historicity of the individual. This means that the Not Yet pole of human dignity functions as a sort of eschatological proviso (see 2.3.3), that is, as a warning against and critique of moral hubris (moralism, see below). The eschatological proviso is a concept also borrowed from theology. In theological use it means, "All forms of human, Christian, churchly effort, stand under the eschatological proviso. They are not the Kingdom of God; they point to it and are motivated by the idea of the Kingdom of God."[24] The eschatological proviso thus critiques any human ideology that claims to be, and embody, the ultimate salvation of humankind. So too, all human pursuit of the ideal of human dignity stands under an eschatological proviso. Human beings have *not yet* achieved the fullness of their dignity, but all their strategies to achieve it, however flawed, point to it, and are motivated by the idea of human dignity, especially insofar at this idea captures the existential desire for the satisfaction of a meaningful life well lived. Yet, no human strategy, be it individual or political, ecclesial or secular, no sets of rights or codes of ethics, can claim to be the absolute, final way to guarantee the fullness of dignity for all. Broad strokes are certainly possible, but the more one drills down into the details, the more one will encounter minor flaws, and 'necessary evils'. Hence, these strategies are always open to, and indeed require, criticism. Nevertheless, they all continue to try to realise the fullness of a proper understanding of human dignity in the world, just as each human being continues to desire the intangible end of their own dignity as a realised sense of self-worth born of morally good behaviour towards others and their dignity.

Moralism (see 2.2.1) is what happens when we do not heed the eschatological proviso, when we are certain that we are right and good and they are wrong and evil. It is a form of moral absolutism that classifies the other as bad or mad before first trying to understand the other as a human person in his or her quest for human dignity, however inappropriate the chosen actions, or his or her understanding of human dignity, may be. To put it in rather trite terms, instead of hating the sin and loving the sinner, moralism hates the sin *and* the sinner.[25] Moralism is a product of an overemphasis on normative ethics to the detriment of descriptive ethics. This can lead to hubris that makes one blind to the inadequacies or inappropriateness of one's own moral behaviour. Moralism makes us blind to the human person, and to the fact that we as human persons are similar in such a fundamental way that we can claim to share in a universal human dignity.

Thus, this book argues that a proper understanding of human dignity, by virtue of the property of the Already and the Not Yet, acts as a correction to any kind of moralism. As a descriptive criterion it enables us first to see and to understand how a person can believe they are acting in a 'morally good' way, even if in fact they are not. Moreover, as a normative criterion, all our own actions, intentions, strategies, and ideas of human dignity and self-worth are constantly critiqued. We have no right to genuine moral pride until we can secure it for everyone, and that, as we have seen, is Not Yet the case. And finally, instead of trying to address the problems of moralism by simply dismissing moral language altogether, the book seeks to retrieve the correct use of moral language in an effort to understand and then evaluate, where possible offering correctives to moral behaviour.

Having briefly considered and offered 'working definitions' for concepts key to the primary thesis that this book intends to defend—among which are: moral, moral event, moral good, moral behaviour, ethics, descriptive ethics, normative ethics, a descriptive category, a normative criterion, the human person, self-worth, desire, the Already and the Not Yet, the eschatological proviso, and moralism—I turn to the multi-dimensional model that this book proposes as a helpful framework within which to properly understand the concept of human dignity.

THE COMPONENT DIMENSIONS OF HUMAN DIGNITY MODEL

In this book, I argue that one of the major problems evident in the arguments of those who criticise the concept of human dignity, and who would like to see it dismissed, is that their understanding of human dignity, or the kind of definition they think human dignity should have, is one-dimensional. Moreover, they tend to emphasise human dignity's purported role as a normative criterion without taking any descriptive properties it may have into account.[26] Their criticism is not invalid, since, as we shall see, human dignity is often used this way, and often seems to be reduced to one or other feature of what it means to be human, e.g., autonomy or biological life. I shall argue, however, that therein lies the flaw that opens the way to those who would challenge the value of the concept of human dignity: the idea that human dignity must be *either* this, *or* that. I shall argue, instead, that like the human person and the moral event to which the concept of human dignity is intimately bound, human dignity is best understood as a multidimensional concept, such that it is not 'either… or' but rather 'both…and'. So, human dignity is Already *and* Not Yet, autonomy *and* life, normative *and* descriptive, and so on. A proper understanding of the dignity of the human person must itself be multidimensional if it is to adequately address the human person that it describes.[27]

Therefore, taking the distinctions between a descriptive category and a normative criterion into account, as well as the multidimensionality of the human person and the moral event, a proper understanding of the dignity of the human person says something about what human persons are, what they are capable of, what they most desire and both how they do (descriptive) and how they ought (normative) to behave in the pursuit of those desires.

A proper understanding of the concept of human dignity is captured in the Component Dimensions of Human Dignity model, which will be elaborated on in detail in Chapter 3. For now, I present a concise overview of the model here so that one can see how what has been discussed so far fits into the thesis regarding the proper understanding of the concept of human dignity that this book intends to demonstrate. The model itself is one of the major outputs of the present research.

In this book, I shall argue that the concept of human dignity can be understood in light of four Component Dimensions of being human. They are 'component' because they are fundamental to the greater meaning of the term dignity of the human person. If the dignity of the human person were bread, then these would be the flour, water and yeast. They are 'dimensions' because they are inadequate on their own. They are aspects of the whole—the dignity of the human person. We eat bread, not flour or yeast.[28]

Furthermore, I have said that each Component Dimension is best understood along the axis of the Already and the Not Yet. In an effort to systematise this, I propose that each Component Dimension is constituted by a Complementary Duality. They are 'dualities' because they represent two poles, i.e., the 'Already and the Not Yet.' They are 'complementary' because both poles are necessary to the proper meaning of each Component Dimension of dignity. One pole of the Complementary Duality is something that is already accomplished; it is a universal objective reality; it is something that *is*. The other pole is still to be accomplished; it requires further action; it is something that should *become*. The example of an apple will illustrate what this means. A complementary duality of an apple is 'seed and tree.' An apple already has a seed. The seed is an objective reality, something that is. An apple can become a tree although it is not yet a tree. This duality is complementary in the sense that an apple is only a seed because it has the potential to become a tree and an apple is only a tree when it has fulfilled the potential in the seed.[29]

The Existential Component Dimension: the Dignity We Have and the Dignity We Acquire

The Existential Component Dimension deals with human existence. It is the most abstract of the Component Dimensions in that it deals with the issue of what constitutes a human person per se. Nevertheless, despite its abstract quality it is grounded in the concrete human experience of being both a reflective, thinking subject and a corporeal being, dependent on and active in a material universe.

The Existential Component Dimension of dignity comprises the Complementary Duality of 'Having Dignity and Acquiring Dignity.' On the one hand, dignity is a given, a universal reality already possessed by all human persons. On the other, dignity is something that can be both lost and acquired.

The dignity we already have is inherent in every human person. Every person has a worth, equal to the worth of every other human person, that rests in his or her *existential potential* to live a reflective, meaningful, morally good life in and through the relationships that the person is embedded in, and encounters in various ways, throughout his or her life. This is possible because human persons have certain capacities—to experience, to reflect on that experience, and to act on the judgements that proceed from this reflection, in an historical social context. Note, however, that the dignity we have is not because of these capacities per se, but rather because of what these capacities imply it is possible for us to become. Moreover, the fact that human persons are meaning-seeking and meaning-giving beings means that there is an existential drive to fulfil this potential and become 'dignified'.

The dignity we acquire is what we become when we fulfil the potential in our capacities. Because we can never fully exhaust that potential, and because our historicity places limits on the degree to which we can live up to that potential, the fullness of acquired dignity always remains Not Yet. The historicity of the human person means, moreover, that this acquired dignity, unlike the dignity we always already have, can be lost or damaged depending on how one lives one's life.[30]

This Existential Component Dimension raises the question of how one turns the dignity one has (the potential) into acquired dignity (the fulfilment). There are three facets to the answer, each constituted by the three remaining Component Dimensions.

The Cognitive-Affective Component Dimension: Inherent Worth and Self-Worth

Having dealt briefly with the Existential Component Dimension, the remaining Component Dimensions tease out various aspects of the corporeal subjectivity captured by the Existential Component Dimension. Thus, the second Component Dimension is the Cognitive-Affective Component Dimension, which reflects the human capacities of reason and emotion, to think creatively, and to form ideas and feelings about oneself, others, and how others think or feel about one. Human beings are thinking, self-conscious beings, and it is this capacity that enables them to act morally and reflect on the meaning and purpose of their existence in the first place. Moreover, they not only need to *think* they have meaning, they need to *feel* like they have meaning. Hence I speak of a Cognitive-Affective Component Dimension: feelings and ideas are both ways in which human beings experience and reflect on their existence.[31]

The Cognitive-Affective Component Dimension is constituted by the Complementary Duality of 'Inherent Worth and Self-Worth.' The pole of Inherent Worth emphasises that all human persons already have a dignity founded upon their uniquely human potential to live a meaningful, (emotionally and cognitively) reflective life in pursuit of the fulfilment of their dignity and the dignity of others. This inherent worth makes a moral claim on society to provide the basic freedoms and goods necessary for the fulfilment of one's dignity. However, affirming the dignity of the human person in an abstract way means very little if people do not concretely experience this dignity.

Contemporary English associates dignity with self-worth, self-respect and pride.[32] Therefore, the pole of Self-Worth refers to the process of becoming cognisant of and fulfilling one's human potential, one's inherent dignity, such that one experiences a sense of one's own value, worth, ability, meaning, and purpose as a human person, i.e., one's acquired dignity. Note that precisely how one conceives of the ideal of self-worth, and what strategies one engages in to develop and bolster one's desired image of oneself will be strongly influenced by one's historicity, the relationships and formative experiences one has, and the mores (moral norms) of one's society and culture. We do not all, in other words, want to become the same person, or even the same type of person. We *do*, however, all want to be able to feel good about the person we are becoming, or have become. The fact that different people may have different ideas of what constitutes a dignified life may lead to conflict with those who disagree. Nevertheless, though they may question the Acquired Dignity of the other, they may never question the Inherent Worth of the other, as this is based in a potential that they all, always, share.[33]

The Behavioural Component Dimension: Moral Good and Morally Good

The Behavioural Component Dimension addresses human behaviour in the world, and the observation that human beings act (a feature of their corporeality), and justify their actions (a feature of their subjectivity), according to societal mores and moral norms. It comprises the Complementary Duality of 'The Moral Good of Human Dignity and The Dignity of the Morally Good.'

The first element of this Complementary Duality underlines that the dignity of the human person[34] is a moral good, i.e., an end in itself,[35] insofar as it is a good end of human moral behaviour (N.B., behaviour is used here as an umbrella term for what occurs in a moral event, that is, it includes the action and the reasoning behind that action). It has been shown, however, in the section defining the Already and the Not Yet, that this notion of the moral good of dignity has a *double* meaning in that it refers both to the dignity we have as inherent worth and to the dignity we acquire in the form of a sense of self-worth.

People generally praise what they believe to be morally good behaviour. Those who engage in such behaviour are similarly praised for being morally good.[36] This brings us to the second element, the Dignity of the Morally Good. Engaging in morally good behaviour and being deemed morally good confers worthiness and esteem, and thus dignity, on the actor. People who are deemed morally good by virtue of their moral behaviour thus acquire dignity over and above that which they inherently have as a human person.

Of course, precisely what counts as morally good behaviour is subject to the social mores and moral norms of a person's culture, and the way in which a person uses his or her given capacities to comply with or rebel against these mores and norms.[37] This in turn will affect the idea of who he or she has to become in order to feel a sense of self-worth. The desired image will be of a person respected for behaving in a particular way according to some agreed moral standard. Thus, dignity is acquired, in the context of a person's relationships, by engaging in what he or she, and others presumably, believe to be 'morally good' behaviour (I put 'morally good' in inverted commas here to illustrate that it may only be thought or believed to be, or represented as, morally good behaviour. This may still be shown to be morally bad or wrong in light of the normative aspects of a proper understanding of human dignity. See the Social Component Dimension below).[38]

The fact that people may engage in different supposedly or subjectively 'morally good' strategies in the pursuit of a sense of self-worth that will be based on the approval they believe they will deserve for their 'morally good' behaviour, means that there is a high degree of variation in how people pursue the fulfilment of their dignity. Some might argue that this necessarily leads to moral relativism, since each actor is operating according to the relative mores and norms of his or her society. Hence, some may argue that no objective ethical discussion of the behaviour is possible beyond a descriptive ethics. The only norms that are relevant are those of the society in which the person lives. I disagree with this position. Although I will accept, and even argue for, a 'relativity' in morally good strategies to fulfil the desire for dignity as self-worth, this does not imply that relativism has to be accepted. Objective normative ethical assessment of a person's idea of who he or she should become in order to have a sense of self-worth, and how he or she should behave, is made possible by the fourth and final component dimension, which allows for relativity, i.e., variations dependent on one's historicity and one's idea of dignity as self-worth, in moral behaviour but critiques the extremes of relativism on the one hand and of moralism on the other.[39]

The Social Component Dimension: Others' Dignity and My Dignity

The Social Component Dimension makes it clear that every individual is inextricably bound-up in the fortunes of others who affect (corporeality) and are affected by the individual (subjectivity) in each of the three aforementioned facets of human existence and experience. It comprises the Complementary Duality of 'Others' Dignity and My Dignity.'

The first pole, Others' Dignity, refers to the dignity of all people, oneself included. This inherent worth, which is associated with the potential to acquire dignity through one's behaviour, implies therefore that all people seek to fulfil this potential by attempting to acquire some form of dignity as self-worth for themselves through engaging in what they believe to be 'morally good' behaviour. Moreover, this first pole emphasises the fact that the inherent dignity that all human persons already have is a moral good.

The second pole, My Dignity, refers to the ideal form of acquired dignity, i.e., to the perfect fulfilment of a person's inherent potential. This is where a proper understanding of human dignity draws its strength from as a normative ethical criterion. This pole captures the 'should', the 'ought', in our ethical discourse: one's own acquisition of dignity *should* not infringe upon the *inherent* dignity of others—i.e., others' potential to lead meaningful, fully human lives—and where possible should facilitate the actualisation of others' *acquired* dignity—i.e., the realisation of the true self-worth associated with leading such a meaningful, fully human life in and through one's relationships. If one denies *others'* dignity, then one cannot truly fulfil the dignity one has by acquiring a genuinely *good* and true sense of self-worth. Since both the dignity we *have* and the dignity we *acquire* are moral goods, one cannot acquire true self-worth if the acquisition of that self-worth is based on a behavioural strategy that diminishes or attacks the inherent worth of others (i.e. prevents others from acquiring dignity); that would entail engaging in morally bad behaviour. And since it is the morally good who acquire dignity, morally bad behaviour cannot be reconciled with a true sense of self-worth. Hence, at an objective normative level, such behavioural strategies, and the ideas of self-worth that inspire such strategies, are not worthy of respect and, therefore, cannot be the basis of a properly *good* sense of self-worth, i.e. a true fulfilment of one's own dignity as a human person. Ultimately, one has only truly fulfilled one's potential, one has only truly acquired dignity, when the dignity of others is not only abstractly affirmed by society but is also concretely experienced as self-worth by all. Of course, this is obviously not yet the case. This means that even moral goodness is insufficient for the full acquisition of human dignity and that even the best examples among us can only ever approximate the ideal (Cf. eschatological proviso above).[40]

To conclude this section, one can summarise what the Component Dimensions of Human Dignity model says as follows.

According to this model, at an existential level all human persons Already *have* dignity because they are human persons, i.e., because they all have certain inherent capacities that constitute a potential to live a meaningful, reflective, and morally good life. The most notable, though not the only, capacities that can be associated with human dignity include the abilities to reason, and to freely act in one's society in a responsible way.[41] Each person, however, in their historical situatedness, will seek to answer the irresistible drive to realise this potential by *acquiring dignity* in a unique manner.

The dignity that human beings seek to acquire is a consequence of, and therefore the fulfilment of, their potential. Their capacities mean that they can become aware of their *inherent worth*. To become aware of one's inherent worth means that a person now has a sense of *self-worth*, i.e., a conscious appreciation of his or her own value in relation to the world in which he or she lives. A person will seek to enhance this sense of *self-worth* through his or her behaviour in society, since life without a sense of self-worth is meaningless and the person will despair.

The person pursues this sense of self-worth through engaging in what she believes to be *morally good* behaviour. Since a society usually honours those who behave in what that society holds to be a *morally good* way, such behaviour is likely to enhance the person's sense of self-worth. This provides the first sense in which human dignity is a *moral good*: the enhancement of a person's sense of self-worth is among the legitimate, though not necessarily always conscious, ends to which his or her '*morally good' behaviour* is directed. In other words, the fulfilment of his or her own dignity is an end in itself.

However, human dignity is also a *moral good* in the sense that, by virtue of their *inherent worth*, all human beings are legitimate ends of moral behaviour. This *inherent worth* means that all people *already* have dignity by virtue of their potential, regardless of whether this potential has been developed in any way (*Others' Dignity*). Nevertheless, all of these others likewise aspire to achieving a sense of self-worth. Thus on a social level, and human beings are inherently social beings, I can never truly fulfil *my dignity* until all others have been able to fulfil their dignity. Thus dignity is a *moral good*, since I can only truly acquire the moral good of *my dignity* by working for the *moral good* of *others' dignity*. And we clearly live in a world in which this is *not yet* the case.[42] In Chapter 4, I consider two case studies to demonstrate the descriptive and normative properties of this model.

METHODOLOGICAL APPROACH AND STRUCTURE

Thus far in this introduction, I have articulated a primary thesis, and elaborated on this primary thesis by way of a more detailed research claim and accompanying definitions of key terms including the proposed Component Dimensions of Human Dignity model. In this section, I outline an important methodological assumption that is crucial to the approach I intend to take in making a case to support the research claim. Then, in light of the methodological approach and the research claim it is intended to support, I provide an overview of the remainder of this book.

Methodological Approach

The overarching methodology that this book uses is designed to be a response to the exaggerated use of a hermeneutic of suspicion that underlies the critique of dignity, and more especially the conclusion that the concept of human dignity should be discarded from ethics (see Chapter 1 with regard to this critique and Chapter 2 with regard to its methodological assumptions).

Introduction

Hermeneutics refers either to the philosophical discipline of the study of interpretation or to a particular way of interpreting, especially with regard to the reading of texts.[43] In general the term will be used in this book in the latter sense, i.e., to refer to particular ways of interpreting. So, for example a feminist hermeneutic involves reading and interpreting texts, for example, the Bible, from the perspective of, or through the lens of, the experience of being a woman in a patriarchal society. Note, then, that since hermeneutics is about interpretation, it is also about meaning, i.e., how people interpret meaning and what they find meaningful.

The overarching methodology employed in this book is founded on the idea that while a hermeneutic of suspicion can be extremely valuable in questioning the assumptions and pointing out the problems that underlie a construct, a hermeneutic of suspicion is less helpful in constructing arguments in favour of a particular idea or construct. In other words, one needs a hermeneutic of suspicion to deconstruct ideas and reveal 'false consciousness', but one also needs an alternative hermeneutic that can make sense of the findings of that suspicion in a constructive way.[44]

Therefore, in conjunction with a hermeneutic of suspicion (Chapter 1), I have opted to use a hermeneutic of generosity (Chapter 3). The terms hermeneutic of suspicion and hermeneutic of generosity warrant further elaboration.

They are used here based upon the understanding of these terms offered by Margaret R. Miles.[45] Miles is a historical theologian, and in an article titled "Hermeneutics of Generosity and Suspicion" draws on her experience of teaching hermeneutics to doctoral students at the Harvard Divinity School. Miles grapples with the challenges faced by offering theological education in a pluralist context, a context in which the students are no longer just white, middle-class males. How should texts and theological discourse be approached in this context?

Miles argues that these "new people" automatically approach texts with a hermeneutic of suspicion[46] that questions the assumptions, hidden biases and prejudices, and the historical context and motivations of the authors they are reading. It is a way of interpreting that seeks, according to philosopher Paul Ricœur, to demystify, to reduce illusion, to "purify discourse of its excrescences, liquidate the idols, go from drunkenness to sobriety, realize our state of poverty once and for all."[47] It is typical of what philosopher Hans-Georg Gadamer characterises as the Enlightenment's "prejudice against prejudice" in pursuit of so-called objective truth.[48] According to Miles, the "new people" engage a hermeneutic of suspicion because they do not immediately identify with the assumptions, biases, etc., coming themselves from very different contexts with very different experiences, often of exclusion by the likes of the authors.[49]

In addressing this problem, Miles identifies *two* types of a hermeneutic of generosity. The first is one that tries to avoid these 'suspicious' questions by appealing to the readers to transcend these problems and only deal with the ideas presented. In other words, it is an appeal to the reader, the interpreter, to renounce her particularity and her interests. In the words of Paul Ricœur, the reader is asked to "participate in the belief in the reality of the … object, but in a neutralized mode; [to] believe with the believer … ."[50] If we were to apply this to the critique on dignity that I shall outline in Chapter 1, it would be equivalent to ignoring the critique and arguing instead for a particular understanding of human dignity based on some or other criterion.[51] For example, the Judeo-Christian idea that human beings have dignity because they are made in the image of God has been criticised because it makes the notion of human dignity inaccessible to non-believers; human dignity is reduced to a matter of faith.[52] The first type of hermeneutic of generosity would ask non-believers to acknowledge that believers' internal argumentation—tradition, reason, faith, and so on—is sound, and so non-believers should just accept that, for believers at least, human dignity is true. This is clearly not a suitable alternative in light of the job that the concept of human dignity is typically asked to do, namely, to function as a normative criterion by which human moral behaviour can be evaluated.[53] To do this, the concept of human dignity has to be based on an argument that can be universally understood and accepted.

Introduction

The second understanding of a hermeneutic of generosity, which is the one that Miles advocates as the solution to the challenges posed by the hermeneutic of suspicion, is one that flows from, rather than counter to, the hermeneutic of suspicion. This means that the 'suspicious' questions allow one to uncover the authors' biases and one's own, such that one can 'generously' approach the text with an understanding of where the author was coming from and why he or she wrote the text in the first place, and how one's own biases play a role in one's interpretation. One is now able to approach the text with 'objectivity', treating the ideas present with a far richer and more qualified rationality.[54] It is this latter understanding of a hermeneutic of generosity that will be applied in this research.

Moreover, I shall use the notion of a hermeneutic to generosity to underscore the idea that an adequate hermeneutical approach cannot be purely 'destructive' but must also be 'reconstructive'. Suspicion alone runs the risk of stopping at destructive reductionism.[55] The result may be a complete loss of meaning. If meaning is to be retained, and I shall argue that such meaning is existentially vital to human life,[56] then a reconstructive hermeneutic is necessary.[57] I maintain that the hermeneutic of generosity captures this reconstructive ideal. To illustrate this, I refer here to Boston College teacher of theological method, Lucretia B. Yaghjian,[58] who, following Miles, summarises the two terms as follows: "A hermeneutic of generosity walks with the theological tradition, accepts it on its own terms, but asks it to account for itself in terms of an accepted theological norm. A hermeneutic of suspicion questions the theological tradition, does not accept it on its own terms, and provides its own norms for the critique of the tradition." Yaghjian has applied this very specifically to theology. For the purposes of this research I would like to rephrase her definition.

The critique in Chapter 1 applies a hermeneutic of suspicion to the concept of human dignity by asking it to account for itself over against external criteria. The norms applied are the norms of law, science, and sociology. Moreover, with Miles, one could say that the critics are like the "new people" she mentions. They look upon the concept of human dignity with suspicion because they themselves do not identify with those who use it to underpin their arguments. Cognitive scientist and critic of the concept of human dignity Steven Pinker, for example, describes the concept of human dignity as "conservative bioethics' latest, most dangerous ploy."[59] His description testifies to his status as a 'new person': he is suspicious of the concept of human dignity because he disagrees with the alleged agenda of those who use it (i.e., so-called "conservative" bioethicists). Nevertheless, the criticisms must be taken seriously, because these "new people" also have to see the value of the concept if the concept of human dignity is going to be of any use. Moreover, the criticisms may indeed reveal an illegitimate use of the concept of human dignity to conceal ideology.

What the critics have not done, however, at least not adequately, is applied a hermeneutic of generosity that asks the concept of human dignity to account for itself using accepted criteria from its own tradition. This can be seen in two ways. First, as I shall argue in Chapter 2, the critiques rely on reductionist views of ethics, the human person, and the moral event. The hermeneutic of generosity that I shall apply will take more holistic views of ethics, the human person, and the moral event into account. Second, and this is important with regard to the idea of hermeneutical ethics (which I also elaborate on in Chapter 2, section 2.3.1), and to the thesis that human dignity can also serve as a descriptive category, the critiques are unable to see how certain conceptions of human dignity can be meaningful for particular persons in particular historical circumstances. Whether these people have a correct understanding of human dignity is only part of the question. First, one must ask what their understanding of human dignity is and why it is meaningful. Then, one can begin to explore whether this understanding of human dignity and the moral behaviour that it inspires is indeed adequate.

This understanding of a hermeneutic of generosity resonates with Gadamer's understanding of the hermeneutical circle. For Gadamer, hermeneutics is not simply about uncovering the biases of others, but also, and very importantly, uncovering one's own biases. Only by uncovering one's own biases is one able to understand the deeper meanings that underlie the other's biases and so move closer to *the* meaning: "... every revision of the fore-projection is capable of projecting before itself a new projection of meaning; rival projects can emerge side by side until it becomes clearer what the unity of meaning is; interpretation begins with fore-conceptions that are replaced by more suitable ones. This constant process of new projection constitutes the movement of understanding and interpretation."[60] The hermeneutic of generosity that I apply here involves precisely the projection of a "new projection of meaning," (the Component Dimensions of Human Dignity model, Chapter 3) following on from a revision of the 'fore-projections' inherent in both the critique and many of the perspectives it criticises, in an attempt to replace this with more suitable 'fore-conceptions' (Chapter 2) that can move us closer to the "unity of meaning".

In summary then, this book takes the critiques seriously, but intends to show that their hermeneutic of suspicion, while helpful in highlighting challenges to the efficacy of the concept of human dignity for ethical discourse, is on its own, inadequate. The inadequacy stems from an unwillingness to adopt a hermeneutic of generosity, which would solve some of the problems with the assumptions upon which the critique's use of the hermeneutic of suspicion rests, particularly its reductionist views of ethics as a legalist *techne* (2.1.1), the human person as one or other feature instead of a complex, multidimensional whole (2.1.3.3), and morality as right and wrong acts (2.1.3.4). The hermeneutics of generosity that I shall apply, then, shall take the building blocks of the critique and reconstruct them according to criteria internal to the concept of human dignity, namely a hermeneutical ethics (2.3.1), the human person adequately considered (2.3.2.1), and the complex layers of the moral event (2.3.2.2).[61]

Structure
This book intends to deepen our understanding of the concept of the dignity of the human person and its relation to human moral behaviour.

In this introduction, I have outlined a research claim that proposes a way of thinking about the concept of human dignity that should enable us to account for, and where necessary overcome, several problems that contemporary critiques have raised with regard to the concept of human dignity. At the methodological core of this claim is the argument that, since we are also concerned with how human dignity is related to human moral behaviour, a proper understanding of human dignity must be founded upon adequate understandings of ethics, the human person, and moral behaviour.

I shall argue that our understanding of these three concepts has a particularly strong influence on our understanding of human dignity in that they constitute assumptions that affect our methodological approach to the problems that the critiques of human dignity raise. In other words, part of the solution to overcoming the critiques is to criticise the methodological assumptions of the critiques themselves, which are a product of the critics' understandings of the concepts of 'ethics', 'human', and 'moral behaviour'.

In what follows, I provide an overview of the chapters of this book, each of which constitutes an important building block in the case being made in support of the primary thesis and research claim.

In order to make such a case, however, it is necessary to first take a step back, and seriously consider the challenges that the concept of human dignity faces at present. Therefore, in Chapter 1 we shall consider the challenges that the concept of human dignity faces in contemporary ethical discourse. By way of introduction, I list them here. I shall demonstrate how these critiques come about in Chapter 1.

- The concept of human dignity has fallen prey to a 'dignity talk' in which its use has become clichéd and it is often only polemically appealed to as an apparently self-evident, argument winning criterion.
- Key international and national documents claim that all human persons have dignity and that this dignity is inviolable. Yet this

universal dignity, and its alleged inviolability, is not always evident in the particular experience of individuals in a world where innocent suffering is rife.

- The concept of human dignity seems sometimes to be used as the basis or ground for human rights, such that human beings have rights or should be good to one another because they already have dignity. At other times human dignity seems to be the goal or end of human rights and morally good behaviour, such that people have a 'right to dignity'. This appears to be a circular argument.

- There is no such thing as human dignity, and when this concept is used in ethical discourse, people actually mean something else, for example, respect for human autonomy, or respect for human biological life.

- Human dignity has become strongly associated with Judeo-Christian ethics. Non-believers have become suspicious of the use of the term by Jewish and Christian ethicists because they sometimes seem to use it in a manner that seems to have more to do with respecting God than with respecting the human person. Moreover, the traditional Judeo-Christian approach of basing the idea of human dignity on the belief that human beings are created in the image of God raises questions for the non-believer who could then argue that, since he or she does not believe in God, why should they believe in human dignity.

- Finally, the aforementioned problems seem to point to a significant degree of confusion about and even vacuity in the concept of human dignity, such that it is not really up to the task of being the kind of rigorous normative criterion that one would expect from something enshrined in international human rights declarations and national constitutions.

These are the challenges that the proper understanding of human dignity proposed in this book will have to account for, and provide a meaningful answer to.

Chapter 2, in line with the methodological approach outlined above, will take an even further step back, so to speak, by looking at the underlying assumptions that lead to the problems encountered in contemporary understandings of dignity (Chapter 1). Hence, Chapter 2 constitutes a 'critique of the critique'. I shall argue that part of the problem stems from the critics' underlying hermeneutic of suspicion, as well as their presuppositions regarding ethics, the human person, and moral behaviour. This 'critique of the critique' arises from the realisation that there are three possible responses to the initial critique in Chapter 1: (1) Agree and dismiss the concept of human dignity; (2) Pick one of the positions, e.g. that human dignity really is based on the fact that we are created in the image of God and that this makes human biological life inviolable; (3) Take the criticisms seriously and search for the truth in all of them so that a better understanding of human dignity, which can indeed serve the purposes required of it in ethics, and which moves towards the "unity of meaning",[62] can be constructed. I have opted to do the latter in this book and the reasons for this will be developed in Chapter 2. The 'critique of the critique' that I shall conduct there will demonstrate that the criticisms in Chapter 1 are valid insofar as they are based on certain assumptions, for example that they rely heavily on a hermeneutic of suspicion, but that these assumptions are themselves only partially true. I shall develop alternative assumptions which will form the methodological justification for the approach I have chosen to take to the challenges faced by the concept of human dignity, i.e., option (3). Key to this, will be the idea that by approaching the problem of human dignity with a hermeneutic of generosity, we can use the building blocks that the deconstruction of the concept of human dignity by the hermeneutic of suspicion leaves us with, to reconstruct a more comprehensive and useful understanding of human dignity.

In Chapter 3, based on the alternative methodological assumptions developed in Chapter 2, and taking the criticisms of Chapter 1 into account, I shall construct the Component Dimensions of Human Dignity model mentioned earlier. To do this, I shall 're-read' Chapter 1 with a hermeneutic of generosity—i.e., taking the criticisms seriously, I shall nevertheless at the same time overcome them using the same material that was deconstructed by the hermeneutic of suspicion using a 'both…

and' paradigm rather than an 'either...or' paradigm. Having developed the multidimensional Component Dimensions of Dignity model, which constitutes a substantial part of the overall thesis of this research that a proper understanding of human dignity means that it can serve as both a descriptive category and a normative criterion, it remains necessary to demonstrate that such an understanding of human dignity is both valid and useful. In other words, though I will have 'reconstructed' human dignity using the internal categories of the original critique, it will be necessary to also show how this understanding can indeed function as both a descriptive category and a normative criterion.

This will be done in Chapter 4 which will consider two case studies. The first will consider the issue of interpersonal violence and base its analysis on the work of psychiatrist James Gilligan. The second will turn to the issue of end-of-life decisions, and particularly the case of a terminally ill woman who chooses to end her own life with barbiturates prescribed by her doctor. This will be considered in light of the ideas of philosopher Ronald Dworkin.

Chapter 5 then turns to a vital issue for a treatise on human dignity, namely the link between what will have been a 'religion-free' reconstruction of a workable understanding of human dignity that is relevant to all domains of ethics, secular and religious, and the belief in God and the idea that human beings are created in the image of God. The chapter will demonstrate that the Component Dimensions of Human Dignity model is reconcilable with the theological anthropology and understanding of human dignity developed in the Roman Catholic Church's 1965 Pastoral Constitution of the Church in the Modern World, *Gaudium et spes*.[63] This document is chosen because is has proven instrumental in the development of the dignity of the human person as a fundamental moral criterion in contemporary Roman Catholic ethics. Much of the first part of *Gaudium et spes* is dedicated to the subject of the human person and her dignity, with the express intention of using this concept as a means of engaging in ethical dialogue with the non-Roman-Catholic world. I shall show that, contrary to the critique that human dignity has no basis without God, the Roman Catholic Church has developed a complex multidimensional notion of human dignity that can be acceptable to both believers and non-believers alike.

The closing chapter, Chapter 6, will revisit the criticisms highlighted in Chapter 1 and mentioned above, and comment on how the revised methodological assumptions developed in Chapter 2 and the resulting multidimensional understanding of the dignity of the human person developed in Chapter 3—the use of which is demonstrated in Chapter 4—can both take these criticisms into account and offer meaningful solutions to the issues they raise.

Endnotes

1. Respectively, Bagaric and Allan, "The Vacuous Concept of Dignity," 257–270; Macklin, "Dignity is a Useless Concept," 1419–1420; Pinker, "The Stupidity of Dignity."
2. Wils, "The End of 'Human Dignity' in Ethics?," 39–54. Wils, a theological ethicist, raises similar concerns in his article. Unlike the three conclusions mentioned above, he concludes that the concept of human dignity is multidimensional. Via an historical-systematic analysis, he seeks to classify various types of dignity according to their methodological presuppositions. This book will likewise argue for a multidimensional understanding of human dignity, but using a different methodology. See the details on the methodology in the relevant section in the introduction.
3. One should note, however, that a distinction is obviously possible, particularly due to the fact that the latter explicitly mentions the 'person'. So, for example, one could make a distinction between 'human dignity' as referring to the dignity of all human life forms, and 'the dignity of the human person' as referring only to those human life forms that demonstrate personhood (however that may be defined). In this book, no such distinction will be made, since, whichever term one uses, it must refer to an anthropology, i.e., to an idea of what constitutes a human person. Thus, the debate should focus more on what constitutes the human person to which both the terms 'human dignity' and 'dignity of the human person' can refer. For example, usage in the German debate seems to make little distinction between *Menschenwürde* (human dignity) and *Würde der Person* (dignity of the person). Instead, the focus is on what constitutes the human person, i.e., can one make a distinction between *Mensch* and *Person*? In a contribution aimed at addressing the role of the concept of the person in solving bioethical problems, the German philosopher and biomedical ethicist Dieter Birnbacher points out that in biomedical ethics there are two 'schools' of thought in this regard. The first he calls the *Äquivalez-doktrin,* which holds that all human beings (*menschlichen Wesen*) are persons from conception to death, e.g. philosopher Robert Spaemann. The *Nichtäquivalez-doktrin* argues that a human being is only a person if they display certain capacities, e.g. philosopher Peter Singer. Interestingly, in both cases, Birnbacher states that it is *Menschenwürde* that is ascribed to the relevant notion of person. Hence, I too make

no distinction between the 'dignity of the human person' and 'human dignity', though I shall elaborate an explicit anthropology to which human dignity properly understood should refer. Birnbacher, "Hilft der Personen Begriff bei der Lösung bioethischer Fragestellungen?," 31–32. See also, among others, Spaemann, "Sind Alle Menschen Personen? Über neue philosophische Rechtfertigungen der Lebensvernichtung," 133–147; Singer, *Practical Ethics,* 2nd ed. (Cambridge: Cambridge University, 1993), chapter 4; Mieth, "Das Proprium Christianum und das Menschenwürdeargument in der Bioethik," 252–271.

4. *OED Online,* s.v. "moral, *adj.*", accessed June 30, 2009, http://www.oed.com/view/Entry/122086, "4. a. Of a person, a person's conduct, etc.: morally good, virtuous; conforming to standards of morality."

5. Ibid., "1. a. Of or relating to human character or behaviour considered as good or bad; of or relating to the distinction between right and wrong, or good and evil, in relation to the actions, desires, or character of responsible human beings; ethical."

6. Regarding the distinction between good and bad versus right and wrong, see, among others, Frankena ("McCormick and the Traditional Distinction," 146), who notes the importance of distinguishing between, "moral goodness ... as a predicate both of actions and of agents, their motives, character traits and so forth, from moral rightness as a predicate of actions ... . For actions may be right—do the right thing or what one ought to do —and yet not be morally good."

7. The objectivity of moral norms is a matter of some debate, especially considering that moral behaviour is always performed by an historically situated acting subject who may indeed act according to norms, but the norms may themselves be historically relative, e.g., norms regarding the permissibility of slavery. See the comments regarding formal norms and concrete material norms in Chapter 2, section 2.3.2.2, and the discussion on the eschatological proviso in 2.3.3.

8. See Chapter 2, section 2.3.2.2 A Multidimensional Understanding of the Moral Event for further explanation of this point.

9. See, for example, Wallach and Wallach, *Rethinking Goodness,* 41: "To say that something or someone was *agathos* (in various linguistic forms) meant, essentially, that they served well a desired end or function. This corresponds to an important non-moral sense of 'good' today—as one might speak of a 'good knife' or of a 'good teacher.'" See also, the discussion concerning Aristotle's understanding of 'good'—*agathos*—by Irwin (*s.v.* "good," in Glossary in *Nicomachean Ethics,* 332), who iden-

tifies three different understandings of good in Aristotle's *Nicomachean Ethics* "These three uses are related. What makes a knife a good knife (3), depends on what good (1) we want the knife to achieve, and that will depend on what the knife is good (2) for. Similarly a good (3) person will be able to achieve goods (1) that depend on what is good (2) for a person—his final good or happiness." Note that, sometimes, especially among so-called proportionalists, non-moral has the same meaning as pre-moral or ontic. Richard McCormick, for example, states, "Before we know whether it was justifiably caused, it is said to be ontic, premoral, or nonmoral evil." McCormick, *Notes on Moral Theology: 1981 through 1984*, p. 61, n. 33.

10. See, among others, Gula, *Reason Informed by Faith*, 269: "... all human actions contain some features which enhance our humanity and some features which restrict it. To the extent that these features enhance the potential for human goodness and growth, they are premoral or ontic goods. To the extent that these features frustrate the full potential for promoting the well-being of persons and of their social relations, these features are premoral or ontic evils." Louis Janssens opts for the language of ontic evil and ontic good in his article "Ontic Evil and Moral Evil," but, in his article "Norms and Priorities in a Love Ethics", he uses—apparently with the same meaning—premoral values and premoral disvalues. The advantage of the latter terms is, in my opinion, that they avoid the confusion that can arise concerning the words 'good', 'bad' and 'evil'. Hence in section 2.3.2.2 of this book, in describing the multidimensionality of the moral event, I opt for 'values' and 'disvalues' rather than 'goods' and 'evils'.

11. See also Knauer, "The Hermeneutic Function of the Principle of Double Effect," 132–162, who provides a similar example, though he uses the term 'physical evil' rather than 'pre-moral evil' to distinguish a description of the event from an assessment of the morality of the event. Note too, that I use the word amputation, which is a morally neutral description, rather than more morally-loaded terms like mutilation. The same applies to other terms like killing and murder, the latter being morally loaded by implying unjustifiable killing. In such cases a moral evaluation of the intention is implied in the definition of the word used to describe the physical action itself. See Westberg, "Good and Evil in Human Acts (Ia IIae, qq. 18–21)," 95.

12. Coppens, *A Brief Text-book of Moral Philosophy*, 16, and also 31–32. The 'useful' and the 'pleasurable' can be seen as somewhat equivalent to terms used here, i.e., non-moral and pre-moral goods respectively.

13. Cf. ibid., "But moral good is not good because it is useful; on the contrary, it is useful because it is good, *i.e.*, because it tends to make man more perfect, and hence better fitted to attain his last end" (p. 32); and, "... that which perfects a free being, as such, we call a *moral good*" (p. 29). See also pragmatist philosopher John Dewey's understanding of a moral good, *Lectures on Ethics, 1900–1901,* 54. Dewey argues, using truth-telling as a model example, that the reason it is a moral good, and is hence treated as an end in itself, is because it is found to be an "unqualified condition" for various other goods that we seek to realise (social life, business life, friendship, and so on). Truth-telling becomes a symbol for all those other goods we want to realise, and hence, instead of having to work out why we should tell the truth each time, it becomes a principle that we ought to tell the truth. Thus, it becomes possible to think of it like an end in itself, because we do not always connect it to the multiple other ends that we know implicitly it is a pre-condition for. Therefore, anything we call a moral good, e.g., saving life, "is not to be resolved either into a condition of getting the maximum of pleasure, nor is it to be conceived as something having worth entirely apart from all other goods or values. In each case it represents what has been found to be the key to the situation, the controlling factor in a variety of other experiences which are desirable."
14. Curran, "Absolute Moral Norms," 78.
15. "*Ethics* is a generic term for various ways of understanding the moral life." Beauchamp and Childress, *Principles of Biomedical Ethics,* 1–2. According to Beauchamp and Childress, ethics can be divided into normative and non-normative ethics. The former includes general normative ethics and practical or applied ethics, and the latter includes descriptive and meta-ethics. Therefore, the line they draw is between ethics as being concerned with making moral evaluations, versus ethics as being concerned with understanding moral behaviour. My terms—normative, to denote the former, and descriptive to denote the latter—are intended to make a similar distinction between moral evaluation and understanding. See also Frankena (*Ethics*), who distinguishes between descriptive, normative, and meta-ethics. Meta-ethics is concerned with answering "logical, epistemological, and semantic questions like: What is the meaning or use of the expressions '(morally) right' or 'good'? How can ethical and value judgments be established or justified? Can they be justified at all? What is the nature of morality? What is the distinction between the moral and the nonmoral? What is the meaning of 'free' or 'responsible'?" I would say then, that, in many respects, one could

describe this book as a meta-ethical enquiry into the concept of 'human dignity', and indeed even the distinction between descriptive and normative ethics is a meta-ethical one based on the distinction between ethics that seeks non-judgemental insight into moral behaviour and ethics as the art of making moral evaluations.
16. Beauchamp and Childress group descriptive ethics and meta-ethics under non-normative ethics because "their objective is to establish what factually or conceptually *is* the case, not what ethically *ought to be* the case." *Principles of Biomedical Ethics,* 2. See also Driver, *Ethics,* 4: "Descriptive ethics is not evaluative—for example, an anthropologist studying the ethical beliefs prevalent in a given culture will describe those beliefs and practices, but will not evaluate them and will not (generally) endorse or criticize them."
17. See, among others, Kagan, *Normative Ethics,* 1–11. According to Clark Professor of Philosophy at Yale, Shelly Kagan, normative ethics is concerned with how we should live, and hence involves theories that aim to provide substantive answers to questions like, "Which acts are morally better or worse than others? Which acts are morally permissible, which ones morally required, and which ones morally forbidden—and what makes them so?" (p. 7). Driver clearly sets up the distinction between descriptive and normative ethics as non-evaluative versus evaluative: "Normative claims are evaluative. In ethics, the kind of evaluations that occur are those that have to do with moral value and disvalue, moral rightness and wrongness." Driver, *Ethics,* 5. Note, Driver here uses the terms value and disvalue at a moral level. I would use them, following Janssens, "Norms and Priorities," to make pre-moral descriptions.
18. The words of a convicted criminal quoted in Gilligan, *Violence* 106.
19. See, among others, Janssens, "Artificial Insemination: Ethical Considerations," 3–29.
20. See Frankfurt, "Freedom of the Will and the Concept of a Person," 5–20. See also Browning, "Human Dignity, Human Complexity and Human Goods," 302–303.
21. See also section 3.4.4. The Behavioural Component Dimension: The Moral Good of Dignity and the Dignity of the Morally Good.
22. See sections 2.3.2.1.2, 2.3.3.1, and 3.4.1.
23. See, among others, Knauer, "The Hermeneutic Function."
24. Fries, *Fundamental Theology,* 439, see also 152 and 154. See also, among others, Metz, *Zur Theologie der Welt,* 143–146; Metz, "Religion and Society in the Light of a Political Theology," 513, 514 and 517.

25. See, among others, Baier, "Moralism and Cruelty: Reflection on Hume and Kant," 436–437; Taylor, "Moralism and Morally Accountable Beings," 154; Mansfield, *Manliness,* 120.
26. See the discussion on ethics as legalistic *techne* in 2.1.1, and the discussion on reductionism in 2.1.3.
27. See the discussion on multidimensionality in 3.1.1.
28. See the discussion on the four Component Dimensions and how they relate to an adequate multidimensional anthropology in 3.3.
29. The notion of a Complementary Duality is discussed at length in 3.4.1.
30. See the detailed discussion of the Existential Component Dimension and its Complementary Duality in sections 3.3.1, and 3.4.2 respectively.
31. Joseph A. Selling of the Faculty of Theology at the Katholieke Universiteit Leuven was helpful in pointing out the need to take the affective aspects of the human person into account.
32. See, for example, Murray, *In Pursuit: Of Happiness and Good Government,* 112–113. See also, s.v. "dignity," in, among others, *Merriam-Webster Online Dictionary* (www.Merriam-Webster.com, 2007); *The American Heritage Dictionary of the English Language,* 4th ed. (Houghton Mifflin Company, 2004); *Compact Oxford English Dictionary of Current English,* 2nd ed. (Oxford: Oxford University, 2003); *Oxford English Dictionary,* 2nd ed. (Oxford: Oxford University, 1989).
33. The Cognitive-Affective Component Dimension and its Complementary Duality of Inherent Worth are discussed in detail in 3.3.2, and 3.4.3 respectively.
34. The dignity of the human person, properly understood, is defined by the Component Dimensions of Human Dignity model being proposed in this book. Often, however, when referring to the dignity of the human person as a moral good, texts are referring specifically to the dignity we have, that is, the Already pole.
35. See, among others, Bradley, *Ethical Studies,* 142.
36. Cf. Frankena, *Ethics*: "The sorts of things that may be morally good or bad are persons, groups of persons, traits of character, dispositions, emotions, motives, and intentions—in short, persons, groups of persons, and elements of personality."
37. Paul Ricœur has developed similar ideas with regard to the relationship between self-esteem, morally good behaviour, and the social institutions with which one engages. See, for example, Ricœur, *Oneself as Another,* 180, 203, and 262.

38. See the detailed description of the Behavioural Component Dimension and its Complementary Duality of the Moral Good of Human Dignity and the Dignity of the Morally Good in 3.3.3, and 3.4.4.
39. See the detailed discussion of moral relativism and its problems, as well as how a multidimensional understanding of human dignity helps to overcome these challenges in 2.2.2, 2.3.3, and Chapter 4.
40. See also, for a more detailed treatment of the Social Component Dimension, 3.3.4, 3.4.5 and Chapter 4.
41. Following Martha Nussbaum, I actually favour a far broader range of 'capacities' as constitutive of inherent human worth. See Nussbaum, *Women and Human Development*, 78–80; Nussbaum, *Frontiers of Justice*.
42. This summary is similar to that which appears in Kirchhoffer, "Become What You Are," 64–65.
43. See, for example, Gadamer, *Truth and Method*, 157: "The classical discipline concerned with the art of understanding texts is hermeneutics." For a brief overview of the historical development of hermeneutics see Bernasconi, "Hermeneutics," 429–431. For a feminist perspective see Schüssler Fiorenza, *Sharing Her Word*, 95–100. An accessible introduction is Jasper, *A Short Introduction to Hermeneutics,* especially, 114–115.
44. See, among others, Kearney, *On Paul Ricœur*, 27–29; Schüssler Fiorenza, *Sharing Her Word*, 95–100. Gadamer, "The Hermeneutics of Suspicion," 64; Ricœur, "Two Essays by Paul Ricœur," 203–204; Ricœur, "The Language of Faith," 224.
45. Miles, "Hermeneutics of Generosity and Suspicion," 34–52.
46. See also Chapter 2, section 2.1.2 for a more detailed discussion of the hermeneutics of suspicion, based particularly on the work of philosopher Paul Ricœur.
47. Ricœur, *Freud and Philosophy*, 27. See also pp. 32–36. Ricœur is often credited with coining the term 'hermeneutics of suspicion', particularly through his analysis of those whom he calls the 'masters of suspicion': Sigmund Freud, Karl Marx, and Friedrich Nietzsche. See Chapter 2.1.2 of this book.
48. Gadamer, *Truth and Method*, 273.
49. For an example how these "new people" engage a hermeneutic of suspicion see Burrow, *James H. Cone and Black Liberation Theology*, 46–54.
50. This is similar to what Ricœur would call a hermeneutics of faith. A hermeneutics of faith is characterised by "the manifestation and restoration of a meaning addressed to me in the manner of a message, a proclamation, or as is sometimes said, a kerygma." It "first puts the accent on

the object, then underscores the fullness of symbol, to finally greet the revealing power of the primal word." Ricœur, *Freud and Philosophy*, 27–32.
51. See Chapter 2, section 2.2 of this book for further objections to this response to the critique.
52. See Chapter 1, section 1.6 for further details of this criticism of the concept of human dignity.
53. See also Gadamer, *Truth and Method*, 270–271, who highlights the fact that we all always approach a text or a communication of any sort with our own fore-understandings and fore-meanings. These can entail problems for our ability to understand the message, even if the message has its own biases. The first possibility of overcoming this problem that he addresses is very similar to this first meaning of a hermeneutics of generosity, and his criticism of it is also very important: "There can, of course, be a general expectation that what the text says will fit perfectly with my own meanings and expectations. But what another person tells me ... is generally supposed to be his own and not my opinion; and this is what I am to take note of without necessarily having to share it. Yet this presupposition is not something that makes understanding easier, but harder, since the fore-meanings that determine my own understanding can go entirely unnoticed." Thus this first understanding of a hermeneutic of generosity is of no use in that it brings neither the 'new people' nor the old closer to an understanding of their own biases and how these affect their interpretation. The result is that it also does not open up any further horizons of meaning, which is the essence of the hermeneutical enterprise.
54. This understanding of the hermeneutic of generosity is similar to what is still called by some authors, particularly feminist and liberation theologians, a hermeneutic of suspicion. For these authors, the hermeneutic of suspicion must include this 'generous' rereading that tries to re-appropriate the meaning of the texts for the reader free of the biases inherent in the world of the author. Nevertheless, for the sake of clarity, and because I use an understanding of the hermeneutic of suspicion more closely associated with Ricœur and his analysis of the masters of suspicion, I have opted to use the notion of the hermeneutic of generosity to clarify this difference. For examples of the aforementioned understanding of the hermeneutics of suspicion among feminist and liberation theologians, see, among others, Kearney, "Between Tradition and Utopia," 68; Stone, *Effective Faith: A Critical Study of the Christology of Juan Luis Segundo*, 37, 55, 90–92, and 158; Schüssler Fiorenza, *Sharing Her Word*, 95–100.

55. See 2.1.3 for a detailed discussion of the problem of reductionism in relation to the critique of human dignity.
56. See 2.1.1, 2.3.1, 2.3.2.1.1.
57. See also Ricœur "Two Essays," 203–204; and Ricœur, *Freud and Philosophy*, 55, who states that interpretation (hermeneutics) mediates "between myth and philosophy ... . But that mediation is not given, it is to be constructed." I have chosen to stick to the term 'hermeneutic of generosity' in this book because it avoids some of the ambiguity in Ricœur's various terms for this reconstructive process: hermeneutics of faith, affirmation, re-appropriation, among others.
58. Yaghjian, *Writing Theology Well*, 67.
59. Pinker, "The Stupidity of Dignity."
60. Gadamer, *Truth and Method*, 269.
61. For more on this 're-reading' of the meanings in Chapter 1, see my comments regarding method in 3.2.
62. Cf. Gadamer, *Truth and Method*, 269.
63. Another important Roman Catholic document, promulgated on the same day and based on the understanding of human dignity developed in *Gaudium et spes* is the Second Vatican Council's Declaration on Religious Freedom (*Dignitatis humanae*), which even bears the concept of human dignity in its conventional title (the first words of the Latin text). Reference will also be made to this important document in Chapter 5.

CHAPTER 1

QUESTIONING DIGNITY

APPLYING A HERMENEUTIC OF SUSPICION TO THE CONCEPT OF HUMAN DIGNITY

The concept of human dignity is widely used in legal and ethical discourse today. This is largely due to the institutionalisation of the concept in international declarations and national constitutions.

Nevertheless, the concept of human dignity has recently been called into question by several authors. Though the authors in question never suggest that they are approaching the concept of human dignity with a hermeneutic of suspicion, I maintain that this is indeed what they are doing. I believe that this suspicion is justified and lays bare real problems in the way that the concept of human dignity is being used and abused in contemporary ethical discourse. Nevertheless, I disagree with the solution proposed by some authors which calls for the dismissal of the concept of human dignity. In this book I argue instead for a revitalisation of the concept on the basis of a clarification of its meaning. However, in order to do so, I believe it is first necessary to take a serious look at the challenges that any useful understanding of the concept of human dignity will have to take into account. Hence, this chapter gives serious consideration to some of the key criticisms that can be levelled at the concept of human dignity and its contemporary usage. This chapter will, in other words, approach human dignity with a justifiable hermeneutic of suspicion.

The critics' suspicions, and indeed my own suspicion, have their origin in the use and even apparent abuse of the concept of human dignity to justify opposing courses of moral behaviour. I shall term this sort of usage 'dignity talk'. The concept of human dignity has come to be used as a sort of ethical weapon: an argument settling normative criterion that no one can challenge. That would be fine, if all the parties involved were in agreement about what the concept of human dignity actually meant. In reality, however, like the professors of law, Mirko Bagaric and James Allan have noted in their critical article titled "The Vacuous Concept of Dignity", "it is clear that in many instances the concept is simply assumed to have some meaning and weight. Often judges and legal commentators mention and use the concept without any elucidation or elaboration at all."[1] Herein, in many respects, lies the crux of the problem: the concept of human dignity seems to be in danger of taking on an almost 'magical' character, such that it can be invoked at will as a legitimate justification for a particular course of action.[2] The upshot of all this is that several authors have called for human dignity to be dismissed as a concept of any value to ethical and legal discourse, calling it vacuous, stupid, and useless.[3]

In this chapter, I shall demonstrate the 'rise of human dignity' as an ethical criterion in international and national, secular and religious documents (1.1). I shall then show how this use of human dignity as the basis of human rights has led to situations in various areas of ethical discourse where the concept of human dignity has been used to justify opposing courses of moral behaviour, what I shall term 'dignity talk' (1.2–1.4). Since, as Bagaric and Allan have pointed out, this is an untenable situation if human dignity is to be expected to function effectively as a normative criterion, I shall look at some of the possible bases put forward for human dignity (1.5). Among the bases that will be mentioned are those that ground the concept of human dignity in religious beliefs, such as the Judeo-Christian belief that human beings are created in the image of God.

Such religious groundings of human dignity bring with them their own set of challenges in a secular and pluralised world. These are addressed in 1.6. This chapter will conclude with a summary of the key challenges facing the concept of human dignity that any significant defence of the concept and its continued relevance would have to take into account (1.7). I would like to reiterate that in this chapter I shall employ a hermeneutic of suspicion, i.e. a critical questioning of the way in which human dignity is both used and understood in contemporary ethics, particularly insofar as it gives rise to 'dignity talk', in order to reveal the many challenges that I believe a proper understanding of the concept of human dignity must be able to overcome if it is to be of any value to ethics.

1.1. The Widespread Use of the Concept of Human Dignity

The horrors of World War II, its enormous death toll, and particularly the Nazis' attempt to exterminate the Jewish people, raised serious questions about what it means to be a human being. How could such violence be perpetrated on such a vast scale against other human beings? How could people do this to each other? And how can people prevent it from happening again? One could argue that the latter question led to a variety of answers that would in turn lead to efforts to ensure peace in the future. Consider, for example, the many branches of the United Nations Organisation aimed at bringing about, or safeguarding peace by diplomatic, political, social, humanitarian, and even military means. But, the most significant answer to the above questions must be the rediscovery of the notion of 'the dignity of the human person'.[4] According to the professor of history of law, Joern Eckert, "The idea of human dignity was decisively strengthened by developments after the Second World War. After the terrible crimes and contempt towards mankind by the Nazis, there was a sudden surge for stronger protection of human dignity."[5] The concept of human dignity came to be hailed as one of the reasons why such horrors should never happen again. The concept of human dignity is an affirmation of the worth of every human being, such that none should be subjected to cruel treatment.[6]

Thus, after the Second World War, the concept of human dignity came to form the basis of an ever increasing number of ethical and legal instruments. In what follows I shall provide a representative, and in no way exhaustive, overview of just a small sample of the instruments that make use of the concept.[7]

Among the first, and possibly the most influential, are the 1945 *Charter of the United Nations* and the 1948 *Universal Declaration of Human Rights* (UDHR). The *Charter* clearly states that one of the United Nations Organisation's founding principles is a determination to "reaffirm faith in ... the dignity and worth of the human person ...." The UDHR makes more frequent mention of human dignity, most notably in its preamble and Article 1. The preamble states that "recognition of the inherent dignity and of the equal and inalienable rights of all members of the human family is the foundation of freedom, justice and peace in the world." Article 1 states, "All human beings are born free and equal in dignity and rights. They are endowed with reason and conscience and should act towards one another in a spirit of brotherhood."

The United Nations' 1966 *International Covenant on Economic, Social and Cultural Rights* (ICESCR), 1966 *International Covenant on Civil and Political Rights* (ICCPR), and 1984 *Convention Against Torture and Other Cruel, Inhuman, Degrading Treatment or Punishment*, all state in their preambles that the recognition of the inherent dignity of the human person is "the foundation of freedom, justice and peace in the world ...." Furthermore, they all state that the inalienable rights to which all human beings are entitled "derive from the inherent dignity of the human person."

The United Nations' 1979 *Convention on the Elimination of All Forms of Discrimination Against Women* emphasises, in its preamble, that all human persons are born equal in dignity, regardless of sexual differences, and therefore all discrimination against women is a violation of this human dignity.

The United Nations' 1989 *Convention on the Rights of the Child*, likewise, bases its claim that "childhood is entitled to special care and assistance" on the idea that all human beings have inherent dignity.

Interestingly, though there is no reference made to human dignity in the Council of Europe's 1950 *European Convention on Human Rights*, reference is made to human dignity in the European Union's 2000 *Charter of Fundamental Rights of the European Union*. The preamble claims that the Union is founded upon, what it calls, "the indivisible, universal values of human dignity, freedom, equality and solidarity." Accordingly, article 1 of the charter states, "Human dignity is inviolable. It must be respected and protected."

The prominence given to human dignity in the charter just mentioned makes sense when one takes into account the importance placed on human dignity in the constitutions of several of the states that are now part of the European Union and to which this charter would thus apply. For example, Germany's 1949 (amended in 2006) *Grundgesetz für die Bundesrepublik Deutschland* also puts the inviolability (*Unantastbarkeit*) of the dignity of the human person in its article 1, stating, moreover, that the protection of human dignity is a duty for all state agencies (*staatlichen Gewalt*). The 1999 *Constitution of Finland* states that the constitution "shall guarantee the inviolability of human dignity." Likewise, the preamble of the 1937 (amended in 2004) *Constitution of Ireland* states that the constitution is intended to assure, among other things, the "dignity and freedom of the human individual ...." Similar statements are also made in the constitutions of Poland, Belgium, Bulgaria, Hungary, Sweden, Spain, Portugal, and Greece, among others.

The use of human dignity in national constitutions is, however, not reserved to European states. Since the United Nations' ICESCR and ICCPR mentioned above have been ratified by 158 and 161 countries respectively, this should hardly be surprising.[8]

The widely acclaimed 1996 *Constitution of the Republic of South Africa*, for example, names human dignity as the first of the state's founding values. Furthermore, in the second chapter of the constitution, namely, the Bill of Rights, article 10 states, "Everyone has inherent dignity and the right to have their dignity respected and protected." South Africa is not the only African state to make use of the notion of human dignity in its constitution. For example, others include Angola, Ethiopia, and Nigeria.[9]

In South America, Brazil's 1988 constitution states, in article 1, that the democratic state of Brazil is founded upon, among other things, the dignity of the human person. And the 1993 Peruvian constitution names "the protection of the human person and respect for his dignity" as "the supreme goal of society and the State."

Canada and the United States of America, are, interestingly enough, less explicit in their use of the term dignity. Perhaps this has something to do with the time in which they were first established and their respective constitutions were written. As already pointed out, it is really only following World War II that the notion of the dignity of the human person has really flourished in international and national law. Nevertheless, the concept is not entirely absent in these countries either. For example, the dignity of the human person has been called upon by courts in the United States to ground certain rights. In Canada, the respect for the inherent dignity of persons has been said to underpin the rights and freedoms listed in the Canadian Charter.[10]

The 'rise of human dignity' is also not limited to secular documents. The Roman Catholic Church, for example, has also come to embrace the notion of human dignity and its associated language of human rights, particularly in its so-called social teachings. Two key documents in this regard are both outcomes of the Second Vatican Council that took place between October 1962 and December 1965.

The 1965 *Pastoral Constitution of the Church in the Modern World*,[11] commonly referred to using the opening words of the Latin text, *Gaudium et spes* (GS), dedicates its first chapter to elaborating the idea of the dignity of the human person in order to then use this concept as the basis for a vision of how the Church should engage with the modern world and the challenges that it faces. "Everything we have said about the dignity of the human person, and about the human community and the profound meaning of human activity, lays the foundation for the relationship between the Church and the world, and provides the basis for dialogue between them" (GS, 40).[12]

The way in which *Gaudium et spes* intends the concept of dignity to be used is then illustrated in the second key document, the 1965 *Declaration on Religious Freedom*, or *Dignitatis humanae* (DH). Many commentators consider this declaration to represent a paradigm shift in Catholic thinking regarding other religions, or at least, membership of other religions. This is because it argues for the right to religious freedom, and it does so by basing its argument on human dignity: "The council further declares that the right to religious freedom has its foundation in the very dignity of the human person as this dignity is known through the revealed word of God and by reason itself" (DH, 2).[13]

All of these charters, covenants and constitutions claim that dignity is the ground of rights that, when assured, will ensure peaceful coexistence; and/or that the constitution, and the powers of the state or Church, are designed to protect human dignity. The aim, in the latter, is, again, a just and peaceful society. What is remarkable, however, is that very few of the documents actually define what human dignity is.[14] Unsurprisingly, this can lead to problems when it comes to the adjudication of which rights flow forth from dignity, or which rights will realise its flourishing in society.

1.2. Rights Talk and Human Dignity

Professor of law Mary Ann Glendon, in her influential book *Rights Talk*, points out that one seems to be able to claim a human right to just about anything nowadays. Glendon argues that the proliferation of "rights talk" has led to a concurrent diminishment of emphasis on duties and responsibilities resulting in an unhealthy political situation that has rights claims without shared norms to guide them.[15] Bagaric and Allan, who have already been mentioned, likewise point out the apparent proliferation of what they also call "rights talk", arguing that this language seems to dominate moral discourse today. Bagaric and Allan cite several interesting, and indeed almost comical examples that they have come across in their research, such as the right to a sex break, the right to cheap gasoline, and the right of English football supporters to FA Cup tickets.[16] Even if none of these were true, it is conceivable that such claims could be made, such is the ubiquity of rights talk.[17]

Naturally, this ability to make any claim potentially undermines the power of human rights in ethical discourse. Since rights claims may be found on both sides of an argument, one needs some way of evaluating various conflicting rights claims. Or put another way, one needs to find a "concept that can explain and justify the existence of rights." Without such a concept, human rights themselves are just "vacuous at the epistemological level." Often, in trying to find this sound basis for rights claims, an appeal is made to the dignity of the human person.[18] Mary Ann Glendon, for example, shows how the West German Constitutional Court ruled against the right to abortion in 1975 on the basis that the obligation to respect human dignity suggested that the right to life took priority over personality rights.[19] The German *Grundgesetz* is, of course, included in the list of legal instruments compiled above; the fact that this list is even possible illustrates the appeal made to human dignity as the basis of rights. Most of the documents mentioned claim either that rights are designed to protect human dignity or that human dignity is the ground of human rights and the claims they make.

Yet, as an attempt to ground various rights claims and judge competing rights claims, is the appeal to the concept of human dignity any better than an appeal to a plethora of rights in the first place? In other words, is human dignity a concept so clearly defined and accepted that it functions effectively as a criterion in judging various claims?[20] Critics, like Bagaric and Allan, maintain that it is not. As Bagaric and Allan note, "What is clear ... is that the concept of human dignity is easily able to be used as some sort of empowering notion, one that confers rights and entitlements and protects interests .... Yet the same concept of dignity is equally easily able to be used as a sort of constraint on action ...."[21] Similarly, in their recent book, *Human Dignity in Bioethics and Biolaw,* professors of law Deryck Beyleveld and Roger Brownsword observe that public debates seem to be characterised by two opposing conceptions of human dignity, that both nevertheless place fundamental importance on respect for human dignity:

> One conception, 'human dignity as empowerment', treats human rights as founded on the intrinsic dignity of humans and, characteristically, this issues in a reinforced plea that individual autonomy should be respected. The other conception, 'human dignity as constraint', is more concerned with human duties than with human rights. Treating this conception ... as an umbrella term for a number of duty-driven approaches, we can find not only a duty to respect the dignity of others but also a duty not to compromise our own dignity as well as to act in a way that is compatible with respect for the vision of human dignity that gives a particular community its distinctive cultural identity.[22]

Moreover, as I shall illustrate in the various examples that follow, the proliferation of rights talk and the appeal to dignity as the basis of those rights claims, combined with an apparent lack of clarity with regard to what human dignity actually is, has led to the rise of 'dignity talk', where human dignity is used as a self-evident, argument winning criterion.

1.3. The Rise of 'Dignity Talk' in Contemporary Ethical Discourse

The moral philosopher Stephen Toulmin penned an important article in 1982 in which he argued that the challenges of new developments in medicine in the 1960s marked a shift in the role of the moral philosopher. Ethicists were now being asked to address concrete issues in a way that would bridge the gap between relativists (inspired largely by the social sciences) on the one hand and absolutists (inspired largely by religion) on the other. Ethicists were pulled out of the world of meta-ethics, which was concerned with what kinds of issues should be considered moral, into a world which asked them for a "rational" way of settling ethical disputes.[23]

What was true then remains true today, especially with regard to the challenges facing the concept of human dignity: biomedical issues seem to be the driving force behind much of the debate surrounding the question of human dignity. That said, however, there are other areas of ethical reflection that could be considered. For example, globalisation and issues of global justice have also raised questions about human dignity and what it means. Philosopher Marjolijn Drenth von Februar notes how human dignity can be used to back seemingly opposite courses of action and sets out to define a practical understanding of human dignity in response to the challenges raised by globalisation.[24] In the interests of space, however, I shall not deal with globalisation any further. In this section, I shall introduce a few illustrative examples of how human dignity is being called upon, and challenged, as a foundational ethical criterion. In addition to the biomedical context (1.3.1 and 1.3.2), and in order to demonstrate that the concerns regarding the validity of the concept of human dignity are not only limited to that field of ethics, I shall also provide an example of how the concept of human dignity has been used (or abused) both as justification for and an argument against violent behaviour (1.3.3).

1.3.1. Human Dignity and Stem-Cell Research
In 2003, American professor of medical ethics, Ruth Macklin, wrote a controversial editorial titled, "Dignity is a useless concept."[25] In it, she argues that dignity really means nothing more than respect for persons and their autonomy, and should hence be abandoned in favour of what she maintains are more precise terms. Her editorial is a response to what she believes is an unnecessary recourse to the concept of human dignity to argue against developments in genetics or biotechnology. Needless to say, her editorial provoked a significant response, inspiring both backers and

opponents to address the value of the concept of dignity in medical ethics. It should be noted that scepticism with regard to the concept of human dignity, and particularly in the context of advances in stem-cell research, is not limited to the English-speaking world. For example, German philosopher Dieter Birnbacher, among others, has also raised concerns, particularly with the tendency to ascribe human dignity to fertilised human ova.[26] In this book, however, I shall focus on developments primarily in the English language literature.

One of the most important responses to Macklin's article in the United States of America came in the form of a volume titled *Human Dignity and Bioethics: Essays Commissioned by the President's Council on Bioethics.*[27] In the introductory chapter, Adam Schulman, a senior research consultant at the President's Council on Bioethics, twice mentions Macklin and notes that "Her approach may have the virtue of simplicity, but it does not explain *why* all persons are entitled to respect; and it is far from clear that all present and future controversies in bioethics can be resolved merely by providing informed consent, honoring confidentiality, avoiding discrimination, and refraining from abuse."[28] In the second introductory chapter, F. Daniel Davis, the executive director at the President's Council on Bioethics, makes it clear that one of the aims of the collection of essays is to "take up the challenge implicitly issued by American medical ethicist Ruth Macklin, who bluntly asserted four years ago that 'dignity is a useless concept in medical ethics and can be eliminated without any loss of content.'"[29] Apart from Davis's contribution, at least two other essays in the volume aim to deal explicitly with Macklin's claim, those of Daniel P. Sulmasy, professor of medicine and director of the Bioethics Institute of New York Medical College, and Rebecca Dresser, professor of law and professor of medical ethics at Washington University.[30]

Though the Council's intention was to provide an in-depth reflection on human dignity in order that most people, upon reflection, would come to reject Macklin's claim that dignity is a useless concept,[31] the volume nevertheless attracted further criticism, most notably from cognitive scientist and Harvard professor of psychology Steven Pinker. He was invited to present his criticisms to the Council on March 7, 2008,[32] and also published them in an article in the *New Republic*, tellingly titled "The Stupidity of Dignity: Conservative bioethics' latest, most dangerous ploy," on May 28, 2008.[33]

In both his address to the council, and his article, Pinker argues that the council has failed to achieve its aim with this volume for two reasons. First, because, he maintains, despite their efforts, the essays seem to highlight how "ambiguous, slippery, and vague," dignity is, rather than provide a sound basis for dignity. And second, and this point is particularly important with regard to the rise of 'dignity talk' in biomedical ethics, Pinker suggests that the volume in question suffers from a lack of perspective: though many of the authors claim they respond to Macklin, Macklin herself was not invited to defend her position; and, Pinker argues, the list of contributors is weighted in favour of conservatively-oriented, religiously-motivated thinkers who argue, often on religious grounds, for an understanding of dignity that would provide a basis for them to argue against, or even ban, what they believe to be discomforting advances in biomedical technology. In contrast, Pinker maintains that "as a superficial signal of worth rather than worth itself, dignity should not be fetishized. It should not be treated as an absolute value. It should not be used to ratify vague feelings of unease at new developments. It should not be used as a justification for the exercise of arbitrary power, and it should not be used to stifle advances in human well-being."[34] He adopts even stronger language in his article:

> The report does not, the editors admit, settle the question of what dignity is or how it should guide our policies. It does, however, reveal a great deal about the approach to bioethics represented by the Council. And what it reveals should alarm anyone concerned with American biomedicine and its promise to improve human welfare. For this government-sponsored bioethics does not want

medical practice to maximize health and flourishing; it considers that quest to be a bad thing, not a good thing.[35]

Remarkably, despite his criticism of the use of dignity by 'conservative bioethics', he himself disagrees with Macklin, at least insofar as her idea that dignity is a useless concept that should be abandoned. He believes the concept of dignity is of value to bioethics, provided that it is specifically defined. Not surprisingly, *his* definition of dignity, unlike those he criticises, tends to support advances in biomedical technology. He argues that dignity is an attribute that causes other people to respect one another, and may be composed of, for example, signs of composure, cleanliness, maturity, attractiveness, and control of the body. The flipside of this is that we want our dignity to be respected. This, Pinker argues is what makes dignity morally significant.

> ... people generally want to be seen as dignified. Dignity is thus one of the interests of a person, alongside bodily integrity and personal property, that other people are obligated to respect. We don't want anyone to stomp on our toes; we don't want anyone to steal our hubcaps; and we don't want anyone to open the bathroom door when we're sitting on the john. ... When the concept of dignity is precisely specified, it becomes a mundane matter of thoughtfulness pushing against callousness and bureaucratic inertia, not a contentious moral conundrum. And, because it amounts to treating people in the way that they wish to be treated, ultimately it's just another application of the principle of autonomy.[36]

Bizarrely, Pinker then ends his article with an appeal to human dignity, perhaps tongue in cheek, to oppose 'conservative bioethics' and the so-called 'theocons'.[37]

> Worst of all, theocon bioethics flaunts a callousness toward the billions of non-geriatric people, born and unborn, whose lives or health could be saved by biomedical advances. Even if progress were delayed a mere decade by moratoria, red tape, and funding taboos (to say nothing of the threat of criminal prosecution), millions of people with degenerative diseases and failing organs

would needlessly suffer and die. And that would be the biggest affront to human dignity of all.[38]

The point of this section was to highlight how, in one particular example, in one particular area of ethical debate, 'dignity talk' is on the rise. I believe that Pinker and Macklin, among others, are right to be suspicious of this trend, particularly if there is, as suggested, no consensus as to what human dignity actually entails. Nevertheless, Pinker, too, seems to fall into the same trap, offering an understanding of dignity that suits his agenda, just as the 'theocons' use their own version of dignity to underpin theirs.[39] In the next section, we shall look at the rise of 'dignity talk' in the context of another biomedically related issue, namely the area of end-of-life decisions.

1.3.2. *Human Dignity and End-of-Life Decisions*

It is not surprising that the concept of human dignity has come to be used in the debate surrounding end-of-life decisions. Though choosing how and when one dies obviously has moral implications, those who help one die also potentially face legal prosecution. Hence, the questions concerning the ethics and morality of end-of-life decisions inevitably became questions regarding the legality of such decisions, especially for those who help in the process. Since, as shown in the list of instruments already mentioned, the concept of human dignity has found its way into constitutional law in many countries, it has likewise become one of the main criteria appealed to by those both in favour and opposed to allowing people to choose to die.

To demonstrate this, I shall consider the use of the word dignity in a few representative arguments for and against. These are not scholarly arguments, which makes them all the more important with regard to the point that is being made here regarding the rise of 'dignity talk', a rise that is one of the main reasons that the concept of human dignity has been called into question.

Questioning Dignity

Basically, the argument can be summarised like this. Those in favour of allowing a person to choose to end his or her own life say that this is the ultimate expression of respect for the dignity of the human person. To not allow them that choice, is an offence to dignity. Those against allowing a person to end his or her life say that suicide, or mercy-killing, or aid in dying is an offence to human dignity and therefore should not be allowed. It is clear that there is a problem. Both arguments rely on what seems to be a common concept of human dignity, and yet they reach different conclusions. Let us look at some of the public rhetoric to get a better grasp of the problem.

At one end of the spectrum we have those who argue that human beings have a right to die with dignity. This is best captured in the name given to the landmark law passed in Oregon, USA, in 1994, and successfully defended against a repeal effort in 1997, the so-called Death with Dignity Act. This act permits, so-called physician-assisted suicide, or the more palatable term used by the American Public Health Association, 'aid in dying.' The best way to illustrate what this means is to refer to the case of the first person who made use of this act: in 1998, "a woman in her 80s who was near death from breast cancer legally ended her life with barbiturates prescribed by an Oregon doctor."[40]

One of the most vocal pressure groups in favour of extending such legislation to other states is the Death with Dignity National Center. Their website provides us with an insight into the association of dignity with the idea that one has a right to choose how and when one dies.

> The greatest human freedom is to live, and die, according to one's own desires and beliefs. The most common desire among those with a terminal illness is to die with some measure of dignity. From advance directives to physician-assisted dying, death with dignity is a movement to provide options for the dying to control their own end-of-life care.[41]

This association of human dignity with the power to choose how and when one dies is not only a North American phenomenon. For example, in

Belgium, the second country, after the Netherlands, to legalise euthanasia (the third if one counts the legal jurisdiction of Oregon), Jean-Jacques De Gucht, a member of the liberal party (OpenVLD) in Belgium, clearly states on his personal website that a dignified end to one's life is a fundamental human right, whereby everyone has the right to determine how their life will end. He furthermore maintains that the 2002 Belgian euthanasia law went a long way to guaranteeing that right.[42] Likewise, in the Netherlands, the first country to legalise euthanasia, the Dutch Association for a Voluntary Ending of Life (*Nederlandse Vereniging voor een Vrijwillig Levenseinde*), or Right to Die-NL, as they call themselves in English, makes a plea for a further criterion to be considered as legitimate grounds for euthanasia, namely, a loss of dignity.[43]

At the other end of the spectrum, human dignity is used as a criterion to oppose euthanasia, arguing that human beings have no right to take their own or others' lives. For example, the Salvation Army in New Zealand, in response to what they perceive to be a growing threat that euthanasia may become protected by law in New Zealand, states, "The Salvation Army believes that euthanasia and assisted suicide undermine human dignity and are morally wrong regardless of age or disability. Euthanasia is not 'death with dignity'."[44]

And, although the latter position is typically associated with religious groups, in a response to the Voluntary Euthanasia Society changing its name to Dying with Dignity, the "Association of Palliative Medicine accused the organisation of trying to suggest dignity in terminal illness can only be won by euthanasia."[45]

The examples briefly mentioned above are interesting in another way, namely, not only do they use the notion of dignity to support opposing positions regarding end-of-life decisions, but the understanding of human dignity itself is unclear. Are they talking about human freedom, self-respect, respect by others, value in the eyes of society, value regardless of the eyes of society, or the inviolable value of biological life itself? For example, the Association of Palliative Medicine's understanding of dignity seems to have more in common with the Death with Dignity National Center's understanding, in that both seem to refer to a sense of pride and honour, than it does with the Salvation Army's, even though both the Association of Palliative Medicine and the Salvation Army oppose euthanasia. The Salvation Army's understanding, by contrast, seems to have more to do with some inviolable universal worth shared by all human beings that inheres in biological life itself. And where it is legal, it would seem to be based on respect for human autonomy more than anything else. So which of these things is human dignity?

I shall return to this question in section 1.5 after considering one more context in which the rise of 'dignity talk' seems to jeopardising the value of the concept of human dignity for ethical and legal discourse, namely, how dignity is used to argue both against violence and apparently in favour of it.

1.3.3. Human Dignity and Interpersonal Violence
The fact that the horrors of the first half of the twentieth century played a decisive role in the increased use of the concept of human dignity as the basis of international and national human rights declarations and constitutions, seems to suggest that human dignity is something that stands opposed to violence against other human beings. By violence, I mean intentionally causing physical or psychological harm to another human being for one's own or for a third party's benefit. The acts of a soldier in a just war (however that may be defined) may be considered necessary, but they remain violent acts because, even if justified, for example in rightful defence of one's country, the enemy is intentionally physically harmed. The fact that the concept of human dignity rose to prominence after the Second World War is precisely to assert that such violence is always abhorrent, and something which works against the good of human dignity, but which may, in an imperfect world be necessary, as in cases of self-defence. Nevertheless, it should never be seen as an ideal way to behave. The concept of human dignity came to be hailed as one of the reasons why such violence should never again occur. Human dignity is an affirmation of the

worth of every human being, such that no one should be subjected to cruel treatment. In other words, the 'dignity of the human person', which underpins such important documents as the *Universal Declaration of Human Rights* and *Gaudium et spes*, would seem to provide a justification for *not* being violent.

For example, in the *Universal Declaration of Human Rights*, the preamble states that "recognition of the inherent dignity and of the equal and inalienable rights of all members of the human family is the foundation of freedom, justice and peace in the world." Article 1 states, "All human beings are born free and equal in dignity and rights. They are endowed with reason and conscience and should act towards one another in a spirit of brotherhood." These are strong words. Because human beings have dignity, they should act towards one another in a spirit of brotherhood. One would be hard-pressed to legitimately associate violent behaviour with living in a spirit of brotherhood, hence, human dignity stands opposed to violence. Likewise, in the preamble, the idea that human dignity forms the basis of peace also suggests that dignity and violence are incommensurate.[46]

Gaudium et spes, paragraph 39, states, "For after we have obeyed the Lord, and in His Spirit nurtured on earth the values of human dignity, brotherhood and freedom, and indeed all the good fruits of our nature and enterprise, we will find them again, but freed of stain, burnished and transfigured, when Christ hands over to the Father: 'a kingdom eternal and universal, a kingdom of truth and life, of holiness and grace, of justice, love and peace.'" From this we can again infer that human dignity is associated with justice, love and peace, rather than with any kind of violence.

A concrete example of the use of the concept of human dignity against violence can be found in the opinion of Justice Kate O'Regan of the South African Constitutional Court in a landmark case that outlawed the death penalty in South Africa on grounds that it was an offence to human dignity. She argued that dignity is very specifically about affirming the value of all human beings as human beings. In other words, it is not simply about being alive, but about being able to live in a certain way, namely, in a way that is worthy of a human being. She argues that this is particularly important in the South African context where Apartheid set out precisely to dehumanise and therefore to deny the inherent dignity of many human beings. One of the tools used to enforce this denial was the death penalty.[47] Hence, the death penalty was outlawed as unconstitutional on the basis that it is contrary to one of the foundational values of South African society, namely, human dignity.

So, given that the concept of human dignity is used in ethical discourse as the basis for peaceful, 'brotherly' behaviour towards others, the following quote is quite shocking. Here, a convicted prisoner justifies his continually violent behaviour in prison by appealing to some understanding of human dignity.

> Pride. Dignity. Self-esteem. And I'll kill every mother-fucker in that cell block if I have to in order to get it! My life ain't worth nothin' if I take somebody disrespectin' me and callin' me punk asshole faggot and goin' 'Ha! Ha!' at me. Life ain't worth livin' if there ain't nothin' worth dyin' for. If you ain't got pride, you got nothin'. That's all you got! I've already got my pride.[48]

The use of dignity in this way is discomforting to say the least. How can one of the foundational principles of modern human rights law be turned into a weapon? The way that this man uses and understands human dignity must surely be wrong. The point is, however, whether he is right or wrong, there is a fundamental problem, much the same as the problems that have already been mentioned with regard to the debates surrounding end-of-life decisions and stem-cell research, namely, some version of the concept of human dignity is being appealed to in order to justify apparently opposite courses of action. Whilst Martin Luther King, Jr. appealed to human dignity as the basis for African Americans to stand up and be counted as 'a somebody' through non-violent civil protests, his contemporary, Malcolm X, stated that human dignity was the reason that black people could violently rise up in an act of self-defence to claim their identity.[49]

Moreover, the appeal to human dignity is seen to put a self-evident end to the argument, without the concept itself being unpacked or explained. The South African Constitutional Court ruled that the death penalty was illegitimate because it went against human dignity; the violent criminal, however mistaken he may be, believes that his dignity justifies the killing of someone who disrespects that dignity.

I shall return to the respective meanings of dignity that these arguments entail shortly. First, however, I would like to consider another example in which violence is an issue. In this case, however, human dignity is not used to justify anything. Instead, it is dismissed as irrelevant. It is, in that sense, the opposite problem, or perhaps a problem that results from the kind of ambiguity that has been discussed so far, namely, that though human dignity is affirmed in theory, it has no power or relevance in actual behaviour.

1.4. The Consequence of 'Dignity Talk': Dignity Becomes Relative

From the preceding section (1.3.3) the 'dignity of the human person', as understood in the post-Second-World-War context, would seem to be a criterion by which we are able to judge violent behaviour as unjust, wrong, or immoral. Hence, I concluded that it was surprising that the violent criminal made an appeal to human dignity to justify his crime. What may be far worse, however, and in the long run far more detrimental for the value of the concept of human dignity for ethical discourse, is that the concept of human dignity is often ignored by the states that claim to uphold it in their constitutions. The result is that though human dignity is proclaimed as a universal truth, the particular reality of lived experience makes it hard to see or even to affirm human dignity as really universally true. How do we account for the idea that all human beings have dignity despite the apparent lack of dignity in a world where suffering is rife; and how do we account for the desire, expressed by so many people, to live a dignified life if we claim that everyone already has dignity? As former chief justice of South Africa and president of the South African constitutional court Arthur Chaskalson has asked, "Why do [these horrible things] continue to happen, if respect for human dignity is indeed a universal social good?"[50]

To understand this problem with the concept of human dignity, I shall first demonstrate how human dignity is indeed thought to be a universal good, before showing that despite this belief, proclaimed in international rights documents, actual practice calls this value into question as something relative, irrelevant, or even non-existent.

1.4.1. Human Dignity Is an Inviolable, Universal Moral Good
A moral good is an end in itself. This means that such a good is good in itself and does not need to be a means to some other good to be good. Immanuel Kant claimed that human beings qualified as such moral goods. Kant expressed this in terms of his categorical imperative which states that a human person should always be treated as an end and never only as a means. Human beings are hence of absolute worth rather than relative worth. Things, and beings other than rational beings, have, according to Kant, a relative worth insofar as they are desirable or necessary to an acting subject.[51] "On the other hand, rational beings are called persons inasmuch as their nature already marks them out as ends in themselves, ... which are thus objects of respect."[52] Kant's objective in describing human beings this way was precisely to set up an objective principle that could serve as the basis of a practical law. Otherwise, Kant feared, without anything of absolute value, no such objective law would be possible.[53]

This Kantian notion of human beings as ends in themselves and hence as moral goods is clearly present in some understandings of human dignity. For example, the Victorian Law Reform Commission states,

> The concept of human dignity is often invoked to justify the idea that human beings should not be treated as if they are things, that is, that they should not be commodified. The categories of person

and property are, according to modern legal orthodoxy, distinct: if one is a person, one is not property. ... Treating a person or part of a person simply as an object or a thing to be traded would strip a person of his or her dignity.[54]

My intention here is not to address Immanuel Kant's understanding of human dignity, which is of course more complex than the above quote.[55] Nevertheless, this quote illustrates what it might mean to speak of the human being and his or her dignity as a moral good. There is something about human beings that makes them different from other objects that one may encounter and this difference is universally worthy of respect. To quote the Victorian Law Reform Commission again: "Dignity is the quality of human beings which distinguishes us from things: human beings are not things, but people; not objects, but subjects."[56] Hence, the desire to protect or ensure human dignity, this end in itself, underpins the legal and ethical instruments reviewed earlier. The result is statements like those found in the European Union's 2000 *Charter of Fundamental Rights of the European Union* quoted earlier: "Human dignity is inviolable. It must be respected and protected."

Of course, precisely what constitutes this inviolable dignity, or why indeed it is inviolable at all, is not really made clear.[57] I shall return to that problem shortly. For now, it is sufficient to note that the concept of human dignity is normally used in a manner that implies it is a moral good that is hence inviolable.

1.4.2. Human Dignity Is, in Reality, Violable
I would propose that it is this alleged inviolability that has led to the rise of 'dignity talk'. After all, who can argue against a claim that is based on an inviolable universal moral good? However, the very fact that human dignity has been proclaimed inviolable, and subsequently given rise to 'dignity talk' means that the efficacy of the notion of human dignity itself is jeopardised when actions by those who are supposed to uphold

Questioning Dignity

and protect the inviolability of human dignity seem indeed themselves to violate it.

The list of instruments that make use of the concept of human dignity is interesting, in this regard, in that despite human dignity being an acknowledged or even central value for a number of countries, many of these same countries have a track record of human rights violations, and hence, one could argue, violations of human dignity. For example, among the countries that have ratified the 1966 *International Covenant on Economic, Social and Cultural Rights* (ICESCR), and the 1966 *International Covenant on Civil and Political Rights* (ICCPR) are Rwanda (which acceded to the covenants in 1975), the Sudan (which acceded in 1986), and Zimbabwe (which acceded in 1991). In all three cases you will notice that the year of accession is prior to the grave threats to human dignity that have taken place in recent years in these countries.[58] The genocide in Rwanda that took place between April and June 1994 resulted in between 800,000 and 1 million deaths and can only be seen as total denial of the worth of other human beings. Tutsis and moderate Hutus were, in the eyes of the Hutu mob, so worthless and so lacking in any sense of dignity that they were slaughtered on sight.

Moreover, one should not think that only African countries are guilty of disregarding human dignity. The actions of the United States of America have recently come under scrutiny with regard to the treatment of suspected terrorists, particularly concerning the use of questioning techniques that may constitute torture.[59] On September 6, 2006, in a speech defending the prosecution of suspected terrorists by military commission, and a Central Intelligence Agency (CIA) 'program' that developed "an alternative set of procedures"[60] for questioning suspected terrorists who had been trained to "resist interrogation," the then president of the United States of America, George W. Bush, said,

> ... the Supreme Court's recent decision [in June 2006] has impaired our ability to prosecute terrorists through military commissions, and has put in question the future of the CIA program. In its ruling

on military commissions, the Court determined that a provision of the Geneva Conventions known as 'Common Article Three' applies to our war with al Qaeda. This article includes provisions that prohibit 'outrages upon personal dignity' and 'humiliating and degrading treatment.' The problem is that these and other provisions of Common Article Three are vague and undefined, and each could be interpreted in different ways by American or foreign judges. And some believe our military and intelligence personnel involved in capturing and questioning terrorists could now be at risk of prosecution under the War Crimes Act—simply for doing their jobs in a thorough and professional way.[61]

While I sympathise with Bush's concern regarding the apparent 'vagueness' of the notion of personal dignity itself—something that this chapter indeed intends to illustrate—I would argue that the *Geneva Convention* is fairly clear in its particular understanding of human dignity, regardless of what other understandings might be available. Article 3 states,

> To this end the following acts are and shall remain prohibited at any time and in any place whatsoever with respect to the above-mentioned persons:
>
> (a) Violence to life and person, in particular murder of all kinds, mutilation, cruel treatment and torture;
>
> (b) Taking of hostages;
>
> (c) Outrages upon personal dignity, in particular, humiliating and degrading treatment;
>
> (d) The passing of sentences and the carrying out of executions without previous judgment pronounced by a regularly constituted court affording all the judicial guarantees which are recognized as indispensable by civilized peoples.[62]

From the above quote, it is, I think, clear that regardless of what personal dignity might mean the notion certainly precludes humiliating and degrading treatment. In addition, the convention quite clearly forbids cruel treatment and torture. I would argue that so-called 'waterboarding', one of the procedures used in questioning suspected terrorists, fits within this ambit.

Bush, however, was not so easily defeated, and essentially argued that since such interrogation techniques are necessary, and save lives, and since personal dignity is vague, if the US Congress passed laws that clearly stated what is and is not legal, then Americans would be safe from prosecution for war crimes:

> As we work with Congress to pass a good bill, we will also consult with congressional leaders on how to ensure that the CIA program goes forward in a way that follows the law, that meets the national security needs of our country, and protects the brave men and women we ask to obtain information that will save innocent lives. For the sake of our security, Congress needs to act, and update our laws to meet the threats of this new era. And I know they will.[63]

The implication, of course, is that the concept of personal dignity, due to its 'vagueness', is, according to Bush, open to interpretation by the laws of a particular government at a particular time to "meet the threats of this new era" and is thus not a universal criterion that can be used always and everywhere to judge the moral quality of human behaviour.

Thus, not only is human dignity a potentially ambiguous idea, i.e., because it appears to both justify and condemn opposing actions, but it may even be a completely irrelevant term, used when appropriate and otherwise ignored. One only need return to the wording of article 1 of the *Universal Declaration of Human Rights* to see the problem: "All human beings are born free and equal in dignity and rights. They are endowed with reason and conscience and should act towards one another in a spirit of brotherhood." The word 'should' reveals this problematic aspect of the notion of dignity. Many of the aforementioned legal instruments speak of human dignity as inherent, inviolable or inalienable, and yet, we are faced with a world where this supposedly universal quality of the human person is not apparent, i.e., we do not live in the 'spirit of brotherhood' that the

Universal Declaration of Human Rights claims that we 'should' live in by virtue of our inherent human dignity. If one acts in a way that ignores the dignity of someone else, for example, as the criminal quoted above does, then one not only damages or denies the dignity of one's victim but also, according to the definition in the *Universal Declaration of Human Rights*, one seems to ultimately damage or deny one's own human dignity because one does not act like a brother or a sister, and by that of course is meant the best kind of brother or sister. The actor's 'immoral' behaviour thus diminishes the dignity of the victim and the actor.

Thus, this begs the question: is the use of the notion in all these documents actually nothing more than a nice sentiment, a normative idea that is in fact often contrary to the realities of human life and experience?

In their critique of the concept of human dignity, Mirko Bagaric and James Allan conclude, "Dignity is a vacuous concept. The notion of dignity should be discarded as a potential foundation for rights claims unless, and until, its source, nature, relevance and meaning are determined."[64] While I disagree with them that the notion of dignity should be discarded, I agree that we ought to work towards a clearer understanding of its source, nature and relevance. The widespread use of the concept of human dignity, the rise of what I have called 'dignity talk', and the apparent relativity of the concept in the face of what some might call *realpolitik*,[65] make the need to clarify and strengthen the concept of human dignity all the more urgent if it is to continue to serve any meaningful function in contemporary ethical discourse.

What then are the possible bases for human dignity? I shall provide a brief overview of several possible bases in the next section in order to demonstrate the apparent lack of consensus in this regard. If people do not agree on the basis for human dignity, then this may be one of the key reasons for the problems discussed so far.

1.5 The Many Possible Bases for Human Dignity: Grounds for Dismissal?

Bearing in mind that the intention in this chapter is to approach the concept of human dignity with a hermeneutic of suspicion, the fact that the concept of human dignity is used by two opposing sides of an ethical debate should not be cause for one to end the enquiry. On the contrary, the hermeneutic of suspicion requires one to dig deeper in an attempt to find a reason for this apparent confusion. What one discovers is that though the various parties may all appeal to the concept of human dignity, they seem in fact to have very different understandings of what human dignity actually means.

In this section I shall provide representative examples of some of the many possible grounds offered for human dignity. This is not intended to be a comprehensive bibliographic survey of the issue. The examples provided here are just that, examples, and this may mean that other authors or variations on a theme are left out. Moreover, I shall not enter into detailed discussion regarding the efficacy of the various grounds offered for human dignity by these examples at this stage. The aim here is to demonstrate the point made by critics of the concept of human dignity that the very fact that there are so many grounds offered, and no apparent agreement between them, suggests, according to the critics, that human dignity is of little use to contemporary ethics.

1.5.1. Is Dignity Something We Have or Something We Acquire?

The first important distinction to note is that conceptions of human dignity can be divided into two broad categories. First, there are those that associate human dignity with some ontological or metaphysical feature of humanity such that human dignity is always, already and forever, inviolably and inalienably present in every human being; dignity is something all human beings supposedly have. And second, there are those that associate human dignity with the way a person lives, the kind of moral life he or she leads, such that dignity is something that can be won and lost depending on how the person lives or how he or she is treated by others; dignity in this latter sense is apparently something human beings acquire.[66]

This apparent confusion regarding what human dignity actually means is not confined to ethical debate. Indeed, it may have its source in mixed messages found in the constitutional and rights documents that lie behind the rise of 'dignity talk' in the first place.

For example, as stated already, article 1 of the *Universal Declaration of Human Rights* states that all human beings are born free and equal in dignity and rights. In other words, all human beings already have an equal dignity from birth onwards. The preamble likewise speaks of *inherent* dignity. Yet article 22 can be read in a way that puts a different spin on the concept of human dignity, "Everyone, as a member of society, has the right to social security and is entitled to realization, through national effort and international co-operation and in accordance with the organization and resources of each State, of the economic, social and cultural rights indispensable for his dignity and the free development of his personality." One could read this as saying that dignity is not the ground of rights, but the end of rights. A person has dignity when certain basic rights are met that are "indispensable for his dignity and the free development of his personality." The implication of course would then be that a person's dignity might not be an ontological given, but something that is enhanced or diminished depending on the circumstances in which she lives and how she responds to these circumstances.

A second example of this apparent confusion between dignity as something human beings inherently have versus something that human beings acquire through their behaviour and circumstances, can be found in *Gaudium et spes* (GS). On the one hand, GS states that human beings have dignity because they are "made to the image of God". They have been crowned with glory and honour (par. 12). On the other hand, according to GS 16, it would seem that human dignity is not something that all human beings already have but rather something that results from obeying the law written by God in their hearts: "For man has in his heart a law written by God; to obey it is the very dignity of man; according to it he will be judged." This is the law by which human beings will be judged, presumably suggesting that a favourable judgement means they have secured dignity, an unfavourable one, shame: "Conscience frequently errs from invincible ignorance without losing its dignity. The same cannot be said for a man who cares but little for truth and goodness, or for a conscience which by degrees grows practically sightless as a result of habitual sin." Thus, by loving God and loving one's neighbour, the essence of the law, one acquires dignity.[67]

Strikingly, in an apparent contradiction of what has just been quoted, GS, 28 then states that human dignity is something that can never be lost, regardless of how one behaves: "But it is necessary to distinguish between error, which always merits repudiation, and the person in error, who never loses the dignity of being a person even when he is flawed by false or inadequate religious notions."[68]

Thus, a cursory reading of two key documents reveals to the suspicious mind an ambiguity: is dignity something we already have or is it something that we acquire? The documents that make reference to dignity seem at first sight to be unhelpful in resolving this problem. Moreover, the fact that even in such core documents different readings are possible such that they result in different understandings of human dignity may explain, to some extent, why this duality arises in public ethical debate.

These two understandings of dignity often seem to be on opposite ends of ethical debate. So, in the case of stem-cell research, the understanding of dignity as an inherent and inviolable worth is used for arguments against, while the understanding of dignity as something we look to advance through the way we behave may be used for arguments for; in the case of end-of-life decisions, the former may be used against, while the latter may be used for; and in the case of interpersonal violence, the former may be used against and the latter may be used for.

That said, however, precisely what constitutes the ground or basis for the inherent or the acquired versions of dignity can also differ. In what follows, I shall list an illustrative sample of some of the possible bases of these respective understandings of human dignity.

1.5.2. Dignity as Something We Already Have

Within this group, a further distinction can be made between two broad categories that are characterised by what they emphasise as being the most important constitutive feature or features of human dignity. I shall call the first the ontological group, and the second, the capacity group. Both of these groups imply that dignity is something inherent to the human person, as well as something that cannot be taken away. In the case of the capacity group, however, there may be limitations placed on who can be said to have dignity since it may limit its understanding of which human beings constitute human persons. The absence of particular capacities may call the claim that a particular individual has dignity into question. Note, however, that the emphasis is on the capacity, not on whether or not the capacity has been realised to any extent. In what follows I shall provide examples of these two groups.

1.5.2.1. Dignity as Some Ontological Given

Foremost among the ontological group are religiously, and particularly Judeo-Christian inspired ideas of human dignity that claim, as we have seen already with reference to *Gaudium et spes*, that all human beings have human dignity because they are created in the image of God.[69] For some interpreters, this in turn has come to mean that the very biological existence of a human being, at whatever stage that life may be, is inviolable because it is a gift from God. Likewise, human DNA, as the matter that constitutes human life becomes something that should not be experimented with, ostensibly because it would be an offence to human dignity. For example, Joseph Cardinal Bernardin, the then archbishop of Chicago, in one of his many public addresses on the idea of a consistent ethic of life, said, "A consistent ethic of life is based on the need to ensure that the sacredness of human life, which is the ultimate source of human dignity, will be defended and fostered from womb to tomb, from genetic laboratory to the cancer ward, from the ghetto to the prison."[70]

Boston College Theologian Stephen J. Pope dedicates an entire chapter of his book, *Human Evolution and Christian Ethics,* to the subject of the dignity of the human person. His aim in this chapter is to counter claims that evolution is at odds with the notion of the dignity of the human person.[71] Such a claim holds that if human beings are descended from more primitive organisms, and therefore not divinely created, then they have no claim to a special dignity over and against other organisms. Pope claims that this is not the case, and that even if we accept evolution and the notion of common descent, i.e., that human beings are descended from more primitive organisms, the concept of the dignity of the human person remains valid.[72]

So, how does Pope explicitly define human dignity? Pope states at the beginning of his chapter that his concern is "intrinsic human dignity as opposed to worth based on particular traits, such as social status, racial identity, income or talent."[73] To illustrate the kind of dignity he claims to be talking about, Pope turns to the United Nations' 1948 *Universal Declaration of Human Rights*. Pope affirms that rights are said to "have their moral justification in human dignity." Pope summarises the concept of human dignity as it appears in the *Universal Declaration of Human Rights* as follows: "Appeals to human dignity affirm that each person has intrinsic value and therefore ought to be protected from certain kinds of harm. Because people have dignity, they have rights that shield them from certain kinds of harms ... and that require them to be given certain kinds of benefits ... ."[74]

Furthermore, Pope seems to base the idea of the intrinsic dignity of the human person on the Christian belief that the human being is created in the image of God.[75] This inherent, or intrinsic, worth is what entitles the person to certain rights, or put differently, entitles a person to be treated in a way that is special and different to that of animals, a way that is never purely instrumental.[76] In other words, as Pope himself quite clearly states, "We should not confuse the dignity of the person with the dignity of various human traits." And further, "Human nature has intrinsic value and so do all who partake in it, regardless of the extent to which they instantiate or manifest the various traits that give humanity its special nobility."[77]

In addition, Pope acknowledges that contemporary discussions have suggested making a distinction between persons, as possessing some or other criterion such as rationality or consciousness, and human life in general, which includes embryos and the profoundly mentally handicapped. Nevertheless he counters this simply by saying that "Christian ethics needs to retain its affirmation of the equally intrinsic value of every member of the human race. In this way Christian ethics remains centrally grounded in the narrative and teachings of Jesus."[78]

Stephen Pope, however, while giving voice to an ontological religiously-inspired notion of human dignity that is shared by every human being does not simply base this human dignity in biological life. His focus remains the idea that human beings are created in the image of God. However, one can identify a trend towards reducing the idea of the gift of dignity to the gift of life, and hence an equation between dignity and biological life. To demonstrate this, I shall perform a brief analysis of recent statements by Pope Benedict XVI.[79] These statements have occurred in various forums and do not necessarily constitute authoritative Roman Catholic teaching. Nevertheless they echo sentiments that are expressed on pro-life websites[80] and even in some of the essays in the President's Council on Bioethics' collection that Steven Pinker so heavily criticised.[81]

Consider the following quotes from Benedict's discourses.[82] The quotes that are used here are not chronological, so in that way, the apparent shift that seems to take place here is somewhat synthetic. Nevertheless, there would seem to be a tendency to equate, supersede or even merge the dignity of the human person with the dignity of human biological life, and the quotes have been put in this order to illustrate this tendency as clearly as possible.

"… the heart of the economic, social and cultural development of each community is a proper respect for life and for the dignity of every human person."[83] In this quote Benedict has put respect for life and respect for dignity alongside one another as values that must be upheld in order for communities to flourish. At this point, the values appear to be distinct from one another.

However, Benedict is apparently concerned that the flourishing of society is at risk: "In a certain number of countries, we are actually seeing the appearance of new legislation that calls into question respect for human life from its conception until its natural end at the risk of exploiting it as an object for research and experimentation, and thereby striking a serious blow to the fundamental dignity of the human being."[84] Again, there are two values, but life from conception to natural end is subordinated to dignity. The fact that a threat to life is a threat to dignity, does not exclude other things from being a threat to dignity that may not be a threat to life, for example, inadequate access to education or having to live in a society in which one's religious freedom is curtailed.

In response to this threat, Benedict XVI points out that "the Church wants to make her own contribution to serving the human community by shedding more and more light on the relationship that unites each person to the Creator of all life and is the basis of the inalienable dignity of every human being, from conception to natural death."[85] The Church thus calls on human beings to "respect the sacredness of the human person and his dignity, because his life is a divine gift. We are concerned to see that some branches of science are experimenting on the human being, without respect for either the dignity or the integrity of the person in all the stages of his life, from conception to his natural end."[86] So, the dignity of the person, from conception to natural death, is affirmed. There are those who may contest this on various grounds, for example, some of the 'capacity group' arguments may argue that a fertilised egg does not have human dignity, but that is not the point here. The point is that human life, which is a gift from God, seems to be presented here as the basis of human dignity.

Now, in a further criticism of the sciences by Benedict XVI, there seems to be a trend towards making human biological life an absolute norm, i.e. an ultimate moral good that is an end in itself and that can never be subordinated to another end: "In fact, this research advances through the suppression of human lives [i.e., human beings who already exist, even though they have not yet been born] that are equal in dignity to the lives of other human individuals and the lives of the researchers themselves."[87] What is remarkable here is that the unborn are not equal in dignity to the researchers, but the *lives* of the unborn are equal in dignity to the *lives* of the researchers. Is this just a stylistic slip of the tongue? Further quotes show that this may not in fact be accidental. In the following quotes, it is the dignity of human life that Benedict apparently sees threatened, not the dignity of the human person: "Sadly, the modern world is marked by an increasing number of threats to the dignity of human life;"[88] "When faced with the demand, which is often expressed, of eliminating suffering even by recourse to euthanasia, it is essential to reaffirm the inviolable dignity of human life from conception to its natural end;"[89] "[The Church] feels in duty bound to insist that science's ability to predict and control must never be employed against human life and its dignity ... ."[90]

Thus, Benedict seems to be saying that human life is an absolute value, and an end in itself. Indeed, it would seem that the dignity of the person is meaningless without life, and that life should be preserved regardless of what the implications may be for, for example, autonomy and self-respect. In other publications,[91] I have argued that Benedict XVI's public discourse in fact displays a much more complex understanding of human dignity that does indeed take these other factors into account. This is why Benedict's apparent tendency to associate dignity with human life demonstrated here is all the more puzzling. Nevertheless, it remains important because it is an essential part of his public discourse and is used in the public discourse of other organisations. For example, Richard Doerflinger, deputy director of the United States Conference of Catholic Bishops' Secretariat for Pro-Life Activities, states on their website, "To be sure, the debate on 'cloning for research' demonstrates that there will be much outright destruction of life along this path as well. But this willingness to destroy life is a symptom of a new level of disdain for human dignity, a mentality that treats other human beings as objects for our control. Nothing could be more alien to the attitude needed to build a culture of life."[92]

Allied to the association of human dignity with human life are ideas that associate human dignity with the human species. Such ideas no longer, necessarily, depend on a religious claim that human beings are created or loved by God and hence have dignity. Instead, human beings have dignity, and therefore moral value, because other human beings somehow intuit that this is so by virtue of their being members of the same species. A ground for human dignity could not possibly be more vague, and yet, there seems to be something essentially true about it. My discomfort at reading how the violent criminal maligns the 'sanctity' of the term dignity by using it to justify actions that are themselves an offence to the dignity of others may be evidence of this intuition. But exactly what this intuition is or where it comes from, or even whether it is valid, is all still up for debate. This idea of an intuition that affirms that all human beings have dignity simply because they are human beings has been dealt with by Dan Egonsson, professor of practical philosophy at Lund University, Sweden. He calls this intuition the "Standard Attitude", but seems reluctant to actually define exactly what it is or how we come to have it.[93] In the end, Egonsson concludes that the Standard Attitude is best understood as "an attitude towards the direct importance of being a member of the biological species *Homo sapiens.*"[94] Essentially, Egonsson argues for "the thesis that given subjectivism and the existence of an intuition or preference to the effect that a human being has a special moral standing precisely in virtue of being human, then we have a foundation of the idea of human dignity."[95]

Francis Fukuyama, professor of international political economy at Johns Hopkins University, in his book *Our Posthuman Future*, makes another attempt at grounding dignity in an ontological way in the human species in an effort to challenge those who favour unbridled biotechnological progress. Fukuyama argues that though human beings evolved from animals, there was an "ontological leap" in our evolution that gave rise to a unique set of characteristics that distinguishes us from animals and provides us with a nature that is uniquely human, and hence worth respecting. Nevertheless, Fukuyama is reluctant to specify any particular feature as essential, and instead refers to a "Factor X". Says Fukuyama, "Factor X cannot be reduced to the possession of moral choice, or reason, or language, or sociability, or sentience, or emotions, or consciousness, or any other quality that has been put forth as a ground for human dignity. It is all of these qualities coming together in a human whole that make up Factor X." Nevertheless, though referring to 'qualities', Fukuyama's position remains distinctly ontological: "Every member of the human species possesses a genetic endowment that allows him or her to become a whole human being, an endowment that distinguishes a human in essence from other types of creatures."[96]

Thus, within this ontological group there are ideas that associate dignity with creation by God, human life, and being a member of the human species. Fukuyama's reference to certain capacities such as moral choice, reason, etc. provides a convenient point of transition to the second group of ideas regarding human dignity, namely, those that situate dignity in some or other feature of being human. These are distinct from the ontological group just discussed in that they may consider certain human beings, or stages of human life, as not having human dignity. This does not mean however that they necessarily discount certain human beings or stages of human life as not possessing human dignity.

1.5.2.2. Dignity as Some Given Capacity
The association of human dignity with human life may, indeed, seem to be a very concrete factor, even though in the real world there are in fact still ongoing debates about when a person is actually clinically dead.[97] 'Dignity is life' is a clear and simple formula, but it takes none of the

Questioning Dignity 83

complexity of what it is that makes us human into account. The constitutions and declarations already mentioned in Section 1.1 do indeed aim to protect human life, although the precise definition of what a human life is may still be debated, but they also protect or advocate a certain minimum quality of life. For example, one might argue that life without freedom is pointless and also does not reflect dignity. Legal and political philosopher Ronald Dworkin, who develops an interesting argument regarding the 'sanctity of life' in his book *Life's Dominion,* nevertheless affirms, "Freedom is the cardinal, absolute requirement of self-respect: no one treats his life as having any intrinsic, objective importance unless he insists on leading that life himself, not being ushered along it by others, no matter how much he loves or respects or fears them." [98] People like Dworkin are obviously aware of the value of life, but life itself is not absolutely valuable. Life's value is dependent on other features of the human person. In this section we shall consider a few examples that locate human dignity in given human capacities such as autonomy, reason, and action.

In a book chapter that surveys the historical development of the idea of human dignity and the threats posed to it by modern science, Münster professor of philosophy Kurt Bayertz notes how the historical philosophical development of the idea of human dignity sought to separate the human person from dependency on the divine by affirming the rationality, perfectibility and autonomy of the human being. The human being thus became a self-determining subject, "its own master".[99] Bayertz explains how during and after the Renaissance three qualities of the human being — rationality, perfectibility, and autonomy—became the ground for a new confidence in the human ability to counter the supposed misery of the human condition, prevalent in medieval theology, and "improve this world and the human being's Fate within it."[100]

Rationality describes the ability of the human being to be conscious of her own existence, ask questions about it, and use the knowledge thus acquired. Bayertz states, "According to [John Stuart] Mill, open discussions with the greatest questions which can occupy humanity raises 'even persons of the most ordinary intellect to something of the dignity of thinking beings.'"[101]

The second facet, perfectibility, leads on from the first. Bayertz points out how the human being is the least physically determined of all higher animals, but her capacity to think makes her the most versatile and adaptable. Rational knowledge can thus be used by human beings to alter their condition for the better, in almost any circumstances.

This then leads logically to the third facet—autonomy. According to Bayertz, in the Renaissance idea of human dignity, the human ability to use reason to improve one's situation implies that the world is not a determined place. Human beings can change it. Nature offers no fixed *telos*. The human being is thus free to choose whichever end she wishes. By choosing a particular goal, the human being creates her own norms and values. Immanuel Kant believed that this moral self-legislation was the primary reason for a notion of human dignity, and Bayertz quotes Kant by way of illustration, "Autonomy is therefore the ground of the dignity of human nature and of every rational nature."[102]

In their recent book, *Human Dignity in Bioethics and Biolaw,* professors of law Deryck Beyleveld and Roger Brownsword, argue for a dignity-based approach to law that relies heavily on the moral philosophy of University of Chicago professor of philosophy Alan Gewirth. They state, "the essence of the dignity of agents resides in their capacity to choose, to set their own ends ... ."[103]

This view corresponds to the Kantian view mentioned above. Nevertheless, it is a view of human dignity that is treated with suspicion by feminist thinkers. For example, Margaret Farley, emeritus professor of Christian ethics at Yale, notes that feminist theory is more concerned with the imbeddedness of human beings in relationships, and, moreover, that these relationships are often about caring rather than conquering the other. Farley then looks to construct a feminist basis for respect for persons more in line with this observation. She states, "The capacity of persons to love one another and the world, and (as theologians and philosophers of religion must surely add) their capacity to love and to love freely what is sacredly transcendent and immanent, makes them worthy of respect."[104] Farley, therefore, seems to prefer to ground, or at least to emphasise as the most important feature of any grounding of human dignity, the human capacity to love. It is the capacity to love, she argues, that enables us to have freedom in the first place. Note, it is the capacity that makes human beings worthy of respect, not whether or not the capacity is actualised in anyway. An atheist may not love God, but this would not mean that she no longer has dignity.

This, emphasis on capacities as the basis for human dignity is not only found in secular philosophical discourse. Indeed, the doctrine that human beings are created in the image of God can also be interpreted in a way that grounds human dignity in the capacities that are deemed constitutive of this image. So, for example, Stephen J. Pope, despite apparently arguing for a 'traitless' dignity as we have seen above, nevertheless elsewhere affirms evolved human capacities as constitutive of human dignity: "The essential Christian affirmation of human dignity, the claim that we are created in the image of God, need not be undermined by evolutionary origins. The evolutionary process generated the development of important and distinctive human capacities, notably to understand and to love, that constitute the natural basis of the affirmation that we are made in God's image."[105]

As mentioned already, this emphasis on certain human capacities as constitutive of human dignity may mean that those who do not demonstrate these capacities, who do not, for example, have the potential to reason, choose, act, or love, may not be deemed to possess human dignity. If they nevertheless deserve respect, it cannot be grounded on human dignity. A representative of this position is professor of law and ethics at Chicago Martha Nussbaum.

In her contribution to the collection of essays commissioned by the President's Council on Bioethics, Nussbaum links human dignity with her 'capability theory'. She is suspicious of the Stoic account of dignity that associates dignity with the capacity for rationality alone. Her concern is that this leads to a denial of "any dignity or end-like worth inherent in those human capacities in which animals also partake, such as sentience, everyday (non-moral) practical reasoning, emotion, and the capacity for love and care." Moreover, according to Nussbaum, the Stoic account, like the ontological accounts mentioned in the previous section, make dignity something invulnerable to the challenges of daily life. No matter what happens, one can never lose one's dignity. Nussbaum is concerned that such a ground is of little value in bringing about real justice in the world, something which human rights, and particularly the so-called positive rights which are meant to guarantee social goods like education and healthcare, are meant to achieve. Thus, one could say that Nussbaum shares Margaret Farley's concern that certain accounts of dignity do not take seriously enough the existential relational 'situated-ness' of the human person. That said, however, Nussbaum nevertheless believes that the Stoics are right to affirm the need for a concept of inalienable dignity, but that they are wrong to do so by locating it internally in higher reason. She prefers to locate it in human beings' "capacities for various forms of activity and striving." She says that "[t]hese capacities are preparations for activity, and it is necessary for a flourishing human life, a life worthy of those capacities, that there be opportunities to use them in activity." Moreover, she is reluctant to base dignity in any single capacity, since this may lead to abuse where some people are deemed not to have this capacity, for example, severely mentally handicapped people. It must, in other words, "respect the many varieties of human beings." For Nussbaum, then,

> ... full and equal human dignity is possessed by any child of human parents who has any of an open-ended disjunction of basic capabilities for major human life-activities. At one end, we would not accord equal human dignity to a person in a persistent vegetative state, or an anencephalic child, since it would appear that there is no striving there, no reaching out for functioning. On the other end, we would include a wide range of children and adults with severe mental disabilities, some of whom are capable of love and care but

not of reading and writing, some of whom are capable of reading and writing but severely challenged in the area of social interaction. So the notion of 'basic capabilities' still does some work in saying why it is so important to give capacities development and expression, but it is refashioned to be flexible and pluralistic, respectful of human diversity.[106]

In conclusion then, looking at this section with a hermeneutic of suspicion, for those who talk of human dignity as something all human persons already have, there seems to be little agreement as to what actually constitutes the basis of this dignity. Moreover, while ontological grounds may range from divine origins to being members of the human species, and capacity-based grounds may range from the more traditional 'reason' or 'autonomy' to a broad range of human capabilities, including the capacity to love, none of them provide clarity as to who precisely has dignity. For example, there is nothing about the species model that precludes abortion or allowing a person to opt for physician-assisted suicide, and as mentioned already, the capacity-based model runs the risk of precluding those who can be said not to possess a given capacity. The picture is further complicated when one considers that human dignity also has another possible foundation, something that the 'ontological group' and indeed even the Stoic rationalism that Nussbaum describes, seem keen to avoid, namely that dignity is something that human beings acquire through their behaviour. Here it is no longer human origins or human capacities that confer dignity, but rather what human beings make of them that matters.

1.5.3. Dignity as Something We Acquire

At the beginning of this section on the various bases for dignity, I made it clear that critics of the concept of human dignity already point out that there is a discrepancy in the use of the term such that sometimes people seem to talk about dignity as something human beings already have—an inherent good—and at other times as something that human beings somehow acquire—an end to be attained. Section 1.5.2 then considered a small sample of the bases for dignity that would ground it as something human beings already have. The present section will now consider arguments that talk of dignity as something that human beings somehow acquire. Here too, one could consider this from two related perspectives. The first I shall call the 'psychological group,' and the second the 'social group'. The psychological group concerns the self-conscious subject's appreciation of his or her own dignity. Here, dignity is associated with ideas of pride, self-respect, and integrity; dignity has more to do with how one thinks of oneself than how others think of one, though of course, how others think of one affects how one thinks of oneself. In other words, dignity is the psychological experience of one's own worth. The social group is based on social norms and mores. A person who lives up to or somehow emulates these norms in a society is considered by that society (i.e. the community of people who share those norms and mores) to have dignity. Such a person is, hence, worthy of respect. The two groups are of course related in that the way in which one thinks of one's self as having worth will in part be determined by how one believes one lives up to the norms of society such that one feels that one has a right to demand respect.

1.5.3.1. Dignity as a Psychological Phenomenon

Several authors point out that when we speak of dignity we often mean a personal sense of pride and worth. This is apparent from the use of the term in the English language. The word dignity in contemporary English usage does indeed carry the notion of pride or self-respect. The *Compact Oxford English Dictionary,* for example, defines dignity as, among other things, "a sense of pride in oneself."[107]

The word dignity occurs several times in the work of psychiatrist, James Gilligan. Gilligan was responsible for the psychiatric programme in the Massachusetts state prison system between 1981 and 1991. In his book *Violence: Reflections on a National Epidemic*, Gilligan relates the story of the violent man that I have already quoted in this chapter. When Gilligan asked the man what he wanted so badly that he was prepared to be subjected to severe punishments for his violent behaviour, and even risk death at the hands of other inmates, the man answered, "Pride. Dignity.

Self-esteem." In his book, Gilligan develops the thesis that the primary cause of violence is an overwhelming sense of shame, so overwhelming that life becomes unbearable without it, and a person is willing to risk his life in order to restore his pride.[108]

To many it may at first appear that an act of violence, like murder, reflects neither the dignity of the perpetrator nor of the victim. Yet, this depends on how one understands the notion of human dignity, and particularly its basis. This is indeed partly the point of section 1.5, namely, to show that different bases for dignity have different implications for the way that people use the concept to justify their behaviour. Gilligan's work suggests an understanding of human dignity that reflects not some abstract principle, already ontologically given, but rather something that people can be cognisant of in their own lives. Moreover, the understanding of dignity that Gilligan accords violent criminals implies that dignity is in some sense something that one can lose and that one can acquire through the actions of others and one's own actions. The violent man's sense of dignity shifts between feelings of shame and pride. I shall highlight a few aspects of Gilligan's work and its relationship to the concept of human dignity in what follows.

When discussing the motives for violent behaviour, Gilligan himself makes the connection, as the prisoner quoted above does, between this violence and a particular concept of dignity. Here, dignity, as a subjective category, has everything to do with a person's own sense of pride. Gilligan states, "For we misunderstand these [violent] men, at our peril, if we do not realize they mean it literally when they say they would rather kill or mutilate others, be killed or mutilated themselves, than live without pride, dignity, and self-respect. They literally prefer death to dishonour."[109]

In Gilligan's later work *Preventing Violence,* where he states that his theory deals with shame and its opposite pride, he considers pride to be an umbrella term that incorporates "self-esteem, self-love, self-respect, feelings of self-worth, dignity, and the sense of having maintained one's honour intact."[110] Therefore, Gilligan has specifically named dignity, understood as an appreciation of one's own worth, as the opposite of shame.

One could, quite rightly, argue that the criminal's claim that he has a right to defend his dignity through violence is wrong, because his claim to dignity is obviously at odds with the claims of those he attacks (see 4.1.2). Nevertheless, Gilligan's work is important here in that it demonstrates how dignity is sometimes subjectively grounded in some sense of self-worth. The appropriateness of what a person believes will afford him a sense of self-worth is not the issue here. The point is that there are those who argue for a subjective basis for dignity grounded in a person's sense of self and/or the worthiness of that self for respect by others. Moreover, this dignity, as a positive sense of self, is vulnerable to humiliation, and therefore, unlike the ontological bases of dignity mentioned earlier, obviously violable, or at the very least mutable.

Charles Taylor, a professor of social and political philosophy, in his well-known book, *Sources of the Self: The Making of Modern Identity*, provides a useful insight into the argument that bases dignity in a sense of pride. Taylor calls dignity the "characteristics by which we think of ourselves as commanding (or failing to command) the respect of those around us." By respect, Taylor means the attitude that entails some admiration of the person concerned. "Our 'dignity' ... is our sense of ourselves as commanding (attitudinal) respect."

Taylor considers the question of what our dignity consists in to be fundamentally important because "our dignity is so much woven into our very comportment. The very way we walk, move, gesture, speak is shaped from the earliest moments by our awareness that we appear before others, that we stand in public space, and this space is potentially one of respect or contempt, of pride or shame. Our style of movement expresses how we see ourselves as enjoying respect or lacking it, as commanding it or failing to do so." [111]

Questioning Dignity 91

While Taylor's claims are more general, they are illustrated in the particular case of the violent men that Gilligan deals with. Their violent behaviour (comportment) is related to their demand to be respected by others. Gilligan argues that the source of the need for external respect is an acute lack of self-love. This self-love is lacking, according to Gilligan, because these men never experienced adequate affirmation of their worth when they were children. Indeed, they were often physically and psychologically abused such that their most formative experience is not one of respect, but contempt, not pride, but shame.[112]

Taylor goes on to state that dignity can consist in "our power, our sense of dominating public space; or our invulnerability to power; or our self-sufficiency, our life having its own centre; or our being liked and looked to by others, a centre of attention. But very often the sense of dignity grounds in some of the same moral views I mentioned above. For instance, my sense of myself as a householder, father of a family, holding down a job, providing for my dependants; all this can be the basis for my sense of dignity. Just as its absence can be catastrophic, can shatter it by totally undermining my sense of self-worth." [113]

What is evident from Taylor's description of what dignity can consist in, is that when dignity is understood as self-worth, precisely what this self-worth is attached to, i.e., what it is about a person that she herself deems worthy of the respect of others, is open ended. This potentially makes dignity relative and hence even more problematic as an ethical criterion by which to judge the moral quality of a behaviour, or to evaluate rights claims. Gilligan's criminal, for example, associates it with his being seen as powerful, a product, Gilligan maintains, of living in an honour culture in which men are expected to be strong, independent, and sexually potent.[114] But Martha Nussbaum illustrates an alternative vision, which corresponds to Taylor's claim that dignity can be associated with *invulnerability* to power. Nussbaum says that though some people identify themselves as victims and ask for the help of the powerful, there are others among those disempowered people who may rightly insist,

"We have our pride and our strength. We are complete in ourselves. No whining and complaining for us. We are more beautiful, ultimately, than those who oppress us." As an illustration of this, Nussbaum points to the disability-rights movement's resistance to the idea that their disability implies a deprivation.[115] Nussbaum, of course, argues that an idea of inherent dignity based on a broad range of capabilities is necessary to be able to make such a claim. However, if, as Taylor suggests, dignity is grounded in a person's *idea* of what makes them worthy of respect, then it is dignity as a sense of self-worth that makes the claim possible. In other words, the people in Nussbaum's example have chosen to associate their dignity with the fact that they have inherent capacities, or even a sense of self that is invulnerable to oppression, but they could have associated their dignity with any number of other ideas. The real basis of dignity, then, in this psychological account of dignity, is not the capacities, but the conscious association of one's worth with those capacities, or with the idea that one is created by God, or with the idea that one can hurt other people, or with some other idea that one believes will confer worth on one in the eyes of one's society and confirm one's worth for oneself.

What is important to note, however, is that whatever it is that is considered to justify the claim of having dignity, that thing is considered admirable, if not by everyone, then at least by the person in question.[116] Taylor notes that the life of dignity is always something set apart, something admirable, otherwise it is meaningless.[117] This resonates with Gilligan's claim that violent men would rather kill or be killed, or even take their own lives than face a life of indignity, or shame.

Advocates who argue for the right to end their lives, like professor of medicine, psychiatry, and medical humanities Timothy Quill, often do so on the basis that *not* to allow them to do so would be an offence to their dignity.[118] At first, this seems irreconcilable with Gilligan's claim: Gilligan's criminals will kill themselves because they feel they have *no* dignity; the advocates of the right to die will kill themselves as an expression *of* their dignity. However, when one realises this still has to do with an idea that grounds dignity in a sense of self-worth, this apparent difference is dissolved. The advocates of the right to die want to be allowed to take their own lives because to go on living would expose them to shame. At a psychological level, then, this is very similar to Gilligan's criminal who is prepared to die rather than to live in shame. Moreover, in both cases, how they act conforms to an ideal of what constitutes a dignified life, a life that one can be proud of, a life that is admirable, a life that is meaningful.

In arguments for a right to die, dignity is often linked to autonomy. Ruth Macklin, for example, argues that to respect a person's autonomy in such instances is the same as respecting a person's dignity. In other words, dignity is nothing more than autonomy.[119] This would seem to put such arguments in the 'capacities group'. But, it is not that simple, because what is being argued for by these advocates of the right to die is not simply respect for the inherent capacity to be autonomous, but respect for the product of the exercise of that autonomy, i.e., for the person that they have become through the choices that they have exercised throughout their lives. For example, Lennart Nordenfelt, professor of philosophy of medical ethics at Linköping, Sweden, describes this dignity as the dignity "we attach to ourselves as integrated and autonomous persons, persons with a history and persons with a future with all our relationships to other human beings. Most of us have a basic respect for our own identity, although it need not be at all remarkable from a moral or other point of view. But this self-respect can easily be shattered, for instance by the cruel acts of other people."[120] Nordenfelt points out though, and this is particularly relevant to the debates regarding end-of-life decisions, a person's dignity, i.e., their sense of who they are as an integrated whole, can also be shattered through the 'cruelty' of biology, illness, and the approach of death.

Nordenfelt's position here is interesting in that it pushes the boundaries of the idea of dignity as a psychological sense of self-worth to encompass a person's entire existential conception of his or her life. In this case, dignity is not based in the fleeting moments of feeling proud or feeling humiliated but in the sum of all of those experiences as an integrated whole and how that sum reflects an integrated identity over time and the values that a person has chosen to hold dear.

A similar position is put forward by professor of medical ethics at Memorial University of Newfoundland, Daryl Pullman, who argues for an aesthetics of dignity. "This sense of dignity is dependent upon the unity and integrity of a life narrative that is at once both personal and communal. Maintaining a unified and meaningful life narrative is both a moral and an aesthetic project. Suffering occurs when any aspect of the person is threatened or is perceived as undergoing disintegration. Such aesthetic upheaval is often referred to as a loss of dignity."[121]

Pullman's argument shares similarities with that of legal and political philosopher Ronald Dworkin who, in his book, *Life's Dominion*, also tends to associate dignity with an aesthetic of a meaningful life well lived. Dworkin argues that Western political culture is dominated by a "belief in individual human dignity: that people have the moral right—and the moral responsibility—to confront the most fundamental questions about the meaning and value of their own lives for themselves, answering to their own consciences and convictions."[122] Dworkin justifies this perspective by providing the example of the abolition of slavery in the United States. He argues that dignity framed the most powerful arguments of both religious and secular abolitionists: "the cruelest aspect of slavery was its failure to recognize a slave's right to decide central issues of value for himself."[123] Thus, though the capacity for autonomy is important, the emphasis is not on the dignity we have because of this capacity but on the dignity that we acquire by using this autonomy, and all our other capacities, to live a meaningful life, to adequately honour, as Dworkin would put it, "the sanctity of life."[124]

In summary then, what I have called the 'psychological group' grounds dignity in the psychological experience of one's own worth, either as a sense of pride associated with the respect that one believes one deserves from others, or as an existential attachment to a life meaningfully and beautifully lived. Nevertheless, you will have noticed that in both cases the sense of self-worth is associated with behaviour or a way of living that would be considered admirable, not only by the actor, but by others in society. This brings us to the second group of ideas that ground dignity in something we acquire, what I have called the 'social group'.

1.5.3.2. Dignity as a Social Phenomenon

Again, here I shall only mention a few illustrative and interesting representatives of this group. This group can be defined as those who ground human dignity in human behaviour, rather than human psychology. Dignity is associated with the degree to which a human being uses his capacities to conform to some societal norm of morally good behaviour. A person who has dignity is a person who is morally admirable in the eyes of his or her society.

In his critique of the President's Council on Bioethics Report on Human Dignity already mentioned, Steven Pinker states that dignity is relative. The kind of dignity he describes, and indeed advocates, as the only useful concept of dignity is one based on the social mores of the society in which it is situated:

> One doesn't have to be a scientific or moral relativist to notice that ascriptions of dignity vary radically with the time, place, and beholder. In olden days, a glimpse of stocking was looked on as something shocking. We chuckle at the photographs of Victorians in starched collars and wool suits hiking in the woods on a sweltering day, or at the Brahmins and patriarchs of countless societies who consider it beneath their dignity to pick up a dish or play with a child.[125]

Pinker argues that this is related to evolved traits that inspire the individual to respect another human being; the outward signs trigger esteem. Though Pinker does not explicitly say so, the above quote also shows that the actual content of these signs may vary. This has to do with changes in social mores regarding what constitutes a dignified manner. Dignity, and hence, respect, is afforded to those who display these signs. For Pinker, then, in ethics, the value of this understanding of human dignity is that we should not put people in circumstances that force them to behave in a way that is undignified, for example, having to parade through a hospital corridor in one of those open-backed gowns. A rectal examination can be awkward and embarrassing for the examinee due to the mores surrounding the indignity of having to expose one's 'private' parts, and so, according to Pinker, doctors and medical personnel should be aware of this and treat the person with due respect and sensitivity.

Cambridge psychologist and theologian Fraser Watts makes a similar point, suggesting that dignity seems to assume that we respect people for their positive qualities, in particular their rationality. Nevertheless, he notes, what society holds to be positive qualities may change. So, whereas it may have been considered dignified not to weep in public, today one might think that this shows a lack of sensitivity rather than dignity.[126] In this understanding of human dignity, a person, therefore, has dignity to the extent that they demonstrate the kind of comportment (to use Charles Taylor's word) that society, which functions as the conferrer of dignity, deems admirable.[127]

Michael J. Meyer, professor of philosophy at Santa Clara University, argues for a virtue of dignity. To illustrate what he means by the virtue of dignity he offers the examples of Martin Luther King's marching at Selma and Mahatma Gandhi's marching for the Salt Satyagraha. According to Meyer, their actions confer on them a dignity of character worthy of respect, because they are neither too humble not to act for the good, nor too proud to think it beneath them to do so.

Tellingly, Meyer then also provides the example of the 'dignified' butler. The challenge that he admits this poses for his idea of a virtue of dignity is that the butler's dignity is due to the mores of the aristocratic society he inhabits, not despite it (as in the case of King and Gandhi).[128] A moral relativist might point out that the dignity Meyer ascribes to King and Gandhi is likewise a product of a set of mores regarding what constitutes dignified behaviour, in this case standing up for one's rights and the rights of others in a non-violent way.

Nick Bostrom, professor of philosophy and director of the Future of Humanity Institute at Oxford University, describes himself as a transhumanist, which means that he "holds that current human nature is improvable through the use of applied science and other rational methods, which may make it possible to increase human health-span, extend our intellectual and physical capacities, and give us increased control over our own mental states and moods. Technologies of concern include not only current ones, like genetic engineering and information technology, but also anticipated future developments such as fully immersive virtual reality, machine-phase nanotechnology, and artificial intelligence."[129] Bostrom, like Steven Pinker, opposes the use of human dignity by so-called bioconservatives, like Leon Kass and Francis Fukuyama, to prevent such enhancements or research into the possibility of such enhancements. Instead he offers an alternative understanding of dignity to that "invoked by bioconservative commentators to argue against enhancement."[130]

The central thrust of Bostrom's understanding of human dignity is that dignity can be understood as denoting some "special excellence or moral worthiness, ... something that current human beings possess to widely differing degrees. Some excel far more than others do. Some are morally admirable; others are base and vicious."[131] This view of dignity, according to Bostrom, emphasises not our DNA, not our origins, but what we are and what we can become. He argues, in essence that through enhancement we can, and indeed have already, become 'better' people. If, for example, genetic engineering were to enable us to give birth to children who had a better chance of survival, better chances of success, better quality of life, then not to allow such enhancement would be tantamount to child abuse. Bostrom says, "In any case, if the alternative to parental choice in determining the basic capacities of new people is entrusting the child's welfare to nature, that is blind chance, then the decision should be easy.

Had Mother Nature been a real parent, she would have been in jail for child abuse and murder." The point is that Bostrom has taken the idea that the capacities for autonomy and perfectibility are the grounds for the claim that all human beings share equal dignity (see 1.5.2.2), and inverted it, such that a person has dignity to the degree that they strive for and can be said to have realised autonomy and perfectibility in themselves and others.

1.5.3.3. Religious Positions That Describe Dignity as Something Acquired

In order to avoid the conclusion that the polarity between arguments that understand human dignity as something human beings have versus something human beings acquire is simply between religious arguments that ground human dignity in some ontologically inherent worth of the human being and secular humanist (or relativist) arguments that ground it in conscious human experience and progress, I shall provide an example of a religiously-inspired grounding of human dignity that also associates dignity with some conception of self-worth and behaviour in accordance with some moral norm.

German moral theologian and longtime professor of moral theology at the Pontifical Gregorian University in Rome, Klaus Demmer MSC, maintains that central to moral theology is how human dignity manifests itself in action.[132] He shows that the Second Vatican Council's attempt to communicate with the world about God and morality led to a formulation of the concept of dignity that makes the idea of God's plan for moral behaviour implicitly present for all human beings. Demmer says, "Contemporary sensibility regards the appeal to conscience as extremely important; conscience stands for the person's dignity and for individual responsibility in moral life. This notion is particularly important in the context of a pluralistic and tolerant society that has made the duty to actively respect the other's conscience—including in cases of disagreement—a central component of its political program." For Demmer, linking human dignity with the idea of conscience means that a human being realises his or her dignity and freedom to the extent that he or she responsibly obeys, and hence acts on, the truths known to this conscience: "Only the awareness of God's judgement can grant ultimate freedom from the judgement of others. The very dignity of the person consists in being judged by God only and in living in harmony with her or his own conscience."[133]

The idea that human dignity amounts to living in harmony with one's conscience is seen in the Second Vatican Council's important *Declaration on Religious Freedom, Dignitatis Humanae*,[134] which states, "A sense of the dignity of the human person has been impressing itself more and more deeply on the consciousness of contemporary man, and the demand is increasingly made that men should act on their own judgment, enjoying and making use of a responsible freedom, not driven by coercion but motivated by a sense of duty" (par. 1). The declaration goes on to say, "It is in accordance with their dignity as persons—that is, beings endowed with reason and free will and therefore privileged to bear personal responsibility—that all men should be at once impelled by nature and also bound by a moral obligation to seek the truth, especially religious truth. They are also bound to adhere to the truth, once it is known, and to order their whole lives in accord with the demands of truth." Thus, human dignity is not simply associated with the idea that human beings already have the capacities of reason and free will, but with how those capacities are used in the responsible pursuit of truth, a pursuit that is guided by one's conscience, which Demmer calls, "the privileged place in the person where God dwells."[135]

Thus, when *Dignitatis Humanae* bases the right to freedom of religion on the dignity of the human person, the emphasis is clearly on the association of human dignity with a person's own sense of integrity and authenticity,[136] an idea that sounds similar to those of Nordenfelt, Pullman, and Dworkin discussed earlier. Moreover, a person is said to realise their dignity to the extent that they do indeed live such an authentic and meaningful life in pursuit of the truth. Thus, here we have an idea that seems similar to the notion of a virtue of dignity described by Meyer.

1.5.4. The Critics Call for the Dismissal of the Concept of Human Dignity

A word of caution is necessary here. The consideration of various grounds for dignity presented in Section 1.5 is very brief, and certainly not complete. Moreover, it could be argued that it does not consider the full depth and detail of the arguments offered. I shall argue in Chapter 2 that this is indeed a consequence of certain methodological assumptions made by the critics of the concept of human dignity, and inherent to their hermeneutic of suspicion. Moreover, this kind of superficial treatment is typical of appeals made to human dignity in public debate, where rhetoric and soundbites, and simple, apparently powerful formulas that associate human dignity with 'life' or 'autonomy', backing it up by quoting a line from some supposedly 'authoritative' source like the pope or Kant, are the order of the day.

Nevertheless, the analysis performed here does at least demonstrate that human dignity can be and indeed is associated with a wide variety of facets of what it means to be human, ranging from religious claims about creation, through arguments based on the capacities that separate us from animals, to conscious perceptions of personal worth, both of oneself and others based on the norms of society and the pursuit of a meaningful life.

Critics of the concept of human dignity draw two conclusions from this. First, Bagaric and Allan rightly point out that none of the ideas or qualities associated with or proposed as bases for the concept of human dignity can easily be said to be wrong: "We are in a situation in which anything goes, or at least appears to go."[137] They argue that this certainly does not help the situation. If anything it only weakens dignity as a concept that can underpin rights claims, and therefore, I would add, also weakens its value as a criterion by which moral behaviour can be evaluated. Hence, they conclude that, "The notion of dignity should be discarded as a potential foundation for rights claims unless, and until, its source, nature, relevance and meaning are determined."[138]

Second, Ruth Macklin draws a different and far more radical conclusion. She sees no point in even trying to clarify what we mean by dignity. For Macklin, the analysis above would simply prove that when people use the term dignity they actually mean something else. Her solution is that instead of using the notion of dignity at all, arguments would be a lot clearer if people said what they meant instead of hiding it behind the façade of dignity.[139] So in the case of end-of-life decisions, for example, Macklin would argue that there are not two different arguments both based on human dignity, but instead an argument based on the sanctity of biological life as a gift from God versus an argument based on respect for the autonomy of the person.

The example just provided raises a final area that needs to be taken into account in the critique of the concept of human dignity, namely, the association of human dignity with religious faith. Many of the criticisms of human dignity arise because the critics argue that the concept of human dignity is being abused by those who seek to impose religious beliefs on people against their will. This criticism will be addressed next.

1.6. Human Dignity and God
Bagaric and Allan point out that one of the challenges that the concept of human dignity faces is that many of its advocates base their arguments on statements of faith regarding the creation of human beings in the image of God. Bagaric and Allan are perhaps correct in saying that, "In more secular times, though, many find that source implausible." And, of course, if they find that source implausible, why should they accept the validity of the idea that all people deserve certain rights because they have something called inherent dignity?

Steven Pinker is even more scathing in his attack on those who seek to ground human dignity in the tenets of religious faith. Pinker argues that the collection of essays on human dignity produced by the President's Council on Bioethics, which he criticises as biased in favour of religiously-inspired intellectuals, represents "a movement to impose a radical political agenda, fed by fervent religious impulses, onto American biomedicine." He states that he finds it extraordinary that the volume "finds room for seven essays that align their arguments with Judeo-Christian doctrine," and asks rhetorically, "How did the United States, the world's scientific powerhouse, reach a point at which it grapples with the ethical challenges of twenty-first century biomedicine using Bible stories, Catholic doctrine, and woolly rabbinical allegory?" The notion of human dignity, he maintains, is attractive to these so-called 'theocons' because it is the "natural ground on which to build an obstructionist bioethics. An alleged breach of dignity provides a way for third parties to pass judgement on actions that are knowingly and willingly chosen by the affected individuals. It thus offers a moralistic justification for expanded government regulation of science, medicine, and private life."[140]

The problem is evident, namely, if someone is not a believer, then arguments for human dignity based on faith statements will be unconvincing. Some religious advocates of the concept of human dignity are aware of this problem too, and so attempt to make a case for an idea of dignity that expresses their religious convictions but that might appeal to non-believers too. For example, Glenn Tinder, emeritus professor of political science, in his essay *Against Fate: An Essay on Personal Dignity* states that his is an attempt to "cast the Christian view of humanity and history in terms that are new and might thus be persuasive for those not attracted to Christian terms."[141]

There is an additional problem inherent in grounding human dignity in religious ideas. Apart from making it unpalatable for non-believers, it may lead to confusion among believers. This confusion may arise when it is no longer clear whether it is human dignity that is being respected or God. If it is the latter, then Ruth Macklin makes an important point regarding not using dignity at all. If people engage in certain behaviour or condemn certain behaviour as bad because it offends God, then that is what they should say instead of couching it in terms of human dignity. I shall illustrate this point by briefly analysing several statements by Pope

Benedict XVI. I have already shown how there is a tendency in Benedict's language that could be interpreted as equating human dignity with human life (see 1.5.2.1). Here, I shall demonstrate how certain theological arguments for the dignity of the human person may lead to this equation of human dignity with human life, such that the protection of human life at all stages of development becomes an absolute norm.[142]

In his 2007 message for the World Day of Peace, Benedict XVI asserts that the dignity of the human person means that "the person can not be disposed of at will".[143] In the same speech, Benedict then seemingly translates this assertion into an obligation to respect the fundamental rights of the person, in other words, those things that a person requires as the bare minimum in order to fulfil his or her dignity. Two rights are emphasised: life and religious freedom. That is, one has a right to life because it is through living one's life that one realises the potential inherent in one's dignity. Likewise, the right to religious freedom ensures that one can live out one's dignity by appropriately responding to God, which in Benedict's thinking ought to culminate in receiving Christian baptism in the Roman Catholic Church. However, the language of rights here seems inappropriate, because Benedict XVI does not seem to view them so much as human rights as God's rights: "life is a gift which is not completely at the disposal of the subject," and "religious freedom places the human being in relationship with a transcendent principle which withdraws him from human caprice."[144] In other words, this could be interpreted as implying that it is God's right to decide who lives and dies and God's right to call the human person to relate to Him spiritually. Thus it is God's rights that should not be trodden on by either society, from which negative rights normally defend the human person, or by the human person himself. Thus, the dignity of the human person, as free, reasonable, subject, is superseded not by a 'right' to life, but by a dignity of 'life', a sanctity of life. Life in absolute terms becomes more valuable than individual dignity, because it is a precondition of dignity, it is the primary gift of God, and therefore God's right. It would seem then, that the ultimate criterion for Benedict is thus no longer the dignity of the human person, or even the will of God, discernable in revelation and the natural law, but instead, God Himself. Human beings, and their laws, have no right to interfere in domains of existence that are rightfully God's.[145]

Consequences of this tendency are, first, that any value that the dignity of the human person has as an ethical criterion is undermined, and second, the ethical argumentation that replaces it is no longer accessible to all people of goodwill: it is increasingly dogmatic rather than reasonable. This is precisely what irks critics like Pinker, Macklin, and Bagaric and Allan, and something that the hermeneutic of suspicion should rightly reveal when it leads to polemic rather than rational ethical reflection.

Bagaric and Allan make the point not only with regard to religious arguments, but any metaphysical argument to underpin human dignity. "First, simply asserting something does not actually make it so, no matter how often it is repeated and by whom the claim is made. Second, self-evident truths are rare and can only occur in the most limited of circumstances. ... Given that there is no absurdity in the claim that humans (or at least some humans) do *not* have dignity [e.g. if you base human dignity in the presence or realisation of specific capacities], the claim that dignity inheres in all people is certainly not self-verifying."[146] Obviously, this assertion is dependent on what one means by dignity. If, for example, dignity is based on the belief that all human beings are created in the image of God, then dignity is a sort of ontological fact regardless of what experience may tell us. To affirm, on this basis, that all people have inherent dignity is no more or less 'absurd' than affirming that human beings are created by a loving God. However, if dignity is associated with particular capacities or the realisation of these capacities in certain behaviours, then it is certainly not absurd to assert that some people do not have dignity insofar as they are not able to exercise their capacities or are not given their due respect, howsoever those may be defined. Therefore, any defence of human dignity will have to take these particular experiences of a lack of dignity into account regardless of what other basis may be offered for human dignity, divine or otherwise.

1.7. Conclusion: The Challenges That an Adequate Understanding of Dignity Must Take into Account

In this chapter, I have investigated the concept of human dignity using a hermeneutic of suspicion. This suspicion arises from the rise in 'dignity talk' in which human dignity is used as sort of trump card to justify often opposing arguments and courses of action in contemporary ethical debates. As Peter Singer—Australian philosopher, animal rights advocate, and noted critic of the concept of human dignity, which he considers as amounting to speciesism—notes, "Philosophers frequently introduce ideas of dignity, respect, and worth at the point at which reasons appear to be lacking, but this is hardly good enough. Fine phrases are the last resort of those who have run out of arguments."[147]

In this concluding section, I shall summarise the problems that the analysis performed in this chapter, along with the consideration of some of the writings of critics of dignity, like Macklin, Pinker, and Bagaric and Allan, has brought to light, and which will need to be addressed by any adequate defence of the concept of human dignity. I shall return to these challenges in the concluding Chapter 6 where I shall consider whether the multidimensional understanding of human dignity proposed in this book does in fact offer a meaningful response to them.

1.7.1. The Problem of 'Dignity Talk'

The first, and most obvious problem is that of 'dignity talk'. I have shown that, whereas the concept of human dignity rose to prominence as a value that formed the basis of human rights discourse, as human rights discourse has evolved to a 'rights talk' so too the basis of rights claims has fallen prey to 'dignity talk' to the extent that it has become so clichéd that some critics, like Macklin, deem it unhelpful anymore.

An adequate defence of the concept of human dignity will have to be able to explain and offer a corrective to this 'dignity talk'. In other words, an adequate concept of human dignity must be able to identify what is true and what is false about the understandings of dignity appealed to by the protagonists. For example, to associate human dignity with human life is true, but to only associate it with life is a misleading reductionism. The same might be said for the association of dignity with autonomy or any of the other features mentioned.

1.7.2. The Universal Claim Versus Particular Experience
I have shown that an argument can be made not for human dignity's inviolability but indeed for its violability. Governments ignore it to the detriment of their people, or their enemies. Moreover, despite the universal claim that all human beings have dignity, and hence that human dignity is a universal moral good, a newspaper on any day of the week will challenge this claim with reports of atrocities, deprivation, and people struggling to make sense of the suffering in their lives.

An adequate defence of the concept of human dignity will have to account for this ambiguity. How can dignity be something we say that all people already have and yet at the same time something that seems so beyond our grasp in daily life?

1.7.3. Human Dignity Cannot Be both the Ground and the End of Moral Behaviour
This chapter has indicated that there is an ambiguity in the use of the concept of dignity, both in human rights discourse—religious and secular — and in those who use the concept of human dignity to underpin their claims (see section 1.5 where I considered the various possible bases for dignity). This ambiguity consists in claiming on the one hand that dignity is something that all human beings already have and are therefore entitled to certain rights so that they can live a life worthy of that dignity they have, and on the other, that dignity is something that people aspire to and desire, as they desire to be respected and to live meaningful and fulfilling lives.

An adequate defence of dignity must either show that one of these conceptions is false, or account for how human dignity can be both something we already have and something that we seek to acquire. I intend to do the latter.

1.7.4. There Is No Such Thing As Human Dignity

Potentially one of the most telling criticisms is that inspired by Ruth Macklin's critique. Macklin's critique on its own is weak. She argues that respect for human dignity just means respect for autonomy and respect for the person, and that therefore the concept of dignity is useless. What is important about Macklin's critique, however, is that if one takes it further, as I have done in this chapter, by looking at the various possible grounds offered for human dignity, one might conclude that the concept of human dignity is really just a façade, a term that is used to represent another claim, such that when one argues for a particular course of action based on respect for human dignity, one indeed means something else. Macklin mentions autonomy, but one might also mention life, or one's pride, or one's religious beliefs.

An adequate defence of the concept of human dignity will have to show that human dignity cannot simply be reduced to one or other feature of the human person. Moreover, it will have to demonstrate that the concept offers something more to ethics than any of the individual features alone. Otherwise, one will be forced to conclude, as Macklin does, that dignity is a "useless concept".

1.7.5. The Concept of Human Dignity Is Based on Religious Doctrines and Therefore Inaccessible to Non-Believers

Section 1.6 of this chapter showed that the reference to religious beliefs, such as the Judeo-Christian tenet that human beings are created in the image of God, has led to suspicion regarding the efficacy of human dignity as an ethical criterion. The appeal to human dignity is seen as a covert way of forcing a 'conservative' religious moral agenda that is progress and science averse onto 'liberal' societies. This criticism is not without its merits, but its scorn may be misdirected. Rather, what it should call into question is precisely what the notion of human dignity consists of in such 'conservative' arguments. For example, I have shown that such arguments may have more to do with respecting the 'dignity of God' than with respecting the 'dignity of the human person'.

Thus, the critics and the advocates of certain 'religiously-inspired' views of human dignity may both be misrepresenting the Christian theological anthropology that should underpin Christian claims regarding human dignity. Therefore, an adequate defence of human dignity will have to be able to account for these misrepresentations, as well as offer a conception of human dignity that should be acceptable to both believers and non-believers alike.

1.7.6. Human Dignity is Inadequate as a Normative Moral Criterion

Bagaric and Allan, in particular, are concerned that the alleged 'vacuity' of dignity makes it defunct as a normative moral criterion. They argue that its vagueness is not up to the rigorous demands of making legal judgements or as the basis of rights claims.

Thus, an adequate defence of the concept of human dignity will have to demonstrate the concept's normative properties and the usefulness of these properties in adjudicating between rights claims or judging the moral goodness of a particular moral event.

I would add, however, that this criticism raises several more questions. Why should the concept of human dignity only be seen as normative criterion in ethical discourse? Might this emphasis on its normative function be one of the causes for the rise of 'dignity talk'? Might the concept of human dignity not also have a descriptive function in ethics? I contend that it does and that is a claim that I shall seek to justify in the next chapter.

In the next chapter, then, I shall move to a 'critique of the critique' based on an analysis of some of the methodological assumptions that lie behind the criticisms of the concept of human dignity noted in the present chapter, not the least of which are the hermeneutic of suspicion and the emphasis on normative ethics. I shall then offer alternative methodological assumptions that will serve to construct an alternative understanding of the concept of human dignity as a descriptive category as well as a normative criterion.

Endnotes

1. Bagaric and Allan, "The Vacuous Concept of Dignity," 263–264.
2. See also Bayertz, "Introduction: Sanctity of Life and Human Dignity," xvi, who makes a similar point and adds 'sanctity of life' to these argument clinching criteria; and Jan Jans, "Enjoying and Making Use of a Responsible Freedom," 107: "… there seems to be a tendency to use 'human dignity' as a kind of trump card. Once invoked, it stalls further reflection and debate because it seems to be impossible to discuss actions that go against human dignity!" Jans, himself proposes that human dignity should instead be seen as the beginning rather than the end of ethical reflection. I shall argue for a similar position with regard to human dignity's value as a descriptive category and the role of hermeneutical ethics. See also Soulen and Woodhead, "Introduction: Contextualising Human Dignity," 2; and Witte, "Between Sanctity and Depravity," 121.
3. Respectively, Bagaric and Allan, "The Vacuous Concept of Dignity"; Macklin, "Dignity is a Useless Concept"; Pinker, "The Stupidity of Dignity."
4. Obviously, the concept of 'human dignity' dates back much further than the Second World War, but it has arguably never been in such widespread use as since the Second World War. For a useful, concise, overview of the historical development of the concept of human dignity, see, among others, Soulen and Woodhead, "Introduction: Contextualising Human Dignity," 3–14.
5. Eckert, "Legal Roots of Human Dignity in German Law," 52.
6. See also Dicke, "The Founding Function of Human Dignity in the Universal Declaration of Human Rights," 112–113.
7. Cf. Bagaric and Allan, "The Vacuous Concept of Dignity," 261–263; Soulen and Woodhead, "Introduction: Contextualising Human Dignity," 2; Pope, *Human Evolution and Christian Ethics*, 188, who also provides a brief overview in his introduction to a chapter in which he addresses the challenge that Darwinism poses to our understanding of human dignity.
8. United Nations' Office of the High Commissioner for Human Rights, "Ratification and Reservations," accessed May 30, 2008, http://www2.ohchr.org/english/bodies/ratification/ index.htm.
9. Angola Const. of 1992, art. II and XX, accessed May 31, 2008, http://www.angola.org.uk/law.htm; Ethiopia Const. of

1994, art. XXI, XXIV, XXIX, XXX, and XCI, accessed May 31, 2008, http://www.ethiopianembassy.org/constitution.shtml; Nigeria Const. of 1999, art. XVII and XXXIV, accessed May 31, 2008, http://www.nigeria.gov.ng/NR/rdonlyres/D38CF776-EE00-48DF-A09D-C06FE29997DA/0/NigerianConstitution.pdf.
10. Chaskalson, "Human Dignity as a Constitutional Value," 136–137. Chaskalson cites several legal proceedings to back these claims up.
11. Vatican Council II, "Pastoral Constitution of the Church in the Modern World (*Gaudium et spes*)."
12. Official Roman Catholic documents are typically referred to by paragraph number. Hereafter, all such documents will be referred to this way.
13. Vatican Council II, "Declaration on Religious Freedom (*Dignitatis Humanae*)," par. 2.
14. *Gaudium et spes* is a notable exception, but because it bases its definition on the religious belief in creation in the image of God, non-believers may have strong prejudices against the definition. See also 1.6 below where I elaborate on this problem and Chapter 5 where I demonstrate that *Gaudium et spes's* understanding of human dignity can nevertheless be reconciled with a properly multidimensional 'secular' understanding of human dignity as developed in this book. See also Jans, "Enjoying and Making Use of a Responsible Freedom," which investigates some of the theological and philosophical background that led to the understanding of human dignity put forward in *Gaudium et spes* and *Dignitatis humanae*, especially its relation to the idea of 'responsible freedom'.
15. See Glendon, *Rights Talk,* 12.
16. Bagaric and Allan, "The Vacuous Concept of Dignity," 258.
17. See also Wellmann, *The Proliferation of Rights*.
18. Mirko Bagaric and James Allan, "The Vacuous Concept," 260. See also, Drenth von Februar, "A Better Life for All," 19.
19. See Glendon, *Rights Talk,* 61–64. Glendon goes on to point out that this decision nevertheless did not make abortion impossible. In other words, the Court recognised that upholding the right to life did not mean that the interests of woman could be ignored, but the seriousness of the decision to abort had to be emphasised. Hence, it became possible to still have an abortion provided that the woman sought council beforehand regarding the possibilities, and in particular the support that the state offers if she were to continue the pregnancy.
20. This concern is also raised by, among others, Soulen and Woodhead, "Introduction: Contextualising Human Dignity," 15: "... the concept of

human dignity proves remarkably fragile—insufficient to sustain the ethical and metaphysical weight that modern rights-talk would place upon it. ... the price that has been paid has been a gradual weakening of the concept, and a blunting of its power to diagnose and resist contemporary endangerments of the very dignity it strives to secure."

21. Bagaric and Allan, "The Vacuous Concept of Dignity," 267.
22. Beyleveld and Brownsword, *Human Dignity in Bioethics and Biolaw*, 1.
23. See Toulmin, "How Medicine Saved the Life of Ethics," 736–750.
24. Drenth von Februar, "A Better Life for All". See also the other contributions in the same book, especially, Verstraeten, "Globalisation and the Dignity of the Poor," as well as, among others, Loose and Waanders (eds.), *Work and Human Dignity in the context of Globalisation*; Meeks, "The Economy of Grace: Human Dignity in the Market System"; DiSanto, "The Threat of Commodity-Consciousness to Human Dignity".
25. Macklin, "Dignity is a Useless Concept."
26. See Birnbacher, *Analytische Einführung in die Ethik*, 74–76. See also Weber-Hassemer, "'Menschenwürde' im Bioethischen Diskurs," 23–38, for a useful overview of the debates regarding the use of *Menschenwürde* in the German context. See also idem. n. 1 for a useful list of other recent publications in this regard.
27. President's Council on Bioethics, *Human Dignity and Bioethics*.
28. Schulman, "Bioethics and the Question of Human Dignity," 14.
29. Davis, "Human Dignity and Respect for Persons," 19, citing Macklin, "Dignity is a Useless Concept", 1419–1420.
30. See Sulmasy, "Dignity and Bioethics," 469–501; Dresser, "Human Dignity and the Seriously Ill Patient," 505–512.
31. See Davis, "Human Dignity and Respect for Persons," 34.
32. President's Council on Bioethics, "Session 5: Human Dignity and Bioethics: Essays Commissioned by the President's Council of Bioethics."
33. Pinker, "The Stupidity of Dignity."
34. Steven Pinker in the meeting of the President's Council on Bioethics, "Session 5."
35. Steven Pinker, "The Stupidity of Dignity."
36. Ibid.
37. When using the term 'theocons', Pinker refers to a book by Linker, *The Theocons: Secular America under Siege,* which argues that a group of conservative thinkers, led by Catholic priest, Richard John Neuhaus, has had a profound influence on American politics, and especially on the

administration of George W. Bush, such that they threaten to demolish the traditional distinction between church and state.
38. Pinker, "The Stupidity of Dignity".
39. See also Schwöbel, "Recovering Human Dignity," 44–45, who points out that both those for and against genetic research on human embryos appeal to human dignity.
40. Daniel Hillyard and John Dombrink, "Oregon's Death with Dignity Hits 10 Years," *Seattle Post Intelligencer*, March 25, 2008, http://seattlepi.nwsource.com/opinion/356404_dignity26.html.
41. Death with Dignity National Center website, accessed September 17, 2008, http://www.deathwithdignity.org
42. See Jean-Jacques De Gucht's website, accessed September 17, 2008, http://www.jeanjacquesdegucht.be/opinion.html?opinionid = 9.
43. See Nederlandse Vereniging voor een Vrijwillig Levenseinde website, accessed September 17, 2008, http://www.nvve.nl/nvve2/pagina.asp?pagkey = 72345&status = stelling&Stelling ID=4506.
44. See "Euthanasia," Salvation Army, accessed June 20, 2012, http://www.salvationarmy.org.nz/about-us/position-statements/euthanasia.
45. "Anti-Euthanasia Alliance Launched," BBC News Online, January 31, 2006, http://news.bbc.co.uk/2/hi/health/4662312.stm.
46. The International Criminal Court specifies outrages on personal dignity as a war crime. See International Criminal Court, *Elements of Crimes*, 2011, article 8(2)(b)(xxi).
47. Constitutional Court of South Africa, State versus Makwanyane and Another 1995(6) BCLR 665 (CC), par 328.
48. The words of a convicted criminal quoted in Gilligan, *Violence*, 106.
49. See Baker-Fletcher, "Somebodyness and Self-Respect" 11.
50. Chaskalson, "Human Dignity as a Constitutional Value," 137.
51. Cf. Aristotle, *Nicomachean Ethics,* 1094a1–20: "Every art and every investigation, and similarly every action and pursuit, is considered to be aimed at some good. Hence the good has been rightly defined as 'that at which all things aim'." And 1096b10–15: "Clearly, then, things can be called good in two senses: some are good in their own right, and others as means to secure these."
52. See Kant, *Grounding for the Metaphysics of Morals,* 36.
53. See also, Shell, "Kant on Human Dignity," 58–60. Shell discusses Kant's distinction between *Werth* (value) and *Würde* (dignity). The latter is used with reference the persons as ends in themselves.

54. Victorian Law Reform Commission, *Workplace Privacy: Issues Paper*, 15; quoted in Bagaric and Allan, "The Vacuous Concept of Dignity," 264.
55. For a good analysis of Kant's understanding of dignity see Shell, "Kant on Human Dignity"; Shell, "Kant's Concept of Human Dignity as a Resource for Bioethics," 333–349.
56. Victorian Law Reform Commission, *Workplace Privacy: Issues Paper*, 14. Interestingly, with reference to the above quote, the Victorian Law Reform Commission itself cites Immanuel Kant's *Grounding for the Metaphysics of Morals:* "Now I say that man, and in general every rational being, exists as an end in himself, and not merely as a means to be arbitrarily used by this or that will. He must in all his actions, whether directed to himself or to other rational beings, always be regarded at the same time as an end." Kant, *Grounding for the Metaphysics of Morals*, 35.
57. Of course, in Kant's philosophy, a great deal of thought is given to this. The point is that when the concept of human dignity is used in this sort of public discourse, little explanation is usually given.
58. See United Nations' Office of the High Commissioner for Human Rights, "Human Rights by Country", website of the Office of the High Commissioner for Human Rights," accessed June 2, 2008, http://www.ohchr.org/EN/Countries/Pages/HumanRightsintheWorld.aspx for detailed information of the status of human rights in various countries throughout the world. See also the Human Rights Watch website which includes links to the Human Rights Watch's *World Report* which contains information on human rights violations around the world (Accessed June 2, 2008, http://hrw.org).
59. See Human Rights Watch, *Double Jeopardy: CIA Renditions to Jordan*.
60. The CIA has admitted to using a procedure now known as 'waterboarding' which involves "… strapping the person being interrogated on to a board as pints of water are forced into his lungs through a cloth covering his face while the victim's mouth is forced open." The result is a drowning sensation. See Leonard Doyle, "Waterboarding is Torture—I did it myself says US advisor," *The Independent,* November 1, 2007, http://www.independent.co.uk/news/world/americas/waterboarding-is-torture--i-did-it-myself-says-us-advisor-398490.html.
61. U.S. President, "Remarks on the War on Terror, September 6, 2006," 1574–1575.
62. United Nations' Office of the High Commissioner for Human Rights, *Geneva Convention relative to the Treatment of Prisoners of War*.

63. U.S President, "Remarks on the War on Terror, September 6, 2006;" on March 8, 2008, Bush vetoed a bill that would have placed significant restrictions on the interrogation techniques permitted for use by the CIA. In his justification for the veto, he stated "I cannot sign into law a bill that would prevent me, and future Presidents, from authorizing the CIA to conduct a separate, lawful intelligence program, and from taking all lawful actions necessary to protect Americans from attack." U.S. President, "Message to the House of Representatives Returning Without Approval the 'Intelligence Authorization Act for Fiscal Year 2008', March 8, 2008," 347.
64. Mirko Bagaric and James Allan, "The Vacuous Concept of Dignity," 269.
65. "Realpolitik. The word conjures up images of tough leaders and armed forces. The term has also come to imply a certain amorality or immorality in action, choosing a course that may be the most effective but not one overly concerned with what is right or proper. Realpolitik has been used in many ways, some for purely self-serving political interests and others for mere intellectual debate. Regardless, realism (as realpolitik is alternatively known) has been a guiding influence in policy-making across national capitals of the world as well as within the ivory towers of academia." Wayman and Diehl, "Realism Reconsidered," 3.
66. Several authors note this different usage. See, among others, Steven Pinker's comments to the President's Council on Bioethics, President's Council on Bioethics, "Session 5," where he distinguishes between third person (have) and first person (acquired) dignity. Interestingly, the author that Pinker is most critical of, Leon R. Kass (See Pinker, "The Stupidity of Dignity"), also makes a similar distinction between what he calls the basic dignity of human being and the full dignity of being human: "Defending Human Dignity," 299. See also the contribution by bioethicists Weisstub and Thomasma, "Human Dignity, Vulnerability, Personhood," 330.
67. See GS, 16.
68. The reading of GS presented here is obviously aimed at highlighting apparent contradictions. This is typical of the approach taken by the critics mentioned in this chapter. I shall show in Chapter 4, in light of a hermeneutic of generosity, that such a reading is mistaken and that GS does in fact offer a largely coherent multidimensional view of human dignity, based on an equally multifaceted anthropology, that includes both a dignity human beings have and a dignity human beings acquire.
69. Creation in the image of God is not the only religiously based 'ontological' argument for human dignity. Others include the idea of a rational soul,

and, especially among Christians, the idea that Jesus Christ died to save all human beings. I shall not deal with these in any depth however in this book.
70. Bernardin, *Consistent Ethic of Life*, 61.
71. See Pope, *Human Evolution and Christian Ethics*, 189 and 192.
72. See ibid., 188.
73. Ibid. I would like to point out that the fact that Pope clearly states this seems to imply that dignity can indeed be understood otherwise, in other words, in terms of traits, status, and so on. I believe that this aspect of dignity is indeed still implicit in Pope's anthropology, despite his attempt to defend a 'valueless,' intrinsic dignity. See 1.5.2.2, as well as the note regarding Pope in 3.4.2.
74. Ibid., 188–189.
75. See ibid., 208.
76. See ibid., 192.
77. Ibid., 209.
78. Ibid., 210.
79. This analysis also appears in Kirchhoffer, "Benedict XVI, Human Dignity, and Absolute Moral Norms," 586-608.
80. For example, see the United States Conference of Catholic Bishops Pro-life Committee's website where they present a collection of quotes by Pope Benedict XVI (accessed June 9, 2008, http://www.usccb.org/prolife/tdocs/popebquotes2008.shtml). Cf. the Death with Dignity National Center website's entry on religion and spirituality with regard to physician-assisted suicide (accessed June 9, 2008, http://www.deathwithdignity.org/ historyfacts/religion. asp).
81. For example, Leon R. Kass, former chair of the President's Council for Bioethics and fellow at the American Enterprise Institute, in his essay "Defending Human Dignity," (p. 300), states, "In clinical medicine, a primary ethical focus is on the need to respect the equal worth and dignity of each patient at every stage of his or her life—regardless of race, class or gender, condition of body and mind, severity of illness, nearness to death, or ability to pay for services rendered. Defenders of human dignity rightly insist that every patient deserves—from every physician, nurse, or hospital—equal respect in speech and deed and equal consideration regarding the selection of appropriate treatment. Moreover, they also rightly insist that no life is to be deemed worthier than another and that under no circumstances should we look upon a fellow human being as if he or she has a "life unworthy of life" and deserves to be made dead.

The ground of these opinions, and of the respect for human dignity they betoken, lies not in the patient's autonomy or any other of his personal qualities or excellences, but rather in the patient's very being and vitality. Doctors should always respect the life the patient has, all the more because he has entrusted it to their care in the belief that they will indeed respect it to the very last."

82. All quotes are taken from the Vatican's official website (accessed June 9, 2008, http://www.vatican.va/holy_father/benedict_xvi/index.htm). The reason for using this source rather than any other is that, as the official website, it would serve as the first point of contact for many people looking for the pope's statements in English. Thus, since my intention in this research was to consider Benedict's public discourse, I felt it was appropriate to use the most public source. In addition, as evidenced by the fallout surrounding the so-called 'Regensburg address', there seems to be a creeping acceptance of anything that the pope says as having equal authority. I do not support this trend, but I do think that moral theologians and ethicists need to take it into account when analysing the ethical implications of papal discourse. For a useful and concise analysis of this trend, and the role that technology plays in it see, Robinson, *Confronting Power and Sex in the Catholic Church,* 117–124.

83. Benedict XVI, Letter to Card. Walter Kasper on the occasion of the Second Conference on Peace and Tolerance, organized by the Ecumenical Patriarchate of Constantinople in conjunction with the Appeal of Conscience Foundation (4 November 2005).

84. Benedict XVI, Address to the Members of the "Pro Petri Sede" and "Etrennes Pontificales" Associations (30 October 2006).

85. Benedict XVI, Letter to Jean-Louis Cardinal Tauran on the Occasion of the Colloquium organized by UNESCO in Paris (24 May 2005).

86. Benedict XVI, Common Declaration by His Holiness Benedict XVI and His Beatitude Christodoulos, Archbishop of Athens and All Greece (14 December 2006).

87. Benedict XVI, Address to the Participants in the Symposium on the Theme: "Stem Cells: What Future for Therapy?" Organized by the Pontifical Academy for Life (16 September 2006).

88. Benedict XVI, Letter to H.E. Mr. Roh Moo-hyun, President of the Republic of Korea (15 February 2007).

89. Benedict XVI, Letter to the Italian Bishops on occasion of the 55th General Assembly held in Assisi (10 November 2005).

90. Benedict XVI, Address to the Members of the Pontifical Academy of Sciences (6 November 2006).
91. See Kirchhoffer, "Benedict XVI, Human Dignity, and Absolute Moral Norms." The article asks whether interpretations of Benedict's public statements regarding human dignity that would claim that some of these norms are absolute moral norms are in fact correct. Particular attention is paid to the apparent equation or reduction of human dignity to the dignity of human life. The article concludes that though it is possible to read Benedict XVI's normative morality as advocating absolute moral norms, such an interpretation would usually be incorrect in light of Benedict XVI's more comprehensive understanding of human dignity. See also Kirchhoffer, "Pope Benedict XVI on the Dignity of the Human Person."
92. Richard M. Doerflinger, "Human Cloning vs. Human Dignity," United States Conference of Catholic Bishops website, accessed July 28, 2009, http://www.usccb.org/prolife/programs/rlp/03doerflinger.shtml; internet.
93. See Egonsson, *Dimensions of Dignity*, 47–48 and 244.
94. Ibid., 241.
95. Ibid., 244.
96. Fukuyama, *Our Posthuman Future*, 171.
97. See, among others, Arnold and Youngner, "The Dead Donor Rule: Should We Stretch it, Bend it, or Abandon it?"; Youngner, Arnold, and DeVita, "When is 'dead'?"; Youngner and Arnold, "Philosophical debates about the definition of death: who cares?"
98. Dworkin, *Life's Dominion*, 239.
99. Kurt Bayertz, "Human Dignity: Philosophical Origin and Scientific Erosion of an Idea," 77.
100. Ibid., 74.
101. Ibid., 75, quoting Mill, "On Liberty," 234.
102. Kant, *Groundwork of the Metaphysics of Morals*, 103, quoted in Bayertz, "Human Dignity," 77.
103. Beyleveld and Brownsword, *Human Dignity in Bioethics and Biolaw*, 5. Though Beyleveld and Brownsword situate human dignity primarily in human autonomy, this does not mean that they advocate the extreme position of respect for dignity as permission. They argue dignity also requires respecting others' autonomy and that this places limits on what an agent can do. For more on Gewirth's moral philosophy, see Beyleveld and Brownsword, Chapter 4, and Gewirth, *Reason and Morality*.
104. Farley, "A Feminist Version of Respect for Persons," 183–198. See also Mitchell, *Morality: Religious and Secular*, 134.

105. Pope, *Human Evolution and Christian Ethics*, 208.
106. Nussbaum, "Human Dignity and Political Entitlements," 299.
107. *Compact Oxford English Dictionary of Current English*, 2nd ed., s.v. "dignity." See also, for example, Murray, *In Pursuit: Of Happiness and Good Government*, 112–113; Watts, "Human Dignity: Concepts and Experiences," 248.
108. For an elaboration on Gilligan's thesis see Chapter 4, section 4.1 of this book.
109. Gilligan, *Violence*, 110.
110. Gilligan, *Preventing Violence*, 30. See also Gilligan, "Shame, Guilt and Violence," 1155.
111. Taylor, *Sources of the Self*, 15.
112. See Gilligan, *Violence*, 45–55.
113. Taylor, *Sources of the Self*, 15. See also Gilligan, *Violence*, 112.
114. See Gilligan, *Violence*, 230–231: "Men are honored for activity (ultimately, violent activity); and they are dishonored for passivity (or pacifism), which renders them vulnerable to the charge of being a non-man ('a wimp, a punk, and a pussy,' ...)." See Gilligan, *Preventing Violence*, 56–57. See also Jewkes and Abrahams, "The Epidemiology of Rape and Sexual Coercion in South Africa" 1231–1244, for a summary of the causes of rape and sexual violence in South Africa and particularly the role that a culture of male entitlement and power plays in the perpetuation of this violence against women, and violence in general in South Africa.
115. Nussbaum, "Human Dignity and Political Entitlements," 299. See also Broesterhuizen, "Doofheid: beperking of kracht," 53–77, who considers how deaf people have increasingly begun to appropriate their own deafness in a positive way into their identities, rather than seeing it as something that makes them less worthy.
116. See Charles Taylor, *Sources of the Self*, 23–25.
117. See ibid., 23.
118. See, among others, Quill, "Death and Dignity: A Case of Individualised Decision Making," 691–694; Nielsen, "Guidelines for legalized euthanasia in Canada," 314–318.
119. Macklin, "Dignity is a Useless Concept," 1419–1420.
120. Nordenfelt, "The Varieties of Dignity," 69–81.
121. Pullman, "Human Dignity and the Ethics and Aesthetics of Pain and Suffering," 84.
122. Dworkin, *Life's Dominion*, 166.

123. Ibid., 167.
124. Ibid., 215. Though Bagaric and Allan ("The Vacuous Concept of Dignity") quote Dworkin as grounding dignity in the sanctity of life, they are mistaken if they think that this is equivalent to the ontological arguments discussed earlier that only associated dignity with biological life. Dworkin offers a complex understanding of the 'sanctity of life' and uses the word sanctity to explicitly demonstrate the religious nature of the value that we attach to our lives. But the view of life is not as a biological organism but as an aesthetic, meaningfully-lived, narrative whole. I elaborate more on Dworkin's views in Chapter 4 section 4.2.
125. Steven Pinker, "The Stupidity of Dignity"
126. Fraser Watts, "Human Dignity: Concepts and Experiences," 248.
127. Note that Watts points this out as one of the ways in which dignity is understood and used, but it does not represent his own position which is more complex and combines what he calls an absolute (what I call the dignity we have) and a qualitative (what I call the dignity we acquire) sense of dignity.
128. Michael J. Meyer, "Dignity as a (Modern) Virtue". Note that Meyer provides an intriguing defence of his idea by arguing that the difference between the butler, whose dignity relies on a culture of deference, and King and Gandhi, is that the latter stand up for equality, i.e., for the more fundamental moral good of basic human dignity (*Menschenwürde*). Nevertheless, he is used here because his examples demonstrate the importance of social mores in forming ideas (good or bad) about what constitutes dignified (i.e., morally good) behaviour.
129. Bostrom, "In Defense of Posthuman Dignity," 203–214.
130. Bostrom, "Dignity and Enhancement," 173–206.
131. Nick Bostrom, "In Defense of Posthuman Dignity."
132. Demmer, *Shaping the Moral Life*, 2.
133. Ibid., 16.
134. Vatican Council II, "Declaration on Religious Freedom (*Dignitatis Humanae*)".
135. Demmer, *Shaping the Moral Life*, 17.
136. Note that *Dignitatis Humanae* is not advocating relativism, since it still maintains that there is an objective Truth to be known, though the extent to which any human individual can know the fullness of this truth is limited: "Religious freedom, in turn, which men demand as necessary to fulfill their duty to worship God, has to do with immunity from coercion in civil society. Therefore it leaves untouched traditional Catholic

doctrine on the moral duty of men and societies toward the true religion and toward the one Church of Christ" (par. 1).

137. Bagaric and Allan, "The Vacuous Concept of Dignity," 264.
138. Ibid., 269.
139. Macklin, "Dignity is a Useless Concept".
140. See Steven Pinker, "The Stupidity of Dignity".
141. Tinder, "Against Fate: An Essay on Personal Dignity," 12. Tinder appeals to the concept of destiny as opposed to fate to ground his case for human dignity. Whether such a concept would satisfy the likes of Pinker remains to be seen.
142. This analysis is also performed in Kirchhoffer, "Benedict XVI, Human Dignity, and Absolute Moral Norms".
143. Benedict XVI, "The Human Person, the Heart of Peace," Message for the Celebration of the World Day of Peace (1 January 2007), par. 4.
144. Ibid., par. 2.
145. See also *Catechism of the Catholic Church,* par. 2280: "Everyone is responsible for his life before God who has given it to him. It is God who remains the sovereign Master of life. We are obliged to accept life gratefully and preserve it for his honour and the salvation of our souls. We are stewards, not owners, of the life God has entrusted to us. It is not ours to dispose of."
146. Bagaric and Allan, "The Vacuous Concept of Dignity," 268.
147. Peter Singer, "All Animals are Equal," 228.

CHAPTER 2

QUESTIONING 'QUESTIONING DIGNITY'

A Methodological Critique of the Critique

This chapter reconsiders the critique of the concept of human dignity in light of a reappraisal of the methodological assumptions that underlie the said critique. In so doing, it acknowledges the seriousness of the criticisms levelled by the critique, but at the same time points out that these criticisms are themselves based on certain methodological assumptions. By proposing alternative methodological assumptions, this chapter aims to go beyond the conclusions to the critique that would see the dismissal of the concept of human dignity from ethical discourse. Based on these alternative methodological assumptions, this chapter lays the groundwork for a case in favour of the value of the concept of human dignity that nevertheless tries to account for and offer a solution to the problems raised by the critique conducted in Chapter 1.

The critique of the concept of human dignity as it is conducted in Chapter 1 in line with critiques like those of Bagaric and Allan, Macklin, and Pinker—leaves one with three options regarding how to deal with the concept of human dignity: (1) accept the critique and agree with the likes of Bagaric and Allan, Macklin, and Pinker that indeed the concept of human dignity is "vacuous," "useless," and 'stupid'; (2) refuse to accept the critique, choose *one* of the various conceptions of human dignity put forward in section 1.5 of Chapter 1 and argue for it as the correct understanding of human dignity against all the others which must therefore be incorrect; (3) take the critique seriously as demonstrating real problems both in the conception of human dignity and its employment in contemporary ethical discourse, but then, instead of dismissing the concept outright, look for a way to constructively engage these criticisms with a view to developing a better, more comprehensive understanding of human dignity that can both take these criticisms into account and offer a useful tool for ethical reflection.

I have opted, in this book, for the third possibility. In the three sections that constitute this chapter, I shall defend this choice by dealing with each of the three possibilities in turn, thereby demonstrating the problems inherent in options (1) and (2) and building a case for option (3).

2.1. The Problems with Dismissing Dignity Outright

This section argues that the decision to dismiss the concept of human dignity outright relies on certain inadequate methodological presuppositions: a legalistic, *techne*-oriented view of ethics (2.1.1), an excessive reliance on a hermeneutic of suspicion (2.1.2), and an epistemological reductionism (2.1.3). These presuppositions have their methodological uses, for example, in the critical analysis of the challenges facing the concept of human dignity, but they are an inadequate basis on which to make epistemic claims about the concept of human dignity, because they take neither the hermeneutical function of ethics, nor the complex multi-dimensionality of the human person and the moral event adequately into account.

2.1.1. Overemphasis on a Legalistic, Techne-oriented View of Ethics

One of the key criticisms levelled in Chapter 1 is that the concept of human dignity is not up to the task of grounding human rights and adjudicating between competing rights claims.[1] This raises a question as to the operative understanding of ethics behind this criticism.

2.1.1.1. Legalism

The critique's focus on the concept of human dignity's efficacy as a criterion by which one can evaluate behaviour points towards normative ethics, that is, ethics as concerned with the 'objective' evaluation of the rightness and wrongness, goodness and badness, of moral behaviour.[2] Moreover, the criticisms also point to a particular kind of normative ethics, namely legalism. According to the late political theorist and professor of government at Harvard University, Judith N. Shklar, legalism "is the ethical attitude that holds moral conduct to be a matter of rule following, and moral relationships to consist of duties and rights determined by rules."[3]

What is interesting is that both the critics and those they criticise tend to emphasise this legalistic use of human dignity as a normative criterion. This accounts for the rise of 'dignity talk' demonstrated in Chapter 1, i.e., the rise in the use of the concept of human dignity as a criterion by which behaviour can be justified or condemned. Ironically, it is this rise in 'dignity talk', i.e., the apparent use of the concept of human dignity in a legalistic fashion as a normative criterion, that leads the critique to question the value of human dignity in the first place. But the critique never considers an alternative paradigm; it remains in a legalistic paradigm: it dismisses the concept of human dignity because the concept, as a normative concept, does not, apparently, have the kind of internal rigour supposedly required by such a legalistic normative criterion.

2.1.1.2. Avoidance and 'Rational' Moral Calculus

The attraction of a legalistic approach to ethics may be that it turns ethical problems into legal ones, meaning that one is no longer faced with an existential question but with a technical one. In other words, legalism offers the possibility of a 'rational', definitive solution to a problem, such that one is either doing something illegal or not.

In contemporary Western societies, this legalism could be attributed to the 'avoidance' typical of the so-called 'liberal' political quest to offer what professor of theological ethics at the Catholic University of Leuven, Johan Verstraeten, calls a "rational foundation for social regulation." In a survey of the contemporary challenges facing practical ethics from a Christian perspective, Verstraeten notes that in this quest,

> ... they use a radical method of avoidance: every recourse to a normative[4] or metaphysical vision of a 'good society' is systematically rejected, or at least eliminated from the foundation of their political game plan. As sole solution to the fragmentation, they defend a theoretical construction of formal procedures whose only goal is allowing individuals to pursue their personal preferences and interests in as far as they do not impede the freedom of others. Their minimal state no longer has an ethical basis or function.[5]

Philosopher and bioethicist at Radboud University, Hub Zwart, similarly notes that modern society now tends to see the only acceptable form of ethical thought as a sort of moral calculus[6] that weighs the profit and loss of interests. Here, an express choice is made for a "'method of avoidance': fundamentally meaningful questions, such as the moral significance of biological nature, are by definition excluded from the agenda."[7] The result, as shown in Chapter 1, especially Section 1.3 and in the critiques by Macklin and Pinker, is that, according to Zwart, most ethical debates get reduced to an often irresolvable calculus with only two variables—autonomy vs. potential harm (or what Pinker calls first person versus third person arguments).[8]

The result of such an approach is similar to what I have described as the rise of 'dignity talk'. So, as Verstraeten—following Alisdair MacIntyre[9]—says, "It is true that rational moral arguments are still used, [e.g. the moral calculus between autonomy and harm] but they often no longer

Questioning 'Questioning Dignity'

have a basis. They are like scientific formulas that have survived an atomic war but whose meaning-giving framework has been lost. Ethics risks becoming bogged down in pure rhetoric. Strategic, rational arguments are used for sophistic legitimation of private interests."[10] What the critique reveals is that the concepts of human dignity and human rights have, to some extent, become masks for this kind of calculus, such that though people speak of human dignity, they may in fact be talking about autonomy or life, for example (see 1.5.4).[11] The solution the critique proposes, however, is not to find out what human dignity really means for ethical discourse, but instead to 'avoid' the concept entirely so that the debate can be returned to the 'rational' weighing of interests with a limited number of variables often in a legalistic fashion in order to arrive at a credible decision. The alleged 'vacuity' of human dignity means that it is not a viable criterion to underpin such a decision, or to guide the procedures that are necessary to arrive at such a decision.

In the end, however, this means that the critique of human dignity, in its apparent desire for a rational legal foundation for the evaluation of moral behaviour ends up adding nothing to the debate and simply becomes another voice arguing for a perspective that serves its own interests.

2.1.1.3. Ethics as Techne

Yet a legalistic approach to ethics is not the only way that one can turn ethics into an attempt to provide definitive solutions to moral problems. Indeed, the legalism and the moral calculus described above are both symptomatic of a trend towards seeing ethics as a kind of *techne* that philosopher and director of the Centre for Ethics at Radboud University, Paul van Tongeren, has attributed to the rise of professional ethics. Van Tongeren is concerned about the apparent solution-driven trend in professional ethics where a sort of 'ethical engineering' seems to be taking place; people increasingly look to ethicists to provide definitive solutions to problems using a particular ethical technique. Van Tongeren suggests that this technique-oriented approach to ethics (of which one could say legalism is an example, in which the normative procedures of jurisprudence constitute the technique) is one of the biggest problems facing ethics as a discipline. According to Van Tongeren, there is a danger of reducing ethics to *techne*, and the role of the ethicist to that of a technician who comes in with a tool to apply to a given situation that will then provide the affected parties with the right answer.[12]

The reason that Van Tongeren seems opposed to a sort of 'ethical engineering' is that it undermines the very human basis for ethics in the first place, thereby denying human beings the fullness of their humanity, because, according to Van Tongeren, human beings are essentially meaning-beings and social-beings. He says that the philosophical task of ethics is "to conjoin practice and logos adequately." For Van Tongeren, basing himself on Aristotle's *Politics*,[13] the logos is for explaining, indicating the advantageous and disadvantageous, right and wrong, and so on. He says that "the essentially human is the logos, i.e. the ability to understand and produce meaning."[14] This meaning is identified and communicated in and to a community in speech. This communication is necessary because the veracity of a particular meaning is based on the agreement of others.[15] In other words, a meaningful conversation ensues.

To reduce ethics to *techne*, then, strips the moral problem of its meaningful character. It ignores the logos to focus solely on the practice. It ignores the fact that the reason there is an issue in the first place is that one is confronted by experience that begs for interpretation, for it is through interpretation that one comes to self-understanding, to an answer to "the question what is happening to us as moral beings."[16] The kind of legalistic, calculating view of ethics that I argue underpins the critique in chapter 1 is "inadequate to discover the more fundamental questions active"[17] in ethical problems. It essentially muzzles rather than articulates important aspects of experience. For example, Hub Zwart argues that, in the case of using reproductive technologies to cause pregnancy in post-menopausal women, an ethics of *techne* neither allows us to ask nor to articulate why the idea evokes hesitancy in the first place. Similarly, Van Tongeren illustrates what he means by 'meaning' using the example of the applied problem of ethical issues surrounding the application of new reproductive techniques. The *techne* will seek to answer questions about the admissibility of these reproductive techniques instead of using such questions as "an occasion to ask about the meaning of (having) children. Why do people want children? Why do parents love children? How do parents love their children?"[18]

In a sense, then, one could say that resorting to *techne* as a way of solving moral problems is a way of opting out of the world and meaningful living. It is a way for human beings to relinquish their personal responsibility in favour of an impersonal law. This is an attitude that one often encounters in everyday ethical problems. Many people seem to think, or perhaps prefer to think, that if something is not against the law, then it is also not unethical. Consider for example the analysis, in section 1.4.2, of President George W. Bush's attempts to create new laws to protect people who may have been engaging in morally wrong torture practices. Of course, when this happens, moral issues are not given their proper weight, and the meanings inherent in them, the meanings that are indeed the cause of the problem in the first place, are not given the attention they deserve. Ethics is reduced to the procedural at the expense of the reflective.[19]

2.1.1.4. Human Dignity as Normative Criterion or as Descriptive Category?
To bring this discussion back to the concept of human dignity and the challenges outlined in Chapter 1, what is apparent in every instance is that meaning is attached to the term. The concept of human dignity is significant because, for those who use it as part of their ethical argumentation, it says something about who they believe human beings are, and what human beings can or should become. It says something about how they interpret themselves in their world and in their communities.

Therefore, far from simply being just a normative criterion that a legalistic, *techne*-oriented approach can use to judge between competing positions, human dignity is also a descriptive category that contains within it those things that the people who use it believe are meaningful to their moral lives as self-conscious human beings in community. Insofar as these meanings affect practice, is it not also worth considering the concept of human dignity as a window, a hermeneutical key into why people value certain things and choose certain behaviours?

According to Tübingen theological ethicist Dietmar Mieth, understanding constitutes an important part of ethics, and is the condition for judgement. Understanding means being able to explain something, to gain insight, and to interpret the forces behind things.[20] It is this attitude that I believe underpins what I have defined as descriptive ethics in the introduction and it is this attitude that is missing from the critique. The critique longs for a criterion by which it can judge without first seeking to understand.

Thus, I agree with Tilburg moral theologian Jan Jans, when he proposes, "instead of using [human dignity] as a kind of universal stopgap, to consider it really as the beginning and not as the end of concrete ethical involvement." Jans adds, "In other words, the reference to human dignity is not a shortcut allowing to dispense from the handicraft of concrete ethics, but first and most the indication that there are indeed serious ethical questions facing us, questions that challenge us as concrete subjects to bring to bear on them our responsible freedom."[21]

2.1.2. Overemphasis on a Hermeneutic of Suspicion

If one accepts that human beings are interpreting beings, then it is possible to ask what the dominant interpretive paradigm, or hermeneutic, is in the critique conducted in Chapter 1, and, more importantly, underlying a conclusion that would dismiss human dignity from ethical discourse.

I maintain that the underlying hermeneutic is typical of a hermeneutic of suspicion. The understanding of a hermeneutic of suspicion used here is that defined by philosopher Paul Ricœur: a hermeneutic of suspicion can be defined as "the demystification of a meaning presented to the interpreter in the form of a disguise. This type of hermeneutics is animated by suspicion, by a scepticism towards the given, and it is characterised by a distrust of the symbol as a dissimulation of the real." The hermeneutic of suspicion looks upon "the contents of consciousness as in some sense 'false'; [and aims] to transcend this falsity through a reductive interpretation and critique."[22] According to Ricœur, suspicion is the "critical instrument of demystification."[23]

Ricœur calls three modern thinkers, Karl Marx, Sigmund Freud, and Friedrich Nietzsche, the "Masters of Suspicion".[24] The hermeneutic of suspicion unites these three thinkers in that they all seek to uncover a 'false consciousness' that they discern in culture. The 'false consciousness' is a cultural phenomenon and thus it is cultures and their myths that the hermeneutic of suspicion critiques.

Moreover, Ricœur notes that the motivation that underpins the critique of 'false consciousness', and leads to the denunciation of 'false consciousness', is the possibility of unveiling the 'masked consciousness', i.e., the truth that is really there, and that is different from the one first thought to be true. The suspicion, in other words, rests on the assertion that there is a deeper truth that can only be uncovered by an expert who has seen this truth and who can provide the method to reveal it: the truth in the case of Karl Marx, is economic determinism, in the case of Sigmund Freud, a libido, and in the case of Friedrich Nietzsche the will to power, and the methods are respectively, the theory of ideologies, the theory of ideas and illusions, and the genealogies of ethics.[25]

In the critique of the concept of human dignity this hermeneutic of suspicion is likewise evident in the application of 'rational' methods to reveal a truth to which others are blind. For example, Stephen Pinker argues that the concept of human dignity conceals a religious ideology that seeks to impose itself and its conservative agenda on liberal society. For Pinker, the concept of human dignity as used by such 'theocons' is based on "Bible stories, Catholic doctrine, and woolly rabbinical allegory." His method to counter such claims, and to reveal the 'false consciousness' that they constitute, is to appeal to cognitive psychology.

> Dignity is a phenomenon of human perception. Certain signals from the world trigger an attribution in the mind of a perceiver. Just as converging lines in a drawing are a cue for the perception of depth, and differences in loudness between the two ears cue us to the position of a sound, certain features in another human being trigger ascriptions of worth. These features include signs of composure, cleanliness, maturity, attractiveness, and control of the body. The perception of dignity in turn elicits a response in the perceiver. Just as the smell of baking bread triggers a desire to eat it, and the sight of a baby's face triggers a desire to protect it, the appearance of dignity triggers a desire to esteem and respect the dignified person.

Pinker concludes that "because [respect for human dignity] amounts to treating people in the way that they wish to be treated, ultimately it's just another application of the principle of autonomy."[26]

Ruth Macklin's suspicion is likewise that the use of the concept of human dignity only muddies the ethical waters. She is concerned by the proliferation of claims that some kinds of medical research and practices offend human dignity. She asks, "are such charges coherent? Is dignity a useful concept for an ethical analysis of medical activities?" And concludes, "A close inspection of leading examples shows that appeals to dignity are either vague restatements of other, more precise, notions or mere slogans that add nothing to an understanding of the topic." Though she claims her method is a 'close inspection' of leading examples, it remains a somewhat selective inspection, in that the examples she uses lend themselves to her claim that respect for human dignity is either reducible to respect for autonomy or is too vague to warrant attention.

Nevertheless, in Chapter 1, I have expanded on Macklin's limited selection, and on Bagaric and Allan's critique,[27] by presenting a wider array of possible bases for human dignity in Section 1.5. The method used to reveal the masked truth is a deconstruction of the term human dignity. Such a deconstruction is typical of the approach adopted by the hermeneutic of suspicion.[28] The application of a hermeneutic of suspicion in this case leads to the conclusion that indeed, not only do 'theocons' potentially use human dignity to conceal other agendas, but so do 'liberals', 'progressives', and so-called 'transhumanists'.[29] They respectively simply fill in the concept of human dignity with whatever anthropological vision best suits their agenda. Thus, the hermeneutic of suspicion's solution to the problem of the rise of 'dignity talk' is to reveal the truth that the concept of human dignity is either too vague, or refers to something else, and in both instances is nothing more than a polemical tool for competing ideologies. Ricœur, however, argues that such a hermeneutic of suspicion on its own is inadequate.

It is true that the hermeneutic of suspicion, through its deconstruction helps to demystify the use of the concept of human dignity in contemporary ethical discourse. Nevertheless, it offers little more. Either, as in the case of Pinker for example, the results of such a hermeneutic are simply used to further an alternative ideological agenda, or as in the case of Bagaric and Allan, the only conclusion that can be drawn is, "Dignity is a vacuous concept. The notion of dignity should be discarded as a potential foundation for rights claims unless, and until, its source, nature, relevance and meaning are determined."[30]

In order for the results of the hermeneutic of suspicion to really be beneficial, a reconstruction has to follow the deconstruction. As theologians like David Tracy and Elisabeth Schüssler Fiorenza,[31] among others, have asked, why stop there? It is not enough to just reveal the illusions of 'false consciousness'. The hermeneutics of suspicion needs to be complemented by a hermeneutics of affirmation,[32] or by what I have described in the introduction, following Miles and Yaghjian, as a hermeneutics of generosity.[33] It is necessary to reconstruct meaning aware of the failings revealed by the hermeneutics of suspicion.[34]

Ricœur's particular focus is the implication of the hermeneutic of suspicion for religion and for faith. The masters of suspicion have rightly unmasked the sinister 'false consciousnesses', i.e., the idols of religion. Ricœur then says, "In conceiving hermeneutics as a hermeneutic with a *double edge,* I bind in an indivisible way the de-construction of religious language and the restoration of a meaning capable of giving a language to faith." If I paraphrase this statement so as to make it applicable to the discussion of ethics and human dignity, the deconstruction of the concept of human dignity must be indivisibly bound to the restoration of a meaning capable of giving a language to ethical discourse. The concept of human dignity is an integral part of contemporary ethical discourse, even though it seems to be given many meanings. What is necessary is a hermeneutic that makes sense of these many meanings in a way that aids and enriches rather than impoverishes ethical discourse.

In the end, what worries Ricœur is not the hermeneutic of suspicion per se, which he sees as a necessary part of an effective hermeneutics. What worries him is when the hermeneutic of suspicion leads to the wrong kind of affirmation:

> We are thus brought to say that the stake of any discernment, at the heart of ourselves, between the authentic and the inauthentic is the meaning that we give to the *Affirmation.* What do we affirm? What is our source, our resource of affirmation? It is at this ultimate level that I confront the three princes of necessity [Freud, Marx and Nietzsche]: man, they say, must come to love necessity—to love fate—to love things as they are and accept the fact that his life disappears, that reality continues, anonymous and silent. Such is the atheistic *affirmation* of my culture.[35]

In other words, there is a danger inherent in the hermeneutic of suspicion, and in the methods that it uses to reveal the 'truth' it sees hidden behind 'false consciousness'. This danger is that the critique becomes so certain of its own method, and the 'truth' it has revealed, that it can only affirm this outcome as *the* Truth. Inevitably, as Ricœur shows, this can never be the whole truth, but only a part of the truth. If the difference "between the authentic and the inauthentic is the meaning that we give to the *Affirmation*," then the difference between the double-edged hermeneutics envisioned by Ricœur and the hermeneutics of suspicion applied by the masters of suspicion is that the latter reduce all meaning to the affirmation of the 'truths' revealed by their method, whereas for Ricœur, the affirmation should construct new and richer meanings through a "re-reading of the same things in depth and under the heading of ... affirmation."[36]

Hans-Georg Gadamer, another important philosopher who has focussed on the role of hermeneutics, demonstrates this problem of the reduction of meaning in the following example:

> The interpretation of the common world in which we participate is certainly not in the first place the objectifying task of methodical thinking. That may certainly be included, but it is not the raison d'être of our activity. When we are interpreting a text, it is not to prove "scientifically" that *this* love poem belongs to the genre of love poems. That is an objective statement and nobody can doubt it; but if that conclusion is the only result of investigating a poem, then we have failed. The intention is to understand *this* love poem, on its own and in its unique relation to the common structure of love poems. It is an absolutely individualized particular form, so that one participates in the utterance or message which is there embodied by the poet. Participation is indeed a better formulation of what is going on in our life experience than is the foundationalist account of the apodictic evidence of self-consciousness.[37]

Gadamer's example of the love poem can be applied to the way in which Chapter 1 deals with human dignity. Chapter 1 and the critics mentioned in it objectify human dignity using methodical thinking. They prove "scientifically" that *this* ethical term has some problems in the way that it is employed in ethical discourse. To quote Gadamer, "That is an objective statement and nobody can doubt it;" but, to paraphrase Gadamer, if that is the only result of investigating the concept of human dignity, then we have failed. The intention is to understand this concept on its own and in its unique relation to other concepts in ethical discourse, and indeed, to the way in which ethics is done. Bearing in mind what I have said in section 2.1.1 regarding the importance of meaning and the understanding of meaning for the discipline of ethics, we need to be able to participate in the message embodied in a person's particular use of the concept of human dignity, before we can proceed to any judgement of that usage.

To 'translate' what Gadamer is saying into the terms we have seen used by Ricœur, then, simply to affirm that dignity is a problematic concept and that people use it to further their own agendas contributes little, on its own, to the ethical task of meaningful living. To conclude that the dignity of the human person should be discarded is based on affirmations of ethics and of the human person that are the products of the reductionist, objectifying methods employed by the critique. A human person is not reducible to cognitive science, or theories of language, or biological life, or theories of autonomy, any more than ethics is reducible to legalist *techne*. Hence, the conclusion that the concept of human dignity should be discarded is the product of an exaggerated emphasis on the hermeneutic of suspicion at the expense of meaning and participation. No meaningful reconstruction follows the deconstruction. Based on the alternative methodological assumptions I shall propose in Section 2.3, in Chapter 3 I shall offer such a reconstruction using a hermeneutic of generosity that affirms the value of the concept of human dignity for ethical discourse, but that nevertheless takes the valuable criticisms revealed by the hermeneutic of suspicion into account.

Gadamer's example highlights another important aspect of the critique performed in Chapter 1 that should cause one to exercise caution in too quickly accepting the claim that dignity should be discarded, namely, integral to the excessive use of the hermeneutic of suspicion is an epistemological reductionism. I shall deal with this criticism of the critique in the next section.

2.1.3. Excessive Reductionism

The idea that ethics is about being able to judge rights claims in a legal sense, i.e., that ethics is oriented towards *techne*, means that there is also a tendency to want human dignity to be one or other clearly defined thing. The critique wants human dignity to be constituted either by freedom, or life; either pride or some essential value independent of how one feels; either from God or based in human capacities. The problem with this approach to the concept of human dignity should be obvious, namely, it ignores the fact that the issue concerns the dignity of the *human person*, and the human person is *not* reducible to one or other of these features but is rather a *Gestalt* of all of these. Moreover, the human *Gestalt* is always more that the sum of these parts.[38] It is this human *Gestalt* that has dignity. And so it is the *Gestalt* that should be considered. Furthermore, the critique of dignity, and particularly those who would conclude that dignity should be dismissed, ignores the complexity of ethics and the moral event, tending to reduce ethics to what is legal, and morality to the evaluation of particular acts.

Thus, it seems that the critique, by applying a hermeneutic of suspicion, falls into the trap of turning methodological reductionism into epistemological reductionism. In other words it ends up affirming its method and the results of this method as the only truth there is to know. In this section, I shall demonstrate this by first describing the problem of reductionism and then demonstrating how this takes place in the critique in Chapter 1.

2.1.3.1. Types of Reductionism

Theologian Stephen J. Pope, in his books *The Evolution of Altruism and the Ordering of Love* and *Human Evolution and Christian Ethics*,[39] seeks to navigate a path through the sometimes opposing claims of evolutionary biology and Christian ethics. Among his key concerns are the claims the respective fields make about human nature, and what we can know of human nature.

Pope argues that some views of Christian charity and Christian ethics are inadequate in that they do not take a scientifically grounded understanding of human nature into account. By human nature he means "the basic inclinations, desires, needs and other aspects shared by all or most members of the species *Homo sapiens.*"[40] Pope suggests that by ignoring human nature, these theories unnecessarily separate the human person from the wider natural world.[41] Pope seeks to defend the value of scientific insights in the sense that they provide "an important source of information for understanding human nature, human flourishing, the natural law, and the virtues."[42] He explains this in terms of his understanding of Christian ethics. For Pope, the most important aspect of a systematic approach to Christian ethics is the teleological aspect because it concerns how we perceive what is good for humanity, the human good. Moreover, this aspect, if it is to be done properly, is reliant on an account of human nature. Pope argues that an account of human nature that excludes the findings of science would be incomplete and possibly inadequate, leaving us worse off ethically speaking insofar as our ability goes to think teleologically about the human good.[43] Thus, Pope concludes, "Scientific insights into the evolutionary roots of religion are compatible with the Christian view of the person as a self-transcending being made in the image of God."[44]

Pope does not, however, uncritically accept the arguments proposed by evolutionary biologists as constituting all there is to say about *Homo sapiens*. On the contrary, Pope is very careful and, more specifically, rejects a number of the assumptions that many evolutionary biologists make. He affirms that one should not look to science to support or provide the basis for theological beliefs or to provide the content of morality.[45]

Pope's main concern regarding scientific accounts of human nature is the uncritical acceptance, and sometimes advocacy, of extreme forms of reductionism. Hence, Pope's critical appropriation of the insights of evolutionary biology is undertaken in the light of his understanding of three kinds of reductionism. All three kinds of reductionism can occur when one is talking in evolutionary terms about the human being, but, Pope argues, not all three kinds of reductionism are valid.

First, Pope addresses *methodological* reductionism, which has as its premise, "that the natural sciences can explain the workings of physical, chemical, and biological processes without recourse to nonscientific ways of thinking."[46] Moreover, it is particularly concerned with doing so by breaking these processes down into smaller units and investigating how these units affect and limit the operations of other units and the whole. Pope argues that this is a valid and useful method of inquiry in that it helps us to understand how the parts act on the whole, but that we should also always be mindful of its inherent limitations: "It is not always possible comprehensively to explain the actions of a whole by accounting for the traits of its parts."[47] When this caveat is ignored, then epistemological and ontological reductionism can creep in.

Second, *epistemological* reductionism holds, according to Pope, "that traits found in higher levels of complexity can be explained entirely in terms of what is discovered on lower levels of complexity."[48] So, in the case of human evolution, sociobiologists may be tempted to explain all human behaviour in terms of biology, without reference to psychology, intention, motives, or culture, for example. Pope is opposed to this sort of reductionism and instead defends the idea of emergent complexity.[49] That is to say that the whole is always greater and more complex than the sum of its parts (see the idea of a *Gestalt* mentioned above), and, better yet, is qualitatively different, such that the analysis and understanding of its parts through valid methodological reductionism is by no means the only valid means of inquiry, nor the ultimate, all-determining truth. Not only are emergent qualities not simply determined by events at lower levels of complexity, the emergent higher levels, moreover, influence those lower levels in their own right. The capacities of more complex entities cannot simply be derived from their constituent parts. By way of illustration, Pope provides a striking example of how inadequate epistemological reductionism is: "We cannot expect to understand a Vivaldi concerto simply by mapping its sound waves or a Giotto fresco by analyzing its chemical composition."[50]

Third, Pope also rejects *ontological* reductionism. This takes epistemological reduction a step further by asserting that "more complex, higher-level traits or entities are nothing more than a particular way in which simpler traits or entities are organized. It insists that the character of wholes is determined entirely by the traits of their constituent parts. It would seem committed to the claim that only micro-entities are real. ... It asserts that the natural world [matter] is all that exists."[51] Pope argues that this ontological reductionism suffers from a fatal flaw, namely, it has exceeded the boundaries of its method—methodological reductionism—to engage in another discipline, such as theology or philosophy. "At times materialists concede that their position is based on unproven ontological assumptions, or even that they result from a kind of 'faith.'"[52]

Thus, Pope concludes that it is possible to accept the methodological reductionism of scientific enquiry while rejecting the epistemological and ontological claims that this is the only valid form of enquiry and that the material world alone is real, respectively.[53]

2.1.3.2. Reductionism of the Concept of Human Dignity
The critique in Chapter 1 applies a methodological reductionism, in line with the legitimate use of a hermeneutic of suspicion, by breaking the concept of human dignity down into component parts. It considers how the concept is used in different debates and to what end. It furthermore considers the different bases for dignity put forward by various authors. This all aids in the understanding of the challenges that the concept of human dignity faces in public ethical discourse. One of the key challenges identified in this way is that the concept of human dignity functions according to the component parts that are emphasised, for example, ontological groundings or psychological groundings of the idea.

The conclusion that dignity should be dismissed, however, jumps from a methodological reductionism aimed at understanding a larger whole, to epistemological and ontological reductionism. Epistemological reductionism in this case says that one can *only* understand what the concept of human dignity means through an analysis of its parts. And since such an analysis reveals apparent ambiguities—such as dignity being conceived, on the one hand, as something human beings already have, and, on the other, as something that human beings acquire—epistemological reductionism concludes that we cannot understand human dignity and hence the concept should be discarded until such time as we can make sense of the component parts. This position is represented by Bagaric and Allan.

Ontological reductionism is represented by Ruth Macklin. The component parts are the *only* truth. So, this position concludes that human dignity should be dismissed because the concept does not actually exist. Human dignity really means something else. Human dignity is 'nothing more than', e.g., biological life, or autonomy, etc., and hence, since only these are true, only these should be used in ethical discourse.

Those who call for the dismissal of the concept of human dignity, however, are not only guilty of an epistemological or ontological reduction of the concept of human dignity itself, but also of the concepts to which human dignity refers and is important, namely, the human person and the moral event. The reduction of both of these concepts is related to the legalistic view of ethics discussed in section 2.1.1., which is, one could argue, already a reduction of the concept of ethics. Such an understanding of ethics reduces the human person in that it does not take the person as a meaning-seeking being into account, and it reduces the moral event because it tends towards a deontological evaluation of the rightness or wrongness of the act at the expense of goodness or badness of the intention. Moreover, it does not take into account moral behaviour as a locus of meaning-seeking.

2.1.3.3. Reductionism of the Human Person
When speaking of the dignity of the human person, or human dignity, there is a tendency to ask, what is it about the human person that makes him

or her so special as to warrant a special dignity? What is it about human beings that sets them apart from other beings, or even other aspects of reality, so as to imply that they deserve special care, that they have some special worth?

Methodological reductionism may be legitimately engaged at this point to go in search of particular features of or beliefs about human beings that are said to set them apart from other creatures and afford them a special dignity. Religious arguments may, therefore, highlight the biblical revelation that human beings are created by God in his image, or created to have dominion over creation, or that human beings are loved and called by God to communion with him, or that human beings are created with an immortal soul, or that Jesus Christ, God incarnate, sacrificed himself for the good of all humanity. Philosophical arguments might emphasise human rationality, reason, free will, speech, consciousness, love, culture, or moral activity. Biological arguments might emphasise the uniqueness of the human species as reflective creatures capable of consciously influencing their environment and adapting it to their advantage.

Methodological reductionism, however, does not allow one to conclude that only *one* of these features or beliefs is actually true. So, when Bagaric and Allan, at the end of their analysis of the various bases offered for human dignity, admit that, "The telling aspect of this is that none of the bases is manifestly incorrect," there is no reason for them to then conclude that the concept itself should be discarded.[54] There is nothing in methodological reductionism that does not allow all of these features to be true. The problem with the conclusion that the concept of human dignity should be dismissed, and indeed with many of the arguments supposedly in favour of human dignity (see Chapter 1 section 1.5 and Chapter 2 section 2.2.), is that it assumes that *only* one of these features or beliefs can be true, *only* one of these can be the basis for the claim that human beings have dignity. And since, the critique argues, nobody can agree what that one thing should be, human dignity should be discarded.

What those who would dismiss human dignity fail to acknowledge is that the concept of human dignity addresses a multidimensional reality, i.e., the human person. If it is unacceptable to reduce the human person to one feature of one epistemological approach, for example to genes, or to autonomy, or to a soul, should it not likewise be unacceptable to reduce human dignity to one of these things? In the words of physicist and theologian, John Polkinghorne, "Only an account of human nature that locates us within the multidimensional reality of our actual experience can begin to describe a context adequate for anthropological enquiry."[55] And, after all, as Reinhard Marx, theologian and, then, Roman Catholic bishop of Trier, has observed, "Anthropology lays the foundation for ethics. It is, so to speak, ethics' hermeneutical key."[56]

The reductionism of the human person that takes place in the critique of the concept of human dignity is, moreover, somewhat ironic because the concept of human dignity and its rise as a core value in modern post-war ethical discourse seems to be strongly correlated with the rise of personalism and personalist thinking in the twentieth century.[57] Among the many important personalist thinkers, one could mention, to name a few, Americans Borden Parker Bowne and Martin Luther King, Jr., Germans Max Scheler and Edith Stein, Frenchmen Emmanuel Mounier and Jacques Maritain, and Belgian Louis Janssens.[58] Now, while emphases may differ to the extent that one can even discern different schools of personalism, all personalists hold that the central criterion, and indeed the way of knowing the world, is the person who is a subject, and an end in his or her own right, and not an object. Moreover, what is important about personalism, as opposed to say some strands of Kantian idealism, is that it seeks a middle path between individualism (where the subject is absolute) and collectivism (where the subject is at risk of being swallowed up by the collective). The result is a view of the person, based largely on a phenomenological and existential analysis of human experience, that is implicitly or explicitly multidimensional, because the person as acting subject is always situated in a physical, historical reality that is shared with other persons with whom the person is always in relationship.[59]

In section 2.3 I shall present a multidimensional understanding of the human person based on the thought of Louis Janssens that will serve as the basis for rethinking how we can deal with the concept of human dignity.

2.1.3.4. Reductionism of the Moral Event
Finally, with regard to the problems of reductionism in the critique of human dignity, there is the reduction of the moral event that is implied by a view of ethics that emphasises a legalistic *techne* rather than a hermeneutical ethics, or in other words, an ethics that emphasises the normative at the expense of the descriptive.

First, a word is necessary concerning the multidimensionality of the moral event. Roman Catholic moral tradition has long held that there are three so-called sources of the morality of an act. The *Catechism of the Catholic Church* defines morality as the judgment of whether a freely chosen deliberate human act is good or bad. The three sources of morality are (1) the object chosen, i.e., the action performed, (2) the end in view or the intention, and (3) the circumstances. All three have to be taken into account in making judgements regarding the morality of the action as a whole.[60] Since there is often confusion over the word 'act' in that there is debate as to whether it only refers to the physical action performed or the entire sequence of events including the intention and the circumstances, I have opted instead to use Catholic University of Leuven professor of theological ethics Joseph A. Selling's term the 'moral event' as an umbrella term that encompasses all of these sources.[61] Thus, within any given moral event, there are actions, intentions, and circumstances, as well as further distinctions and nuances like formal norms, concrete material norms, pre-moral values and disvalues, and so on,[62] that all contribute to the meaning and morality of the event. A moral event, then, like the human person, is multidimensional.

Precisely which of these sources should play the most important role in determining the morality of a moral event is probably one of the most hotly debated features of both philosophical and Christian ethics. For example, whereas deontologists emphasise duty, law, and obligation, and hence the moral rightness of physical acts, teleologists tend to emphasise the ends or goals to be obtained, and hence the moral goodness of intentions. In its most extreme form the latter becomes so-called consequentialism which measures the goodness of the moral event based on obtaining the maximum good for as many as possible. Nevertheless, even here there is debate, for example, between so-called act utilitarians and rule utilitarians. In Christian ethics, and particularly Roman Catholic ethics, the arguments have centred around the differences in approach by so-called natural law based theories which tend to focus on the physical act such that certain acts become intrinsically evil, and hence are always and everywhere wrong, and the so-called proportionalist or revisionist approach which emphasises the end and introduces the idea of pre-moral, physical or ontic evil as a way to overcome the absolute norms inherent in a so-called 'physicalist' approach. Of course, volumes can and have been written on this subject; but it is not the focus of this book.[63] The point of this section is to illustrate that the moral event cannot be reduced just to acts *or* intentions *or* circumstances, but indeed is constituted by all of these.

In addition to these three constitutive elements, I would like to add the facet of time. Moral events do not occur in a vacuum but in a historical reality. This is partly taken into account by the idea of circumstances. But the time dimension means in addition that behaviours that were thought to be right may turn out to be wrong, or that intentions that were thought to be good may turn out to be bad, or at least mistaken. This is the essence of the notion of tragedy. Without this time component it would be impossible to see the tragedy in someone who believes he is doing the right thing ending up doing very much the wrong thing.[64] Nor would one be able to understand why people see the death of, for example, a young mother as more tragic than the death of an eighty-year-old woman with severe dementia.[65] Nor would one be able to understand the tragedy in someone who "looks back on his life, near the end, and finds it wasted, empty of any real significance, with nothing in which he can take any pride at all."[66] Arthur Miller, writer of the modern American tragedy *Death of a Salesman*, describes the essence of tragedy as follows:

> As a general rule, to which there may be exceptions unknown to me, I think the tragic feeling is evoked in us when we are in the presence of a character who is ready to lay down his life, if need be, to secure one thing—his sense of personal dignity. From Orestes to Hamlet, Medea to Macbeth, the underlying struggle is that of the individual attempting to gain his "rightful" position in his society.[67]

In order to gain his "rightful" position in society, the person engages in moral behaviour. Not once, but throughout his life. And during this process, he justifies and rationalises his behaviour, always convincing himself that he is doing the right thing, that he is a good person, even when we as onlookers, as the audience of the tragedy play so to speak, sense that everything is unravelling around him, as the good he strives for becomes ever more tarnished. Such an appreciation of the moral event, and indeed one could say of an entire human life, cannot be achieved without taking the notion of time into account. In this sense, the ends that a person seeks in a moral event are never fully achieved. They are always somehow just beyond reach, imperfect, and unfulfilled, because by the time the end is 'achieved' circumstances have changed and new ends, and new means, present themselves for interpretation and action.

Time adds another feature, however, namely, that of historicity and historical consciousness. Historical consciousness has made us aware that what one culture or epoch may have thought to be normatively absolute is subject to change with time and place. Concrete material norms are revealed to be strongly dependent on the social mores that govern a particular society at a given time.[68] This explains how in the space of just a few decades, heroes can become villains and vice versa. Consider, for example, how Nelson Mandela was sentenced to life in prison by an Apartheid court for plotting to overthrow the government, and was believed, by generations of white South Africans, to embody the '*Swart Gevaar*' and the '*Rooi Gevaar*' (the black peril and red peril, i.e. communism) that allegedly threatened to engulf and destroy white, Christian, democratic South Africa. Mandela received the Nobel Peace Prize in 1993 and in 1994 became the first democratically elected president of the Republic of South Africa. Today he is revered around the world, including by most white South Africans, as an icon of peaceful reconciliation.

Despite this multidimensionality of the moral event, which includes the physical act, circumstances, intention and the passage of time—with all its implications—the critique of human dignity discussed in Chapter 1 tends to focus on the act and ignore the dimensions of circumstances, intentions, and time. I believe that this is strongly related to the view of ethics that, as already shown in section 2.1.1, tends towards a legalist *techne* and hence an emphasis on human dignity as a normative criterion. Professor of philosophy at Facultés St. Louis in Brussels, Guillaume De Stexhe, points out that "Professional ethics is often only dealt with from a normative angle as if it would mainly be important at first to impose (from the outside) rules for certain actions." Of course when this happens, one risks losing sight of ethics as the interpretation of the meaning of behaviour (see 2.1.1). De Stexhe, likewise asserts, "More fundamental than the question about norms is the question about the sense of action."[69]

The reason that it is easy to focus on legalistic norms is that they deal with concrete actions. Bearing in mind that the concept of human dignity rose to ethical and especially legal prominence following the violence experienced in the Second World War, De Stexhe's link between an ethics of norms and a desire to control interhuman violence and the threat of anarchy makes sense. When ethics focuses on norms as a way to control violence, then "ethics receives a meaning which ... is essentially negative (as a fight *against* a spontaneity which is *a priori* arbitrary and violent), and also essentially normative or *deontologic*."[70] Thus, as far as the use of human dignity as an ethical criterion is concerned in this context, a moral act is right or wrong based on whether it violates some conception of human dignity.

What the critique in Chapter 1 reveals is that this act-centred, control-oriented, understanding of morality as having to do only with the assessment of the rightness or wrongness of acts is also widespread among advocates of human dignity. For example, in the case of end-of-life decisions, a person could argue that ending one's own life or assisting another to end his or her life is morally wrong because it offends the dignity of the human person (in this case based on biological life as a gift from God). On the other hand, a person who argues for the right to die suggests that not to allow her to end her own life is an offence to human dignity (in this case understood as autonomy). What is remarkable is that both arguments only seem to use the concept of human dignity to evaluate the moral rightness or wrongness of the act in question, in this case ending one's own life. The critique, in bringing this to one's attention, is very helpful. It points to one of the causes that may underlie the unbridled increase in 'dignity talk,' namely, that in this discourse, apart from disagreements regarding the basis of human dignity, there is furthermore often an unjustifiable reduction of the moral event to just the physical act.

Where the critique fails, however, is that it seems to accept that this is the correct way to think about morality and human dignity, namely, that morality is concerned only with physical acts and that human dignity is only a normative criterion by which we can assess the rightness or wrongness of particular acts. Hence, the critique takes nothing of the qualitative meaning of these acts into account, the goodness or badness of the intentions they aim to achieve, the circumstances in which they occur, or the time and historicity that affects the way one responds to a moral event. After all, as already mentioned, does one not intuitively and emotionally respond differently to the death of a young mother, than to the death of an eighty-year-old woman with advanced dementia?

In section 2.3, I shall elaborate further on this multidimensionality of the moral event when I consider alternative methodological assumptions for how one might deal the challenges facing the concept of human dignity in ethical discourse.

In the present section (2.1), I have raised and demonstrated several objections to the conclusion to the critique in Chapter 1 that would discard human dignity as a term of any value to contemporary ethical discourse. Among these objections is, first, that such a conclusion is based on a view of ethics that amounts to a legalistic *techne* that ignores the human person as a meaning-seeking and meaning-giving, interpretive being, and hence also ignores ethics' role as a guide to the interpretation of the moral meanings implicit in human activity and striving. Second, that such a conclusion is the product of an exaggerated use of a hermeneutic of suspicion which legitimately deconstructs the concept of human dignity to uncover biases and abuses of the term, but which then denies any possibility of a reconstructive hermeneutics of generosity, instead affirming that the 'truth' uncovered by the hermeneutic of suspicion is the only real truth. And third, that such a conclusion engages in an unwarranted epistemological and even ontological reductionism such that it reduces human dignity, the human person, and the moral event to only one essential feature instead of acknowledging the fact that the human person and the moral event, and hence human dignity, are in fact multidimensional *Gestalten* that incorporate numerous features and are, hence, resistant to epistemological or ontological reductionism.

In the next section, I raise several objections regarding the assumptions that underpin a conclusion that would ignore the critique in Chapter 1 and would argue for one or other conception of human dignity mentioned in the critique.

2.2. The Problems with Ignoring the Critique
In the introduction to the present Chapter, I listed three possible responses to dealing with the critique of the concept of human dignity in Chapter 1. In section 2.1., I raised several objections regarding methodological problems that underlie a conclusion, based on the critique in Chapter 1, that the concept of human dignity should be discarded entirely.

The second possibility, which will be addressed in the present section, is to ignore the critique and instead continue to argue for *one* of the many ways in which dignity is grounded as outlined in Chapter 1 section 1.5. For example, one might insist that human dignity is grounded in human autonomy, or in the capacity to reason, or in the human species, or in biological life, etc. As in the case of the first possible response (2.1 above), this second option also presents a number of difficulties that make it unattractive as a solution to the critique levelled in Chapter 1. First, it does not help to overcome the problem of moralism, and indeed, may contribute to this phenomenon (2.2.1), and second, by not dealing with the problem of 'dignity talk' and the use of the concept of human dignity as a polemical weapon, it may indeed conversely lead to ethical relativism (2.2.2).

2.2.1. The Problem of Moralism

It could be said that moralism seems to have become a 'sign of the times'. James Gilligan, based on his decades of experience as a psychiatrist working in prisons in the USA, defines moralism as the "illusion that 'we' have the monopoly on the knowledge of good and evil … , and that we know that 'we' are good and 'they' are evil."[71] For Gilligan this moralism does not help society to prevent violence but instead encourages violence in various forms, because it justifies, on moral grounds, violent punishment. This moralising tendency has raised new challenges for both religion—because religiously founded forms of morality are identified as the cause of violence inducing moralism[72]—and for ethics—because moral categories, like the dignity of the human person, are seen as irrelevant to solving the ethical challenges at hand.[73] To prevent violence, Gilligan argues, it will be necessary to transcend moralism. In what follows, I shall provide a brief introduction to the problem of moralism as Gilligan sees it, particularly with regard to its alleged role in stimulating violent behaviour.

2.2.1.1. Moralism and Violence

Gilligan argues that cultural identity is a healthy and important component of a person's sense of self-worth. Cultural identity becomes problematic when the culture becomes an in-group in which those in the group are considered to have worth, while the rest of society, the out-group, either does not acknowledge the worth of individuals in the in-group, or the in-group does not acknowledge the worth of those in the out-group. Boston College theologian Stephen J. Pope, makes a similar point when he says, "… it remains the case that pluralistic societies are the scene of very different views about the nature of the human person, the dignity of the human person, and the extent to which that dignity must be protected."[74] This can lead, Pope argues, to a situation where "the evolutionary depiction of our tendency to categorize human beings into 'us' and 'them' seems to find resonance in human experience: 'our' dignity is recognized by us and 'theirs' is not."[75]

Two examples of my own devising will illustrate what I believe Gilligan and Pope are trying to say. The two examples differ based on the size of the in-group. For the first example consider the case of an immigrant *minority* to a European country. A member of an African Muslim cultural group will probably not generally be afforded the same degree of respect by a white, secular/Christian, Western majority as he would be in his own culture. There are of course exceptions to this rule, but many people would be at least suspicious because of his appearance and cultural affiliation (the media and current events obviously also have a role to play in this). Hence, for such a man, strengthening his own cultural identity becomes a means of warding off the feelings of shame[76] experienced by derogatory glances and comments in the streets of society. An alternative example is that of a person in the white, secular/Christian, Western *majority*, who feels that her cultural identity is at risk because these new immigrants do not respect the same values and codes of society, values with which she has come to identify. This person may believe that immigrant minorities come into her society and then claim a right to play by different rules so to speak, i.e., they demand that society affords them respect instead of working for it from within that society's framework of values like everybody else. The above examples present two sides of the same coin. In both cases, a person condemns the out-group as morally bad, since they are not perceived as subscribing to the same set of moral goods and values as the person does. Stereotyping somewhat, the Muslim man might think the Western woman immoral because she wears 'revealing' clothes, and the woman might think the man immoral because she thinks he oppresses women.

This is the phenomenon of *Us* and *Them*. Philosopher and literary theorist, Tzvetan Todorov explains this phenomenon in the context of his recent study into the rise of totalitarianism in the twentieth century, *Hope and Memory*. Todorov's description is helpful in that it demonstrates how the moralism, and the condemnations of the out-group, can lead to violence, which in the case of totalitarian societies in the twentieth century was perpetrated on a massive scale:

> [T]he grammar of totalitarianism has only two persons: *us*, among whom the distinctions between individual *I*s have been suppressed; and *them*, the enemies who must be fought, not to say slaughtered. In a distant future, when utopia will have been made real on earth, *they* will be nothing more than slaves ... or they will have ceased to exist.[77]

As the examples I gave above illustrate, what Todorov says about totalitarian societies can probably occur in almost any society, albeit on a different scale.[78] And for Gilligan, when it comes to violence and the logic of punishment, the same applies: when society punishes criminals with violence[79] it is acceptable, because *they* were a threat to *us*, even though *their* violence, since it was an attack on *us*, was unacceptable.[80]

Apart from the formation of in-groups and out-groups, it is important to understand the role that moralism plays in helping to justify violence. Moralism, according to Gilligan, sees the world of human behaviour in moral terms. To assign legal guilt in a court of law, a moral judgement has to be made as to whether the perpetrator had an evil mind, a *mens rea*. Effectively, in the process, the perpetrator is demonised as 'evil', and 'evil' must be punished.[81] By dehumanising and demonising those one perceives as a threat to one, by calling them morally 'evil', one makes punishment through violence more acceptable because one destroys the sense that they are like one. They are not human and therefore not entitled to the same treatment as one is.[82]

Moreover, the link between moralism and violence is further enhanced by the link between moralistic attitudes and religion. Religious texts are full of violent images, and righteous revenge. One only has to consider the many punishments for crimes in the Old Testament that require violence or death.[83] In extreme cases, literal readings of these texts still inspire 'righteous violence.' Evolutionary biologist and atheist, Richard Dawkins, provides numerous accounts of how religion and violence have been connected. One particular case demonstrates the danger of religiously-inspired moralism, in that the religious convictions only add to the perpetrator's certainty that he is right and good, regardless of what the law may say. In his book, *The God Delusion*, Dawkins relates the case of Paul Hill, a radical Christian anti-abortionist who shot and killed a doctor who performed abortions, "saying he had killed the doctor to prevent the future deaths of 'innocent babies'." Dawkins then adds, "I don't think Paul Hill was a psychopath. Just very religious. ... Dangerously religious. By the lights of his religious faith, Hill was entirely right and moral to shoot Dr Britton. What was wrong with Hill was his religious faith itself."[84] Dawkins's argument is that if the world can be freed from moralistic religion in favour of atheistic rationalism, people would finally be able to live in peace and harmony.[85]

Similarly, Gilligan, though his target is not religion specifically but moralism in general, which can be associated with any ideology, religious or otherwise, argues that until the apparently rational motives for violence can be understood, which requires looking for the tragic and not the moral, the problem of violence in our societies will not be solved.[86] To achieve this, Gilligan proposes a paradigm shift that sees violence as a disease rather than a moral evil.[87] Diseases are evil in the sense that they cause suffering and death, just like violence. But they are not morally evil. The disease does not act with malicious intent. Nevertheless, we try to understand and cure these diseases through rational investigation. If we attach moral values to a disease, such attempts become more difficult. For example, consider the resistance in some quarters to understanding and finding cures for HIV/AIDS some years ago because it was considered a disease of people who were morally corrupt, who through their immoral actions had brought the disease upon themselves and were therefore justly suffering for their sins.[88] The reality is that HIV/AIDS today has implications for everybody, whether one is infected or not. So does violence.

> [Gilligan's] approach to the problem of violence is ... bio-psycho-social: I view violence as a problem in public health and preventative and social psychiatry. My purpose is to arrive at an understanding of the causes of the various forms of violent behaviour, in the hope that understanding will help to clarify how we can most effectively and efficiently prevent such behaviour.[89]

According to Gilligan, to say that a person is violent because they are evil is not an explanation; it is a value judgement. The question of why they are evil remains unanswered. Therefore, in order to engage in a serious investigation of the causes of violence Gilligan chooses to view it as a medical problem, a pathology like cancer that can be investigated for its causes and the causes treated. Simply calling it evil and forbidding it does not prevent it. Gilligan points out that violence has been forbidden as evil for three millennia and yet it still plagues human society. Therefore, according to Gilligan, moral categories are insufficient, hence his turn to a morally neutral, explanatory approach to develop a theory of the causes of violence.[90]

Dawkins and Gilligan both rightly point to the dangers of moralism and how it can lead to exclusion and violence. Both argue that the solution is to approach the problem from a different angle. For Dawkins, it is the exclusion of religion in favour of a so-called rational atheist discourse. For Gilligan, it is the exclusion of moral language and judgement in favour of quasi-medical discourse.

I disagree with Dawkins because I think he misses the point. While he is quite right to argue that religious beliefs and religiously inspired morality can underpin moralistic attitudes of *us* and *them*, as feminist theologian Tina Beattie points out in her book *The New Atheists*,[91] there is nothing that prevents atheist, or so-called 'scientific', rationalism from being equally moralistic and violent. Dawkins's conclusion is based on a selective reading of history and religion. Moreover, he does not see that violence is an anthropological problem and that human beings will use whatever ideological framework necessary, religious or otherwise, in order to rationalise and justify violence if they believe that this represents the solution to their problems. As Beattie notes, "The division today is not between believers and non-believers. Rather, it is between those who see violence as the solution to the world's problems, and those who recognise the urgent need for a more just and peaceful international order."[92]

Gilligan's argument, however, is more persuasive, at least insofar as it asks one to find a way to understand *why* violence occurs before one rushes into making moral value judgements. In other words, Gilligan, unlike Dawkins, seeks to investigate the human causes of violence, and in this sense is interested in an ethical anthropology rather than trying to lay blame at the door of a particular institution or ideology.[93] I also believe that his bio-psycho-social approach is a particularly useful tool in this regard. Nevertheless, I disagree with Gilligan if adopting such an approach means the dismissal of moral language altogether. If it does, then it is likewise guilty of the kind of exaggerated reductionism already described in section 2.1.3. Rather, moral language is meaningful to those who use it, and so, along with a bio-psycho-social approach (as a form of legitimate methodological reductionism), I maintain that a hermeneutical ethical approach is also needed in which the meanings of this moral language are investigated and understood as a cause of moral behaviour before attempts are made to correct any misunderstandings that may be leading to morally wrong behaviour, i.e., before looking to normative judgement. This approach will lead to an active use of ethical and moral language as meaningful, but will avoid the trap of moralism in which both the sin and the sinner are condemned as evil. In other words, a retrieval and rehabilitation of moral and religious language, as I shall propose in this book with regard to the concept of the dignity of the human person, should contribute to breaking the moralistic cycle of judgement and counter judgement that leads to misunderstanding, fear, and violence.[94]

2.2.1.2. Moralism and Human Dignity Discourse

The analysis in Chapter 1 raised suspicions regarding the value of the concept of the dignity of the human person based on what it described as the rise of 'dignity talk'. 'Dignity talk' is characterised by the use of the concept of human dignity as a sort of self-evident, argument winning, polemical weapon whereby its invocation is seen to represent some sort of final word in the matter since human dignity is inviolable. The result is that one often encounters the same concept being used by two opposing sides of an ethical debate to underpin their respective claims. What the analysis in Chapter 1 further demonstrated is that these contradictory appeals to the term may stem from a combination of an alleged vagueness inherent in the concept and/or different understandings of the bases for the concept.

I believe that this 'dignity talk' promotes moralism for four reasons. First, the concept of human dignity is employed in such instances in a polemical way, i.e., it is seen to function as a criterion that decides the case in an absolute and definitive way. The proponents who appeal to it believe that the actions they defend are therefore absolutely morally right, and the actions they oppose are therefore absolutely morally wrong.

Second, the concept of human dignity, as such proponents understand it, is conceived to be an absolute moral good, such that anyone who they claim stands opposed to human dignity (i.e., their understanding of it), must be morally evil. Hence, the concept of human dignity becomes a criterion around which those who conceive of it in a particular way can marshal themselves to form an in-group in which they are right and good and everyone else is wrong and evil.

Third, this moralism is furthermore linked to a legalistic normative view of ethics at the expense of a hermeneutical descriptive view (see section 2.1.1). The result is an emphasis on human dignity's value as a normative criterion without any regard for the value it may have as a descriptive category. Such normative criteria, and especially one which is seen as absolute since it is allegedly 'inviolable', are attractive to moralistic-type arguments. They make no attempt to understand *why* a person may do something wrong; they only want to prove that it *is* wrong.

And, finally, the moralistic use of human dignity is strongly associated with a reductionist view of the human person and hence a reductionist view of human dignity (see section 2.1.3). Such reductionist views are polemically more powerful. For example, if one strongly associates the concept of human dignity with biological life, then to oppose a course of action by claiming that it is against human dignity is tantamount to calling those who support such an action 'murderers'. Moreover, it is more powerful as a criterion for determining that an action is morally wrong because the measurement is very simple, namely is a life ended, yes or no?[95] This kind of polemic is typical of, for example, the abortion debate as demonstrated by the reference to Dawkins above.[96]

Therefore, ignoring the critique in Chapter 1 is not an option if one believes that moralism is a serious and legitimate problem because, to ignore the critique will only increase the propensity for people to use the concept of human dignity as a polemical weapon. Likewise, simply accepting or arguing for one of the many bases described in the critique, while possible, is inadequate since it does not overcome the problem of 'dignity talk,' and hence is likely to only further diminish the value of the concept of human dignity for ethical discourse in the eyes of anyone who uses a hermeneutic of suspicion to uncover the ideology, religious or otherwise, that lies concealed behind such moralistic uses of the concept of human dignity. Which brings me to my second objection to ignoring the critique, namely, that it is not helpful in overcoming the challenges posed by moral relativism. I shall briefly discuss this problem next.

2.2.2. *The Problem of Relativism*

The flipside of moralism, is moral relativism, and so, if ignoring the critique and arguing for a single basis for human dignity does not counter moralism, it is likewise inadequate to counter moral relativism.

2.2.2.1. *Defining Relativism*

Maria Baghramian, a philosopher at University College Dublin, in her book titled *Relativism*, states that at its most general, relativism can be defined as "the view that cognitive, moral or aesthetic norms and values are dependent on the social or conceptual systems that underpin them, and consequently a neutral standpoint for evaluating them is not available to us."[97] If one were to define relativism in negative terms, i.e., what it is not, then, Baghramian maintains, relativism can be defined as denying the following:

(a) the thesis of universalism or the position that there could and should be universal agreement on matters of truth, goodness, beauty, meaningfulness, etc.;

(b) the thesis of objectivism or the position that cognitive, ethical and aesthetic values such as truth, goodness and beauty are mind-independent, 'capable of being presented from a point of view that is independent of the point of view of any human being in particular and of human kind in general' ... ;

(c) the thesis of absolutism or the view that truth, goodness, beauty, etc. are timeless, unchanging and immutable;

(d) monism or the view that, in any given area or on any given topic, there can be no more than one correct opinion, judgement, or norm. Relativism is compatible with local but not universal monism, for a relativist may accept that in any given culture or society there can be no more than one correct view on any topic but deny that one single correct norm or belief can apply cross-culturally.[98]

The focus of the present discussion is obviously morality and ethics. Baghramian shows that all of the aforementioned aspects can play a role in morality, and what one might more specifically call moral relativism. According to Baghramian,

> Moral relativists claim that the truth or falsity, the appropriateness or inappropriateness of an ethical belief, is relative to its socio-historical background and that moral beliefs cannot be assessed independently of their social framework. They point to the existence of diverse moral systems and maintain that moral values are grounded on societal conventions, historical conditions, metaphysical beliefs, etc. which vary from one society or social grouping to another, and argue that there are no neutral standards available to adjudicate these competing claims.[99]

Baghramian further refines the definition of relativism by pointing out that one can make a distinction between different kinds of moral relativism based on what the basis for the relativisation is. Hence, subjective moral relativism is where the "right and wrong of actions, and the acceptability of ethical ... evaluations, are all ... dependent on the beliefs and opinions of individual thinkers and actors—they are expressions of the private psychological states of agents." In the case of social relativism, the emphasis shifts such that rightness and wrongness, etc. are relative to "the prevailing social and cultural conditions." Social relativism is further subdivided into cultural relativism, which holds that there is no "culturally neutral criterion for adjudicating between conflicting claims arising from different cultural contexts", and historicism, which holds that knowledge and hence moral evaluations are "constrained by their historical conditions and bear the imprints of their time and place." Finally, Baghramian mentions conceptual relativism, which "relativises ... our theory of what there is, to conceptual schemes, scientific paradigms, world versions, categorical schemes or frameworks. ... Our knowledge of the world is mediated through a language, a theory or scheme and there is a plurality of such mediatory schemes."[100]

2.2.2.2. The Link Between Relativism and Moralism

Relativism and moralism can be linked in the following way. Jewish ethicist Peter J. Haas, in reflecting on ethics after the Holocaust, has proposed that the best way to understand how the Holocaust could have happened is neither to consider that Germans were somehow all evil, nor that they were just following instructions, but that in fact they were following an ethical conviction, a Nazi ethic.[101] In his view, even though individuals may have experienced personal disgust with what they were asked to do, they did it anyway because they believed that it was for the greater 'good'. Haas, seeking to avoid appearing to advocate moral relativism, suggests that one can make a distinction between an ethic and morality, such that whereas an ethic is only answerable to its internal criteria and consistency, a morality is capable of some sort of objective, context-independent evaluation of rightness and goodness. Hence, the Nazi ethic is not morality, even though those operating within it may have believed it to be.

Pastoral theologian and ethicist at the Catholic University of Leuven, Didier Pollefeyt, in his critique of Haas's position, is uncomfortable with Haas's distinction between morality and an ethic because he feels the morality component tends to lose out to the relativising power of the ethic. Pollefeyt advocates instead a distinction between morality and *Weltanschauung* or ideology. What people bought into, so to speak, was a particular Nazi ideology, not an ethic. Pollefeyt argues that this terminology is better because it better represents the fact that Nazism is not a continuation of a prevailing Western ethic, but rather a perversion of it that distorts and manipulates the Western ethical tradition to its own ends based on an ideological vision inspired by the writings of Adolf Hitler.[102]

I contend that whether one characterises Nazism as an ethic or an ideology, Nazism without doubt constituted a form of moralism rather than morality in that it claimed that German Aryans alone were right and good and all the rest, Jews in particular, were wrong and evil. Characteristic of this was a narrative and symbolism that, and here I agree with Pollefeyt, was a product of a selective, and hence perverse, reading of the historical ethical tradition, such that one ended up with a closed, self-justifying, narrative system of right and wrong, good and bad, that was resistant to external critique.[103]

Moralism breeds relativism and vice versa. The reason for this is because, according to Pollefeyt "A critique of one ethical system can[, then,] only be formulated from within another ethical system that has the same formal characteristics. ... There is no Archimedean point from which all ethical systems can be evaluated as to their content, using a kind of universal standard. As such, it would be impossible to find in Haas's thinking a real criterium by which to judge that Nazism is immoral, because there is no intra- or trans-ethical touchstone for preferring one ethical system over the other."[104] This in turn leads to what Pollefeyt calls "power positivism", where the only way to counter the ethic of one group is to establish an alternative ethic that can enforce and defend the rights of those excluded from the first ethic politically and militarily, i.e. with violence.[105] In effect, then, this just leads to the establishment of another ideology (moralism) in which *thems* become *us-es* and *us-es* become *thems*. Despite Pollefeyt's claim that calling it an ideology rather than an ethic somehow opens up the possibility of universal criteria by which opposing ethics can be weighed, the reality cannot be denied that for many Nazis and for those who opposed them, their subjective belief in their ethic was absolute, regardless of whether such objective universal criteria may exist. In other words, despite the possibility of universal criteria, moralism, moral relativism, and the associated "power positivism" is a reality. This is illustrated most poignantly in the first response to the Holocaust which demonised the Nazi's themselves.

> ... [T]he Holocaust was prepared with great precision by a group of immoral beings who did evil—evil for evil's sake—intentionally. Accordingly, genocide was the outcome of a diabolical plan through which evil was systematically realized and with malice aforethought.[106]

2.2.2.3. Relativism and the Concept of Human Dignity

All of the above can play a role in so-called moral relativism. Relativism poses a challenge to the concept of human dignity specifically because human dignity is set up as a *universal* moral good. Moreover, it is often claimed that all human beings inherently already have dignity, and that this dignity is inviolable (see section 1.4.1). The critique in Chapter 1 revealed, however, that, bold as such claims may be, they are not necessarily borne out by particular human experience. Consider for example the human rights violations perpetrated in and/or by states that are signatories of international human rights conventions grounded on the universal value of human dignity (see section 1.4.2). Moreover, the rise of 'dignity talk' and the fact that various different bases are put forward as competing grounds for human dignity with consequent disagreement on what constitutes morally good behaviour (sections 1.3, and 1.5), further emphasises the apparent relativity of human dignity. This is most graphically demonstrated by the violent criminal interviewed by James Gilligan who claims that his violent behaviour is justifiable based on his claim that he has a right to defend his dignity (see 1.3.3).

If one were to choose the second option and ignore the critique in Chapter 1, one would be no closer to being able to account for this relativism or to countering it. Indeed, arguing for an understanding of human dignity that is based on only one of the positions offered in section 1.5 of Chapter 1 is only likely to add to the risks of relativism and the accompanying dangers of moralism. The second option does not try to make sense of how and why people find apparently opposite courses of moral action meaningful to the extent that they can justify it over against the other. I maintain, on the other hand, that correction can only follow understanding. If one does not understand the problem, one cannot hope to correct it. If one does not understand what leads people to do bad things believing they are good, one cannot correct it.

In the next section, I shall propose alternative methodological assumptions that underpin a third possible response to the critique. I shall demonstrate how, by taking the descriptive hermeneutical value of the concept of human dignity into account, one can develop an understanding of the concept that takes relativity in human moral behaviour into account without becoming relativism, and can take normativity into account without becoming moralism.

2.3. The Case for a Multidimensional Understanding of Human Dignity

Thus far in this chapter, I have considered the problems associated with two of the three possible responses to the critique presented in Chapter 1.

With regard to the first response that would conclude that human dignity should be dismissed, I have raised the problems inherent in the critique, and indeed in some understandings of the concept of human dignity, which emphasise ethics as legalist *techne*, overemphasise the hermeneutic of suspicion as a methodological approach leaving no room for reconstruction, and engage in unjustifiable epistemological and ontological reductionism of both the human person and the moral event.

With regard to the second response that would ignore the critique and opt to argue for an extant one-dimensional understanding of human dignity grounded in one of the many bases mentioned in 1.5, I have argued that it is inadequate since it does not take the problems of moralism and relativism seriously, both of which are only worsened by such a response.

It is important to note that characteristic of the entire critique of the concept of human dignity presented in Chapter 1 is a tendency to look at things in 'either...or' terms rather than 'both...and' terms: ethics must be either descriptive or normative; hermeneutics must be either suspicious or faithful; the moral status of a moral event must be determined either by the action or the intention; personhood must be based either in life as a gift from God or the autonomous pursuit of meaning; and so on. Such a view of the world is of course attractive to the extent that it provides the illusion of certainty, of sure answers to questions. However, as I have demonstrated in the discussion of reductionism, such a view is often misleading, because it does not take the multidimensional complexity of reality into account. Therefore, I reject an 'either…or' approach to the concept of human dignity in favour of a 'both…and' approach.[107]

In light of the criticisms of the first and second options dealt with in sections 2.1 and 2.2 respectively, in the present section I put forward a third response to the critique in Chapter 1, based on alternative assumptions, that takes the critique of the concept of human dignity seriously, on the one hand, but seeks to make a case for the concept's continued value for contemporary ethics, on the other. At the core of this response is the view that 'both…and' is often a more accurate depiction of reality than 'either…or'. How this view is incorporated into my proposed response will become apparent in the sections that follow. For now, let it be said that it finds expression in the central claim of this book, namely, in the idea that human dignity is a *multidimensional* concept that can serve *both* a descriptive *and* a normative function in contemporary ethics. The alternative methodological assumptions upon which this claim will be based will be detailed in the present section as follows.

First, in 2.3.1, in response to the legalist *techne* of the critique, I argue for a retrieval of hermeneutical ethics that takes the descriptive value of the concept of human dignity into account based on a view of the role of the ethicist as someone who tries to offer a person insight into the meaning of their moral behaviour rather than simply to provide black and white answers to the problem. This will enable me, in Chapter 3, to take the meanings ascribed to dignity in the critique, not as answers, but as meaningful to those who understand it that way, and in turn to reconstruct, using a hermeneutic of generosity, an understanding of the dignity of the human person as a descriptive category that can make sense of those meanings.

Second, in 2.3.2, in response to the reductionism of the critique, I shall provide the basis for a multidimensional understanding of human dignity by outlining multidimensional understandings of two important concepts to which dignity refers, the human person and the moral event. Common to both of these, and something largely overlooked by the critique in Chapter

1, is the dimension of time, something to which I shall give expression by appealing to the idea of the Already and the Not Yet.

Third, in 2.3.3, I shall address how the adoption of a hermeneutical ethics and a multidimensional understanding of the human person and the moral event addresses both relativism and moralism, and introduce, as an important concept in this regard, the notion of the 'eschatological proviso'.

2.3.1. Hermeneutical Ethics

In section 2.2.1 above, I argued that the critique of the concept of human dignity, and indeed some of human dignity's advocates, tend towards viewing ethics as a legalist *techne*, which philosophers like Van Tongeren and De Stexhe have attributed to the rise of so-called professional ethics. Moreover, I argued that such a view overlooks an essential feature of the human person as a meaning-seeking and meaning-giving social being. By not taking meaning seriously, ethics tends to run the risk of seeking to judge before first seeking to understand. In the reconceptualisation of the concept of human dignity that I shall undertake in Chapter 3, this taking-meaning-seriously becomes an important methodological assumption. Hence, in order to provide some grounding for this claim, in addition to what has already been said in section 2.2.1, I would like to flesh out the idea of a hermeneutical ethics, and the role of the ethicist as a guide to the interpretation of meaning, rather than as judge or technician.

2.3.1.1. Ethics as Theoria

In an effort to preserve the place of meaning in ethics, Paul van Tongeren makes a plea for a hermeneutical ethics, arguing, first, that human beings are beings that understand and express meaning, and therefore, second, that ethics is at least in part a hermeneutical enterprise that attempts to explore in conversation with society and tradition the meanings that underlie and constitute a problem. Hence, according to Van Tongeren the task of the ethicist is to help moral agents to reflect on the various meanings at stake in a problem such that the agents are able to do justice to the real implications that their decisions will entail for what it means to be human.[108]

While aware of the fact that ethics "is about human practice, and it is for the sake of human practice and its improvement," Van Tongeren, nevertheless, argues that ethics is always oriented towards insight, *theoria*, rather than *techne*.[109] Van Tongeren's understanding of *theoria* is a Nietzschean one, rather than a Platonic or Aristotelian one. Whereas the latter use *theoria* to refer to the contemplation of pure forms, according to Van Tongeren, Nietzsche retrieves a pre-Platonic understanding of *theoria* in which, though still taking a certain distance from daily life, it nevertheless seeks to influence and provide stability to activities and experiences of everyday life.[110] Thus, *theoria* remains practice-oriented.

Similarly, Tübingen moral theologian Dietmar Mieth, also highlights the importance of 'insight' (*Einsicht*) for ethics, and thereby also highlights the value of a hermeneutical ethics. Mieth maintains that ethics concerns the investigation of the meaning of reality (both as actual reality and possible reality), experience, and praxis.[111] Therefore, for Mieth, insight, which Van Tongeren calls *theoria*, cannot be separated from praxis, or indeed from ethics as such.[112] This is, moreover, true, according to Mieth, because ethics is always contextual. It is 'involved'. And because this involvement arises from the fact that ethics entails the interpretation of moral experience and communicative (cf. notion of logos in 2.1.2) praxis, this involvement, this contextuality, is not something external to ethics, but is something intrinsic to ethics itself. This means that contextuality is, therefore, not something that can be avoided in favour of a detached rationalism. According to Mieth, a reductionist ethic does not do justice to 'the ethical' as it reveals itself in reality. For this reason, for Mieth, a hermeneutical ethics must mediate between judgement, experience, and praxis. And it must do so by first seeking understanding, that is, seeking to explain, to gain insight (*theoria*), and to interpret the forces at play.[113]

2.3.1.2. Hermeneutical Ethics and the Role of the Ethicist

How does one go about obtaining understanding? The answer lies in Van Tongeren's claim, based on Aristotle's *Politics* and *Nicomachean Ethics*, that the human person is a meaning-seeking and meaning-communicating social being.[114] This means that all meaning is constituted in a context of communicated meanings, in the conversation, which may consist of spoken words, texts, or actions.[115] The person interprets these meanings based on a desire to be good, and to live a good life.[116] In other words, the person engages in the construction of a self-image that she can hold in esteem based on the meaningfulness of ethical actions that she engages in, i.e., actions that have moral meaning, and hence implications for the person's sense of her own goodness or badness.[117] The actions, interpretations, meanings, and images of the self combine to form a narrative history of the self, which is itself situated in a communal tradition of interpretation, that is communicated to others and that itself becomes the basis for further interpretation and judgement of appropriate moral action for the persons involved.[118] Therefore, when people act according to pre-existing (traditional) ethical norms, or justify their actions in terms of such norms (for example in the case of 'dignity talk') they do so to the extent that such norms, or indeed their interpretation of the meaning of such norms, can be coherently integrated into the self-image that they seek to construct through the way they live out their lives. This means that both the person's actions and the norms he invokes to justify them, can be interrogated for the meaning that he intends these norms and actions to bestow on his self-image as a good person.[119] In other words, a hermeneutical ethics can ask what do the manifold aspects involved in a particular ethical decision or action mean for one's life as a whole? According to Van Tongeren, hermeneutical ethics, therefore, aims "to reach, through the appropriation of meaning, a morally meaningful and inhabitable world. ... In doing this, by bringing up the ethical questions that are behind the applied ethical problems, it contributes to the design of a structure of moral meaning, where answering so-called applied ethical questions belongs."[120]

This, then, has implications for the role of the ethicist. The ethicist is no longer seen as a judge, or a technician, but as an investigator or explorer of ethical meaning. As such his or her role becomes one of helping people to ask questions about the meaning of their moral behaviour and convictions, and helping them to engage in the conversation that precedes them in a search for meaningful answers to those questions.[121]

The notion of hermeneutical ethics, and the necessity of insight and understanding for the formation of a morally meaningful world, therefore, forms the basis of the claim made in this book that the concept of the dignity of the human person can, and should, be understood in part as a descriptive category. That is to say that an interrogation of how the 'normative' concept of human dignity is understood in particular cases can provide insight into how a person interprets both the meaningfulness of moral behaviour and the notion of a good, meaningful life. Moreover, by considering human dignity as a descriptive category, one opens the way to confronting a person's own sense of meaning and the apparent integrity of her life story, with other meanings that challenge the person's self-understanding.[122] As Van Tongeren points out, ethics confronts one with other meanings, which teaches us to see ourselves with other eyes.[123] In so doing, a person can make responsible, free decisions to engage in moral behaviour, the rightness and wrongness of which can never be proven beyond doubt, but which should at least move closer to an adequate vision of the good.[124]

Taking into account this view of ethics and the role of the ethicist, it becomes clear that it might be useful to develop a systematic framework, or a model, that can assist in unpacking the meanings inherent in the concept of human dignity; what Van Tongeren is perhaps hinting at with the phrase "the design of a structure of moral meaning." Though such a model can never exhaust the possible meanings, it can provide a lens through which one can gain insight into specific meanings as well as compare various understandings of the concept of human dignity. Since human dignity refers to the human person, it makes sense that a logical starting point for such a model might be found in an adequate anthropology.

2.3.2. The Human Person and the Moral Event
In 2.1.3.3 and 2.1.3.4 I criticised the reductionism of the human person and the moral event that takes place both in certain understandings of human dignity, as demonstrated by the critique, and in the critical conclusion to the critique that would seek to discard the concept of human dignity. In this section I shall propose a multidimensional anthropology and conception of the moral event that will serve as the basis of a hermeneutical framework within which we can approach a meaningful reconstruction of the concept of human dignity in Chapter 3.

2.3.2.1. A Multidimensional Anthropology
Since the concept of human dignity refers to the human person, in order to understand human dignity, it is necessary to have a meaningful anthropology to which it can refer. The fact that such an anthropology is necessarily multidimensional was already worked out in 2.1.3.3. Here, the focus will be on detailing an appropriate anthropology. This anthropology covers several different aspects of the way human beings phenomenologically and existentially experience their being human.

Leuven moral theologian Louis Janssens describes eight facets of the human person. According to Janssens a human person is only adequately considered when all of these features are taken into account. Moreover, although he distinguishes different features he insists that they remain interrelated in such a way that even these distinctions remain artificial abstractions.[125] What follows is a concise summary of these eight features as described by Janssens.

(1) "*The human person is a subject*, not an object as are the things of the world." That is to say that a human person is a conscious being who possesses the capacity to knowingly and wilfully act. This conscious action, especially in moral matters, is an expression of inherent human

freedom. The flipside of this freedom is the responsibility that a person accepts for the actions that she performs.[126]

Constitutive of human subjectivity is self-awareness. "Man is a being who knows, and who knows that he knows."[127] The person becomes aware of herself, from the earliest stages of her life, through her interaction with others, and the world around her. This means that a person is aware of herself and her own existence as a subject because she is able to intentionally focus her awareness on other things. In other words, it is through knowing and wilful action that the human person is aware of herself.[128] Direct and total self-awareness is therefore impossible. A person is not a pure subject. "In other words, insofar as we are open to all that is, our being transcends the world; yet we cannot state the question of being except on the basis of our participation in the world."[129] I shall return to this important statement later.

A second important constitutive element of this subjectivity is human freedom, which can be distinguished into two kinds, ontological freedom and categorical freedom.[130]

A human person is ontologically free because, as a being conscious of herself, she belongs to herself and is able to dispose of herself.[131] She is what Janssens calls an "intentional wholeness", which includes not only this conscious self-awareness but also the fact that it is always in relation to the world, as I shall explain below. As an intentional wholeness, her ontological freedom means that she is capable of determining the meaning of her own life and of orienting herself towards self-fulfilment.[132] Through the exercise of her ontological freedom, the person makes a *"fundamental choice*, or in its enduring state, *fundamental intention."*[133]

The fundamental choice is a choice for a desire that the person chooses to realise as the fulfilment of her intentional wholeness, as the meaning she chooses for her life. Desire is the manifestation of the "intentional wholeness" of the human person. Janssens mentions, for example, the desire for success, for possessions, for knowledge, and sexual desire. Each of these desires are partial aspects of a person's intentional wholeness. How a person orders these desires as partial manifestations of her intentionality will define her fundamental choice.[134]

A short digression into the notion of desire here might be helpful. One can distinguish between two kinds of desire. On the one hand, there are so-called first-order desires, or appetites, like the desire for food, sex, survival, and even knowledge or success. But these are desires that human beings have in common with other creatures. Animals also have first-order desires for, e.g., food, sex, and survival. Human beings, however, unlike other animals, can be said to have second-order desire, and I would equate this notion of second-order desire with Janssens' understanding of the fundamental choice. Second-order desire denotes the human capacity not simply to want, or to want to do certain things, but to want to desire certain things. It is the self-reflective capacity to evaluate one's preferences and purposes and to want them to be different than what they are. In this sense, a second-order desire is that desire that directs the ordering of first-order desires such that they come to manifest the idea of a meaningful, purposeful and fulfilling existence.[135]

Returning to Janssens, apart from ontological freedom, he also talks of categorical freedom. First-order desires, or what Janssens calls "tendencies" or "intentional dynamisms"[136] are the source of particular actions, and these particular actions are where categorical freedom comes into play. This is the freedom to choose between particular courses of action or to prefer some actions to others. Moreover, it is the freedom to choose particular first-order desires as legitimate motives for such behaviour, whereby these first-order desires are integrated into the person's second-order desire, or fundamental choice. In other words, the fundamental choice (i.e. that which the person deems to constitute a meaningful fulfilment of her intentional wholeness) is only real to the extent that it is incarnated in the particular choices of categorical freedom. Or put differently, a person's second-order desire animates her particular acts and is fulfilled in them.[137] This has implications for a person's temporal historicity which I shall return to below.

Before moving on to Janssens' second facet of the human person, I would like to point out the similarity between these ideas and the ideas developed in section 2.3.1.2 on hermeneutical ethics, in which the human person was characterised as a meaning-seeking and a meaning-giving being. I propose that what has just been said regarding self-awareness, freedom, desire, and the fundamental choice should be seen as an explication of this basic anthropological point. After all, as asserted above, the person seeks and interprets meaning in and through moral activity.

(2) "The person is a subject in corporeality."[138] Though a subject, the human person is an incarnate, bodily subject, such that her physical body has a defining impact on her subjectivity. A person is a unity of body and soul.[139] The person's body is essential and not accidental to her existence.[140]

(3) "*Our body forms* not only part of the subject who we are, but also, as corporeal, *a part of the material world.* Through this very fact, our being is a being-in-the-world."[141] The being-in-the-world expresses the human person's fundamental relatedness to all that is. A person cannot be anything other than related to a physical universe through the limitations of a personal body. It is through the physicality of the body and in the physicality of the world and the concrete relationships that this entails that the human person exercises her freedom of choice or categorical freedom in an effort to realise the fundamental choice of her ontological freedom. Moreover, the opposite is also true. How a person experiences this physicality, for example, losing a leg, or getting a brain lesion, will affect the way the person formulates and gives expression to her fundamental choice. As Janssens puts it, "Moral attitudes are determined by the answer to the question: what do the things of this world *mean* for the person whose body is part of the subject he is?" (my italics).[142] And, "the way in which we fulfill our relationships with the reality outside ourselves determines, the way in which we fulfill ourselves."[143] This relationality can be further

fleshed out into specific kinds of relationships, which are represented by the next four aspects of the human person as identified by Janssens.

(4) "Human persons are essentially directed toward each other."[144] This point resonates with, and reiterates, the point made earlier regarding hermeneutical ethics, that human persons are social beings. This is most evident in the fact that children become individuals with unique identities through their formative contact with other human beings who have themselves already become conscious moral subjects. It is through these encounters that human persons become moral subjects as they learn the values and norms of social interaction.[145]

Something which Janssens does not mention, however, but which I think is important to add, is that it is also in these formative interactions with others that human persons experience their own vulnerability to the capriciousness or ill-will of others. So, just as Janssens emphasises the indispensableness of tenderness, security, safety and genuine love from and for others,[146] one should also realise that one can experience violence, danger, fear, hatred, and disrespect at the hands of others in a way that is far more significant for the formation of one's fundamental choice than, say, the vulnerability that one experiences in the face of natural occurrences, like a thunderstorm.[147] Similarly, while Janssens points out that it is through relationships dominated by objects, for example, the exchange of goods and services, that the human person learns about morals in terms of justice, loyalty, fair play, truthfulness and the like,[148] I would add that here too people also experience injustice, being betrayed, being cheated, and being lied to, and can learn through these experience to do the same, nevertheless incorporating them into some fundamental choice, some meaningful idea of what it means to be a fulfilled human person. Apart from being a victim of physical violence, for example by an abusive parent, people may also experience the violence and disregard of societal structures, like class, racism, and sexism.[149]

These negative experiences of interpersonal relatedness, like those positive ones of tenderness, etc. will influence how a person morally seeks to fulfil themselves as human subjects. It is perhaps through interpersonal relatedness, more than any other aspect of being-in-the-world, apart from maybe the realisation that one must inevitably die, that one most experiences the contradiction of affirmation of one's subjectivity by others on the one hand, and the negation of one's subjectivity by others on the other. The flipside of both of these, I believe, is that one's moral response to these experiences will always seek to affirm one's own subjectivity, whether that is done through diminishing others' subjectivity or affirming others' subjectivity.

According to Janssens, "the way in which we fulfil our ... relationships determines the way (moral or immoral, truly human or inhuman) in which we fulfil ourselves as human persons."[150]

(5) "*Human Persons* are not only essentially social beings because they are open to each other in the I-Thou relationship, but also because they *need to live in social groups* and thus in appropriate structures and institutions."[151] Such structures and institutions include, among other things, the family, marriage, laws, and political structures.[152] One might add language, schools, stories and histories, and religions. According to Janssens these 'cultural realities outside ourselves' constitute the goods of objective culture. "Every human person needs objective culture in order to fulfill his subjective culture, the unfolding of all his capabilities and possibilities as a human subject." Again, the way in which a person morally responds to these social institutions, contributing to them with his talents for the good of others, or using them for his own good, will both affect and reflect how he understands his fundamental choice and in turn the way in which he fulfils himself as a human person.[153]

(6) "Created in the image of God, the human person is called to know and worship Him ... and to glorify Him in all his attitudes and activities ... ."[154] This wording is strongly confessional, and while appropriate to a Christian anthropology, could perhaps nevertheless be worded in such a way as to take into account how it is that not everyone is a believing Christian.[155]

Janssens nuances this somewhat in the article "Personalist Morals" by suggesting that metaphysics "endeavours" to demonstrate that the human person's being-in-the-world, i.e. essential relatedness, is itself a reference to God. He then adds "If it is true that God is the source of our being in the world, the Absolute of our relationships with others, we must recognise that our existence is a gift we have received from God." What is interesting here is that he has formulated a conditional statement here. Likewise, in discussing the notion of the fundamental choice in the same article, he considers how this fundamental choice might be articulated for the atheist or agnostic, the non-Christian, and the Christian.

Nevertheless, I feel that in both of these accounts, he is relying on a metaphysical analysis of the human person rather than a phenomenological one, and hence, it seems somewhat at odds with the other facets he identifies of the human person adequately considered. Therefore, it is not surprising that two of Janssens' former students at Leuven, themselves now both theological ethicists, have nuanced Janssens' language in this regard.

Joseph Selling calls it an openness to "the totality of reality, to the transcendent, to God." He fills in the concept of God by describing it as "that which transcends even the totality of reality itself." According to Selling, "Any person who seeks 'the meaning of life' is searching for a dimension of being human that is accessible to all while simultaneously transcending each individual." For the theist, this is God. "Others will describe the relationship to the transcendent in terms appropriate to their belief system."[156] Similarly, Jan Jans states, "I would appeal ... for an anthropologically more inclusive view by including commitment to meaning or openness to the transcendent as one of the essential characteristics of the humanly desirable."[157]

I would like to add to these two more nuanced positions that this relatedness and openness to transcendence might be understood in terms of the experience of awe, i.e., the mixture of fear and wonder, that accompanies the realisation that one is in fact always and already in relation to the totality of reality in all its dimensions, dimensions that are transcendent since they extend well beyond, both temporally and spatially, anything one could ever hope to know or experience oneself. At the same time, the fact that one can experience this sense of awe testifies to one's own unique subjectivity in this vast network of infinite relations, and in so doing affirms the givenness, or, in theological terms, the gift, of one's own unique experience of that reality. The combination of the two, awe and givenness, becomes the stimulus for the search to live out that givenness meaningfully in relation to the transcendent reality.

(7) "The human person is a historical being."[158] The historicity of the human person contains two dimensions. The first which Janssens points out is that a person's life is a history composed of stages in which different possibilities present themselves. "Therefore it is, for instance, essentially important to begin with the meaning of youth to morally judge behaviour within that stage of life."[159]

The second is that a person is imbedded in a historical reality, a cultural history that includes a given social milieu. This means that an individual person is exposed to and influenced by the norms and values of a particular society at a particular time. At the same time, however, as scientific developments regarding what humankind knows of its universe as well as technological advances show, these norms and values may be challenged and changed in the light of new reflections on how society can better serve the flourishing of human beings.

This historicity of the human person implies that prudence[160] is required both in the evaluation of change, and in the moral judgement of particular individuals who, though ontologically free, are always influenced in the formation of their fundamental choice and the categorical choices they make for moral behaviour by the historical values and experiences of their stage in life and the society in which they are imbedded.[161]

Moreover, this temporality means that the realisation and fulfilment of a person's fundamental choice can only take place through a temporal sequence of concrete moral actions under the direction of categorical freedom.

(8) "All human persons are fundamentally equal, but at the same time each is an originality."[162] As the anthropology developed by Janssens suggests, all human beings are fundamentally equal because they share the same human condition. "Knowing, feeling, desiring and acting we can be caught up in the same values. Everything that is human can interest us … . Fundamental equality explains why moral demands are universalizeable, that the same moral obligations apply to all."[163]

At the same time, each human person, by virtue of his own unique historical situation, with differing capacities, drives, and temperaments, will develop as an "original personality with its individual character".[164] Going back to what Janssens said about freedom, the person develops this character in line with a fundamental choice by means of his individual, temporally and spatially limited, moral behaviour in the context of his relatedness to all of reality. This unique personality that each human person constitutes stands as a further critique of reductionism and legalist *techne*.

In light of Janssens' understanding of the human person adequately considered, I shall next distil two additional points that will be particularly relevant to the reconsideration of the concept of human dignity to be performed in Chapter 3.

2.3.2.1.1. The Desire for Self-Worth
In addressing the notion of the free, self-aware subject, and her use of her ontological freedom to make a fundamental choice, I drew a parallel, between the notion of the fundamental choice and second-order desire. Hence, put differently, one could say that all human persons desire to become someone, to be able to meaningfully realise in some way in the concrete world what they experience as their own subjectivity.

I quoted what I believe to be a vitally important sentence by Janssens, "In other words, insofar as we are open to all that is, our being transcends the world; yet we cannot state the question of being except on the basis of our participation in the world."[165] This statement articulates a paradox that I already gave some expression to when discussing the experience of awe in the face of one's relatedness to all reality, namely that one is aware of one's own subjectivity, but one is at the same time aware that this subjectivity is only possible because of its relatedness to everything else. So, when one takes the relatedness to the world, to others, to institutions, to transcendence, and to time (historicity) into account, depending on one's experiences, these relationships may be judged a threat to one's subjectivity, such as when one is facing death, or as an affirmation of one's subjectivity.[166] And since death, and the end of one's subjectivity must be, in most cases, undesirable, one will engage one's categorical freedom in moral behaviour that affords some sense of affirmation to one's own subjectivity. Interestingly, a person might even choose death if that death somehow affirms something about who they want to be, about what they want to become, about the fundamental choice that they have made regarding how best to live out and fulfil their subjectivity.[167]

Hence, I would like to suggest that anthropologically, one can say that all human persons experience a desire for self-worth that motivates both their fundamental choice and their categorical choices, such that they can say that their individual subjectivity is meaningful and fulfilling in the face of an infinite number of relationships. This idea of the desire for self-worth also resonates with the idea of the human person as a meaning-seeking and communicating social being. To find meaning and purpose is to affirm the worth of one's own subjective existence.[168] To reiterate Janssens, "the way in which we fulfil our relationships with the reality outside ourselves determines the way in which we fulfil ourselves."[169]

2.3.2.1.2. *The Already and the Not Yet*
The second observation I would like to make concerns the relationship between the self-worth that the person desires—the fundamental choice

that she seeks to realise in her life—and the fact of historicity. As Janssens notes, "the human being is temporalized in the sense that his fundamental choice is developed only in the succession of his particular actions." Moreover, because one lives in a historical world, and therefore, though open to all of reality, is in fact at any one point only exposed and impacted by much more specific relationships and circumstances, the extent to which one can fully realise one's fundamental choice is limited by one's historical reality, all the more because that historical reality will also have consequences for how one interprets one's fundamental choice and the meaning of one's life. The concept of tragedy, which I have discussed before with regard to time and historicity, is helpful in this regard, because it reveals how even the most perfect and noble fundamental choice may go unrealised due to events beyond one's control, like a terrible accident, or the violent acts of others, or a natural disaster.

Moreover, insofar as the fundamental choice and a person's conception of what constitutes a meaningful life worthy of respect are formed by and through the relationships with the physical world, other persons, institutions, and the transcendent over time, within human society different conceptions of the good fundamental choice and the right way to realise it may be in conflict. What Janssens calls morally evil fundamental intentions, such as subordinating the realisation of the fullness of relatedness to the fulfilment of specific first-order desires for, e.g., pleasure, sex, or material possessions,[170] are probably not thought to be morally evil by those who have chosen these to be their fundamental choice.

Therefore, I would like to introduce the concept of the Already and the Not Yet[171] to explain this relationship between fundamental choice and historical time (see also the introduction to this book). What Janssens' anthropology affirms is that all human persons *already* have an ontological freedom, and experience a desire to fulfil their intentional wholeness in and through their relationships, which they do by making a fundamental choice about who they want to be which leads them to making categorical choices in the form of concrete moral behaviours. On the other hand, historicity and the limitations of time, space, and how one experiences one's interpersonal and cultural milieu (bearing in mind the point about the historicity of cultural norms and values) means that no person's fundamental choice is ever fully realised. It always remains *'not yet'*. I believe this is also expressed in the understanding of desire. What we desire is never fully attained, especially since this desire is born out of the experience of being in relationship to other things that always place pressure on what one desires. A person who desires material wealth can never have enough because he is always confronted by others who have more, or by the possibility that he might lose it. Likewise a person who desires and 'finds' meaning and purpose in life always finds that meaning questioned by events in life, to which he each time anew has to reaffirm his fundamental choice and decide once more to make a categorical choice for a particular moral behaviour in line with the meaning he perceives his life to have.[172]

2.3.2.2. A Multidimensional Understanding of the Moral Event
In section 2.1.3.4, I described how a moral event should be understood as a multidimensional combination of features that include intention, circumstances, action, and time. I also mentioned how critics of the concept of human dignity, as well as many of those who defend it, tend to emphasise its value as a normative criterion by which to judge whether a physical act is right or wrong.

In light of the multidimensional anthropology just outlined, I propose that a proper understanding of human dignity should take the other features of the moral event into account. In other words, the multidimensionality of the moral event will facilitate a better understanding of the concept of human dignity's value as a descriptive category. What follows is an attempt to state simply what is often a very complicated subject in the literature.

I have already shown that the human person is an intentional, meaning-seeking being. I have also suggested that this arises from the paradox of experiencing one's subjectivity as dependent on one's relationship to all of reality. Hence, I have suggested that this meaning-seeking can be called the desire for self-worth.

Louis Janssens speaks of formal norms, which are norms about what fundamental choice *ought* to be.[173] Thus, the most basic of these formal norms might be, in Christian terms, to love God and neighbour, or in more philosophical terms to do good and avoid evil. Or, in light of the above remarks, there exists a formal norm that one ought to realise a meaningful sense of self-worth in relationship to reality through one's moral behaviour.

But formal norms do not provide the content of concrete material actions. This content is a product of the intention, that is, the choice of action and end that is judged to realise the fundamental choice,[174] which may be guided by concrete material norms.[175]

This is where the difficulty starts to arise because there are moral and pre-moral aspects of all of these things. Pre-moral refers to concrete values and disvalues in a given situation. For example, health, pleasure, material resources, are pre-moral values or goods. They have no moral content in themselves. They only describe things that are desirable and welcomed. Hence, concrete material norms can be formulated that prescribe actions that promote these goods. Other things, like hunger, thirst, pain, violence, death, ignorance, are pre-moral disvalues. Again, they have no moral content, but they are undesirable and would be avoided if possible. Likewise, concrete material norms can be formulated that forbid actions that contain these disvalues.[176]

The person weighs these values and disvalues to make a moral decision regarding a course of action to realise a particular end that he *believes* will contribute to the fulfilment of his fundamental choice. I emphasise the word 'believes' because no amount of reflection and evaluation can ever exhaust the possible permutations of what could happen as a result of the action. Hence, I would say that every moral behaviour is, in a sense, an act of *faith* that one *hopes* is right, where right refers to the extent that the action realises one's good (*loving*) fundamental choice.[177]

However, this may also mean that the person sometimes considers it necessary to perform a pre-moral disvalue, for example, causing pain and suffering by cutting off another person's leg, in order to realise a pre-moral value that is deemed greater, e.g. saving the life and health of a person with a gangrenous leg. The whole event in this case would be deemed morally good because the doctor's intention chose an appropriate concrete material course of action (amputation) to realise an end (saving the life of the patient) that is in accordance with the doctor's fundamental choice to lead a meaningful life by promoting the health of others.[178] Moreover, the concrete material norm that normally forbids causing pain to another is superseded by the greater value implied by the concrete material norm that prescribes the promotion of life and health. In this sense, unlike formal norms (e.g. do good), which are absolute, concrete material norms can be relative.[179]

The point I am making here is twofold. First, the doctor, though aware that he would cause pain, *believed* that he was doing good both for the patient and in terms of the realisation of his fundamental choice, i.e. the meaning and purpose that he finds in life. Second, despite the fact that he caused pain, in light of his intended end and his fundamental choice, a third party can nevertheless evaluate the doctor's behaviour as morally right, because it is in line with his morally good fundamental choice to do good ('do good' is the formal norm that makes his fundamental choice morally good).

In other words, in the concrete working-out of one's fundamental choice, or the self-worth one pursues as a human person, in the concrete moral actions that one engages in during one's pursuit of a meaningful life, one may end up engaging in pre-moral disvalues, and nevertheless be pursuing what one believes to be good. And of course, sometimes, how one concretely fills in one's fundamental choice, i.e. the intentions that one develops, may result in actions that are objectively morally wrong (because they involve unjustifiable disvalues), even though one subjectively still believes and intends them to be morally good (cf. notion of tragedy in section 2.1.3.4).

The importance of this multidimensionality of the moral event for the reconstruction of the concept of human dignity that I shall perform in Chapter 3, is that when people use the concept of human dignity in their ethical discourse, they may be using it at any one of these levels. Moreover, they may be using it to refer to themselves, to others or to both. And finally, when they use it they will be implying a particular understanding of the human person that they deem meaningful for the realisation of their self-worth. So, for example, one might say that a person has a fundamental choice to realise the fullness of human dignity; or that there is a formal norm that human dignity should not be violated; or that there is a formal norm that human dignity should be realised; or that in choosing a particular concrete material action a person believes that this will realise human dignity (her own or that of others); or that a particular action is objectively at odds with human dignity; and so on. Therefore, a person's understanding of human dignity will affect how she behaves morally and vice versa. The model I propose in Chapter 3 will aid in describing these various understandings of human dignity and how they affect a person's moral behaviour based on where she considers the concept of human dignity to be most relevant with regard to the various dimensions of the moral event, as well as, what anthropological aspects she emphasises as most meaningful to the concept of human dignity.

At first sight, it may appear that the notion of a hermeneutical ethics developed so far, combined with the idea that a person engages in an existential quest for self-fulfilment in and through manifold relationships by engaging in what he believes to be morally good behaviour in order to realise his fundamental choice, is advocating ethical relativism. It may appear, in other words, as if in the attempt to describe and understand, any claim for universal normativity is given up, such that 'anything goes.' In the next section I shall demonstrate that this is not the case.

2.3.3. Ethical Relativity Rather Than Relativism

The methodological assumptions I am setting up here regarding ethics, the human person, and the moral event are intended to provide a middle road between ethical relativism and moralism, as well as a more realistic depiction of moral life than those offered by the legalist *techne* so often mistaken for ethics.

Nevertheless, the criticism may arise that what I have proposed is tantamount to relativism anyway, especially with its emphasis on understanding and interpretation, on the freedom of the subject, and on the idea that a person may engage in morally wrong behaviour believing it to be a morally right fulfilment of her morally good disposition. In other words, it might appear that I am advocating a purely 'subjective' ethics that locates the moral goodness of a person's behaviour and ideas in the subjective beliefs of the individual alone. In addition, by highlighting the relevance of historicity, both in terms of the development of the individual, and the provisional nature of historical cultural norms, it may seem as if I am allowing for no universally normative critique of ethical behaviour, since the person is only accountable to the historical cultural norms of her society, or indeed even only to her own subjective interpretation of these norms, and hence her existential idea of the life worthy of respect and a sense of self-worth.

I am not advocating relativism; I am however advocating relativity.[180] I am not advocating the absence of universal norms; I am however highlighting the unattainabilty and hence the critical nature of such norms on concrete material behaviour.

First, with regard to hermeneutical ethics, Van Tongeren addresses the problem of relativism as follows. The fact that meaning exists within the moral interactions of the human person and his interpretations of morally meaningful events, does not imply that meaning coincides with that particular interaction or interpretation. In other words, the accusation of relativism with regard to hermeneutical ethics is no different from the relativism that it criticises, in that both assume that they can step out of the discussion about meaning (out of the interrelatedness that is essential to human existence). In fact, however, in saying anything, one is already part of the discussion about meaning among various interpretations. To say anything is to offer an interpretation of meaning. This means that the meaning to which one is referring coincides neither purely with the interpretation, nor with the discussion between interpretations. Meaning transcends both. Meaning remains distinct from the discussion and from the interpretation even though it exists in these. Thus, it is true to say that all norms are only known through the discussion about meaning, which is why a hermeneutical ethics is so important, because it seeks to find what is most significant and meaningful in guiding moral action.[181]

This indeed poses the risk of falling into relativism. In utter frustration one might choose to accept that all interpretations are valid. Or, in a misguided attempt to counter this, insist that only one's own interpretation is absolutely valid (what I have elsewhere called moralism, see 2.2.1).[182]

But, because, as Van Tongeren has shown, meaning remains distinct from the discussion about it, and the individual interpretation of it, I would argue that both relativism and moralism are wrong, because the former identifies meaning with the discussion, and the latter with individual interpretations. Therefore, I say that meaning escapes both of these, but, nevertheless, by virtue of the historical and relational nature of the human person, must and can only be sought through discussion and interpretation. Meaning is thus the transcendent goal that is always Already in the conversation, but Not Yet realised in human life. This transcendence of meaning functions as a perpetual critical corrective to both moralistic and relativistic positions.

Second, turning now to the description of the human person and the moral event, the above discussion of meaning can be applied to the question of moral norms. You will recall that a distinction was made between formal norms and concrete material norms. Formal norms are absolutely normative, e.g. do good and avoid evil. But, they are also vague and open to interpretation. They provide little content for precisely how one should go about realising them in a meaningful way. The content is provided by historically conditioned concrete material norms that develop through tradition and experience as the best way to maximise pre-moral values and minimise pre-moral disvalues. And, whereas these concrete material norms are usually a good guide, the task of ethics is to explore their meaning when they become potentially problematic by, for example, resulting in greater pre-moral disvalues. For example, one should not intentionally tell falsehoods, but in certain circumstances, like being questioned by a known enemy, to tell falsehoods (a pre-moral disvalue) may be the right thing to do if it saves the lives (pre-moral values) of one's comrades. Thus, to a certain extent, concrete moral norms are relative.[183]

This does not mean that concrete material norms are relativistic, such that any action is the right action as long as the subject believes it to be right (though, as I have said, part of the task of a hermeneutical ethics it to try to understand *why* the subject sometimes believes it is right). It means that in seeking to realise her fundamental choice, depending on any number of historical circumstances, a person may fill in her understanding of concrete material norms and act according to or against them based on the relation between pre-moral values and disvalues, as she perceives them at a given moment.

Nevertheless, in contrast to relativism, her concrete actions are always open to criticism from the formal norms that her fundamental choice and moral behaviour claim to embody. Likewise, her interpretation of these formal norms is open to criticism by the meaning of the formal norms that transcends the limits of the historical discussion and interpretation of them. Moreover, some norms contain internal criteria by virtue of the definition of the terms used themselves that make them virtually absolute. Janssens provides the example of rape.[184] Because rape involves using violence to force a person to have sex, it is contrary to the formal norm that associates the full realisation of the human value of sexual intercourse with the mutual self-giving expression of love. Thus in light of this formal norm, one can formulate a norm regarding rape: rape is, by the very definition of the word, always prohibited. I propose that the concept of human dignity functions in a similar way to the formal norm that associates the full realisation of the value of sexual intercourse with mutual love. Though particular interpretations of the concept of human dignity may seek to realise a person's fundamental choice in a particular way, the term itself both as a formal norm, and by its very definition, always critiques those interpretations and the moral actions they inspire, just as the formal norm regarding sex and love critiques rape. This will become clearer in Chapter 3 and especially in Chapter 4.[185]

Twentieth-century political theology provides a useful term that captures many of the elements of what has been said about how a hermeneutical ethics combined with multidimensional understandings of the human person and the moral event avoids relativism and moralism, while at the same time acknowledging the possibility of universal formal norms and the relativity of the concrete material realisation of these norms. This term is the 'eschatological proviso'.

2.3.3.1. The Eschatological Proviso

The concept of the eschatological proviso is usually attributed to the political theology of Johann Baptist Metz. For Metz, theology is eschatological,[186] i.e., it is concerned with the coming of the Kingdom of God. But, for Metz, this hoped for vision of the Kingdom also serves a critical function. Since the Kingdom of God is not "pure utopia achieved by means of human progress but the gift of God in response to our effective solidarity with the victims of society,"[187] no human system is an adequate representation of the Kingdom, even though such systems may aspire to bringing about the Kingdom. Thus, the eschatological proviso critiques political reality by pointing to its historical and provisional nature. "A political theology does not, for example, advocate a particular political party or a particular program of reform, because the danger exists that Christianity will be identified with a particular party or program."[188] According to Metz, "The promises to which this 'eschatological proviso' refers [freedom, peace, justice, reconciliation] are not an empty horizon of religious expectation;[189] neither are they only a regulative idea. They are, rather, a critical liberating imperative for our present times … . [The orientation toward the promises] puts us and impels us again and again into a new critical, liberating position over against the present social milieu around us and its established conditions."[190]

Though, as is clear from the paragraph above, the eschatological proviso is a theological concept, I believe it can nevertheless be helpful in the context of ethics and particularly in the present attempt to reconsider the value of the concept of human dignity. The human person makes a fundamental choice in the context of her inherent relatedness to realise a meaningful life in a certain way. This will be expressed in her moral behaviour, which will, she hopes, reflect the meaningful life she desires to lead as an ontologically free subject. Nevertheless, as already mentioned, the nature of historicity, and the specifics of individual moral events, where countless circumstances as well as errant interpretations of the meaning of certain concepts and criteria by the agent can affect the outcome, mean that the full realisation of the fundamental choice often remains beyond the individual's grasp. Full realisation can never be absolutely achieved. The desire for the full realisation of the fundamental choice, and the formal norms that guide it, can never be absolutely fulfilled and hence remain 'not yet'. The fundamental choice, remains, so to speak, an 'eschatological promise'.

At the same time, however, a person engages in moral behaviour hoping that this will contribute to the realisation of that meaning, of that promise, of her fundamental choice. Now, the point I would like to make is that this fundamental choice, and the formal norms that guide it, should always also stand as a critique of particular, concrete moral behaviour. No interpretation of the fundamental choice is ever perfectly adequate, nor can any individual concrete material action fully realise it, hence, one should always be prudent in one's ethical interpretation and action, aware of the fact that one might be wrong, or at least never entirely right.[191]

The implications of this 'eschatological proviso' are that those who sit in judgement of others, using for example some or other particular, and inappropriately one-dimensional interpretation of the dignity of the human person as an absolute moral criterion, should always be cautious of falling into the trap of moralism. Because moralism, as discussed above, is no longer prepared to accept the critique of its own eschatological hope, and rests instead on arrogant certainty of its moral goodness and rightness. What I hope the reconsideration of the concept of the dignity of the human person in Chapter 3 will show is how, with regard to human dignity, moralistic attitudes do not reflect a proper understanding of the concept, especially since they ignore the provisionality of the present historical reality and its associated concrete material norms and social mores.

Endnotes

1. See, among others, Bagaric and Allan, "The Vacuous Concept of Dignity". See also section 1.7.6.
2. See the definition of normative ethics offered in the introduction to this book.
3. Shklar, *Legalism: Law, Morals, and Political Trials*, 1.
4. Here, 'normative' refers to a vision of the ideal kind of society that we should aim for rather than a legalistic society. For example, a society in which people act towards one another in a spirit of brotherhood (see article 1 of the *Universal Declaration of Human Rights*). See also the distinction between formal norms (of which this usage of normative is representative) and concrete material norms (which are more characteristic of the normativity of legalism) in Janssens, "Norms and Priorities in a Love Ethics," 207–238. See also section 2.3.2.2.
5. Verstraeten, "An Ethical Agenda for Europe," 5.
6. Cf. Heidegger, *Gelassenheit*, 12, who makes the distinction between calculating thought and hermeneutical thought.
7. Zwart, "The Moral Significance of our Biological Nature," 72. Cf. Pinker, "The Stupidity of Dignity."
8. Zwart, "The Moral Significance of our Biological Nature," 72 and 74.
9. MacIntyre, *After Virtue*, 6.
10. Verstraeten, "An Ethical Agenda," 6.
11. See also Macklin, "Dignity is a Useless Concept," 1419–1420.
12. See Van Tongeren, "Ethics, Tradition and Hermeneutics," 119. A similar point is made by Selling, "(In Search of) A Fundamental Basis for Ethical Reflection," 13. Selling maintains that people often simply resort to tools such as ethical guidelines, codes, or policies to make decisions without questioning where these tools come from. Moreover, the tools tend to become hyper-specialised, leading to the assumption that unless someone has the necessary technical expertise they cannot make an ethical decision in that field. Selling is concerned about this development because it seems to mistakenly suggest that no fundamental basis common to all ethical reflection exists.
13. Aristotle, *Politica*, 1252b28—1253a19. "For what each thing is when fully developed, we call its nature … . Besides, the final cause and end of a thing is the best, and to be self-sufficing is the end and the best. Hence it

is evident that the state is a creation of nature, and that man is by nature a political animal. ... Now, that a man is more of a political animal than bees or any other gregarious animals is evident. Nature, as we often say, makes nothing in vain, and man is the only animal whom she has endowed with speech. And ... the power of speech is intended to set forth the expedient and inexpedient, and therefore likewise the just and the unjust. And it is a characteristic of man that he alone has any sense of good and evil, of just and unjust, and the like, ..." I shall not go into whether Van Tongeren correctly interprets Aristotle here. My interest is in the anthropology that Van Tongeren develops and its ethical implications.

14. See also Ricœur, *Freud and Philosophy*, 46. "Reflection is the appropriation of our effort to exist and of our desire to be, through the works which bear witness to that effort and desire."
15. See Van Tongeren, "The Relation of Narrativity and Hermeneutics to an Adequate Practical Ethics," 58. See also Taylor, *Sources of the Self,* 112, who describes the human being as having the nature of "a self-interpreting animal." See also Wils, *Handlungen und Bedeutungen: Reflexionen über eine hermeneutische Ethik,* 59. Wils argues that human behaviour is characterised by a self-reflection mediated by symbols.
16. Van Tongeren, "The Relation of Narrativity and Hermeneutics," 60.
17. Zwart, "The Moral Significance," 77.
18. See Van Tongeren, "The Relation of Narrativity and Hermeneutics," 62. See also Hub Zwart's example of the how the moral significance of biological nature, i.e., what our biology means to us as reflective meaning-seeking beings, is avoided by rationalistic weighing of profit and loss. Zwart, "The Moral Significance," 72.
19. See Zwart, "The Moral Significance," 75.
20. See Mieth, "Sozialethik als hermeneutische Ethik," 225.
21. Jans, "Enjoying and Making Use of a Responsible Freedom," 108. Jans's vision of human dignity is strongly based on the Catholic Church's Declaration on Religious Freedom, *Dignitatis Humanae,* which Jans claims defines human dignity as 'responsible freedom'. Furthermore, Jans argues that the scope of the concept of human dignity should be *restricted* to the beginning of ethical discourse. This seems to suggest that he sees no normative value in the concept and instead sees its value only in its hermeneutical/descriptive function. While agreeing with Jans regarding the descriptive value of human dignity, I shall argue that it also serves a normative function in helping to evaluate moral events. Moreover, I shall

argue that such a normative function is not counter to but integral to a hermeneutical ethics (see Chapter 4).
22. Thompson, editor's introduction to *Hermeneutics and the Human Sciences,* by Paul Ricœur, 6.
23. Ricœur, "The Critique of Religion," 205.
24. Ibid.
25. See ibid.; Dreyfus, "Beyond Hermeneutics: Interpretation in Late Heidegger and Recent Foucault," 66–83; Palmer, "On the Transcendability of Hermeneutics (A Response to Dreyfus)," 88. For the essays in which Ricœur conducts his detailed analyses of Freud, Marx and Nietzsche, see Ricœur, *Hermeneutics and the Human Sciences.*
26. Pinker, "The Stupidity of Dignity." See also sections 1.3.1 and 1.6 in Chapter 1.
27. See Bagaric and Allan, "The Vacuous Concept of Dignity;" Macklin, "Dignity is a Useless Concept."
28. See Ricœur, "Two Essays by Paul Ricœur," 203–204.
29. See, for example, the work of transhumanist Nick Bostrom, "In Defense of Posthuman Dignity," and "Dignity and Enhancement."
30. Bagaric and Allan, "The Vacuous Concept of Dignity," 269.
31. See Tracy, *Plurality and Ambiguity,* 106–108; Fuchs, "Points of Resonance," 8.
32. See Ricœur, "Two Essays," 203–204; idem., "The Language of Faith," 224; and also Kearney, *On Paul Ricœur,* 27–29.
33. See the section on methodology in the Introduction to this book. I opt for the term hermeneutics of generosity rather than hermeneutics of affirmation because Ricœur seems to use several terms to describe this process of reconstruction. Moreover, he argues that the masters of suspicion themselves use a hermeneutics of affirmation, but that theirs is limited to affirming only what their methods reveal, which is in the end a very reductionist view of the human person and culture. Hence to avoid confusion I have chosen to use the notion of a hermeneutics of generosity. See also section 3.1 in Chapter 3 for more on the application of a hermeneutic of generosity in this book. See Ricœur, "The Critique," 205.
34. Cf. Schüssler Fiorenza, *But She Said,* 5.
35. Ricœur, "The Language," 224.
36. Ricœur, "Two Essays."
37. Gadamer, "The Hermeneutics of Suspicion," 64.
38. See Wertheimer, "Gestalt Theory," 2. "The fundamental 'formula' of Gestalt theory might be expressed in this way. There are wholes, the

behaviour of which is not determined by that of their individual elements, but where the part-processes are themselves determined by the intrinsic nature of the whole. It is the hope of Gestalt theory to determine the nature of such wholes."

39. See Pope, *Evolution of Altruism and the Ordering of Love*.
40. Pope, *Evolution of Altruism and the Ordering of Love*, 34.
41. For more details on the theories of charity that Pope criticises, i.e. pre-Vatican II scholasticism, personalism-existentialism, and liberation theology, see ibid., 19–31.
42. Pope, *Human Evolution and Christian Ethics*, 93.
43. See ibid., 86 and 92–93.
44. Ibid., 30.
45. See Ibid., 6.
46. Ibid., 56–57.
47. Ibid., 57.
48. Ibid., 61.
49. For more details of the idea of emergent complexity see ibid., 111–112, 124–128 and 308. See also, among others, Stewart, *Does God Play Dice? The New Mathematics of Chaos*, 366–382; Polkinghorne, "Anthropology in an Evolutionary Context," 94.
50. Pope, *Human Evolution and Christian Ethics*, 64; see also 61–69.
51. Ibid., 69–70.
52. Ibid., 71; see 69–75 for a more detailed explanation of Pope's dismissal of ontological reductionism. See also, Dennett, *Darwin's Dangerous Idea*, 82. "Good reductionism," is, according to Dennett, "the commitment to non-question-begging science without any cheating by embracing mysteries or miracles at the outset." Reductionism is bad when its "overzealousness leads to falsification of the phenomena."
53. See Pope, *Human Evolution and Christian Ehics*, 72.
54. Bagaric and Allan, "The Vacuous Concept of Dignity," 264.
55. Polkinghorne, "Anthropology in an Evolutionary Context," 101. See also Welker "Theological Anthropology versus Anthropological Reductionism."
56. Marx, "Sozialethik als hermeneutische Ethik," 246. "Die Anthropologie bildet die Grundlage der Ethik. Sie ist sozusagen deren hermeneutischer Schlüssel."
57. See, among others, Munro, "The Universal Declaration of Human Rights, Maritain, and the Universality of Human Rights;" Jeannot, "A Postsecular Exchange: Jacques Maritain, John Dewey, and Karl Marx."

58. For more details on some of these authors, see the concise survey by De Tavernier, "The Historical Roots of Personalism."
59. See, among others, ibid.; Bengtsson, *The Worldview of Personalism*, 203; Cuddeback and Taboada, "Introduction," in *Person, Society and Value: Towards a Personalist Concept of Health*, 4–5; Burrow, *Personalism: A Critical Introduction*, 1; See also Muelder's foreword to *Personalism* by Burrow, x–xiii.
60. See, among others, *Catechism of the Catholic Church*, par 1750, 1755, and 1757. It should be noted that these three sources are not without their problems, especially in that the *Catechism* bases itself on the writings of Thomas Aquinas which themselves have inconsistencies. Thus, what is precisely meant by object, intention, and circumstances and how they might coincide with or relate to each other is hotly debated. For a critical overview of some considerations with regard to the *Catechism's* interpretation of Thomas, and the notions of object, intention, act and circumstances, see, Hughes, "Our Human Vocation (Paragraphs 1691–2051)," 345–348.
61. Selling, "The Context and the Arguments of Veritatis Splendor," 40 and 58. See also Ashby, "Teleology and Deontology in Ethics," 769–770, who describes the constituent elements of the "moral event" from a deontological and teleological perspective.
62. See, for example, Janssens, "Norms and Priorities."
63. See Curran, "Absolute Moral Norms," 78–79. For more on these debates and the issues surrounding them, see, among numerous others, Ashby, "Teleology and Deontology;" May, *An Introduction to Moral Theology;* Selling and Jans, *The Splendor of Accuracy;* Curran and McCormick, *Natural Law and Theology;* Finnis, *Moral Absolutes: Tradition, Revision, and Truth;* Grisez and Shaw, *Fulfillment in Christ;* Hoose, *Proportionalism: The American Debate and Its European Roots.*
64. See Gilligan, *Violence*, 6–8 and 23. According to Gilligan, the subject of tragic drama is always violence. Unlike a morality play, a tragedy seeks to avoid categories of innocence and guilt. Rather, tragedy is concerned with the difficulty of too easily categorising violence into good and evil, right and wrong, guilty and innocent. The tragic hero is always convinced that he knows the difference between good and evil. The tragedy is that, in the hero or heroine's pursuit of good and desire to destroy evil, they destroy themselves and often 'innocent' others with them. It is a tragedy for both the victims and the perpetrators.
65. See Dworkin, *Life's Dominion*, 85–86.

66. Ibid., 202–203.
67. Miller, "Tragedy and the Common Man," *New York Times*, February 27, 1949.
68. See Curran, "Absolute Moral Norms," 77. See also Janssens, "Artificial Insemination: Ethical Considerations," 10–11. For a useful, introduction to the development of the idea of historicity, see Schockenhoff, *Natural Law and Human Dignity*, 80–114.
69. De Stexhe, "The Sense of Ethics in Human Existence," 65.
70. Ibid., 73.
71. Gilligan, *Violence*, 246. See also, among others, Baier, "Moralism and Cruelty;" Taylor, "Moralism and Morally Accountable Beings," 154; Mansfield, *Manliness*, 120.
72. See, among others, Dawkins, *The God Delusion*, e.g. 242–243, and 303–304. Among the many responses to Dawkins, see, in particular, Beattie, *The New Atheists*.
73. See James Gilligan, *Preventing Violence*, 7, 12–18.
74. Stephen J. Pope, *Human Evolution and Christian Ethics*, 211.
75. Ibid., 212.
76. Shame is a very important concept for Gilligan. I elaborate on this in more detail in Chapter 4, section 4.1.
77. Tzvetan Todorov, *Hope and Memory*, 39.
78. See also Pope, *Human Evolution and Christian Ethics*, 227.
79. Gilligan defines *violence* as follows: "I use the term violence to refer to the infliction of physical injury on a human being by a human being, whether oneself or another, especially when the injury is lethal, but also when it is life-threatening, mutilating, or disabling; and whether it is caused by deliberate, conscious intention or by careless disregard and unconcern for the safety of oneself or others." *Violence*, 98.
80. Gilligan, *Preventing Violence*, 14. "Once we have labelled someone as 'evil' there is often no limit to the cruelty and violence we feel justified in administering to him, ... all in the name of morality, law and justice."
81. See Ibid. 13–14.
82. See Gilligan, *Violence*, 67–69.
83. See, among numerous others, Leviticus 20:1–16; 26:14–39; Deuteronomy 20:10–18. See also Ausloos and Lemmelijn, *The Book of Life*, especially chapters 3.1 and 4.1; originally published in Dutch as *De bijbel: een (g)oude(n) gids*. See also Vervenne, "'Satanic Verses'? Violence and War in the Bible," which includes a concise but significant bibliography on war and violence in the Bible.

84. Dawkins, *God Delusion,* 294–298.
85. See Ibid. 1–2. Dawkins is not alone in this belief. Similar arguments are put forward by other atheists. See, for example, Hitchens, *God is Not Great*; Harris, *The End of Faith.*
86. See Gilligan, *Violence,* 8–9.
87. See Ibid., 25.
88. See, for example, Weitz, "Living with the Stigma of AIDS;" Wister, "Fragile Outcasts: Historical Reflections on Ministry to People with AIDS;" Kopelman, "If HIV/AIDS is Punishment, Who is Bad?"
89. Gilligan, *Violence,* 17.
90. See Ibid., 89–94; See also Gilligan, "Punishment and Violence: Is the Criminal Law Based on One Huge Mistake?"
91. Beattie, *The New Atheists,* 76–97.
92. Ibid., 94.
93. Gilligan, of course, does blame institutional systems, be they religious, social, legal, and so on to the extent that they encourage moralism. However, his accusations are based on an understanding of the causes of violence in the human individual, most importantly, the extreme experience of shame. To the extent that moralistic institutions increase shame in a society they contribute to violence (see Chapter 4, section 4.1).
94. I am not so naive as to think that what I propose presents some sort of ultimate solution that will end all forms of moralism and violence. Nevertheless, I maintain that (a) since the options proposed by Dawkins and Gilligan are inadequate because they ignore moral meaning and don't take the human person as a meaning-seeking being into account, and (b), since ignoring the problem of moralism simply perpetuates a cycle of misunderstanding and violence, the only meaningful solution that presents itself is (c) one that rehabilitates moral language on the basis of an adequate anthropology that takes both the danger of moralism and the human search for meaning seriously.
95. Though such arguments seem seductive in their apparent simplicity, they rarely are as simple as they seem. Consider, for example, the debates surrounding the provision of artificial nutrition and hydration for patients in a persistent vegetative state. Is such a person dead or alive, and does the removal of hydration and nutrition constitute murder, or 'letting die'? In this regard, see among numerous others, Christie, *Last Rights*; Hamel and Walter, *Artificial Nutrition and Hydration and the Permanently Unconscious Patient.*
96. See Dworkin, *Life's Dominion,* 20–21, 42–44.

97. Baghramian, *Relativism*, 3.
98. Ibid., 2.
99. Ibid., 6–7.
100. Ibid., 7–8.
101. See Haas, "Doing Ethics in an Age of Science," 110–111; Idem., *Morality After Auschwitz*; Pollefeyt, "The Morality of Auschwitz?," 119–124.
102. See Pollefeyt, "The Morality of Auschwitz?" 126–127, 130. Cf. Fackenheim, "Nazi 'Ethic', Nazi Weltanschauung and the Holocaust."
103. See Pollefeyt, "The Morality of Auschwitz?" 131–133.
104. Ibid., 125.
105. See ibid., 126, cf. Rubenstein, *The Cunning of History*.
106. Pollefeyt uses the term 'diabolization' rather than demonisation. Pollefeyt, "The Kafkaesque World of the Holocaust," 217.
107. With regard to a 'both … and' approach in the hermeneutics of Elisabeth Schüssler Fiorenza, see Fuchs, "Points of Resonance," 5, 8, and 17. With regard to the importance of the 'both…and' approach in Catholic moral theology, see Curran, *Catholic Moral Theology in the United States*, 133–135.
108. See Van Tongeren, "Ethics, Tradition and Hermeneutics," 122–129.
109. See ibid., 119.
110. See Van Tongeren, Schank, and Siemens, *Nietzsche Wörterbuch*, 315.
111. See Mieth, *Moral und Erfahrung II*, 31; idem., "Sozialethik als hermeneutische Ethik," 223.
112. Cf. the notion of praxis and the hermeneutic circle of liberation theology. Though liberation theologians emphasise praxis, insight remains an integral part of praxis insofar as praxis involves a hermeneutical circle. For example, Juan Luis Segundo says that the hermeneutic circle begins with the experience of oppression as a catalyst to questioning received ways of understanding reality; the community then goes back to the sources of these received traditional understandings, which for Segundo is especially the Bible, and seeks to reinterpret them in light of their experience. This in turn leads to new understandings of reality and to new praxis, which results again in new experiences and the circle begins again. See Segundo, *The Liberation of Theology*, 9.
113. See Mieth, "Sozialethik als hermeneutische Ethik," 223 and 225. See also idem., *Moral und Erfahrung*, 124–128.

114. See Van Tongeren, "Ethics, Tradition and Hermeneutics," 124. See also, Aristotle, *Nicomachean Ethics,* 1097b, p.11: "man is by nature a social being."
115. See Van Tongeren, "The Relation of Narrativity," 59; Wils, *Handlungen und Bedeutungen,* 59 and 74.
116. See Wils, *Handlungen und Bedeutungen,* 89.
117. See ibid., 90.
118. See ibid., 74, and Van Tongeren, "Ethics, Tradition and Hermeneutics," 126–129.
119. See Wils, *Handlungen und Bedeutungen,* 74, 77, and 80.
120. Van Tongeren, "The Relation of Narrativity," 62.
121. See also, Selling, "The Polarity of Ethical Discourse." Selling states, "… 'ethics' refers to the study of how persons make and carry out ethical decisions." And further on he states, "Ethicists don't tell people what to do or not to do. They provide information or awareness about the things that people might take into account in determining their own decision-making and behavior."
122. See Van Tongeren, "The Relation of Narrativity," 62. See also Jans, "Enjoying and Making Use of a Responsible Freedom", 108: "… the reference to human dignity is not a shortcut allowing to dispense from the handicraft of concrete ethics, but first and most the indication that there are indeed serious ethical questions facing us, questions that challenge us as concrete subjects to bring to bear on them our responsible freedom."
123. See Van Tongeren "The Relation of Narrativity," 59.
124. This would appear to suggest that ethical behaviour is relative, and is right and good as long as it is consistent with a person's narrative, and hence, that no universal norms or truths exist. I shall demonstrate, in section 2.3.3, that this is not entirely true and that a distinction needs to be made between relativity and relativism.
125. See Janssens, "Artificial Insemination," 4.
126. Ibid., 5.
127. Janssens, "Personalist Morals," *Louvain Studies* 3, 1 (1970): 5-16, at 8. Cf. Fuchs, *Human Values and Christian Morality,* 105.
128. See Janssens, "Personalist Morals," 7.
129. Ibid., 8.
130. Moral theologian Josef Fuchs calls these basic freedom and freedom of choice. See Fuchs, *Human Values,* 93. See also, Rahner, "Theology of Freedom."

131. Janssens, "Personalist Morals," 9. See also Fuchs, *Human Values,* 95–96; Rahner, *Foundations of Christian Faith,* 26–31, 96–97.
132. Janssens, "Personalist Morals," 9.
133. Ibid.
134. See Janssens, "Personalist Morals," 9–10. See also, among others, Kopfensteiner, "The Theory of the Fundamental Option;" Graham, *Josef Fuchs on Natural Law,* 116–124.
135. See Frankfurt, "Freedom of the Will and the Concept of a Person." See also Browning, "Human Dignity, Human Complexity and Human Goods," 302–303.
136. Janssens, "Personalist Morals," 9 and 10.
137. See ibid., 10–11.
138. Janssens, "Artificial Insemination," 5.
139. Ibid.
140. Janssens, "Personalist Morals," 11.
141. Janssens, "Artificial Insemination," 6. For more on the concept of 'being-in-the-world' see, Heidegger, *Being and Time,* especially 78–85.
142. Janssens, "Personalist Morals," 12.
143. Ibid., 6. See also Selling, "The Human Person," 99: "The human person ... stands in relation to everything, to the whole of reality."
144. Janssens, "Artificial Insemination," 8.
145. See Janssens, "Personalist Morals," 6.
146. See Janssens, "Artificial Insemination," 8.
147. See also the following, among others, which link the experience of violence in childhood with the practice of violence in adulthood: Gilligan, *Violence,* 45–47, 50–55; Palmer, *A Study of Murder,* cited in James Gilligan, *Violence,* 49. For a more recent empirical study of the link between childhood abuse and later violence, see Maxfield and Widom, "The Cycle of Violence," 390–395, who show that verified victims of child abuse are 30 percent more likely to be arrested for a violent crime.
148. See Janssens, "Personalist Morals," 6.
149. See, among others, Otten et al., "The effect of known risk factors on the excess mortality of black adults in the United States," 845–850; McCord and Freeman, "Excess mortality in Harlem," 173–177; Brenner, *Mental Illness and the Economy*; Brenner, "Personal Stability and Economic Security," 2–4; Kohler and Alcock, "An Empirical Table of Structural Violence." For a more recent survey, see Thomas L. Leatherman, "Poverty and Violence, Hunger and Health."

150. Janssens, "Personalist Morals," 6.
151. Janssens, "Artificial Insemination," 9.
152. See ibid.
153. See Janssens, "Personalist Morals," 6–7.
154. Janssens, "Artificial Insemination," 9. See also, Janssens, "Personalism in Moral Theology," 98.
155. This observation also applies to Rahner (*Foundations*), and Fuchs's (*Human Values*) notion of the fundamental option, which is also evident in Janssens' understanding of the fundamental choice. See Janssens, "Personalist Morals," 9–10.
156. Selling, "The Human Person," 97–98.
157. Jans, "Personalism: The Foundations of an Ethics of Responsibility," 152.
158. Janssens, "Artificial Insemination," 10.
159. Ibid. See also Roger Burggraeve's ideas concerning an ethics of growth which takes this historical development of the human person into account, in among others, Burggraeve and Van Halst, *Al de Vragen van Ons Leven*, 15; Burggraeve, "Meaningful Living and Acting. An Ethical and Educational-Pastoral Model in Christian Perspective (Part I);" *idem.*, "Meaningful Living and Acting. An Ethical and Educational-Pastoral Model in Christian Perspective (Part II);" Keenan, "Roger Burggraeve's Ethics of Growth in Context."
160. On the virtue of prudence and its importance to a relational anthropology see, among others, Keenan, "Towards an Inclusive Vision for Moral Theology Part II: An Agenda for the Future," 80.
161. See Janssens, "Artificial Insemination," 10–11; *idem.*, "Personalist Morals," 14–15.
162. Janssens, "Artificial Insemination," 12.
163. Ibid. In this regard, Janssens is most likely referring to the universalisability of formal moral norms, which assert what a human person's disposition ought to be—i.e., the most appropriate fundamental choice—rather than concrete moral norms which tend to be very particular, specific, and subject to the imperfections of historicity. See Janssens, "Norms and Priorities," 207–238.
164. Janssens, "Artificial Insemination," 12.
165. Ibid., 8.
166. Cf. Niebuhr, *The Nature and Destiny of Man*, 3–4. "The obvious fact is that man is a child of nature, subject to its vicissitudes, compelled by its necessities, driven by its impulses, and confined within the brevity of the

years which nature permits its varied organic form, allowing them some, but not too much latitude. The other less obvious fact is that man is a spirit who stands outside nature, life, himself, his reason and the world."
167. See Frankl, *Man's Search for Meaning*, 122, who shows how people believe it is important to have something worth dying for. And p.129 where he argues that people may commit suicide when they find their lives to be empty and meaningless. See also Gilligan, *Violence*, 45–47, who argues that people are prepared to risk their own lives, and even prepared to die if they believe it will replace a sense of shame with a sense of pride.
168. See, among others, Frankl, *Man's Search for Meaning*. "Man's search for meaning is the primary motivation in his life and not a 'secondary rationalization' of instinctual drives. This meaning is unique and specific in that it must and can be fulfilled by him alone; only then does it achieve a significance which will satisfy his own *will* to meaning" (p. 121). And "As each situation in life represents a challenge to man and presents a problem for him to solve, the question of the meaning of life may actually be reversed. Ultimately, man should not ask what the meaning of his life is, but rather he must recognize that it is *he* who is asked. In a word, each man is questioned by life; and he can only answer to life by *answering for* his own life; to life he can only respond by being responsible" (p. 131).
169. Janssens, "Personalist Morals," 6.
170. See Janssens, "Personalist Morals," 9–10.
171. The Already and the Not Yet is a theological notion used to describe the paradox of the claim that salvation was accomplished by the death and resurrection of Jesus Christ, and yet the world continues, and sin and death are still present. St Paul tries to deal with the problem and finds a solution in the idea of salvation as a process that has *already* begun in the death and resurrection of Jesus Christ, but that is *not yet* complete, and will only be completed with Christ's second coming. Paul thus sets up an eschatological tension between what is Already and what is Not Yet. Despite its being a theological concept, I believe it is valuable here to describe the paradox of being a person who has made a fundamental choice, and the reality that due to historicity that fundamental choice can never be fully realised. For more on the theological use of this concept see, among others, Dunn, *The Theology of Paul the Apostle*, 461–493.
172. See also Mieth, *Moral und Erfahrung II,* 31, where Mieth describes ethics as the tension between reality and the realisation of possible

worlds which are 'not yet' (*noch nicht*), but which are nevertheless hoped for.

173. See Janssens, "Norms and Priorities," 207. Janssens does not actually talk about 'fundamental choice' in this article. Nevertheless, he states, "Norms of this category [i.e., formal norms] assert what our disposition ought to be." He also calls 'disposition' our 'inner attitude'. Janssens continues, "We call them formal norms, because our inner attitude or disposition is the formal, animating element of our conduct." In "Personalist morals", 11, Janssens states, "Thus, our fundamental choice animates our particular acts and is fulfilled in them. So the human being is temporalized in the sense that his fundamental choice is developed only in the succession of his particular actions (the foundation of historicity)." So, Janssens appears to use the notion of 'fundamental choice' in a way synonymous with 'disposition' in that both 'animate' behaviour. Therefore, I have chosen to stick with the term 'fundamental choice' though I believe one could just as easily substitute it with the terms disposition or inner attitude.

174. See Janssens, "Norms and Priorities," 208–209. "In other words, in our action our good disposition is the principle of our motives, of our intention, and of its effectiveness. Thus our intention already involves the choice of the action which, according to our prudent judgement of conscience, is appropriate for the actualization of our good disposition or is able to realize in a truly human way the end aimed at by our intention."

175. Janssens in ibid., 210. gives the example of the norm, 'you shall not kill'. It is concrete because it applies to a series of definite actions, and it is material because it addresses the external material content, the 'what is done' of the action.

176. Ibid. 210–211, and 216.

177. See also Kirchhoffer, "Sacrament and Being," in which I explain this understanding of the cardinal virtues—faith, hope, and love—in the context of the challenges posed to sacramentology by the critique of ontotheology.

178. For other examples, see Janssens, "Norms and Priorities," 214–216.

179. See ibid, 217: "Consequently, concrete, material norms are relative in the sense of conditional. They are not binding, if there is a proportionate reason why the case at issue is not governed by them."

180. See also Janssens, "Personalist Morals," 10, who says that part of the mission of moral theology is to show "the relativity of what has already been accomplished" with regard to the extent to which we have fulfilled

the fundamental choice for a communion of Agape with God in the context of our historical relatedness. See also idem., "Norms and Priorities", 216–218, regarding the relativity of concrete material norms.
181. See Van Tongeren, 'Ethics, Tradition and Hermeneutics,' 130–132. See also Selling, "(In Search of) A Fundamental Basis," 13: "In order to function as an ethical foundation, a source of objectivity, a ground for ethical appeal, whatever we invoke, whatever we accept (on faith) or believe to be the ultimate criterion, in order to remain free of falling into mere subjectivism and wish-fulfillment, there must be something more to this criterion than that which is evident, observable, explainable or provable."
182. See Van Tongeren, 'Ethics, Tradition and Hermeneutics,' 130–132.
183. See Janssens, "Norms and Priorities," 214–218.
184. See Janssens, "Norms and Priorities," 217–218.
185. See especially sections 3.4.4, 3.4.5, 4.1.2., and 4.2.2.
186. See Phan, "Roman Catholic Theology," 227.
187. Ibid.
188. Livingston and Schüssler Fiorenza, *Modern Christian Thought*, 291. See also Metz, "Religion and Society in the Light of a Political Theology," 513.
189. This counters the critique levelled against political theologian's like Metz and Jürgen Moltmann by liberation theologians like Gustavo Gutiérrez. See Livingston and Schüssler Fiorenza, *Modern Christian Thought*, 292; and, among others, Gutiérrez, *A Theology of Liberation*, 124.
190. Metz, "Religion and Society," 513–514.
191. See also Selling, "(In Search of) A Fundamental Basis," 17, who argues that "*whatever* we conclude to be the most fundamental criterion for ethical reflection will describe the content of what we must ultimately call a 'faith statement'. We cannot 'prove' that all human persons are fundamentally equal. Ultimately we make some kind of a decision to accept such a proposition—we believe it. ... If the working hypothesis that we are using becomes fixed, static, thought to be entirely complete, we will probably be deceiving ourselves."

CHAPTER 3

THE COMPONENT DIMENSIONS OF HUMAN DIGNITY MODEL

In the introduction to this book, I stated the following primary thesis: the dignity of the human person is a valuable, multidimensional concept for contemporary ethical discourse, because, properly understood, it can serve both as a descriptive category and normative criterion. The concept, thus, provides the basis for a framework that can help to both understand and evaluate human moral behaviour.

In the present chapter, I shall elaborate on what such a proper understanding might look like by presenting the Component Dimensions of Human Dignity model as an interpretive framework for understanding the multidimensional reality of the concept of human dignity.

In the book so far, in Chapter 1, I have provided an overview of the main thrust of the critique that has been levelled at the concept of human dignity in recent years. This critique has led some authors to conclude that human dignity is vacuous, stupid and hence useless to ethical discourse.

The criticisms raised in Chapter 1 are important ones because they legitimately point out challenges to the concept of human dignity that call its value for contemporary ethical discourse into question. There are three ways in which one can respond to the critique.

The first would be to accept it and conclude that the concept of human dignity is indeed vacuous, etc. and so discard it as a term of any practical value in ethical discourse. In Chapter 2, I raised a number of issues that call such a conclusion into question, demonstrating, in particular, that such a conclusion is based on certain inadequate methodological assumptions: ethics is reduced to legalist *techne*; there is an exaggerated reliance on a hermeneutic of suspicion without a concomitant reconstruction using a hermeneutic of generosity; and there is an illegitimate epistemological reductionism of the human person to one or other specific feature, and of the moral event to the physical action.

Chapter 2 likewise criticised the second possible response to the critique in Chapter 1, namely, to ignore the critique and simply continue to argue for one of the positions critiqued and evident in the rise of 'dignity talk'. Here too, there is often a tendency towards reducing human dignity to a single feature of the human person and the moral event either to the action or to the intention. In other words, it does not take one of the most important findings of the critique seriously, namely that there is apparent disagreement regarding the basis and therefore the function of one of the most fundamental concepts in ethical discourse today. As a result, the second option is of no help in overcoming the problem of 'dignity talk' and the associated and interrelated risks of moralism and moral relativism.

The third possible response to the critique in Chapter 1 is to take the criticisms seriously as the result of a legitimate application of a hermeneutic of suspicion and methodological reductionism, but then to use these findings to strengthen the case in favour of the value of human dignity as a criterion for ethical discourse by offering an enriched, reconstructed understanding of its meaning using a hermeneutic of generosity.

Chapter 2 section 3 provided the methodological grounding for this third option:

The Component Dimensions of Human Dignity Model   207

- First, it elucidated the value of a hermeneutical ethics, the role of the ethicist as a guide and interpreter in the human search for meaning in the 'conversations' that are constituted by moral events, and the importance of gaining descriptive insight before engaging in normative judgement;
- second, it offered a multidimensional understanding of the human person as a historically situated, meaning-seeking and -giving, corporeal subject who is always inherently in relationship, and who therefore seeks to acquire a sense of self-worth, i.e. the sense that he or she has lived a meaningful life that he or she can be proud of, in and through the moral interactions with the relationships in which he or she is embedded;
- third, it shed light on the multidimensionality of the moral event and the importance of taking various aspects including, among others, the intention, action, and circumstances, into account when describing and evaluating moral behaviour or when weighing one's moral options, because the goodness and badness, rightness and wrongness, of the event as a whole can be affected by all of these aspects;
- finally, based on the importance of time as a relativising influence in both the moral development of the human person, and the validity of concrete material norms, it offered reinterpretations of the theological notions of the Already and the Not Yet, and the eschatological proviso. The notion of the Already and the Not Yet, applies to both the human person and the moral event in that both already move towards desires that are (always) not yet realised. The notion of the eschatological proviso takes this Not Yet element of human morality into account by acting as a criterion that calls into question all human moral strategies and ideals (which are always historical and therefore limited). In so doing it helps to avoid the trap of moralism by encouraging a hermeneutical ethics that first seeks to understand; and it helps to avoid relativism by holding up a formal norm, e.g., do good and avoid evil, as a goal always desired, though, due to the necessity of concrete interpretation, not yet fully realised.

In light of the critique in Chapter 1 and the 'critique of the critique' in Chapter 2, the present chapter will develop a multidimensional model that can facilitate our understanding of human dignity as a descriptive category and a normative criterion.

The chapter is structured as follows. Section 3.1. will elaborate on the idea of a multidimensional model, how such a model should be understood in relation to the reality it models, and how the model is intended to function. In 3.2., I make several methodological remarks regarding the construction of the proposed model. In 3.3, I discuss the Component Dimensions and how they are related to the anthropology outlined in Chapter 2. In 3.4., I discuss how each of the four Component Dimensions is constituted by a Complementary Duality situated on a temporal axis of the Already and the Not Yet. Each of these Complementary Dualities will be defined in relation to a re-reading of the critique in Chapter 1 (see 3.2 on method). Obviously, the model and its key concepts have already been presented in some detail in the introduction. The aim of this chapter, then, is really to demonstrate how this model can be arrived at based on both the critique in Chapter 1 and the 'critique of the critique' in Chapter 2. Chapter 4 will consider the descriptive and normative value of the concept of human dignity in light of the model derived here using case studies focussing on interpersonal violence and end-of-life decisions.

As the focus of attention in this chapter is the Component Dimensions of Human Dignity model, it is already presented here in Table 2 for ease of reference. I shall refer back to it regularly during the course of this chapter.

Table 2. The component dimensions of human dignity model.

Component Dimension	Complementary Duality	
	Already	Not Yet
Existential	Have (Potential)	Acquire (Fulfilment)
Cognitive-Affective	Inherent Worth	Self-Worth
Behavioural	Moral Good	Morally Good
Social	Others' Dignity	My Dignity

3.1. On Multidimensionality and the Relevance of a Model

3.1.1. Multidimensionality: 'Both...And' rather than 'Either...Or'

The alternative methodological assumptions developed in Chapter 2 section 3 can best be summarised as an option for a 'both...and' worldview rather than an 'either...or' worldview. Whilst the 'either...or' position, which is typical of the critique and indeed many of the positions regarding human dignity that it criticises, is attractive because it seems to present the world in the sharp contrast of black and white, it is nevertheless, as demonstrated in Chapter 2, an inaccurate and inadequate depiction of the world, of ethics, of the human person, of the moral event, and of the concept of human dignity. The world is not black and white; it is not one- or even two-dimensional. The world is full of colour, in innumerable shades and combinations. The world has dimensions of depth and time and sound and taste and touch such that nothing is ever the same. And the world is always observed by a subject such that no two subjects ever have exactly the same experience of the world. The world and one's experience of it is, in other words, always multidimensional even though one can only attend to a few of these dimensions at any one time. Thus, though, in attending to *either* this dimension, *or* that one, the illusion may arise that the world is 'either...or', it remains, in fact, a multidimensional 'both...and'.

3.1.2. The Relevance of a Model: of Eyes and Lenses

Sticking with the analogy of the multicolour visual perception of the world for a moment, it is obvious that one needs eyes to see. One's eyes allow one to perceive not only the multidimensionality of the world as a whole, but to focus on the details of particular dimensions while remaining aware of other dimensions. Even while focussing on reading this page, for example, one will still pick up movement in one's peripheral vision.

In hermeneutics—that is, the study of interpretation—people often speak of a hermeneutical lens. This lens consists of the assumptions through which one interprets the world. Sometimes, the implication is that this lens leads to biases, in the negative sense of the word, as in the English expression, "he's looking at the world through rose-coloured glasses." Nevertheless, this lens can also be thought of in a more constructive way as something that helps one to see what would otherwise not be apparent. For example, polarised sunglasses help one to see better by cutting out glare reflecting off the surface of water, glare that would otherwise blind one to what lies beneath the surface.

Combining the analogies of the lens and the eye, the point I am trying to make is that for a hermeneutical ethics to be effective, it is helpful to have a constructive lens, through which to look, that can allow one to focus on particular details while at the same time remaining aware of the other dimensions of the object that one is observing. This is different from a technique, a *techne*, in that, although one is employing a tool, the aim is still insight and understanding, not simply the application of a technique or formula to arrive at a simple solution.

In keeping with this idea, then, of the need for a lens, an eye, or a tool, in this chapter I shall propose a model that can assist in revealing and understanding the multidimensionality of the concept of human dignity on the one hand, and human dignity's practical value for both descriptive and normative ethics on the other.

The notion of a model, like that of a lens, means that the model itself is not reality. The model I present is not human dignity, nor even a definitive definition of the concept. It is an abstract representation of the depth and complexity of concept in the form of a practicable framework of related ideas that will enable one to explore the various aspects of human dignity in a constructive way. In other words, the model is an attempt to distil the essential features of the concept of human dignity and relate them to one another. It is, like the lens of the eye, a tool that can help the user to see particular features of the concept of human dignity and how they are related to each other and to the multidimensional whole. Nevertheless, at the same time, the concept of human dignity, and certainly human dignity itself, cannot be reduced to the model, and more especially, not to one of the interrelated aspects of the model, just as reality cannot be reduced to the eye, or even to what the eye focuses on.

Finally, it should be borne in mind, that the model is itself based on the assumptions summarised above and detailed in Chapter 2 regarding the multidimensionality of ethics, the human person, and the moral event, such that the resultant understanding of human dignity, as a concept addressing multiple multidimensional realities, is in turn itself a multidimensional, 'both…and' concept. This will become clearer as I develop the various aspects of what I have called the Component Dimensions of Human Dignity model.

3.2. A Note on Method

Section 2.1.2 dealt with the critique's overemphasis on the hermeneutic of suspicion and its acceptance of the 'truths' revealed through the application of a deconstructive method as the only truths available. The difference between the double-edged hermeneutics envisioned by Ricœur and the hermeneutics of suspicion applied by the masters of suspicion is that the latter reduce all meaning to the affirmation of the 'truths' revealed by their method, whereas for Ricœur, the affirmation should construct new and richer meanings through a "a re-reading of the same things in depth and under the heading of … affirmation."[1] This is precisely what I intend to do here, though, rather than use the term affirmation, I have called it a hermeneutic of generosity.

This chapter will, therefore, 're-read' the same things that were read in Chapter 1, especially in section 1.5 regarding the different bases that have been put forward for human dignity. The difference is that this 're-reading' will take place not under the heading of suspicion, but under the heading of generosity. By generosity, the following should be understood.

First, the goal of a hermeneutic of generosity is to restore a meaning to the concept of human dignity that is capable of making it more meaningful to ethical discourse, while, at the same time, dissolving the clouds of 'false consciousness', which in the case of human dignity applies particularly to those understandings of human dignity that reduce it to a single one-dimensional feature of the human person in order to use it as a weapon to further a particular ideological agenda. In other words, as explained in the introduction to this book, a hermeneutic of generosity flows from, rather than counter to, a hermeneutic of suspicion.

Second, in order to achieve this goal of a richer ethical language, generosity focuses not on the fact that there are discrepancies in the various understandings of human dignity delineated in 1.5, but instead, in line with a hermeneutical ethics, focuses on the fact that these understandings of human dignity are nevertheless morally meaningful to those who use them, and therefore important enough to be taken seriously.[2]

Third, at the same time, however, taking this moral meaning seriously does not mean simply making an 'ought' out of an 'is'. In other words, because a particular understanding of human dignity is morally meaningful to a particular person does not necessarily imply that it is the right understanding. That would be accepting the position of the second option discussed in Chapter 2.2 which opens the way to moralism and relativism. It would not, in other words, flow from a hermeneutic of suspicion but would instead ask the reader to ignore suspicion in favour of faith (see the section on methodology in the introduction where this is identified as an inappropriate understanding of generosity). Instead, generosity avoids this trap by ensuring that this moral meaningfulness is appropriately situated in a broader context of a multidimensional reality, particularly with regard to the anthropology and to the understanding of the moral event that these meanings imply. In other words, though descriptively meaningful on their own, these meanings are really only valuable to enhancing the understanding of human dignity as a rich descriptive and normative ethical concept insofar as they are related to each other in the context of an appropriately multidimensional anthropology. To reiterate what was said in the introduction, then, a hermeneutic of generosity asks for the concept of human dignity to account for itself using accepted criteria from its own tradition. The criteria of primary importance in this regard are an adequate multidimensional understanding of the human person and the moral event, and an understanding of ethics that is hermeneutical and that includes both descriptive and normative aspects.

3.3. The Four Component Dimensions and Their Relation to an Adequate Anthropology

I shall use capital first letters to denote technical terms of the proposed model so as to distinguish them from their common meanings. Table 3.1 lists four Component Dimensions: the Existential, the Cognitive-Affective, the Behavioural, and the Social. Their relevance to the understanding of the concept of human dignity is that they focus our attention on the relationship between the concept of human dignity and different aspects of the multidimensional concepts of the human person and the moral event.

These aspects, however, are all interrelated, such that though they can help us to consider things from a particular angle, they can never be separated from one another; they mutually enhance the understanding of each other, and the whole. This is why they are called Component Dimensions. 'Dimension' refers to the fact that they are each qualitatively different aspects or perspectives of a whole, in this case the concept of human dignity. 'Component' refers to the fact that though we can consider each 'Dimension' in turn, it is also always related to the other 'Dimensions' such that the whole cannot be validly understood without taking them all into account. In other words, the 'Component Dimensions' serve a function similar to the eight facets that Louis Janssens identifies with regard to the human person adequately considered. Each of the eight facets helps one to consider a different aspect of what it means to be a human person, but a human person is only adequately considered in the light of all eight facets and the relationships of these facets to one another and the idea of the whole (see section 2.3.2.1).

In what follows I shall relate these Component Dimensions to the anthropology and considerations of the moral event developed in 2.3.2.

3.3.1. *The Existential Component Dimension*

The Existential Component Dimension addresses the relationship between the concept of human dignity and the existential aspects of the human person. The term 'existential' is used here to refer to two related ideas.

First, 'existential' pertains to existence, i.e., to a human person's lived reality: "it implies that existence cannot be set aside from consideration of the human condition. ... The world is presupposed and is essential and integral in all existential philosophising, since human beings exist fundamentally in a world."[3] Furthermore, Protestant existentialist theologian Paul Tillich, defines 'existential' as an attitude to thinking in which the object of thought is involved rather than detached.[4] In the case of human dignity, then, one is concerned with thinking about human dignity as involved with, rather than detached from, the human person as a creature living an involved existence at many levels of interaction. And, a person cannot be detached from his existence in a world, i.e., from the expression of all his faculties and consciousness as a whole living organism.[5]

Thus, this first sense of the term 'existential' corresponds with the description of the human person, based on Louis Janssens' thought, offered in section 2.3.2.1 as the basis of an adequate anthropology for the consideration of the concept of human dignity. The human person's lived reality was defined as the experience of being a historically situated corporeal subject who is always already a being-in-the-world, and as such, always already in relationship to the physical world, to other human subjects, to institutions. He is open to the experience of transcendence. He is both fundamentally equal to others in that they all share this existential reality, but he is also a unique originality.[6]

The second idea to which the term 'existential' gives expression in this context is related to the philosophy of existentialism and to existential psychology. The most important aspect in this regard is where these have to do with the human subject's search for meaning, significance and purpose in life.

The Component Dimensions of Human Dignity Model   215

The philosophy of existentialism can be defined as, "A doctrine that concentrates on the existence of the individual, who, being free and responsible, is held to be what he makes himself by the self-development of his essence through acts of the will (which, in the Christian form of the theory, leads to God)."[7] Paul Tillich elaborates on existentialism as follows, "The common point of all [existentialisms] is that man's existential situation is a state of estrangement from his essential nature." Human beings seek reconciliation with their true being (the essential nature).[8] One could link this notion of reconciliation with that of "self-development ... through acts of the will" mentioned above; one wilfully seeks self-development in an attempt to achieve reconciliation.

Tillich continues, "Reconciliation is a matter of anticipation and expectation, but not of reality. The world is not reconciled, either in the individual ... in the society ... or in life as such." As such the historically situated human being is faced with "a series of unreconciled conflicts, threatening man with self-destruction. The existence of the individual is filled with anxiety and threatened by meaninglessness." Existentialism is, in short, the formulation of "the question implied in existence," namely, what is the meaning of existence?[9]

Self-development through acts of the will can be seen as the ongoing human attempt to answer that question. This corresponds to what was said in 2.3.1. and 2.3.2 about the human person as a meaning-seeking and meaning-giving being, and more especially with the idea that this meaning-seeking can be understood in terms of a desire for self-worth. The human person as a conscious subject is nevertheless repeatedly confronted with situations that call the subjectivity of his 'I' into question by making him the object of a relationship rather than its subject. He needs food, other people, institutions, etc. in order to survive. Without them, he is nothing. The result is a paradox of being everything and nothing at the same time—an apparently irreconcilable existential predicament—that threatens him with meaninglessness. To overcome this, he is compelled to seek meaning in and through his relationships in a way that directly or indirectly affords him a sense of self-worth. For without such a sense of self-worth, or at least the anticipation of such a sense of self-worth, he will be swallowed up by a sense of worthlessness and meaninglessness. Life will no longer be worth living.[10]

Moreover, Tillich's definition of existentialism, especially the idea that reconciliation is about anticipation, not reality, also corresponds with the ideas formulated in section 2.3.2.1.2 regarding the Already and the Not Yet. If one accepts that the search for a meaningful sense of self-worth in and through one's relationships expresses an attempt to answer the "question implied by existence", one must also accept that this attempt is *ongoing*. The attempt is ongoing precisely because it is, on one hand, always faced with the threat of meaninglessness, and on the other, always defined by anticipation and expectation of reconciliation, of the final realisation of meaning and of the fullness of self-worth. Such a final state, however, would no longer express the state of existence, and hence, in existential terms, always remains Not Yet.

In short, then, the second sense of the term 'existential' expresses the idea that a human person, as a historical being in relationship, is always *already* confronted by the potential meaninglessness of life, and in response wilfully engages in and through these relationships in moral behaviour in an effort to acquire a sense of meaning and self-worth. However, since existence is always historical, the anticipated sense of self-worth, or reconciliation to use Tillich's term, is always anticipated and expected, and therefore always remains *not yet* a reality.

The Existential Component Dimension, therefore, addresses the human person in the broadest sense as a meaning-seeking corporeal being in relation. The remaining component dimensions deal with finer aspects of what this entails in terms of human experience.

3.3.2. *The Cognitive-Affective Component Dimension*
If the Existential Component Dimension concerns *what* a human person is in existential terms—the human person as corporeal, meaning-seeking,

historical subject in relationship—then the Cognitive-Affective Component Dimension concerns *how* this person experiences this existential reality and the associated existential desire for meaning and self-worth.

The term 'cognitive' obviously refers to cognition, i.e., the faculty of knowing taken in its widest sense, including sensation, perception, and conception, as well as the rational faculty. Cognition, however, is often considered distinct from feelings or affections, and emotions.[11] Therefore, in order to be clear that feelings and emotions are also an important part of *how* human persons experience the world and their self-awareness, the term 'affective', which refers to emotions and affections, is also used to describe this Component Dimension. Affections or feelings have to do with inner sensations or agitations that *affect* one's emotions. Emotions in turn are states of mind (conscious or otherwise), such as desire or aversion, pleasure or pain, hope or fear.[12]

Both cognitions and emotions are by default engaged with each other and the world. They are necessarily engaged because they both display the quality of intentionality, that is, they are about something, whether real or imagined. For example, in terms of emotion, one is angry about something, or one is in love with someone; similarly, in terms of cognition, one sees, hears, or thinks something. Moreover, they are inseparably interrelated: what one perceives and thinks, affects how one feels; how one feels, likewise, affects what one perceives and thinks.[13]

The fact that both cognition and affection are necessary components of human self-awareness and interaction with the world is also evident from research in developmental psychology. As an illustrative example, among numerous others, psychologist and cognitive neuroscientist, and professor of social-emotional development at the University of Geneva, Gisela Labouvie-Vief, has developed a 'Cognitive-Affective Developmental Theory'. Labouvie-Vief maintains that human beings start out with a high level of fairly undifferentiated emotional content dominating their cognition, such as basic 'hardwired' fears and desires. As other cognitive capacities develop, especially language, the person is able to develop increasingly complex and differentiated emotions, always relating them at the same time to her cognitive experience of the world. Moreover, with increasing cognitive and emotional complexity, the person is also able to articulate and comprehend emotional states of others, as well as others' affective responses to her. The emotional states themselves, like feelings of pride or shame, thus also come to reflect interior states in relation to how a person experiences the world around her, and especially her interactions with other 'cognitive-affective' people. In addition, as cognitive-affective development increases so a person is able to relate emotionally to abstract notions, such a norms and values, ideologies and social mores.[14] Labouvie-Vief summarises the findings of one of her studies, which investigated cognitive-affective transformations in individuals aged 10–80, as follows.

> We coded participants' description of their emotions and their selves into qualitative levels of differing *cognitive-affective complexity*. Findings showed that from adolescence to middle adulthood, individuals acquired more conscious insight into aspects of emotions that previously were unconscious, gained clearer differentiation of self from others, and blended distinct emotions, especially ones involving positive and negative contrasts … . These developments allowed many (but not all) adults to carve out a renewed sense of self that was complex, was historically situated, and entailed a more distinct sense of their individuality.[15]

The point here is not to enter into a discussion on the validity of various developmental theories.[16] Instead, the reference to Labouvie-Vief's work is intended to demonstrate that a person's perception of the world and her identity as a unique, meaning-seeking 'I' in the world are always mediated by a complex combination of emotions and cognitions. In other words, put in very simplistic terms, *how* a person experiences her existential reality and the associated existential desire for meaning and self-worth is through a complex combination of cognitions and emotions.

In terms of the anthropology developed in section 2.3.2, this means that a person experiences both her own subjectivity, on the one hand, and her necessary interrelatedness as a being-in-the-world, on the other, through a combination of cognitions and emotions. She is a subject because she can know that she knows (cognition). And, one could add, because she knows that she feels (affection), and even feels that she knows.

Her cognitive and affective capacities are what enable her to interpret her world, its conversations, and its events, at the sensory, emotional, and intellectual level. The cognitive capacity of language is important here because it enables her to articulate for herself—and to communicate with others—how she interprets, in light of her experiences and her cognitive-affective reflections upon those experiences, the meaning (or desired meaning) of her own life and action.

Furthermore, her cognitive-affective capacities enable her to direct herself as an intentional wholeness (bearing in mind that cognition and affection display the property of intentionality) towards a fundamental choice that will offer her a sense of self-fulfilment in her historical relationships. Both what she experiences herself to be already, and what she desires to, but has not yet, become, are experienced and expressed in cognitive-affective terms.

The historicity of the human person should not be forgotten here. Both what she *can* and what she *does* think and feel about herself are historically conditioned. What she *can* think and feel is conditioned by her historical physical and psychological development over time. A child has different emotional and cognitive capacities to an adult, as demonstrated earlier in the work of Labouvie-Vief. What she *does* think and feel is conditioned by her unique experiences, her cultural milieu, her society's social mores, and the outcomes of her ongoing process of interpretation, action and reinterpretation in this context. Thus, though over time, as she develops her cognitive-affective capacities, she may be able to articulate a fundamental choice in the light of formal norms, and even give expression to concrete material norms that coincide with that vision, the concrete expression of that fundamental choice and those formal norms in moral behaviour will be limited, and may even be (partly) mistaken, due to the conditioning effect of her historical situatedness on the actual cognitive-affective process of interpretation.

In the classic cycle of 'see, judge, act,'[17] the Cognitive-Affective Component Dimension addresses the 'see, judge.' We turn now to the 'act'.

3.3.3. *The Behavioural Component Dimension*
The Behavioural Component Dimension focuses on the human person as a moral being capable of choosing and acting toward a good end in a morally right way.

As corporeal beings-in-the-world, human beings are always in action even when they are inactive. To breathe, even just to occupy physical space, can in the broadest sense be considered an act to the extent that it has a physical effect on the world and, simultaneously, an effect on a person's experience of the world. The Behavioural Component Dimension is *not* concerned with 'action' in this broadest sense of the word, i.e., as a physical property of corporeality. There are many such actions, such as sleeping, digesting food, or walking into somebody by accident. Classical scholastic moral theology, strongly influenced by the work of Thomas Aquinas, calls such an act an *actus hominis*, i.e. act of a human being. Such acts have no direct moral dimension because they do not make use of moral reason, intention and will.[18]

The Behavioural Component Dimension, on the other hand, is intended to express that dimension of human action that has to do with moral behaviour, i.e. actions that are part of a moral event and that hence influence evaluations of moral goodness and badness of the person's intentions, and moral rightness and wrongness of the action itself. Scholastic moral theology distinguishes such an action from an *actus hominis* by calling it an *actus humanus*, i.e., a human act. "The use of deliberative reason that aims at a moral purpose proper to the human person provides the key to making an act a genuine *actus humanus* and thus a 'moral' act."[19]

So, whereas the Existential Component Dimension has to do with what a human being is, and the Cognitive-Affective Component Dimension has to do with how a person experiences his existential reality, the Behavioural Component Dimension is concerned with how, in light of this cognitive-affective experience of being human, the person behaves in a morally meaningful way.

The behaviour is morally meaningful in that it gives expression to the person's fundamental choice and his desire to realise a consistent sense of self-worth, which are articulated at the cognitive-affective level (see 2.3.2). Moreover, the behaviour is morally meaningful because it affects others and is situated in a historical context of social mores and values that say something about the moral meaning of the action involved. Thus, both the person acting, and the people and institutions with whom he is in relationship will make moral evaluations of the person's behaviour. These self-evaluations and external evaluations of behaviour will in turn affect evaluations of the person's character. Morally right behaviour lends itself to a positive appraisal of the actor as a person of morally good character.[20] Likewise, morally wrong behaviour calls that person's character into question. Either way, both the individual and his society are engaged in an ongoing process of action and interpretation that have a determinative effect on how the person experiences his life as meaningful and himself as worthy. Put simply, a meaningful life and accompanying sense of self-worth is pursued through morally good behaviour.[21]

It should also always be borne in mind, however, that the moral event, like an individual human life, is subject to time, and hence to historicity. The historicity of the human person also means that his moral behaviour is historically situated. The result is a dynamic tension between what he deems good on the one hand, and what others and his society deem good on the other; as well as between the abstract good of his fundamental choice to live a meaningful life—including the formal norms that give this choice expression, such as 'do good and avoid evil'—and the concretely realisable ends that his individual behaviour can achieve (see the idea of the eschatological proviso in section 2.3.3.1).

3.3.4. The Social Component Dimension
The Social Component Dimension is really quite self-explanatory. It highlights the fact that a human person as corporeal subject is always already situated in historical relationships with the world, with others, with institutions, with time, and with transcendence.

Unlike the other three Component Dimensions—which, though all aware of this Social Component Dimension, tend to focus on the person as an experiencing, reflecting, and acting existential subject—the Social Component Dimension shifts the focus to the person's context and especially the effect that the person has on her context. The reason being, as discussed regarding the Behavioural Component Dimension above, a person acts in light of her context, and in so doing has an effect on her context. This effect in turn modifies the way the context relates to the person, and so the cycle continues.

In short, the Social Component Dimension emphasises the importance of taking context into account. On one hand, context plays a formative role on how a person conceives her fundamental choice and the appropriate ways to realise it. As such it has a limiting function on the human person's ability to realise the fullness of the meaning she seeks as a human person in the world. On the other hand, context is the conditio sine qua non of being able to form a fundamental choice in the first place, and certainly of any attempt to realise it. Without context, one cannot speak of a human person.[22]

3.4. The Component Dimensions of Human Dignity: Re-Reading the Critique of Human Dignity
Having described the Component Dimensions as they relate to an adequate anthropology, this section now turns more specifically to the concept of human dignity. The assumption that human dignity properly under-

The Component Dimensions of Human Dignity Model   223

stood says something about the multidimensional whole that is the human person, means that it should be possible to consider the concept of human dignity on the level of each of the aforementioned Component Dimensions, i.e. Existential, Cognitive-Affective, Behavioural, and Social. That said, like the considerations of the human person, none of these considerations of human dignity can be isolated from the others. They remain mutually constitutive.

3.4.1. Defining a Complementary Duality in Light of the Already and the Not Yet

Just as the human person is Already and Not Yet, so too, human dignity is Already and Not Yet. That is to say, the concept of human dignity makes both a universal claim about what human persons already are by virtue of their being human, and about what they ought to become in the way that they live out their particular, historically-situated existence. This will become clearer as the model is discussed in more detail. The point here is that the Already and the Not Yet enables one to take the time dimension, as well as its implications regarding historicity, into account in a way that is "both…and" rather than "either…or" (see section 3.1.1).

In light of this time dimension, each Component Dimension can be said to be constituted by a Complementary Duality, of which one pole of the duality can be said to be Already, and the other can be said to be Not Yet. They are 'Complementary' because both poles are necessary for a proper understanding of each Component Dimension of human dignity. Nevertheless, they are 'Dualities' because, like the concept of the Already and the Not Yet, what is Already, though a condition for the Not Yet, can never be the Not Yet, and vice versa. They remain distinct and yet interrelated in such way that they are constitutive of each other.

Aristotle is helpful in understanding this dynamic tension between the poles of the Complementary Dualities. Two aspects of his thought are useful here: his ideas on change, and his ideas on potential.

First, regarding change, Aristotle says that though a substance may change in quality, it remains the same substance.[23] An unripe apple becomes ripe, but it is still an apple.[24] So too, I would say that as time passes, which after all is only measurable in terms of change, the human person changes and to a degree, through the exercise of freedom, even directs the way he changes. Young becomes old; ignorant becomes knowledgeable. The human person nevertheless remains essentially a human person, though that personhood is qualitatively different.

If one applies this idea on qualitative change to the Complementary Duality of each Component Dimension of Human Dignity, then when speaking of, for example, the Existential Component Dimension, one could say that one can speak of qualitatively different existential aspects of human dignity such that on one hand one is describing qualities that are Already, and on the other qualities that will become, but are Not Yet. Nevertheless the qualitative difference between the present and future tenses, for example, though modifying the understanding of the Existential Component Dimension of Human Dignity, are nevertheless still talking about the same 'substance', i.e., the Existential Component Dimension of Human Dignity.

Second, Aristotle distinguishes between potentiality and actuality as a way of explaining how what is not-A can become A. A seed is not actually, but is nevertheless potentially a tree.[25] So, again, when talking about qualities, to say that a person is not actually knowledgeable also implies that they nevertheless have the potential to be knowledgeable, just as an actually unripe apple nevertheless has at the same time the potential to become ripe.

Aristotle also applies this notion of potentiality and actuality to morality. Human beings are naturally constituted to receive moral virtues, but human beings are not by nature already actually virtuous. Virtue must be developed. Human beings acquire virtue by exercising virtue. A person becomes actually virtuous by exercising his potential for virtue over the course of time. And, depending on how the human person exercises virtue, the quality of his virtuousness will change as he becomes more or less virtuous based on the way he behaves in relation to other people.[26] After all, as Aristotle says, "... work reveals in actuality what *is* only potentially."[27]

Applying this idea of potentiality and actuality to the notion of the Complementary Duality can be explained as follows. The Already pole actually exists. At the same time, this already extant actuality also contains the potential to actualise a state that is Not Yet. Thus, the Not Yet pole, like the tree, exists as potential in the Already pole, the seed. The Not Yet pole could not be were it not for the Already pole. Conversely, the Already pole is in part defined by the potential that it holds. A seed is an apple seed because it has the potential to grow into an apple tree; an apple seed can never grow into an oak tree. By this logic, both poles of each Complementary Duality are mutually defining, such that to speak of one implies the other and vice versa.

All of this will become clearer as the details of each Complementary Duality are discussed in what follows.

3.4.2. The Existential Component Dimension: The Dignity We Have and the Dignity We Acquire

In 3.3.1, I defined the Existential Component Dimension as dealing with the human person's existential experience of reality as an historical subject in relationship and the associated quest for meaning. When applied to human dignity, this Existential Component Dimension is constituted by the Complementary Duality of 'The Dignity We Have and the Dignity We Acquire.' 'The Dignity We Have' is grounded in the fact that human beings, as situated historical subjects in relationship, have a number of capacities—among which are capacities of perception and experience, cognitive-affective reflection, and moral action. These capacities constitute an existential potential that can be actualised by engaging these capacities. Therefore, 'The Dignity We Have', though grounded in these capacities, does not inhere in the presence of the capacities per se, but in the fact that these capacities, by their very nature, imply something about what a human person desires and can become. Thus, as Aristotle's seed is partly defined by the tree it can become, so the 'The Dignity We Have' is partly defined by 'The Dignity We Acquire'. The 'Dignity We Acquire' is then driven by our existential desire for self-worth, and for a meaningful life, and is the product of the engagement of our capacities (our potential) in the context of our historically situated relationships. Hence, as the tree is partly defined by the seed, so too the 'Dignity We Acquire' is partly defined by 'The Dignity We Have', i.e., our historical existential reality, the capacities we have, and the opportunities we have to fulfil them. Similarly, our historicity also means that the ultimate fullness of acquired dignity always remains beyond the temporal grasp of an individual (since nobody can fully realise the potential in all of their capacities all of the time), though it may be approximated.

I shall demonstrate this by re-reading parts of the critique in Chapter 1 in line with the methodological assumptions outlined in 2.3. and in 3.2.

Chapter 1 revealed two problems with the way in which the concept of human dignity is used that might lead critics to suggest that it would be better if the concept was discarded. The first of these problems is that human dignity is claimed to be a universal inviolable given on the one hand, and yet is experienced as threatened, violable quality in concrete particular reality. The second problem is that human dignity seems to be described either as something all human beings already have, or as something that human beings acquire or lose based on how they live their lives. I shall briefly recapitulate these two apparent problems.

Chapter 1, section 1.4, discussed how one of the chief consequences of the rise in 'dignity talk' has been a relativisation of the concept of human dignity, such that people use it when it suits their cause, and redefine it, or ignore it, when it does not. This brought to light a seemingly problematic paradox: on one hand, documents like the *Universal Declaration of Human Rights* and *Gaudium et spes* claim that all human beings already have human dignity, a human dignity that is, moreover, held to be supposedly inviolable (1.4.1); on the other hand, a quick look at just about any newspaper in the world on any day of the week will reveal that people are forced, or even seemingly choose, to live in conditions, and behave in ways that certainly do not reflect a universal notion of human dignity, of equal human worth, however one may define it (1.4.2). How often one comes across the phrases, "they were treated like animals," or "he behaved like an animal." Both these phrases are used to describe behaviours or circumstances that are not reflective of some high-minded notion of the human person. Instead, they describe behaviours or circumstances that reflect some allegedly base animality in which the universal claim of human dignity with regard to both the actors and the victims is called into question by the very word 'animal'. To be treated like an animal means to be treated as less than human, as not being of the same worth as a human person, and hence as not being entitled to the same respect and concern, as a human person. Likewise, to behave like an animal is to imply behaviour that is inhuman, or unworthy of a human person, and hence unworthy of respect by other human persons.[28] In short then, one is faced with an apparent contradiction between a universal claim of human dignity on the one hand, and a particular, concrete lack of human dignity on the other, which in turn calls the claim into question (see also section 1.7.2).

The second potential problem was highlighted in section 1.5.1 with regard to the various bases offered for human dignity. Namely, on the one hand, there are those bases, and indeed uses of the concept of human dignity, that imply that human dignity is something that is inherent to the human person as well as something that cannot be taken away; on the other hand, there are those that seem to refer to dignity as something that can be acquired, lost, or relativised based on how one lives one's life and how others treat one. Examples of the former were presented in 1.5.2, where I made a further distinction between an ontological group (1.5.2.1) and a capacity group (1.5.2.2). Examples of the latter were presented in 1.5.3, where I made a further distinction between the, nevertheless related, psychological group (1.5.3.1) and social group (1.5.3.2).

I propose that the first problem, namely, of universal inviolability versus particular violability of human dignity, can be solved by treating the second problem, namely, of dignity as something we have *versus* dignity as something we acquire, differently.

As the critics Bagaric and Allan observe, none of the bases offered for human dignity can be said to be patently wrong. Nevertheless, they interpret this as cause to discard the concept of human dignity.[29] Critic Ruth Macklin takes it a step further and suggests that talk of dignity only confuses the issue because in fact, as evidenced from the discussion of the various bases in 1.5 human dignity is really just a cover for these respective bases, which are the real criteria that one should appeal to, e.g. autonomy, or life (see also 1.5.4, and 1.7.4).[30]

In Chapter 2, I discussed several problems with concluding that human dignity should be dismissed as a concept of any value. Chief among these problems are a legalistic, *techne*-oriented view of ethics (2.1.1), an overemphasis on a hermeneutic of suspicion (2.1.2), and an excessive reductionism of the human person and the moral event (2.1.3). I then went on to formulate alternative methodological assumptions that countered these problems by including a hermeneutical view of ethics, a hermeneutic of generosity, and holistic, multidimensional views of the human person and the moral event (2.3). Taken together, these assumptions make a case to approach the concept of human dignity as a multidimensional, 'both… and' concept rather than, as the critics do, a one-dimensional, 'either… or' concept (see also 3.1.1).

Bearing these alternative assumptions in mind, I turn now to the aforementioned second alleged problem of human dignity: human dignity as something human beings have *versus* human dignity as something that human beings acquire. Thus, in light of the alternative assumptions, whereas the critics, operating from an 'either…or' paradigm must emphasise the *versus*, such that human dignity can only *either* be something human beings have *or* something they acquire, I propose, that operating from a more appropriate 'both…and' paradigm, one could legitimately

The Component Dimensions of Human Dignity Model 229

describe human dignity as *both* something that human beings already have *and* as something they can and do acquire. To illustrate this, I shall briefly summarise the various things that human dignity is associated with both as something human beings *have* (1.5.2) and as something they *acquire* (1.5.3) and then relate them with the view of the human person to which they all refer highlighted by the Existential Component Dimension (3.3.1).

First, several authors argue on various grounds for the notion of human dignity as an intrinsic worth, which inheres in every human person, but which is nevertheless not associated with any specific feature of being human other than sharing in human nature itself. Thus, as found in article 1 of the *Universal Declaration of Human Rights,* they affirm that "All human beings are born free and equal in dignity and rights." To support their arguments they may base their claim, as Stephen J. Pope does, on a religious belief that human beings are created in the image of God or, as Pope Benedict XVI sometimes seems to do in his public discourse, and as pro-life activists certainly do, that human life is a sacred, and hence inviolable, gift from God.[31] Others, like Dan Egonsson and Francis Fukuyama, link human dignity to the human species in a more explicit way, by suggesting that as members of the same species we intuit the inherent value of other members of the species precisely because we ourselves are members of the species.[32] Together these positions all usefully affirm the idea that there is something about human beings per se that makes them worthy of a special kind of respect and concern that is qualitatively different to the concern that other objects in the world may legitimately invoke. According to this position, membership of the human species is sufficient to warrant the claim that a living human entity has inherent human dignity, and is hence worthy of special respect. Indeed, some of these authors go so far as to afford the same dignity, and hence rights, to all human life from the moment of conception to death, which the *Universal Declaration of Human Rights,* by stating, "are born" does not explicitly do.[33]

While I agree with these authors insofar as I can see the value in invoking an idea that human beings ontologically possess an inherent worth by virtue of their being human, I feel that this idea alone is insufficient to properly describe what we should mean by human dignity. On its own, this perspective is problematic for two reasons. First, this perspective's ontological nature tends to situate dignity outside the historically situated human person, such that regardless of what happens to her, regardless of her circumstances, regardless of how she may in reality be violated or violate, her essential inherent dignity always remains intact.[34] The danger then is that the claim of human dignity loses any practical relevance other than as a nice sentiment.[35] The second problem is that, in an attempt to firm up this perspective of dignity, especially in public rhetoric, against accusations that its ontological ground makes it nothing more than a nice sentiment, its advocates may end up resorting to reductionist approaches that, for example, purely associate human dignity with human biological life and the state of being physically alive.[36] The problems with this approach were considered in Chapter 2, where I criticised the so-called second option to the critique of dignity which would involve ignoring the critique to argue for one of the positions highlighted in 1.5. As demonstrated in Chapter 2, arguing for a single extant position, in this case, for example, that dignity is life, opens the door to moralism (2.2.1) and relativism (2.2.2). The solution lies, instead, in a multidimensional understanding of human dignity.

Therefore, there seems to be no valid reason for why this claim that all human beings have inherent worth must be made independent of actual human capacities. Section 1.5.2.2 listed various arguments that associated dignity with an assortment of human capacities, tending thereby to imply, in line with critics like Bagaric and Allan, that only this capacity *or* that capacity could be a legitimate ground for human dignity. However, in light of the 'both…and' paradigm being put forward in this book, there is no reason not to advocate a wide array of such capacities as all somehow contributing to the case for the inherent dignity of the human person.

The Component Dimensions of Human Dignity Model

The human person is not just a subject capable of rationality, perfectibility or autonomous action,[37] but also a subject always in relationship. This latter facet of being human brings with it a whole lot of other features that can all contribute to the idea that the human person has dignity simply by virtue of her being human. Margaret Farley and Stephen J. Pope draw attention to the human capacity to love and care for others in relationship,[38] and Martha Nussbaum lists ten 'capabilities' which are reflective of human capacities that are constitutive of human dignity and hence make a claim on the relationships in which the human person is imbedded to allow or help the person to realise these capabilities and hence her dignity as a human person. Nussbaum's ten capabilities are: life; bodily health; bodily integrity; senses, imagination and thought; emotions; practical reason; affiliation; other species; play; material and political control over one's environment.[39] By her own admission, however, there is no reason to limit these to ten.[40] She describes her list as "a long list of opportunities for functioning, such that it is always rational to want them whatever else one wants. If one ends up having a plan of life that does not make use of all of them, one has hardly been harmed by having the chance to choose a life that does."[41] What is important, then, is that when one speaks of human dignity inherent in the existential human condition, there are a number of capacities "for various forms of activity and striving" which, when exercised have the potential to contribute to the flourishing of human life.[42]

What has been discussed so far is in accordance with the anthropology developed based on Louis Janssens' idea of the human person adequately considered. A human person is a conscious corporeal subject, possessing both ontological and categorical freedom. This reflects the ideas regarding rationality, autonomy, and perfectibility. Moreover, as a being-in-the-world, the human person is also always a being already in relationship to the world, to people, to institutions, to history, and to the experience of transcendence. It is because of the human person's corporeality and relatedness to the world that she is also capable of love, attention to others, affiliation with others, working with others for common goals, and so on.

Moreover, not only is she capable of these things, but it is through these interactions that she finds, articulates, and realises meaning and purpose in a life well lived.

Nevertheless, the fact that the Already pole of 'The Dignity We *Have*' focuses on capacities, i.e., on the human *potential* for flourishing, rather than the fulfilment of that potential, means that one can still make an ontological claim that the human person has inherent worth.[43] And Nussbaum's point that no *one* capacity should be seen as *the* ground for dignity means that even if certain capacities are missing, or only potentially present, one can nevertheless still assert the existence of a certain basic intrinsic dignity that is shared by all members of the human species that confers on them a worth that deserves to be considered with appropriate gravitas.

Situating inherent human dignity in an array of capacities implies that there is a potential for something more. Thus, as capacities imply the potential to fulfil these capacities in a meaningful life, so too, 'The Dignity We Have' (inherent potential) implies the potential to fulfil this dignity in the dignity we acquire (actualised fulfilment). Chapter 1, section 1.5.3 has already provided some insight into what this acquired dignity might entail. The point here, again, however, is to re-read these various descriptions of dignity from a 'both...and' paradigm. When this is done the indissoluble existential link between dignity as something human beings already have and dignity as something human beings have not yet fully acquired becomes obvious.

First of all, with regard to the idea that this realised dignity has to do with the fulfilment of one's capacities, I think the observations I made with regard to the ideas of transhumanist Nick Bostrom, are particularly useful here. Dignity is not because one *has* capacities of autonomy and perfectibility, but dignity is a product of how one uses these to become better. For Bostrom, this involves employing transhumanist technologies.[44] I am not suggesting that this is necessarily the way to use one's capacities for autonomy and perfectibility, though it does offer *one* way,

The Component Dimensions of Human Dignity Model 233

which is itself not without potential ethical challenges. Nevertheless, the point is that the dignity one acquires is linked to the dignity one has in that the former can be seen as the fulfilment of the latter.

Nordenfelt, Pullman, and Dworkin's ideas that link dignity to one's sense of having lived one's life as a meaningful, integral, and beautiful narrative whole are useful here, too. A human existence is a moral and existential project in which meaning is found and given through the way the person lives and the beliefs and values she seeks to embody. Moreover, the historical situatedness of the human person means that the behaviours she engages in and the values she seeks to embody in order to fulfil her dignity, both as an inherent potential and as a realised sense of self-worth, are partially determined by how she relates to the mores of her society, particularly since, as a social being, she is susceptible to practicing those mores and upholding those values that win her praise from her society and hence enhance her feelings of self-worth and her idea of what it means to be dignified (1.5.3.2).

Having considered differently the second problem of having dignity *versus* acquiring dignity identified in Chapter 1, by considering how, in light of a multidimensional anthropology and the notion of the Already and the Not Yet, dignity can be considered *both* as something human beings have *and* as something they acquire, I would like to return briefly to the first problem identified in Chapter 1 and mentioned earlier in the present section: the universal claim that all human beings have dignity on the one hand versus the particular experience of a lack of dignity on the other. By treating dignity as something we have in the form of a potential inherent in human capacities as well as something we acquire through the appropriate use of these capacities, it becomes possible both to make a universal claim that all human beings already have dignity, and account for why that dignity is not yet always present in every particular circumstance. All human beings have the potential to realise the dignity inherent in the capacities that make them human beings. However, at the same time, as historically situated beings in relationship, this realisation can always only ever be a partial realisation due to the temporal and historical limitations placed on human moral behaviour by the human being's existential reality. Therefore, the full realisation of acquired dignity remains Not Yet, and this explains the apparent lack that we sometimes observe in particular human behaviour. Nevertheless, it is still possible to affirm an inherent dignity that is universal and hence should be honoured as much as possible. I shall return to this issue when I discuss the Social Component Dimension and its Complementary Duality of Others' Dignity and My Dignity below.

In summary, then, the Complementary Duality of 'The Dignity We Have and the Dignity We Acquire' that constitutes the Existential Component Dimension of the Component Dimensions of Human Dignity model can be described as follows: All human person's already have dignity based on the potential that is inherent in an assortment of capacities—among which are the capacities to experience, reflect on that experience, and act in accordance with the outcomes of that reflection—and thereby to strive to realise the fullness of that potential dignity by appropriately employing these capacities in and through the historical relationships which the human person finds herself imbedded in the pursuit of an existential quest for meaning, purpose, and self-worth.

Though a summary, the above paragraph remains very dense, much like the Existential Component Dimension itself, which, because it deals with the human person's existential reality tends to use somewhat abstruse terminology. In order to concretise some of this, then, one can ask specific questions about the Existential Component Dimension of Human Dignity that lead one into the remaining Component Dimensions. First among these, one can ask for more specifics on what actually constitutes this acquired dignity (The Cognitive-Affective Component Dimension), how is it acquired (The Behavioural Component Dimension), and how does it relate to the relationships in which the human person is always already embedded (The Social Component Dimension). I turn now to the first of these, namely, the Cognitive-Affective Component Dimension of Human Dignity.

3.4.3. The Cognitive-Affective Component Dimension: Inherent Worth and Self-Worth

The Cognitive-Affective Component Dimension of Human Dignity is constituted by the Complementary Duality of 'Inherent Worth and Self-Worth'. All human beings already have an Inherent Worth by virtue of their capacities and the potential implied in these capacities to live a meaningful and dignified human life. At the same time, however, at the level of the particular subject, this potential is realised in concrete form in the cognitive-affective appreciation of the person's own Self-Worth as a human person who is not only potentially capable but also actually does lead a morally meaningful life in and through the relationships in which he or she is embedded.

I shall not elaborate a great deal here on the Already pole of Inherent Worth. Enough has been said in this regard in section 3.3.2 above concerning the Complementary Duality of 'The Dignity We Have and The Dignity We Acquire'. The point is that all human beings have inherent worth because they have the potential to strive to realise a good and meaningful human life in relationship, a potential that inheres in a number of capacities among which are cognitive-affective capacities.

The Not Yet pole of Self-Worth, however, deserves further elaboration. It has already been argued in the definition of the Cognitive-Affective Component Dimension in 3.3.2, that a person's perception of the world and his identity as a unique, meaning-seeking 'I' in the world are mediated through a complex combination of emotions and cognitions. It is these capacities that enable him to interpret his experiences of the world and to modify his behaviour based on what he deems to be the most meaningful way to live his life. At the core of this cognitive-affective experience and reflection lies a fundamental choice to live a good, meaningful life that confers a sense of self-worth. Of course, precisely how this fundamental choice is articulated and concretely realised is open to interpretation in the context of a person's concrete lived experience. It would be absurd if everybody deemed being a baker to be the best and most meaningful way to realise their fundamental desire for self-worth. There would just be too many people wanting to be bakers and not enough people to appreciate them for being bakers. This of course also means that different visions of what constitutes self-worth may come into conflict, for example, when the baker believes that his profession means that he has more of a claim to the respect of the community than the blacksmith, or the nurse, or the teacher, or the baker's own wife. I have already addressed how this desire for self-worth operates at an anthropological level in section 2.3.2.1.1. What I shall now do is relate it to the way that the concept of human dignity is used by various authors discussed in Section 1.5.

Section 1.5.3.1 clearly shows that the concept of dignity can be interpreted as referring to, to quote the *Compact Oxford English Dictionary,* "a sense of pride in oneself." Moreover, authors like James Gilligan and Charles Taylor clearly associate dignity with the human subject's psychological experience and interpretation of his own worth. This self-perception in turn influences how one behaves. In living out one's autonomy one engages in behaviours and pursues goals that one believes will be admired by others and that one can admire oneself.[45] Dignity is, moreover, associated with a person's perceived sense that he has a right to demand respect. Charles Taylor, for example, clearly defines dignity as those "characteristics by which we think of ourselves as commanding (or failing to command) the respect of those around us." Hence, "Our 'dignity' ... is our sense of ourselves as commanding (attitudinal) respect."[46] Thus, there is a twofold sense to this notion of dignity as being worthy of respect: first, the respect that one has for oneself, and second, the respect that one believes one does or should receive from others.

The image of the kind of person that one deems worthy of respect, and hence the image of the kind of person that one desires to become is always open to modification by one's ontological freedom in the form of the fundamental choice one makes and categorical freedom in the way that one sets about achieving that choice. At the same time, however, it is strongly conditioned by the kind of person that one's society deems to be worthy of respect, and hence to have acquired dignity. Fraser Watts's example of how it was once considered undignified to cry in public and might now be considered to demonstrate a lack of sensitivity not to cry in public speaks to this point, as does Meyer's example of the 'dignified' butler in an aristocratic society, and more tellingly, Gilligan's example of the violent man who was himself a victim of violence and abuse as a child.[47]

The fact that this notion of dignity as self-worth is reflective of a fundamental choice, or what I have also referred to as a second-order desire, and hence is something that not only plays itself out throughout one's life but remains always Not Yet, is evident in the accounts of human dignity already referred to offered by Nordenfelt, Pullman, and Dworkin. In various ways, these authors associate dignity with the integral narrative that one creates through the way in which one lives as reflective of one's fundamental choice. This idea is also evidenced in Klaus Demmer's reference to conscience and *Dignitatis Humanae's* reference to truth. For Demmer, as pointed out in Chapter 1, a human person's dignity is realised when he lives according to the truths known to his conscience. Similarly, *Dignitatis Humanae* states that human beings as free and responsible beings are impelled to seek the truth, and to live according to that truth once they find it.[48] Of course, one could argue that the fullness of that truth can never be found by an individual and hence the truth that one chooses to live by, the form that one chooses to give to one's fundamental choice is undertaken in good conscience. In doing so, one develops a sense of self-worth insofar as one can honestly say that one is someone who is doing the best one can to live according to conscience and truth (i.e. the values that one holds to constitute the basis of a meaningful life).

Having considered how the Complementary Duality of 'Inherent Worth and Self-Worth' helps one to see how third-person claims of inherent worth find concrete relevance in the first-person, cognitive-affective experience of self-worth based on one's image of oneself and the image that one thinks others have of oneself, I would like to now turn to the next question that poses itself. Namely, between making a fundamental choice to become a certain kind of person, and the approximate realisation of that dignified ideal, what goes into making one what one longs to become? The answer lies in the consideration of the Behavioural Component Dimension of Dignity.

3.4.4. *The Behavioural Component Dimension: The Moral Good of Dignity and the Dignity of the Morally Good*

In effect, this entire book is intended as a response to the criticism that the concept of human dignity is of little value as a criterion by which one can evaluate moral behaviour. However, in order to understand how the concept of human dignity is even relevant to the area of moral behaviour it might be useful to know how the two are in fact related. This task falls to the Behavioural Component Dimension of human dignity and its constitutive Complementary Duality of 'The Moral Good of Human Dignity and the Dignity of the Morally Good'.

First, on the Already pole lies the claim that dignity is a moral good. Section 1.4.1 showed how the concept of human dignity is often held to affirm the status of the human subject as a moral good, i.e., as an end in itself. Hence, one finds formulations like those in numerous human rights documents and constitutions affirming the inviolability of human dignity, meaning, of course, that it should not be violated. As a moral good, as an end in itself, the human person has a unique dignity and hence may never be only a means to someone else's ends, never be treated as merely an object.[49]

A strong component of this affirmation of the dignity of the human person as a moral good is the insistence on individual rational autonomy. According to Immanuel Kant, "Hence autonomy is the ground of the dignity of human nature and of every rational nature."[50] It is, in other words, because a person is capable of being a rational autonomous subject that to treat her as an object would be morally wrong. The emphasis on rational autonomy, however, also brings to light an interesting feature of the discussion regarding the bases of human dignity offered in 1.5, namely, that autonomy was offered as a foundation for human dignity both among arguments that saw dignity as something that all human beings already have and among arguments that consider dignity to be something that human beings acquire.

Among the bases offered for human dignity as an inherent worth that all human beings *already* have, it was noted that Deryck Beyleveld and Roger Brownsword, like Kant, seem to situate this inherent dignity in the *capacity* for autonomy: they state, "the essence of the dignity of agents resides in their capacity to choose, to set their own ends ... ."[51] Bayertz also lists the capacity of autonomy, along with rationality and perfectibility among the post-Renaissance bases for human dignity.

At the same time, however, autonomy was also a dominant feature of those arguments that suggested that dignity was something acquired through the way a person behaves, both in terms of her own psychological sense of self-worth, and in terms of the respect of her society. In the case of the former, for example, advocates of the right to die suggest that to not allow a person to legally end her own life is an offence to her dignity because it does not respect the way she has autonomously chosen to live and to end her life in a manner that reflects those ideals, a manner which she autonomously deems more dignified than the alternative.[52] (N.B., I think that such arguments, like those that solely situate dignity in biological life, lack the necessary complexity that I am arguing a proper understanding of human dignity should have. See also Chapter 4, section 4.2.) In the case of the latter, i.e., in terms of the respect one receives from society, this respect is given to the extent that one is judged by society to have autonomously engaged in morally good behaviour, especially when such behaviour is deemed also to be of benefit to society. The link between autonomy and moral behaviour has already been made in the elaboration on the Behavioural Component Dimension of the human person in 3.3.3. There, a distinction was made between an *actus hominis,* i.e., the ordinary, non-moral actions of a human being, and an *actus humanus,* i.e., the human actions that result from deliberation and free choice and are hence subject to moral evaluation as part of a moral event. Moral behaviour, therefore, by definition must involve the autonomy of the individual if it is to be considered moral (I use the word 'involve', rather than proceed from or some other stronger, more definite term in order to make space for the nuances of circumstances and historicity in determining the extent to which an action can be truly said to be autonomous). Illustrative of dignity being conferred on a person by virtue of her morally good (and, by definition, autonomous) behaviour are: Charles Taylor's comments regarding the fact that the life of dignity always involves something admirable, for if the life were not admirable, it would be either meaningless, or detestable, and hence hardly dignified;[53] Michael J. Meyer's examples of Martin Luther King, Jr. and Mahatma Gandhi, and their respective actions for civil rights, as exemplifying what he calls the virtue of dignity;[54] and Nick Bostrom's comment that dignity denotes some "special excellence or moral worthiness … . Some [human beings] excel far more than others do. Some are morally admirable; others are base and vicious."

This presence of the idea of autonomy as integral to the notion of human dignity in both those positions that tend to represent dignity as something that all human persons already have and those that tend to represent dignity as something that human persons acquire through the way that they exercise their autonomy, means that the idea of human dignity as a moral good can be interpreted in two ways, depending on how one interprets the role that autonomy plays. In line with the 'both…and' approach, I intend to show that both are valid and necessary to a proper understanding of human dignity.

The first of these two ways is where the emphasis is on autonomy as a capacity. There is a sort of third-person affirmation of human dignity as a moral good such that, since all human beings possess rational autonomy, this should be protected as a basic condition of good human life. Kant argues for such a moral good thus: "The ground of such a principle is this: rational nature exists as an end in itself. In this way man necessarily thinks of his own existence; thus far is it a subjective principle of human actions. But in this way also does every other rational being think of his existence on the same rational ground that holds also for me; hence it is at the same time an objective principle ... ."[55]

Whilst I agree with Kant's reasoning, I disagree that this affirmation of the principle of human worth as an end in itself, and hence as the basis for Kant's categorical imperative, should be limited to the capacity of autonomy, or to a 'rational nature'. If one were to only limit human dignity to autonomy, then Ruth Macklin would have a point. The moral good would not be human dignity, but human autonomy. To say that human dignity is a moral good is to say more than just that human beings have a capacity for autonomy or rational decision making. Rather as we have seen from other arguments, most notably, those of Nussbaum and Farley, human dignity is a moral good because it is constituted by numerous capacities which make it possible for human beings to engage in moral behaviour and strive to realise a meaningful life. Each of these capacities is a good in a non-moral (useful) or pre-moral (pleasurable) sense, as is the employment of them.

Moreover, these capacities are often pre-conditional for the realisation of other goods. For example, one has to be alive, one has to be able to think, and care, and decide, and act, if one is going to realise the moral good of saving the life of a drowning child.[56]

The ideas of pragmatist philosopher John Dewey are helpful in this regard. Dewey was unhappy with the polarity set up in moral philosophy between teleological, utilitarian ideas which equated the moral good with the maximisation of pleasure, and deontological ideas, like Kant's, which located the moral good in the thing itself such that one could say that it was an end in itself and hence never to be used as a means to maximise, for example, pleasure. Dewey considers this polarity to be a false dichotomy. As a solution, Dewey found a way of explaining how something could come to be treated like an end in itself, and hence like a deontological principle, while at the same time still be considered useful to teleological ends. Dewey argues, using truth-telling as an exemplar, that the reason truth-telling is a moral good, and is hence treated as an end in itself (i.e. one ought to tell the truth for the sake of telling the truth), is because truth-telling is found to be an "unqualified condition" for various other goods that we seek to realise (social life, business life, friendship, and so on). Truth-telling becomes a symbol for all those other goods we want to realise, and hence, instead of having to work out why we should tell the truth each time, which would be a waste of energy, it becomes a principle that we ought to tell the truth. Thus, it becomes possible to think of truth-telling like an end in itself, because we do not always connect it to the multiple other ends that we know implicitly it is a pre-condition for. Therefore, anything we call a moral good "is not to be resolved either into a condition of getting the maximum of pleasure, nor is it to be conceived as something having worth entirely apart from all other goods or values. In each case it represents what has been found to be the key to the situation, the controlling factor in a variety of other experiences which are desirable."[57]

If one applies Dewey's reasoning to the concept of human dignity, then one can say that human dignity is a moral good because it "represents what has been found to be the key to" all the other goods that constitute a human person and that as human persons we want to realise. The human dignity that we have, as constituted by a number of capacities, as well as the existential experience of being an historical subject in relationship and the accompanying desire for self-worth and a meaningful life, is an "unqualified condition" for the other goods, and indeed for the realisation of our dignity as self-worth.

In light of Dewey's solution, and expanding on Kant's more limited basis in rationality alone, it is therefore plausible to affirm a sort of third-person human dignity as a moral good such that, in line with Martha Nussbaum's thinking, since all human persons possess assorted capacities and seek to live them out (in other words they possess an inherent potential),[58] society should be structured in such a way as to provide opportunities for them to do so. One can objectively affirm a third-person dignity that all human persons inherently have by virtue of their capacities and their striving, based on the fact that one experiences oneself in this way. This is of course similar to the manner in which Louis Janssens affirms the fundamental equality of all human beings, which is basically the same as affirming the inherent worth of all human beings. Janssens, of course, and I agree with him in this regard, expands on the argument that focuses purely on autonomy or rationality by arguing that since all human beings share the same multidimensional human condition as corporeal subjects in historical relationships, there is a fundamental equality that makes it possible to formulate universal moral demands.[59]

There is a second way in which one can think of dignity as a moral good. Kant's argument quoted above also helps to illustrate this second way that dignity is a moral good, which for Kant is indeed the first and more obvious way, namely as a subjective end rather than as an objective one. Kant's point is that every human being first experiences their own existence as an end in itself, a moral good, and then extrapolates that to include other rational subjects. So, in this case, the moral good is not so much others' dignity, but first and foremost one's own. Nevertheless, in line with the 'both…and' approach, Kant's own argument contains both a subjective and an objective aspect to the moral good of human dignity, i.e. it is good for a person to fulfil their own dignity, their own desire for a sense of self-worth, but this is best done by taking into account the dignity that all other human persons, as ends in themselves, also already have. Hence, Kant's formulation of the categorical imperative (italics and comments added for emphasis): "Now I say that man, and in general every rational being, exists as an end in himself, and not merely as a means to be arbitrarily used by this or that will. He must in all his actions, *whether directed to himself or to other rational beings*, always be regarded at the same time as an end."[60] Therefore, dignity is a subjective moral good insofar it is good to direct one's actions to the actualisation of one's own dignity as a sense of self-worth, and an objective moral good insofar as in such a pursuit one should take into account the inherent dignity that all other human beings possess by virtue of their similar desire and capacity for such a dignified self-actualisation.

This leads to the Not Yet pole of 'The Dignity of the Morally Good'. I have already shown how dignity is attributed to those who engage in morally good behaviour. And since both the dignity that others already have and the dignity that one aspires to realise in one's own life can, according to the above argumentation, be said to be moral goods, it makes sense that one can acquire the moral good of one's own dignity through the morally good behaviour of acting for the moral good of others' dignity. 'Translating' this into the language of the multidimensional anthropology laid out in section 2.3.2.1, the person uses her ontological freedom to make a fundamental choice to pursue the realisation of her own desire for dignity as a sense of self-worth, i.e., the fulfilment of her intentional wholeness. She does so by engaging her categorical freedom to order her first-order desires and to choose to perform concrete moral actions that she believes will 'incarnate' her fundamental choice, i.e., the realisation of her own dignity. And since a formal norm can be established that the dignity of others (both as capacity and as desire) is also a moral good, one way in which she can define her own behaviour as morally good is by acting not only for her own sense of self-worth but for the good of others' dignity.

Nevertheless, this is not without its problems, because what precisely constitutes morally good behaviour, beyond the formulation of formal norms, is often difficult to define and is furthermore subject to historicity. Hence, moral perfection and the associated perfect actualisation of one's dignity is never possible, and can only at best be approximated. This becomes especially evident in the Social Component Dimension which also provides the basis for the concept of human dignity's efficacy as a normative criterion.

The Component Dimensions of Human Dignity Model 245

3.4.5. The Social Component Dimension: Others' Dignity and My Dignity

The Social Component Dimension is intended to highlight the implications of the fact that the human person is always already situated as a historical, corporeal subject in relationship. Moreover, this Component Dimension is where the value of the concept of human dignity as a normative criterion is most evident. In terms of human dignity and the axis of the Already and the Not Yet, the Social Component Dimension is constituted by the Complementary Duality of 'Others' Dignity and My Dignity'.

The Already pole of Others' Dignity affirms the idea that is it possible to claim that all human persons already have dignity, in the sense of an inherent worth, based on an assortment of capacities (e.g., among others, Bayertz, Farley, Beyleveld and Brownsword, and Nussbaum) and desires (e.g., among others, Gilligan, Taylor, and Dworkin), as well as on the common existential human condition that they share (Janssens), which together constitute the human potential to live a meaningful and morally good life. This inherent worth is a moral good and hence deserves the protection and respect of society. Moreover this inherent worth, by virtue of its constituting a potential for a meaningful and morally good life, is a condition sine qua non for human and societal flourishing.[61] This concurs with the kind of universal claims that are made in various secular and religious documents concerning universal human rights, as well as in the constitutional documents of numerous countries (1.1). In making human dignity—both in terms of capacities and in terms of efforts to realise those capacities—a moral good, the necessary gravitas is given to each individual's effort to live-out a meaningful existence in their historical circumstances, while at the same time holding up an ideal that critiques and corrects all these efforts. This gravitas is what makes the concept of human dignity so important for ethical discourse, and I shall return to it in Chapter 4, especially in section 4.2.2.

This leads to the Not Yet pole of My Dignity. This pole deals again with the subjective pursuit of dignity as a realisation of self-worth and a meaningful life through morally good behaviour. However, its relationship to the Already pole of Others' Dignity means that any dignity that one feels one has acquired is conditioned and qualified by how that relates to the dignity of others'. In essence, I can only say that I have fully achieved dignity when all others have fully achieved dignity, since human dignity, as a moral good in the double sense described above, means that my dignity is an illusion if it does not enhance the dignity of others.

Therein lies the difference between Meyer's example of Mahatma Gandhi and the violent criminals with whom James Gilligan deals. Gandhi acts for the moral good of the dignity of his fellow countrymen, and moreover, by using non-violent means, does so in a way that does not diminish the inherent dignity of their oppressors; though at the same time he rightly challenges the oppressors' own beliefs regarding their acquired dignity as a sense of self-worth. Gandhi's moral behaviour challenges people to see that dignity, that human worth, is not reserved for the British, or for white people, or for soldiers and policemen, or for the rich, or for Christians, or for any other historical category, and it is certainly not reserved for those who violently oppress others to secure their own sense of self-worth. The violent criminal, on the other hand, respects no one's dignity other than his own. He pursues only his own sense of self-worth with no concern for any dignity his victims may have. They are only a means to the acquisition of what he believes is a legitimate fulfilment of his desire for self-worth, which, I maintain, can be put down to the false equation of fear and true respect. I shall deal with the violent criminal again in more detail in the next chapter, as he offers a useful case study with which to demonstrate the descriptive and normative properties of a proper understanding of the concept of human dignity as illustrated by the Component Dimensions of Human Dignity model just presented.

Endnotes

1. Ricœur, "Two Essays by Paul Ricœur," 203–204.
2. Cf. Ricœur's idea of the 'world in front of the text'. *Time and Narrative*, 81.
3. S.v. "Existential" in Van Deurzen and Kenward, *Dictionary of Existential Psychotherapy and Counselling*.
4. See Tillich, *Systematic Theology*, vol. 2, 26.
5. See s.v. "existential" in Oxford English Dictionary, 2nd edition (1989).
6. See Janssens, "Artificial Insemination."
7. S.v. "existentialism," in Oxford English Dictionary, 2nd ed. (1989).
8. See Tillich, *Systematic Theology*, 25–26.
9. See ibid.
10. See the discussion in 2.3.2.1.1. See also Janssens, "Artificial Insemination," 8; idem. "Personalist Morals," 6; Niebuhr, *The Nature and Destiny of Man*, 3–4; Frankl, *Man's Search for Meaning*, 121–131; Gilligan, *Violence*, 45–47.
11. See, s.v. "Cognitive," "Cognition", *Oxford English Dictionary*, 2nd ed. (1989).
12. See the introductory survey of answers to the question "What is an emotion?" by Solomon, "The Philosophy of Emotions," 10–11. See also s.v. "Affective", "Emotion," *Oxford English Dictionary*, 2nd ed. (1989.); s.v. "Affection," *Oxford English Dictionary*, Draft Revision (Sept 2009).
13. Solomon, "The Philosophy of Emotions," 10–12
14. See Labouvie-Vief, "Dynamic Integration," 201–206. For a survey of Labouvie-Vief's theories on cognitive-affective development, see Magai, "Long-Lived Emotions," 380–381.
15. Labouvie-Vief, "Dynamic Integration," 202.
16. For more on the role of emotions in various areas in psychology including developmental psychology, see, among others, the extensive collection of essays in Lewis, Haviland-Jones, and Feldman Barret, *Handbook of Emotions*, especially parts III, V, and VI.
17. 'See, judge, act' refers to a method of social analysis usually attributed to the Belgian Roman Catholic cardinal Joseph Cardijn, who founded the Young Christian Workers movement in 1924. The idea is that it facilitates a hermeneutical circle between theory and praxis. To see is to gain all the data possible about a particular situation; to judge is to reflect on and inter-

pret this data in the light of one's tradition; to act is to make a decision and engage in practical action in light of this reflection and interpretation. The cycle then begins again. Obviously, this 'see, judge, act' method shares a great deal with the idea of a hermeneutical ethics discussed in section 2.1.1 and 2.3.1, as well as the idea of the human person as a historically situated subject in relation. The method has found wide application in so-called liberation theology and the social thought of the Catholic Church. See, among others, Verstraeten, "Catholic Social Thought as Discernment," 2; Rowland, *The Cambridge Companion to Liberation Theology,* 41, 146–148; Mich, "Commentary on Mater et magistra," 191, 198, 203, 211.

18. Bretzke, *Consecrated Phrases: a Latin Theological Dictionary,* 5–6.
19. Ibid. See also Thomas Aquinas, *Summa Theologiae,* I–II, q.1, a. 1: "… those actions alone which lie under his control are properly called human. Now he is master through his mind and will, which is why his free decision is referred to as an ability *of reason and will.* Therefore those acts alone are properly called human which are of his own deliberate willing. Others that may be attributed to him may be called 'acts of a man' [*hominis actiones*], but not 'human acts' [sed non proprie humanae], since they are not his precisely as a human being." I–II, q.1, a. 3 goes on to state, "Ambrose writes that *morals are properly called human.* Indeed moral acts and human acts are the same. So then we may add that the end also provides moral acts with their proper specific character."
20. The idea that morally right behaviour leads to positive appraisals of the person has been borne out in studies of prosocial behaviour in the context of evolutionary biology. The question that evolutionary biologists have essentially asked is that if natural selection favours the fittest, how can self-sacrificing behaviour for the good of others be considered to enhance an individual's fitness? Several theories based on empirical data have been proposed, the most important of which with regard to the present topic is so-called 'indirect reciprocity'. Indirect reciprocity holds that prosocial behaviour brings indirect rewards to the actor such as status and respect in society as an honest and trustworthy person. Trust is important in exchange economies and cheats are often punished, even if only by exclusion. Hence, there is material and psychological benefit (the feel-good factor) to being deemed morally good. See, among others, Kirchhoffer, "The Good, the Bad and Those Who Think They Are;" Fehr and Gächter, "The Puzzle of Human Cooperation," 912; Johnson, Stopka and Knights, "The Puzzle of Human Cooperation," 911–912. From a more cynical perspective, though it proves the point about the relationship between

The Component Dimensions of Human Dignity Model 249

morally right behaviour and others' evaluation of one as therefore being of morally good character, one might consider how Machiavelli advises the prince to appear virtuous and thereby win favour, even though in practice, because of his position, there are some vices that he must necessarily undertake for his safety and well-being. The art, according to Machiavelli, is "to be so prudent that he escapes ill repute for such vices as might take his position away from him." Machiavelli, *The Prince*, Ch. 15.

21. Cf. Janssens, "Personalist Morals," 6: "The way in which we fulfil our relationships with the reality outside ourselves determines the way in which we fulfil ourselves."

22. See, among others, with regard to the formative role of context, MacIntyre, *After Virtue*, 198–199; idem., *Dependent Rational Animals*, 14: "What kind of knowledge is this? It is a form of practical knowledge, a knowing how to interpret, that arises from those complex social interactions with others in which our responses to others and their responses to our responses generate a recognition by them and by us of what thoughts and feelings it is to which each is responding. Of course both they and we sometimes make mistakes, some of us more often than others, but the ability to identify such mistakes itself presupposes an ability to be aware of what others think and feel. Interpretive knowledge of others derives from and is inseparable from involvement with others ... ." With regard to the necessity of context for self-realisation, see Janssens, "Artificial Insemination," 8: "In other words, insofar as we are open to all that is, our being transcends the world; yet we cannot state the question of being except on the basis of our participation in the world." Finally, with regard to the role that context plays in moral evaluation, see, among others, Hughes, "Our Human Vocation (Paragraphs 1691–2051)," who describes how something like lying is morally wrong because it is already contextually defined as not telling the truth to someone *who has a right to know*. In other words, lying is distinct from not telling the truth, since not telling the truth to someone who does not have the right to know, e.g., an enemy, cannot be contextually defined as lying.

23. Aristotle, in fact, describes four types of change, (1) of substance, (2) of quality, (3) of quantity, and (4) of place. I shall only address type (2), which is related to (3) and (4) in that in all cases (1) remains constant. The case of substantial change, i.e. (1), is a special one because it involves the coming to be and ceasing to be of a substance. See Aristotle, *Metaphysics* 1067b–1069a14 and *Physics* V, 224a21–226b17; Tredennick, "Appendix 6: Substance and Change," 297–298; Kenny, *Ancient Philosophy*, 191.

24. See Tredennick, "Appendix 6: Substance and Change," 297–298.
25. See ibid, 298.
26. See Aristotle, *Nicomachean Ethics,* 19761103a24–1103b26.
27. Aristotle, *Nicomachean Ethics,* 1168a9.
28. The passage should not be interpreted in any way as advocating that animals have no worth and should not also be accorded due respect. The passage only serves to illustrate how a figure of speech, which may indeed itself also reflect a callous attitude to other non-human creatures, says something about how human beings treat each other. Nevertheless, the worth and rights of animals is not the focus of this book and shall be addressed no further.
29. See Bagaric and Allan, "The Vacuous Concept of Dignity," 264, 269.
30. See Macklin, "Dignity is a Useless Concept," 1419–1420.
31. Note the readings of Stephen J. Pope and Pope Benedict XVI offered here and in Chapter 1 are products of the hermeneutic of suspicion in Chapter 1. That is to say that in fact, though they nevertheless still strongly emphasise this ontological, essential, character of human dignity, they both display far more complex and nuanced understandings of human dignity that are more in line with the multidimensional understanding offered in this book than may at first appear. See especially Pope, *Human Evolution and Christian Ethics,* 132, 148, 212, as well as, Chapter 1 of the present work. Also, in personal correspondence with the author, Professor Pope, says, "All people have a basic human dignity in virtue of being loved by God as human beings created imago Dei, and not because they have 'earned' or 'merited' this love in virtue of some special traits like being smart, beautiful, and even morally good. In that this is characteristic of all human beings, and in that (put concisely) the capacities to know and to love are what characterize us as human beings, then our ontological dignity is located in our evolved capacities. So to be human is not 'traitless' or 'valueless' or a Kantian noumenon." Professor Pope moreover supports the idea of what he calls a "moral" dignity, and what I have called acquired dignity. Again, in personal correspondence, "We can add a kind of MORAL dignity that comes from being a good person. This is the dignity or honor that we give to Desmond Tutu or Gandhi. In this sense, not everyone has equal dignity. Indeed, we can talk of people who degrade themselves in ways that forfeit their MORAL dignity but not their ONTOLOGICAL dignity. The serial rapist still has value qua human being. I agree with … you that there is a basic drive for affirmation or moral worth." Stephen J. Pope, e-mail message to author, July 2008.

For more on the multidimensionality the concept of human dignity in the public discourse of Pope Benedict XVI, see Kirchhoffer, "Benedict XVI, Human Dignity, and Absolute Moral Norms;" idem., "Pope Benedict XVI on the Dignity of the Human Person."

32. Egonsson, *Dimensions of Dignity*; Fukuyama, *Our Posthuman Future*.
33. See Richard M. Doerflinger, "Human Cloning vs. Human Dignity," United States Conference of Catholic Bishops website, accessed July 28, 2009, http://www.usccb.org/prolife/programs/rlp/03doerflinger.shtml; Benedict XVI, Letter to the Italian Bishops on occasion of the 55th General Assembly held in Assisi (10 November 2005).
34. This is not necessarily a bad thing, because, for example, it makes it possible to advocate dignified treatment of criminals, and may facilitate forgiveness. See *Gaudium et spes*, par. 28: "But it is necessary to distinguish between error, which always merits repudiation, and the person in error, who never loses the dignity of being a person even when he is flawed by false or inadequate religious notions."
35. Cf. Martha Nussbaum's criticism of the Stoic idea of human dignity that situates dignity only in human rationality which, according to Nussbaum, suffers from a similar problem. Nussbaum, "Human Dignity and Political Entitlements."
36. For an example of how this might happen, see Kirchhoffer, "Benedict XVI, Human Dignity, and Absolute Moral Norms."
37. See Bayertz, "Human Dignity: Philosophical Origin and Scientific Erosion of an Idea," 77, who recounts the post-Renaissance connection of dignity to these features. See Dworkin, *Life's Dominion,* 239, on the importance of freedom as integral to the notion of sanctity of life, such that freedom and sanctity of life are both part of understanding human dignity. See Beyleveld and Brownsword, *Human Dignity in Bioethics and Biolaw,* 5, on the importance of autonomy.
38. Farley, "A Feminist Version of Respect for Persons," 183–198; Pope, *Human Evolution*, 208.
39. See Nussbaum, *Women and Human Development*, 78–80; idem., Frontiers of Justice.
40. See Nussbaum, *Women and Human Development,* 77, where she clearly states, "Since the intuitive conception of human functioning and capability demands continued reflection and testing against our intuitions, we should view any given version of the list as a proposal put forward in a Socratic fashion, to be tested against the most secure of our intuitions as we attempt to arrive at a type of reflective equilibrium for political

purposes. ... In this sense, the list remains open-ended and humble; it can always be contested and remade."
41. Nussbaum, *Women and Human Development*, 88.
42. Nussbaum, "Human Dignity and Political Entitlements."
43. One can also continue to base this claim on the idea that human beings are created in the image of God, provided that the image of God one is referring to is equally multidimensional and relational, which is certainly true of an adequate image of the Judeo-Christian God. The Bible, after all, is all about the relationality of a personal God with the world and with others, and the doctrine of the Trinity implies that God is, in God's self, a multidimensional, outward-oriented, relationality. See Verstraeten, "Globalisation and the Dignity of the Poor," 101; Kirchhoffer, "Become What You Are;" Ausloos and Lemmelijn, *The Book of Life*.
44. See Bostrom, "In Defense of Posthuman Dignity."
45. See, among others, Gilligan, *Violence*, 45–55, 110, 112; Taylor, *Sources of the Self*, 15, 23–25.
46. Taylor, *Sources of the Self*, 15.
47. See Watts, "Human Dignity: Concepts and Experiences," 248; Meyer, "Dignity as a (Modern) Virtue;" Gilligan, *Violence*, 45–55.
48. See Demmer, "Shaping the Moral Life," 16–17.
49. See Kant, *Grounding for the Metaphysics of Morals*, 36.
50. Ibid, 41.
51. Beyleveld and Brownsword, *Human Dignity*, 5.
52. See also Dworkin, *Life's Dominion*, 239: "Freedom is the cardinal, absolute requirement of self-respect: no one treats his life as having any intrinsic, objective importance unless he insists on leading that life himself, not being ushered along it by others, no matter how much he loves or respects or fears them."
53. See Taylor, *Sources of the Self*, 23.
54. Meyer, "Dignity as a (Modern) Virtue."
55. Kant, *Grounding for the Metaphysics of Morals*, 36.
56. See also Coppens, *A Brief Text-book of Moral Philosophy*, 16, and also 31–32. A moral good is an end "conformable to reason regulating free acts. ... The useful and pleasurable, when they are embraced by the will according to the right order of things, and in a manner worthy of man, share in the nobility of moral good." The 'useful' and the 'pleasurable' can be seen as somewhat equivalent to terms non-moral and pre-moral goods respectively. See also the Introduction to this book.
57. Dewey, *Lectures on Ethics, 1900–1901*, 54.

The Component Dimensions of Human Dignity Model 253

58. Like Nussbaum, I am reluctant to insist on a definitive list of what these capacities should be, or to insist that a person has to present evidence of all of them before they are considered as possessing human dignity and hence subject to the protection and rights that this gives them. Far more important, I maintain, is to emphasise the potential to realise whatever capacities are in evidence. See Nussbaum, "Human Dignity and Political Entitlements," 299. Idem., *Women and Human Development,* 77, where she clearly states, "Since the intuitive conception of human functioning and capability demands continued reflection and testing against our intuitions, we should view any given version of the list as a proposal put forward in a Socratic fashion, to be tested against the most secure of our intuitions as we attempt to arrive at a type of reflective equilibrium for political purposes. ... In this sense, the list remains open-ended and humble; it can always be contested and remade."
59. Janssens, "Artificial Insemination," 12.
60. Kant, *Grounding for the Metaphysics of Morals,* 35.
61. Cf. Dewey's definition of a moral good, *Lectures on Ethics,* 54. See also section 3.4.4 of this book.

CHAPTER 4

A DESCRIPTIVE CATEGORY AND A NORMATIVE CRITERION

The Component Dimensions of Dignity model offers a framework in which to both understand and employ the concept of human dignity as a descriptive category and as a normative criterion for ethical discourse. When understood as a descriptive category, the concept of human dignity helps to overcome moralism and correct the rise of moralistic 'dignity talk'. When understood as a normative criterion, based on this multidimensional model and its accompanying multidimensional anthropology, the concept of human dignity properly understood contributes to overcoming moral relativism by challenging inappropriate understandings of human dignity as well as the morally wrong acts that these inspire.

In the introduction to this book I defined the notions of a descriptive category and a normative criterion, and emphasised the difference with regard to the ideas of descriptive ethics and normative ethics. To briefly recap, a descriptive category is intended to facilitate descriptive ethics by helping the ethicist to describe, analyse, and seek to understand what is happening and why it is happening with regard to a particular moral issue. It describes the operative moral reasoning, moral norms, and moral action in a particular moral event, but it cannot evaluate the objective moral status of these. A normative criterion, on the other hand, facilitates the objective evaluation of the moral goodness or badness of an intention, and the moral rightness and wrongness of an action, so as to arrive at an overall assessment of the moral status of a moral event or behaviour. Of course, in a particular moral event, the actor may appeal to what he subjectively *believes* to be a normative criterion. This does not mean, however, that his understanding of this criterion is necessarily objectively correct or adequate. Thus, when I refer to the use of the proper understanding of the concept of human dignity as a normative criterion, I am also referring to its ability to objectively evaluate subjective appeals to its normative character in a particular moral event, i.e., the particular understanding of human dignity being appealed to at a given point. Hence, as a normative criterion, human dignity, properly understood, can evaluate the morality of an event, and the appropriateness of the operative understanding of human dignity that underpins this event.

Hermeneutical ethics, one of the key assumptions underlying the model of human dignity proposed in this book, is relevant to both descriptive ethics and normative ethics in the sense that, as an attempt to gain insight and understanding, hermeneutical ethics lends itself to descriptive ethics, while at the same time, as an attempt to take seriously the moral meanings of the moral questions and choices that face a human person it lends itself to normative ethics.[1] Thus, just as I have underlined the importance of hermeneutical ethics as integral to ethical enquiry due to its emphasis on gaining insight and understanding into why people do what they do and the existential significance of people's moral convictions and behaviours, I maintain that the concept of human dignity can function as a window through which some insight can be gained into these matters.

In order to demonstrate the descriptive and normative characteristics of the proper understanding of human dignity proposed in this book, it might be helpful to do so in relation to two areas highlighted in Chapter 1 in which a rise in 'dignity talk' was noted. The two areas I shall focus

A Descriptive Category and a Normative Criterion   257

on, by way of illustration, are interpersonal violence and end-of-life decisions.[2] The aim is not to present an exhaustive discussion of these issues, but instead to use the Component Dimensions of Human Dignity model to describe and evaluate the ethical issues in question, particularly insofar as explicit appeals are made in these issues to the idea of human dignity. Therefore, what follows will be based on the writings of two representative authors—James Gilligan on violence, and Ronald Dworkin on end-of-life decisions—who grapple with the issues in question. Such a narrow, and brief, treatment of the respective issues can in no way be said to represent the final word on the matter. Indeed, in using these examples, I am less interested in arguing for a particular position on either of the matters than I am in demonstrating how a proper understanding of human dignity can help to overcome the problem of 'dignity talk' in order to better understand the ethical issues at hand and the existential meanings at play (thereby avoiding moralism), while at the same time offering at least some normative direction about what we ought to do (thereby avoiding relativism).

When using human dignity as a descriptive category, one can ask the following three questions: What is this person's *operative* understanding of the concept of human dignity? What are the social influences, mores, and circumstances that may have contributed to this understanding of human dignity? And how does this person's operative understanding of human dignity affect and provide subjective justification for the moral choices he or she makes, and the behavioural strategies he or she undertakes?

When using human dignity as a normative criterion, one can similarly ask, is this person's operative understanding of the concept of human dignity a *proper* understanding, especially insofar as it constitutes a moral good and therefore an intended end of the person's moral behaviour? Are the social influences, mores, and circumstances that may have contributed to this understanding of human dignity, and are the person's interpretations of these mores, etc., legitimate and correct (do they promote human life, flourishing and happiness and the personal sense that one has lived one's life well), or should they be called into question? And are the moral choices and behavioural strategies that this person's particular understanding of human dignity inspires morally right or wrong?

In what follows, I shall briefly turn to the writings of the aforementioned authors in order, based on these writings, to find plausible, though certainly not exhaustive, answers to these six questions for the cases in question. In so doing, I shall demonstrate the value of a proper understanding of human dignity as a descriptive category and a normative criterion.

4.1. James Gilligan and Violence

James Gilligan is a clinical psychiatrist who specialises in violent criminals. Between 1981 and 1991, he was the "clinical director of a program of psychiatric services throughout the [Massachusetts] state prison system." As a result of this programme, the level of lethal violence in these prisons was reduced to almost zero.[3]

I understand Gilligan's theory on the causes of violence[4] as follows. This summary provides a backdrop against which to examine an individual case of violent behaviour and examine it through the lens of a proper understanding of human dignity.

For Gilligan, shame is "the primary or ultimate cause of all violence, whether towards others or toward the self."[5]

Shame is a lack of self-love, a feeling of worthlessness and impotence. It is the opposite of pride, which Gilligan understands to be a *healthy*[6] sense of self-esteem, self-respect, or self-love[7] that can withstand the minor insults and humiliations of everyday life and enable a person to love others.[8] In violent men, the feeling of shame is triggered by events that constitute a perceived withdrawal or threat of withdrawal of respect by others.[9]

For men, who are most often the perpetrators of violence,[10] respect is still earned in most patriarchal cultures today by being active, indepen-

A Descriptive Category and a Normative Criterion 259

dent, strong, desirable to women, fecund, and economically successful, among other things. Moreover, men are supposed to uphold the norms and values of their culture.[11]

Gilligan claims that perceived withdrawal of respect, or even just the perceived *threat* of withdrawal of respect, reveals to the violent man the extent to which he does not live up to his patriarchal culture's normative model of a man, and leads him, therefore, to doubt his own worth. Furthermore, the withdrawal of respect constitutes the exposure, or the fear of exposure, of this sense of inadequacy to others, leaving the man feeling naked, weak, and impotent.[12]

In order to overcome the shame of his perceived impotence the violent man must invest in actions that will restore his pride, for to live without some sense of pride, even if it is perverse by other standards, is tantamount to the death of self.[13] He turns to the resources that his culture offers him. And since, according to Gilligan, most of these men experience their culture as a patriarchal, honour-based one that implicitly links manhood with violence,[14] the man violently punishes those who disrespect him, or destroys those who threaten to. He then mistakes the fear that people have for him as genuine respect.[15] Violence, in other words, has become the man's means to replace shame with pride[16] (though of course this is not what was described as a *healthy* sense of self-worth as it does not afford him the capacity to love, which would be contrary to the image he *believes* he needs to maintain to be thought a *real* man).

Having summarised Gilligan's theory on the causes of interpersonal violence, I turn now to a particular example that will form the basis of the demonstration of the descriptive and normative properties of the understanding of human dignity developed in this book. It is an example to which I have already referred in both the introduction and in Chapter 1.

During his time as a psychiatrist in the prison system, Gilligan dealt with numerous violent men. One man in particular was caught in a cycle of violence such that the more he was punished by the prison authorities for violent behaviour, the more violent he became, to the point that he was in danger of being killed by other inmates whom he repeatedly attacked, only to again be severely punished by the prison authorities. The man's case is not unique. In fact, Gilligan claims that his is typical of most of the men that he dealt with. Nevertheless, this man's answer when Gilligan asked him, "What do you want so badly that you would sacrifice everything in order to get it?" is particularly interesting. What is both striking, and disturbing about these words is that the violent man appears to be using the concept of human dignity, or at least something like it, to justify his own violent behaviour towards others.

> Pride. Dignity. Self-esteem. And I'll kill every mother-fucker in that cell block if I have to in order to get it! My life ain't worth nothin' if I take somebody disrespectin' me and callin' me punk asshole faggot and goin' 'Ha! Ha!' at me. Life ain't worth livin' if there ain't nothin' worth dyin' for. If you ain't got pride, you got nothin'. That's all you got! I've already got my pride.[17]

4.1.1. Human Dignity as a Descriptive Category

You will recall that I said that when one uses the concept of human dignity as a descriptive category one could ask three questions. I shall ask them again here and, using James Gilligan's work into the 'bio-psycho-social'[18] causes of violence, offer very brief, illustrative, and hence in no way exhaustive answers to them with regard to the man quoted above. In so doing, I intend to show how the concept of human dignity can be helpful as an invitation[19] to begin to *understand* and hence gain insight into why a person engages in a particular course of moral behaviour.

(1) What is this man's own particular understanding of the concept of human dignity?

His answer certainly seems to equate dignity with pride and with a sense of self-esteem.[20] Moreover, his sense of self-esteem, his dignity, is particularly dependent on the extent to which he perceives he is respected by others.[21] And, most importantly, he considers fear to be equivalent to respect for his dignity; he *believes* that he has dignity when other people fear him. A person who fears him would obviously never call him "punk asshole faggot".[22] Or put differently, he believes that he only has dignity, that he can only feel good about himself, when he appears powerful and strong to others. Punk, asshole, and faggot, are labels that, in a masculine, patriarchal world, constitute an accusation of weakness.[23]

(2) What are the social influences, mores and circumstances that may have contributed to his understanding of human dignity?

He may have grown up in an honour culture where a man's dignity is equated with his ability to defend his honour in the face of insult or humiliation;[24] a culture in which to live without this kind of respect is to live in shame—a life not worth living—;[25] and a culture in which the notion of justice is a retributive one that equates justice with retaliation,[26] and the violent punishment of those who offend one's honour, and hence one's dignity.[27]

(3) How does this man's operative understanding of human dignity provide subjective justification for the moral choices he has made, in this case violently attacking other people? This man *believes* he is morally right to attack someone who threatens his dignity. He believes that his dignity is a moral good that can be defended and indeed enhanced through his violent behaviour. Remember, he associates dignity with being seen to be strong and powerful. If people challenge this perceived strength, and call him weak, then he *believes* the best way to show that he his strong is to show them that he is stronger than they are by inflicting pain on them. The fact that he will regularly risk his own life shows that he perceives his idea of dignity to be the ultimate end of a life well lived: "Life ain't worth livin' if there ain't nothin' worth dyin' for. If you ain't got pride, you got nothin'." Moreover, the fact that he bases his own understanding of dignity on the social mores of an honour culture means there are other people, within that context, who subscribe to similar mores, and who will therefore consider his behaviour morally good, indeed, as an act of 'justice', and hence consider him more worthy of their respect. In other words, within

the paradigm of his cultural context and its associated *operative* understanding of human dignity, he is engaging in morally 'good' behaviour ('just' punishment) for the moral 'good' of his 'dignity', which he understands to be his sense of 'self-worth' based on the degree to which other people see him as strong and powerful and hence worthy of 'respect'. Let it be said, then, that he is using a *particular* understanding of human dignity as a 'normative' criterion, in this case as a 'good' end, to justify his behaviour and to choose what he believes to be a morally 'right' course of action (I have used inverted commas in the two previous sentences to emphasise the subjective, culturally and historically situated nature of the understandings of good, just, dignity, etc.).

The above application of a proper understanding of human dignity as a descriptive criterion should in no way be seen as approving of the man's actions. However, I have already argued that for ethics to be useful ethics it is necessary to find a way of making sense of what people do in moral terms and their subjective rationale for why they do it if we are to avoid moralism. This is where the descriptive properties of the Component Dimensions of Human Dignity model come in. That said, however, I have also argued that a proper understanding of human dignity contains normative properties that make it possible to objectively evaluate the behaviour just described.

4.1.2. Human Dignity as a Normative Criterion

You will recall that when I said that a proper understanding of human dignity also serves as a *normative criterion*, I likewise said that there were also three questions one could ask in this regard.

(1) Is this man's operative understanding of the concept of human dignity a *proper* understanding, especially insofar as it constitutes a moral good and hence an intended end of his moral behaviour?

The man does not demonstrate a proper understanding of human dignity, because, first, he overlooks the *multidimensionality* of a proper understanding of human dignity, and second, in overlooking this multidimensionality he falls into a bad vision of self-worth, such that what this man *believes* to be a morally good end, namely, the pursuit of his dignity as self-worth, is in effect morally bad because he equates self-worth with being feared by others. I shall elaborate on this in what follows.

First, inherent to the man's understanding of human dignity is dignity as an acquired sense of self-worth. He speaks of "Pride. Dignity. Self-esteem." The man wants to be able to look himself in the mirror and not feel shame. This is *not* in itself bad, nor inappropriate to a proper understanding of human dignity, as shown by both the Existential Component Dimension which highlights the human drive to live a meaningful life, and the Cognitive-Affective Component Dimension's Not Yet pole of Self-Worth, which suggests that an integral part of this existential quest is a cognitive-affective appreciation of one's own worth. He is, moreover, right insofar as he believes that it is morally good to pursue a sense of self-worth, as demonstrated by the Behavioural Component Dimension's Already pole of Human Dignity as a Moral Good. But, a *proper* understanding of human dignity takes into account *both* this desire for a sense of self-worth, and the potential to fulfil this desire in and through the relationships in which one is embedded. According to the Behavioural Component Dimension, human dignity, properly understood, is thus a moral good in two related respects: (a) dignity as an *acquired sense of self-worth*, as a perceived validation of the meaningfulness of one's existence, is a good, (b) dignity as the *inherent human potential* to realise this sense of self-worth, for oneself and for others (as defined by the Already poles of the Existential, Cognitive-Affective, and Social Component Dimensions) is likewise a good, for without this potential, and the conditions necessary to realise it, the former sense of dignity, i.e. (a), would be absurd. This is testified to in the paradox of the human condition highlighted by the Existential Component Dimension. One can only speak of the Not Yet pole of Acquired Dignity precisely because human beings are, existentially speaking, historical, situated, corporeal subjects in relationship and hence already have a common dignity and a common yearning to live a meaningful and dignified life in a universe in which they are otherwise insignificant. Moreover, point (b) also means that a *proper* sense of self-worth, i.e. acquired dignity, is a consequence of one's positive engagement for the moral good of the dignity of others. This is borne out by the Not Yet pole of the Behavioural Component Dimension, i.e. the Dignity of the Morally Good, as well as the Not Yet pole of the Social Component Dimension, i.e., My Dignity. Therefore, both (a) and (b) are necessary for an adequate understanding of the concept of human dignity. From the descriptive analysis of the man's understanding of human dignity, it is apparent that his understanding is inadequate because, instead of comprising aspects of both (a) and (b), he only considers his own dignity as self-worth to be a moral good, ignoring both the dignity of others and his own potential to acquire dignity by helping rather than hurting others, which is an inadequate understanding of human dignity.

Second, by his ignoring the second sense of dignity as a moral good described in (b) above, the man opens the way to a bad understanding of self-worth (Cognitive Component Dimension) and a wrong strategy of action to acquire it (Behavioural Component Dimension). It is not self-worth that is bad, but *his idea* of self-worth that is bad.[28] He believes that he can only feel good about himself if others fear him, if others give him the kind of so-called 'respect' (i.e. they fear him) that he believes is his due. Thus, *his idea* of what it means to have dignity is self-centred and egotistical, even narcissistic (though he himself would not of course admit this).[29] He is only concerned with *his* dignity, with *his* feelings of worth, with *his* sense of power, and perceived status and respect. The fact that he will kill others to bolster his desired self-image shows that he is in no way concerned about the dignity of the other. He only recognises, as a moral good, as a 'good' end, his own acquired sense of dignity (i.e. the Not Yet pole of the Cognitive-Affective Component Dimension). He neither acknowledges the moral good of the inherent potential of others to also acquire a sense of dignity, nor of his own inherent potential to help others realise their dignity, his potential to contribute to a flourishing community rather than simply to his own ego. Moreover, when one examines the details of his idea of what constitutes self-worth, it in fact involves the active denial and destruction of any dignity (acquired self-worth or inherent worth as potential) that his victim could be said to have. His idea of dignity, the end which he seeks to attain, is therefore in effect opposed to a proper understanding of the moral good of human dignity, since it relies on his willingness to kill the other (and hence to destroy any potential that the other may have had to advance his own dignity or the dignity of others), and is hence, bad. It does not conform then to the normative elements inherent in the Social Component Dimension, namely that My Dignity will only be fully realised when Others' Dignity is also realised.

(2) Are the social influences, mores, and circumstances that may have contributed to this understanding of human dignity, and are his interpretations of these mores, etc., legitimate and correct, or should they be called into question? That is, do they promote human life, flourishing and happiness and the personal sense that one has lived one's life well?

A proper understanding of human dignity can also help us to critique the mores that may have contributed to this man's understanding of human dignity. For example, among the many possible influences one could discuss, and there are too many to go into in detail here, I have said that the paradigm of the honour culture under which he his operating may equate justice with retributive punishment. This is a rather narrow understanding of justice, and one that potentially denies the moral good of the inherent dignity of all human beings, because it only serves the interests of those offended to the detriment of the alleged perpetrators. Therefore, any social convention that advocates this kind of justice should be called into question, as recent attempts to formulate restorative rather than retributive notions of justice have attempted to do.[30] This is not to say that, for example, a dangerous person, like the man in question, should not be locked up. But it is to say that locking him up should as far as possible serve *his* dignity, for example by providing him with alternative, non-violent ways of realising a meaningful sense of self-worth,[31] as well as the dignity of the society who locks him up.[32] 'Locking him up and throwing away the key' shows a disregard for *his* inherent dignity too[33] (even though it may legitimately challenge his idea of acquired dignity, which I have shown above is a bad vision of dignity). And a justice system, if it is to be truly just, if it is to truly serve the good of human dignity, should not disregard anyone's inherent dignity, i.e. everyone's inherent potential to acquire the good of his dignity (as self-worth) by working for the good of others' dignity, even as it seeks at the same time to prevent or correct misguided and dangerous attempts that undermine others' dignity or the inherent dignity of the actor.

(3) Are the moral choices that this person's particular understanding of human dignity inspires right or wrong? Clearly, we can conclude in light of the answers to the above questions, that, though he believes that what he is doing is morally right (descriptive level), what he is doing is objectively morally wrong (normative level). He has chosen to engage in a strategy to acquire dignity that involves actively attacking the inherent dignity of others. A proper understanding of human dignity requires that one work for the good not only of one's own dignity but for the dignity of others. Only then can one truly acquire dignity as a responsible self in relationship.

4.2. Ronald Dworkin and End-Of-Life Decisions

Ronald Dworkin is an American legal philosopher who has taught in numerous prestigious universities both in the U.S.A. and the United Kingdom. In 2007, he received the Holberg International Memorial Prize in the Humanities. In his book, *Life's Dominion: An Argument about Abortion, Euthanasia, and Individual Freedom,* Dworkin turns his attention to the problems posed by so-called end-of-life decisions, which, as demonstrated in Chapter 1, is one of the areas in which 'dignity talk' is widespread. I have chosen to use Dworkin's ideas here because they offer a particularly nuanced understanding of human dignity. Again, this topic really deserves far more space than I can give it here. My intention is not to take a position regarding end-of-life decisions per se but instead to demonstrate how the descriptive and normative properties of a proper understanding of human dignity opens up the issues at stake to overcome simplistic, one-dimensional, moralistic appeals to the concept of human dignity.

However, before doing so, I shall give a brief overview of Dworkin's ideas concerning end-of-life decisions. In order to narrow the scope and facilitate the analysis in this section, instead of treating end-of-life decisions in general, which would include various technically defined categories such as active and voluntary, passive and voluntary, active and involuntary, passive and involuntary, and so on,[34] I shall focus only on the case of a person who is terminally ill with a painful, degenerative disease and who consciously and competently chooses to end her own life with, for example, barbiturates prescribed by a doctor, before the disease progresses to a stage where she is no longer conscious and/or competent.

For Dworkin, "Dignity—which means respecting the inherent value of our own lives—is at the heart of" arguments surrounding end-of-life decisions.[35]

Dworkin argues that Western political culture is dominated by a "belief in individual human dignity: that people have the moral right—and the moral responsibility—to confront the most fundamental questions about the meaning and value of their own lives for themselves, answering to their own consciences and convictions."[36] Thus, for Dworkin, dignity is a composite idea that incorporates several features of human experience. Among these are (1) autonomy, (2) the desire and capacity for self-respect, (3) the capacity to relate to the mores of one's own society, acting with responsible freedom, and finally, (4) the desire for integrity. I shall briefly unpack these important aspects in turn.

(1) Autonomy is expressed in the idea that people have a right to live according to their own consciences in a manner that is meaningful to them.[37] Moreover, not only is autonomy a right (a requirement), it is also a responsibility: "Freedom is the cardinal, absolute requirement of self-respect: no one treats his life as having any intrinsic, objective importance

unless he insists on leading that life himself, not being ushered along it by others, no matter how much he loves or respects or fears them."[38]

(2) The desire and capacity for self-respect[39] relies on autonomy as is apparent from the previous quote. Self-respect is the product of making autonomous choices about (a) the critical interests that represent answers to self-defining questions regarding how best to live out (b) the intrinsic "sacred or inviolable" value[40] of one's own life depending on the weight one gives to (c) human and natural investments in one's life.

a) Critical interests are those about which people feel their lives would be worse off, and mistaken, if they did not recognise and satisfy these interests. They are interests that embody for a person the idea of what should constitute a good life, and hence say something about a person's character.[41]

b) Dworkin argues that these critical interests are an expression of the fact that all human persons believe that human life is sacred, i.e., intrinsically valuable. This allegedly universal belief in the sanctity of individual human life can be found, according to Dworkin, in the fact that people find it tragic when a particular human life, once it exists, is frustrated, i.e., cannot fully flourish or ends prematurely.[42]

c) This intrinsic value (sanctity)[43] is constituted by a respect for a combination of natural investments (e.g. the creative investment of a divine creator or the wonder of an evolutionary process that would give rise to a unique self-reflective human person) and human investments (by parents, family, society and culture in that unique life on the one hand, and by the person herself in the form of critical decisions about the meaning and purpose of her own life, on the other.)[44] In light of this, Dworkin proposes that, although everyone accepts "that it is intrinsically bad when human life, once begun, is frustrated, people disagree about the best answer to the question of whether avoidable premature death is always or invariably the most serious possible frustration of life."[45] This disagreement arises from the different emphases (as a result of autonomous decisions regarding critical interests) that a person may place on the respective natural and human investments that constitute the intrinsic value of human life. A person who emphasises the natural investments will tend to see death as always more serious than any other possible frustration, e.g. pain or incapacitation. A person who emphasises the human investment may consider death a better option if not dying—for example, living on but in a persistent vegetative state—would frustrate other investments that had already been made in that life, for example with regard to the kind of person a person has worked hard to be, or the values that a person has chosen to embody in the way they lived their life.[46]

(3) Dignity also includes the capacity to respond to the mores and values of one's society, hence the line, "moral responsibility" in the initial quote. The reason that end-of-life decisions are so hotly debated is because these decisions not only say something about how we live our lives but how we think all people should live their lives. According to Dworkin, we *should* be concerned about how other people live too, because individual choices create the moral environment.[47] Insuring that people do not suffer an indignity, i.e. that the intrinsic value of their lives is not recognised, requires the mobilisation of community resources and values.[48] It is the community, the moral, social environment that will determine what constitutes an indignity and what resources should be given to prevent that happening. This is of concern to the individual because if what society considers an indignity does not accord with what he considers an indignity, then it calls into question his critical interests and idea of the good life, with implications for his own sense of self-respect and hence dignity.[49]

Dworkin thus makes a crucial distinction within the concept of dignity itself: on one hand, he acknowledges that "dignity is a matter of convention" because different societies will consider different things indignities; on the other, no matter what these boundaries may be, the right to have one's life recognised as having intrinsic value is not a matter of convention, bearing in mind of course that how this intrinsic value is expressed is again open to interpretation.

(4) Finally, Dworkin's idea of dignity, and especially dignity as a right, is closely related to a key idea of his, namely, integrity. Dworkin argues that a human life can best be understood as a literary work with a beginning, middle and end. "People think it important not just that their life contain a variety of the right experiences, achievements, and connections [cf. critical interests], but that it have a structure that expresses a coherent choice among these—for some, that it display a steady, self-defining commitment to a vision of character or achievement that the life as a whole, seen as an integral creative narrative, illustrates and expresses. Of course, this ideal of integrity does not itself define a way to live: it presupposes substantive convictions."[50] According to Dworkin, integrity is linked to dignity such that, a person who does not demonstrate this integrity lacks dignity in a certain sense: "We think that someone who acts out of character, for gain or to avoid trouble, has insufficient respect for himself."[51]

Therefore, when it comes to end-of-life decisions Dworkin proposes that in order to be able to live in character and with dignity, one must be given the freedom to choose how and when one dies because how a book ends is all-important.

> But though we may feel our own dignity at stake in what others do about death, and may sometimes wish to make others act as we think right, a true appreciation of dignity argues decisively in the opposite direction—for individual freedom, not coercion, for a régime of law and attitude that encourages each of us to make mortal decisions for himself. ... Decisions about life and death are the most important, the most crucial for forming and expressing personality, that anyone makes; we think it crucial to get these decisions right, but also crucial to make them in character, and for ourselves. ...
>
> Because we cherish dignity, we insist on freedom, and we place the right of conscience at its center, so that a government that denies that right is totalitarian no matter how free it leaves us in choices that matter less. Because we honor dignity, we demand democracy, and we define it so that a constitution that permits a majority to

deny freedom of conscience is democracy's enemy, not its author. Whatever view we take about ... euthanasia, we want the right to decide for ourselves, and we should therefore be ready to insist that any honorable constitution, and genuine constitution of principle, will guarantee that right for everyone.[52]

I turn now to a specific case that Dworkin mentions in his book that appeals to dignity which I shall analyse using the descriptive and normative properties of a proper understanding of human dignity as I have defined it in this book and in light of Dworkin's perspective on dignity and end-of-life decisions.

Timothy Quill, a medical doctor and now Professor of Medicine, Psychiatry, and Medical Humanities at the University of Rochester School of Medicine and Dentistry, as well as the Director of the Center for Ethics, Humanities and Palliative Care, describes in detail the case of a patient, whom he calls Diane, who was diagnosed with leukaemia. She had previously fought and overcome vaginal cancer, alcoholism, and depression. She was married with a college-age son. She decided not to undergo the proposed course of treatment which would have been extremely painful, with a high risk of numerous complications, and only a 25 percent chance of long-term survival. She asked Quill to prescribe her barbiturates because she was having trouble sleeping. Upon further enquiry he found out that she planned to end her own life with these barbiturates at a time she felt appropriate.

> It was extraordinarily important to Diane to maintain control of herself and her own dignity during the time remaining to her. When this was no longer possible, she clearly wanted to die. ... she had known of people lingering in what was called relative comfort, and she wanted no part of it. When the time came, she wanted to take her life in the least painful way possible. Knowing of her desire for independence and her decision to stay in control, I thought this request made perfect sense. ... I ... felt strongly that I was setting

Diane free to get the most of the time she had left, and maintain dignity and control on her own terms until her death.[53]

4.2.1. Human Dignity as a Descriptive Category

When applying the concept of human dignity as a descriptive category, the aim is to understand what the *operative* understanding of human dignity is and what role this plays in the person's moral decisions and behaviour. One could say, then, that it is an enquiry into what Dworkin, in his discussion of integrity, calls, "substantive convictions."[54] This can be done by answering the three questions already described.

1) What is this woman's own particular understanding of the concept of human dignity?

This is hard to know directly from Quill's article and has to be inferred from what Quill says in his article and from what Dworkin has said about dignity and integrity.

Quill clearly seems to associate her dignity with her sense of self-respect. Moreover, that self-respect is based to a large extent on the sense of autonomous control that she has over her life. She wants to be able to decide when and how she dies. She does not want to linger in an 'undignified state', i.e. in a condition that would limit her autonomy and control and make her a burden or be pitied by others. Her self-respect is thus also dependent on a feeling that other people respect her and her decisions precisely because she is in control, not because she is in need of their help or pity. In Dworkin's terms, then, she associates her dignity with the human investments more than the natural investments in her life. Her life itself is not as important to her as what she thinks it means to live a good life, namely a life in control.

2) What are the social influences, mores and circumstances that may have contributed to her understanding of human dignity?

A great deal could be said, in this regard. I shall highlight only a few points. She lives in the United States of America, where, as is apparent from Dworkin's writings the idea of self-determination is very strong. It is, after all, the 'land of the free' and 'home of the brave'. The preamble to the constitution states that it exists to secure the Blessings of Liberty. Moreover, the U.S.A. largely operate under both a political and economic philosophy of liberalism that holds individual liberty to be paramount.[55] Certain extreme interpretations of this philosophical setting can then lead to the idea that if one is dependent, or not self-sufficient, and not autonomous, then one somehow does not have self-respect or dignity, because one has not 'made something of oneself'.[56] In other words, in Dworkin's terms, one is living 'out of character' in a particular social and economic milieu. One is not living up to the standards of one's society.

Moreover, her previous experiences, in overcoming cancer, alcoholism and depression, may have affirmed for her that she and she alone, her own self-determination, were responsible for her triumphs. Other people may have said encouraging words like, 'you can do it'. Consider for example how Quill describes her (italics are my own for emphasis): "Diane was *no ordinary person* [which can be interpreted as sign of respect] ... . She was raised in an alcoholic family and had felt alone for much of her life. She had vaginal cancer as a young woman. Through much of her adult life, she had *struggled* with depression and her own alcoholism. I had come to know, *respect, and admire* her over the previous eight years as she *confronted* these problems and gradually *overcame* them. She was an incredibly clear, at times brutally honest, thinker and communicator. As she *took control of her life*, she developed a strong sense of *independence* and *confidence*. In the previous three-and-one-half years, *her hard work* had paid off."

3) How does this woman's operative understanding of human dignity provide subjective justification for the moral choices she has made, in this case choosing to end her own life?

First of all, in most discourse dignity is seen as a moral good and is hence a morally justifiable end of moral behaviour. If her understanding of dignity is strongly related to her own sense of self-respect, and she feels that self-respect is gained through the exercise of autonomy precisely because she, firstly, lives in a society that honours such self-determination, and secondly, has herself been honoured as brave, courageous, independent, and so on for overcoming her earlier struggles, then, when faced with a battle she cannot win physically, and a disease that by default will remove her freedom, she believes that she can nevertheless preserve her self-respect by not giving the disease the chance to take it from her. In a sense then, one could describe her behaviour as an act of 'self'-defence, i.e., an attempt to preserve a particular dignified image of herself that she believes is worthy of her own respect and the respect of others in her society.[57] Her final act will be an act of freedom, and in doing so, she will triumph over the disease that would have otherwise taken that freedom from her, and with it, her self-respect, and hence her dignity.

Since, as I have shown, dignity is understood as a moral good, she probably feels that what she has chosen to do is morally good, because she has defended her dignity (as she understands it, i.e. with a strong connection to autonomy) by acting in a free way. Moreover, it might seem strange to think that killing oneself can be considered morally good because, after all, one then ceases to exist as a moral being. Nevertheless, this is where Dworkin and his idea of life as a book is particularly helpful. For this person, being alive is not as important as living the right kind of life, and for her that entails autonomy. She will choose to die rather than to live because her dying will be itself a testimony to what she wants her life to have meant and signified.

This analysis on the level of descriptive ethics should make one at least realise, whether one agrees with what this woman chose to do or not, how what she did was morally justifiable for her in the historical context of her society. Thus, any moralistic condemnation of her as evil would be wrong. In this way, the descriptive aspects of a proper understanding of human dignity help to avoid the trap of moralism and the anti-human, inhumane condemnation that it entails.

Nevertheless, this analysis has still only occurred on the level of descriptive ethics. In other words, the operative norms in her decision and in particular her understanding of them may or may not be morally adequate at an objective normative level. The description of her subjective understanding of human dignity, self-respect, and autonomy, as well as her interpretation of how these function as goods in her society, such that to act in favour of this subjective view is understood by her to be morally good, does not yet mean that her interpretation of human dignity is an adequate one, or that her motives and behaviour can be said to be objectively morally good in light of a proper multidimensional understanding of human dignity. This objective evaluation is necessary if one is to avoid the pitfalls of relativism in which anything goes, although, a degree of relativity may nevertheless be inevitable and acceptable. This objective evaluation falls to a proper understanding of human dignity as a normative criterion.

4.2.2. Human Dignity as a Normative Criterion
(1) Is this woman's operative understanding of the concept of human dignity a *proper* understanding, especially insofar as it constitutes a moral good and hence an intended end of her moral behaviour?

I maintain, based on Quill's account, that the woman does not demonstrate a proper multidimensional understanding of human dignity. Nevertheless, assessing the objective morality of her behaviour is more difficult than in the case of the violent criminal, because it is not immediately apparent how she might be undermining the moral good of someone else's dignity or indeed even her own (what Dworkin might call the natural investment).

To want self-respect, and to want to be respected by others, and to associate that respect with demonstrating autonomy and feeling oneself to be autonomous is not bad in and of itself. After all, both autonomy as a human capacity, and the desire to realise that autonomy in some form of self-worth have been shown to be part of a properly multidimensional understanding of human dignity (Inherent Worth and Self-Worth). Indeed, autonomy is essential to a proper understanding of human dignity insofar as morally good behaviour, by which one acquires dignity as self-worth (The Dignity of the Morally Good), can only be moral behaviour if it is freely chosen. Conversely, one could say that behaviour that is deemed morally good is a testimony to one's autonomy, and hence makes one worthy of respect.

Nevertheless, while it is an essential element of human dignity, the capacity and desire for autonomy and self-respect are not the only features of the human person that afford him or her dignity, inherent or acquired. For example, Margaret Farley's insistence on the capacity to love as part of the basis for the dignity of the human person[58] is important in that it points towards the human capacity to be other-directed rather than purely self-directed. The idea of human dignity as a moral good means that it is a moral good in two ways. First, as the acquired sense of self-worth that one seeks (which the woman in question associates with being able to act and be seen to act autonomously), and second as the precondition, consisting of an array of other goods, necessary to make this acquisition possible. The question then is, has this woman taken the latter sense of dignity as a moral good properly into account, both with regard to her own inherent dignity and that of others?

Obviously, by choosing to end her life she is choosing to sacrifice, in a final human act (*actus humanus*) every inherent human capacity, all other non-moral and pre-moral goods, from which dignity as inherent worth is derived: not only her life, but her reason, her cognitive-affective capacities, her conscious connection to and experience of all her relationships in the world, and so on. So in one sense, she is not taking the moral good of dignity as inherent worth into account because she puts an end to any potential she may have to further her dignity or others'. At the same time, however, one could argue that she does indeed take these aspects into account because she chooses to die while she still has them and is able to use them, thereby pre-empting their loss to her approaching suffering and death. She wants to die with dignity, i.e., precisely with these capacities, with these relationships, still in place and still in a good state. She wants to die with good relationships in place, and good memories of her, rather than relationships soured by resentment, or memories tainted by pain and suffering. Thus, depending on how one looks at it, one could say either that she does not or that she does take her dignity as inherent worth adequately into account.

As to the moral good of the others' dignity, this is more problematic. If she believes, as it seems she does, that dignity largely, or indeed even only, subsists in autonomy and autonomous behaviour, then, as advocates of aid in dying might do, one could say that she has taken the moral good of others' dignity into account, because by exercising her autonomy she somehow makes a stand for the right of others to have their autonomy recognised.[59] However, from Quill's account of her death, it is quite clear that she never intended to be a martyr for the cause of aid in dying. Moreover, from Quill's account, it is not clear that she even considered others' dignity in any way. He does say that she had long discussions with her husband and son about what she intended to do. She seemed to begin the process very carefully too, not wanting to get others into trouble. For example, according to Quill, she initially insisted that her request for barbiturates was to help her sleep. And she asked her husband and son to leave the room before she took them, presumably to make sure that they would not be held responsible for her death, although this is not clear from Quill's account. But in the end, *they* respected *her* decision, not the other way around. This does not, of course, conclusively mean that she did not respect those closest to her, or that she was not concerned about their futures and their inherent worth as well as their sense of self-worth, but it does muddy the waters somewhat. Sometimes, for example, though in this case it is not clear that this is a consideration, a person may say they want to die precisely because they claim they do not want to be a burden on other people, or cause other people to suffer for a lost cause. In such a case the emphasis is on others' dignity and autonomy. The patient's self-respect might, then, depend on being seen to be helpful and considerate of others (morally 'good' behaviour).

In the end, I would say that Diane's understanding of human dignity, as I have outlined it above would be inadequate if indeed it only emphasises individual autonomy. At the same time, one cannot know for sure that her understanding did not contain other elements that would have affected her behaviour in other ways, for example, in her dealings with her relatives. What my attempt to answer this question does demonstrate, however, is the value in the multidimensional Component Dimensions of Human Dignity model itself as a hermeneutical lens that can help us to unpack some of the ethical considerations and their existential meanings, which as I have said elsewhere, is an important part of the task of the ethicist (see 2.3.1.2).

(2) Are the social influences, mores, and circumstances that may have contributed to this understanding of human dignity, and are her interpretations of these mores, etc., legitimate and correct, or should they be called into question? Do they promote human life, flourishing and happiness and the personal sense that one has lived one's life well?

Again, as in the previous example, there are many aspects that could be addressed. I shall focus on one in particular, namely, the apparent normativity of autonomy to which Diane's understanding of dignity seems to be a response.

As said above, emphasising human freedom and autonomy is not only important, it is essential. In this regard, I agree with Dworkin. Nevertheless, an overemphasis on autonomy that neglects other goods and capacities and ways of being (for example, giving up one's autonomy to care for others) can have a significant downside that is a threat to an adequate understanding of human dignity. In particular, an overemphasis on autonomy potentially leads to an excessively narrow, and possibly dangerously self-centred view of dignity and morally good behaviour that does not take other possibilities and goods inherent in the concept of human dignity into account. In so doing, such a view of human dignity may tend to suggest that those who do not have or who no longer have the capacity to make autonomous, rational decisions about their futures

A Descriptive Category and a Normative Criterion 279

also do not have any dignity; or that those who find themselves in circumstances where the development of their autonomy is hampered by inadequate access to goods like education and healthcare and hence do not display the independence and self-sufficiency deemed worthy of society's respect, also do not have dignity, and are instead simply brutish; or that choosing to stay alive knowing that one will slowly deteriorate and lose one's capacities and autonomy, and become increasingly reliant on others is actually undignified. Such a suggestion would not be in accordance with a proper understanding of human dignity which affirms the inherent worth of all human persons by virtue of their being historically-situated corporeal subjects in relationship (see the Already poles of the Component Dimensions discussed in 3.4.). Following Dworkin, for example, a person who no longer demonstrates all of these capacities, like someone with severe dementia, nevertheless continues to have dignity and deserves to be treated as such in relation to her complete life narrative.[60] Moreover, exaggerated ideas of autonomy may promote an extreme form of individualism in which others' interests and well-being are irrelevant and one acts purely for selfish reasons. This too would not be in accord with a proper understanding of human dignity which inextricably ties one's own well-being to the well-being of others via the Social Component Dimension of Dignity.

(3) Are the moral choices that this person's particular understanding of human dignity inspires morally right or wrong?

In my answer to question (1) I pointed out that it would be difficult to say that this woman's idea of dignity is necessarily bad. It does not, for example, obviously rely on damaging someone else's dignity, even though it may nevertheless give inadequate expression to certain aspects of a proper multidimensional understanding of human dignity. Hence, it is likewise difficult to say whether the moral choice she makes to end her own life is objectively morally right or wrong.

The normative aspect of the Component Dimensions of Human Dignity holds, in accordance with the Behavioural Component Dimension, that a person acquires dignity through morally good behaviour in favour of the moral good of human dignity. As I have argued in answer to question (1), I don't believe that one can unequivocally say that her actions do not take into account all aspects of dignity as a moral good, i.e., her own inherent worth, and the worth of other human persons. Her aim is to die with dignity, and in a certain sense, one can argue that she does so. Quill's depiction of her and the last few months of her life, and even of the first few hours that followed her quiet and, hopefully, peaceful death in her home, certainly create the impression that she had a 'dignified' end. There was no embarrassment or shame, no regrets, no lingering in a semi-sedated state to control the pain. In so doing, she died with all the attributes of both her inherent worth and self-worth apparently intact. Moreover, by extension, one could argue that she did not disregard the dignity of others, and even worked for their good, by making sure that no one would be held criminally responsible for her actions or be subjected to the difficulty of watching her suffer a painful deterioration until she eventually died.

But the normative aspect of the Component Dimensions of Human Dignity model also holds, in accordance with the Social Component Dimension, that one's own dignity (My Dignity) can never be fully fulfilled as long as others are unable to fulfil their dignity, and that this is Not Yet the case. Indeed, it may never be the case, which is why this Social Component Dimension captures the eschatological proviso that was discussed both with regards to an adequate anthropology and an adequate understanding of the moral event (see 2.3.3.1). Human dignity can be understood as a formal norm that guides human behaviour as something that ought to be promoted. Nevertheless, the historicity of the human person means that every attempt to achieve the realisation of human dignity by means of concrete moral actions or even in the form of concrete material norms remains open to criticism in the light of differing interpretations of the formal norm of human dignity. The fullness of my human dignity, as a historical human person, is always Not Yet. The eschatological proviso, then, always challenges one to consider not so much whether a particular behaviour affirms human dignity, but whether it is the best way to affirm human dignity.

This latter aspect leaves one with a sense that, though it would perhaps be inappropriate to declare this woman's choice to be morally wrong or her intentions morally bad, her choice is nevertheless somehow self-defeating. She seems to have preserved her dignity by acting for the good of her dignity, and making sure that nobody else was put in jeopardy on account of her actions. But, one could also say that her choice undermined the dignity that she wanted to preserve. If, indeed, one can only truly realise one's dignity when others also realise their dignity, then one is forced to ask whether Diane's choice somehow undermines the Social Component Dimension. Or at least, that her choice was not wrong or bad or undignified, but that it may not have been the better choice, the more dignified choice. Considering the risks that are associated with an exaggerated emphasis on autonomy—as highlighted in the answer to question (2) above—such that those who do not demonstrate this autonomy, or socially acceptable versions of this autonomy may end up being considered undignified and unworthy of equal respect (as we have witnessed in the past for example in the practice of slavery, and racist and sexist laws), would it have not instead been better to accept the pain and suffering that her death would entail? That too would have been a testament to her autonomy (as were her previous struggles against adversity and abuse), but at the same time it would have been a testament to the dignity of all those who can *not yet* make that choice for themselves, for those who suffer indignities on a daily basis through social injustice, war, rape, poverty, and of course disease. It would have better captured the fullness of human dignity as something that encompasses our whole life: it is something we always have, and something we always long for. By choosing to end her life, I believe that Diane believed she could finally possess the dignity she longed for. But one can never fully possess it, because, as long as others live without it, it remains Not Yet. The eschatological proviso holds the fullness of human dignity out in front of us and asks us to live in a way that seeks to realise it for everyone, for in so doing we realise it in ourselves. I fear that in the end, Diane may have opted to realise it only in herself, and in so doing pushed the full realisation of the dignity of all just that little bit further away, made it that little bit more Not Yet.

In this answer to the third question, one can see how a proper understanding of human dignity avoids relativism. Diane did not take her decision lightly. She did not do what she did because she thought she could do as she liked, and that her freedom meant that morally-speaking anything goes. Those who helped her were apparently very much aware of the gravity of what she intended to do, as was she. I hope that the analysis I have performed here shows that I too comprehend the gravity of her choice and condemn neither her, nor it. But freedom comes with responsibility,[61] a responsibility to live a full and meaningful life in one's quest to realise one's dignity and, in the words of Pope John Paul II, as well as of Nietzsche and Pindar before him, 'become what you are.'[62] I believe that Diane honestly sought to live and die in a way that took that responsibility seriously. Nevertheless, one is more than just an autonomous being. One's dignity inheres in more than just one's rationality. One does not live alone. And for that reason, not all understandings of human dignity and not all attempts to realise one's dignity through one's moral behaviour are equally meritorious. Thus, though they may not be wrong, they may not always be the better option. And it is this better option for which we should strive, for in so doing we do more to make more people's lives more meaningful, ethically relevant, and dignified.

To sum up then, with regard to the concept's value as a normative criterion, the fact that it is possible on the one hand to affirm the moral good of the inherent worth that all human beings have means that it is possible to make moral evaluations of human behaviour based on the extent to which that behaviour and the desires that inspire it promote or inhibit the realisation of the dignity of all human persons. Thus, it stands as a corrective to moral relativism and to a purely relativistic, subjective, egotistical pursuit of dignity in which whatever vision of the dignified life one were to choose and whatever behavioural strategy one were to choose to attain that vision would be okay. On the other hand, the historicity of the human person means that all such attempts—that is, all interpretations of what this dignity is or should be, and the associated behavioural strategies employed to realise them, even those deemed morally good—are subject to the critique of a temporally unattainable and ineffable eschatological ideal. As soon as one makes a choice to pursue a particular moral strategy to fulfil one's dignity, one limits the notion of dignity and relativises it to one's own historical life experience. This is not relativism, but it is relative. The fullness of human dignity is always more than what any one person can say about it, greater than any one definition of it, and beyond what even the most exemplary human life reveals it to be. Like the notion of 'The Good', which has been debated in philosophy for millennia from Plato to G.E. Moore, the fullness of human dignity always escapes us and refuses to answer to a particular historical, and hence relative, attempt to realise it.

Endnotes

1. See, for example, the comments by Mieth, "Sozialethik als hermeneutische Ethik," 223 and 225; idem., *Moral und Erfahrung*, 124–128. Mieth maintains that a hermeneutical ethics must mediate between judgement, experience and praxis, and must do so by first seeking insight. See also, in this book, sections 2.3.1, and 2.3.3.
2. I have chosen not to deal with the issues of stem-cell research or abortion because, though human dignity is a concept that often comes up in these debates, I believe that there are too many additional nuances that need to be considered, for example with regard to understandings of potential, if one is going to treat the subject with the requisite thoroughness. Thus, due to space limitations, I have opted to use the other two issues to illustrate the value of a proper understanding of human dignity. That said, however, I do believe that further research with regard to how this applies in cases that involve human zygotes, embryos or foetuses, as well as non-embryonic human tissue, would not only be very enlightening but are also very necessary in the near future.
3. See Gilligan, *Violence*, 26. See also, Lee and Gilligan, "The Resolve to Stop the Violence Project," which provides a quantitative study of the successful implementation of a programme that operates based on the kinds of ideas elaborated on by Gilligan. The programme reduced the number of violent incidents in the experimental group from 24 per year to 1 per year. In the programme,... a consistent 'subculture' is created within the milieu by virtue of being an intensive, 12-hours-a-day, 6-days-a-week programme that teaches male-role reconstitution, accountability, empathy, alcohol and drug recovery, creative expression, and awareness of one's contribution to the community. Understanding the importance of environmental immersion, careful measures are taken to provide structural elements that are favourable to a shift in subculture: (1) direct supervision; (2) consistent supervision; (3) a racial and ethnic composition of instructors that reflect the population; and (4) positive role modelling with sworn staff and service providers so as to maintain a coherent message. This is done with the recognition that the acculturation process is multimodal, involving elements that are simultaneously taught at the conscious and didactic level, as others are absorbed more through the senses and the surroundings.

A Descriptive Category and a Normative Criterion   285

4. Gilligan, *Violence*, 98: "I use the term violence to refer to the infliction of physical injury on a human being by a human being, whether oneself or another, especially when the injury is lethal, but also when it is life-threatening, mutilating, or disabling; and whether it is caused by deliberate, conscious intention or by careless disregard and unconcern for the safety of oneself or others."
5. Ibid., 110.
6. See ibid., 98: "Health refers to those forces or processes within organisms and species that tend to sustain, protect, and preserve life, individual and collective."
7. See ibid., 47–49. Gilligan frequently uses various synonymous terms to make a point which can lead to the charge that he is being imprecise. Nevertheless, I believe his point is clear, despite the impreciseness of his language. So, while one might argue that there is a difference between, say, self-esteem and self-love, they both clearly express a sentiment that is the opposite of shame. In this book, I have opted for 'self-worth' as a generic term to express all of these sentiments. As I shall demonstrate below, because the terms are largely synonymous, what is really important is not the term, but what is meant by the term, i.e., what does a person believe they need to do or be in order to feel positive about themselves and their life?
8. This is why, according to Gilligan, most people are not violent, and even violent people are not violent all of the time: "… most people have non-violent means available to them to protect or restore their wounded self-esteem," such as socially rewarded economic or cultural achievement, or high social status (*Violence,* 112–114). Moreover, a *healthy* sense of self-love, or in my terms self-worth, is necessary in order to be able not only to deal with humiliation, but also to be able to love others at all. According to Gilligan, "Emotional health is not the absence of pain. It is the capacity to bear painful feelings when they occur, without letting them stop us from loving others and continuing to feel worthy of love ourselves. A person can expose himself to the vulnerability of loving another person only if he has enough self-esteem to protect himself from the devastation he would suffer if that love were not reciprocated" (*Violence*, 52–53).
9. Gilligan bases his theory of shame as a significant cause of violent behaviour on intensive interviews with violent criminals during his time working in the Massachusetts prison system. He has also spent time interviewing violent criminals elsewhere in the United States, Canada and the United Kingdom. Many times during these sessions he was

told by prison inmates who had assaulted other inmates that they did it because "'he disrespected me.'" Another prisoner made it clear that death held no fear for him as long as he had no self-respect: "'If you don't have your self-respect, you don't have nothing.'" He would therefore frequently attack other prisoners and guards if he felt they were disrespecting him. No punishment could deter him, as long as he perceived his actions as enhancing his self-respect (*Violence*, 105–107). Gilligan also explains why violence is more common among poorer or more marginalised communities by suggesting that societies are structured in such a way that such groups are permanently subject to feeling disrespected by the rest of society simply by virtue of the social policies in place. Societies with rigid class systems are a good example (see *Violence*, 185–190). See also Gilligan, *Preventing Violence*, 38–55.

10. Statistically, most lethal violence is committed by men against other men. For example, in the United States of America during 2001, 9.4 males per 100 000 were victims of homicide relative to 2.8 females per 100 000. And regarding perpetrators of homicide, "males were almost ten times more likely than females to commit murder in 2002" in the United States. See, respectively, National Center for Health Statistics, *Health, United States, 2004 with Chartbook on Trends in the Health of Americans*, 194; and Fox and Zawitz, *Homicide Trends in the United States*.

11. See Gilligan, *Violence*, 229–230 and 261–267; idem., *Preventing Violence*, 56–68.

12. See Gilligan, *Violence*, 82, 111–112 and 128–136.

13. Ibid. 52–58, 76: "Murder represents (for the murderer) the ultimate act of self-defense, a last resort against being overwhelmed by shame and 'losing one's mind', and attempt to ward off psychosis of 'going crazy.'" And p. 97: "The loss of self-esteem is experienced subjectively as the death of self. People will sacrifice anything to prevent the death and disintegration of their individual or group identity." But, since not all people experience shame to this degree, either because they have significant stores of self-love or because they have other means to feel good about themselves, not all people become violent killers.

14. Gilligan, *Violence*, 231: "Men are honored for activity (ultimately, violent activity); and they are dishonored for passivity (or pacifism), which renders them vulnerable to the charge of being a non-man ('a wimp, a punk, and a pussy,' …)." And p. 276: "The more impotent (and thus vulnerable to shame) people feel, the more they turn to violence, individual or collective, as the quickest way to regain the feeling of power—

even if that feeling is an illusion." See also Barker and Ricardo, *Young Men and the Construction of Masculinity in Sub-Saharan Africa:*, 5: "Young men who do not achieve a sense of socially respected manhood may be more likely to engage in violence, whether in ethnic clashes in Nigeria, in conflicts in Liberia and Sierra Leone, or in gang-related activity in townships in South Africa."
15. Gilligan, *Preventing Violence,* 53: "To feel shamed is to perceive oneself as being disrespected, and the most direct and rapid way to make others respect you is to make them afraid of you. This is, of course, an *ersatz* and costly form of respect which people have no need of when they receive genuine respect from others, or when their feelings of self-respect are strong enough to maintain their self-esteem independent of respect from others."
16. See Gilligan, *Violence,* 111.
17. The words of a convicted criminal quoted in James Gilligan, *Violence,* 106.
18. Gilligan's approach to the problem of violence is "bio-psycho-social." Gilligan states, "I view violence as a problem in public health and preventative and social psychiatry. My purpose is to arrive at an understanding of the causes of the various forms of violent behaviour, in the hope that understanding will help to clarify how we can most effectively and efficiently prevent such behaviour." *Violence,* 17. See also section 2.2.1.1 of the present book where I also argue against Gilligan's proposed avoidance of moral language as the only solution to moralism.
19. Cf. moral theologian Jan Jans's comment that "instead of using [human dignity] as a kind of universal stopgap, to consider it really as the beginning and not as the end of concrete ethical involvement." Jan Jans, "Enjoying and Making Use of a Responsible Freedom," 108.
20. See also Gilligan, "Shame, Guilt and Violence," 1155.
21. See also Pitt-Rivers, "Honor," in *International Encyclopaedia of Social Science,* 503–504: "the withdrawal of respect dishonors, ... and this inspires the sentiment of shame."
22. Gilligan, *Preventing Violence,* 36: "When people lack self-respect, and feel they are incapable of eliciting respect from others in the form of admiration for their achievements or their personalities, they may see no way to get respect except in the form of fear, which I think of as a kind of *ersatz* substitute for admiration; and violence does elicit fear, as it is intended to."
23. Gilligan provides a graphic illustration of this using the case of Ross L., a twenty-year-old man who murdered a former classmate and then

mutilated her eyes and cut out her tongue. Ross L. had been frequently beaten up and called similar derogatory names by other boys when he was growing up. Gilligan holds that the extreme symbolic violence of the murder are meant to convey a very clear message, namely "I am not a wimp, a punk, and a pussy," which Gilligan further paraphrases to say "I am not shameful," "I cannot be shamed by others, I will shame them instead," and so forth. See Gilligan, *Violence*, 59–66 and 75–78.

24. Gilligan, *Violence*, 230: "[The] code of honor requires men to inflict ... violent injuries on others of both sexes, but most frequently ... other males, whether or not they want to be violent ... ." See also Gilligan, *Preventing Violence*, 56–65. See also De Botton, *Status Anxiety*, 187–188, who points out that the most honoured men in Spartan society were soldiers. We still celebrate military heroes in media and reality today in much the same way. In the past, those who did not want to fight were called deserters. Conscientious objection has only recently been given legal protection. The notion of risking one's life to protect one's honour, or the honour of one's family, wife, daughters, and so on, is also evidenced in the practice of duelling, which in the past often ended in one or more of the duellists losing their lives. In popular culture, this idea has been immortalised in the image of a cowboy who saves the town from an evil gunslinger, gets the girl, and is made sheriff, or rides off dramatically into the sunset. See De Botton, *Status Anxiety*, 115; Baldick, *The Duel: A History of Duelling*.

25. Gilligan *Violence*, 110: "For we misunderstand these men, at our peril, if we do not realize they mean it literally when they say they would rather kill or mutilate others, be killed or mutilated themselves, than live without pride, dignity, and self-respect. They literally prefer death to dishonour." See also De Botton, *Status Anxiety*, 115: "In Hamburg in 1834, a handsome young army officer, Baron von Trautmansdorf, challenged a fellow officer, Baron von Ropp, to a duel over a poem that von Ropp had written and circulated among friends about von Trautmansdorf's moustache, stating that it was thin and floppy and hinting that this might not be the only part of von Trautmansdorf's physique imbued with such qualities. The feud between the barons had originated in their mutual passion for the same woman, Countess Lodoiska, the grey-green-eyed widow of a Polish general. Unable to resolve their differences amicably, the two men met in a field in a Hamburg suburb early on a March morning. Both were carrying swords, both were short of their thirtieth birthdays, both died in the ensuing fight."

26. See Hall, *The Ethical Foundations of Criminal Justice*, 195: "This concept of punishment as retribution is traditionally known as the principle of *lex talionis*, or the law of retaliation, which is metaphorically expressed in the Old Testament rule of 'an eye for an eye, and a tooth for a tooth.' ... Under the retributive theory of justice, punishment is justified simply because it is deserved."
27. One thinks immediately in this respect of the culture often seen in criminal gangs (Gilligan, *Violence*, 262–266). Nevertheless, Gilligan, among others, argues that state justice systems and violent criminals operate under a similar logic in this regard. The only difference is that the state engages in legally sanctioned punishment on behalf of the victim (See *Violence*, 18–19). According to Siegel, *Criminology*, 19, one of the arguments used in support of retributive justice systems that involve state-sanctioned punishment, including the death penalty, is that, "By punishing people who infringe on the rights, property, and freedom of others, the law shifts the burden of revenge from the individual to the state... . Although state retaliation may offend the sensibilities of many citizens, it is greatly preferable to a system in which people would have to seek justice for themselves." Nevertheless, within a given society there may also be several sub-cultures in which violent punishment for perceived disrespect is the norm. For example, Vidmar, "Retributive Justice: Its Social Context," 309, notes that "Retributive justice reactions occur in formal and informal settings as diverse as the nuclear family and large corporate organizations." So a boy might learn to violently punish those who disrespect him by watching his father beat his mother for a similar offence. For more on so-called "observational learning of aggression" see Fleisher, "Lost Youth and the Futility of Deterrence," 66.
28. Cf. earlier comments regarding Gilligan's notion of a healthy sense of self-worth versus the kind of pride that these violent men seek to attain which leaves them permanently open to the threat of shame (n. 8).
29. According to Gilligan, *Violence*, 183: "Attitudes such as arrogance, superiority, and self-importance, to which the term 'narcissism' is often attached, and which are so often misunderstood to be the genuine attitudes of the people who hold them, are actually defenses against, or attempts to ward off or undo, the opposite set of feelings: namely, underlying feelings of personal insignificance and worthlessness." Cf. the alternative hypothesis offered by Baumeister, Smart, and Boden, "Relation of Threatened Egotism to Violence and Aggression," 5–33; Bushman and Baumeister, "Threatened Egotism, Narcissism, Self-Esteem, and Direct and Displaced

Aggression," 219–229; Bushman and Baumeister, "Does Self-Love or Self-Hate Lead to Violence?" 543–545. These authors argue that exaggerated self-esteem (narcissism) rather than low self-esteem is a better predictor of violence. I maintain that Bushman, Baumeister et al. simply do not take narcissism back to its underlying cause as Gilligan does in the above quote, though this would be an interesting area of further research.

30. See, for example, among numerous others, Weitekamp and Kerner, *Restorative Justice: Theoretical Foundations*. For a more personal account of Desmond Tutu's experiences with the South African Truth and Reconciliation Commission, see Tutu, *No Future Without Forgiveness*.

31. See, among others, Gilligan, *Preventing Violence*, 114–130. Lee and Gilligan, "The Resolve," provides an overview of a programme implemented in a prison using ideas similar to Gilligan's and which significantly reduced the number of violent incidents. Other 'experimental' prisons that have recorded reductions in both prison violence and re-offending include the Barlinnie Special Unit, Grendon, and Blantyre House in the United Kingdom. See, among others, Cavadino and Dignan, *The Penal System: An Introduction*, 239–242; Duguid, *Can Prisons Work?*; and the autobiography of a notorious criminal who claims he was reformed by his experience in Barlinnie, Jimmy Boyle, *A Sense of Freedom*. For an extensive bibliography of studies into alternative sentencing and therapeutic jurisprudence, see the website of the International Network for Therapeutic Jurisprudence, under the directorship of Distinguished Research Professor Emeritus of Law David B. Wexler, accessed 27 October 27, 2009. http://www.law.arizona.edu/Depts/upr-intj/intj-cb.html.

32. See also Dworkin, *Life's Dominion*, 236, who argues that the right to dignity is the right to expect other people to acknowledge that your life matters, even though your chosen values may be flawed or dangerous. Your life has intrinsic value. Thus, when society puts people in prison it can still insist that in doing so it respects the dignity of the prisoner as a human being, struggling like we all are to make sense of life. But it imprisons the person because the particular convictions that the prisoner has chosen are dangerous to the intrinsic value of the lives of others. It is not just useful for us to lock him up and throw away the key. That would undermine his right to dignity. We must realise the gravity of what locking him up entails. Demanding that he be treated with dignity means that we still take his future, his ability to have critical interests and to desire integrity, seriously. We worry about what will become of him.

33. One could, following Kant, argue the opposite, namely that punishment is a moral good precisely because it respects the dignity of the human person as a responsible subject. As a responsible subject, he freely engaged in this course of action for which the consequences are the appropriate punishment. To not punish him would be to deny that he acted freely and responsibly, and hence would deny his human dignity. For a summary of this argument see Bedau, *Death is Different*, 16–17. Apart from the fact that the violent man might be following a similar logic in his own rationale, this deontological view of punishment and dignity is problematic in that it too is not based on an adequately multidimensional understanding of the human person. It does not take the historical situatedness of the subject into account which places limits on his freedom, and even his rationality, but which is nevertheless integral to what I have defined as a human person's inherent worth in line with Janssens' anthropology. The Kantian position makes no allowance for error, or circumstances, or for rehabilitation or reformation. Indeed, it even does not allow for a utilitarian argument that punishing the man acts as a deterrence to create a safer society, which would mean treating him as a means.
34. For one way of categorising various end-of-life decisions see, among others, Broeckaert, "Ethical Issues at the End of Life," 385–401; Broeckaert and Núñez Olarte, "Sedation in Palliative Care," 166–180.Dworkin himself categorises the different kinds according to the state of the person in question as follows. (1) Conscious and competent comprising (1a) unassisted (e.g. person poisons himself), (1b) assisted passive (turning off life-support machines of a conscious person) (1c) assisted active (a doctor administering a lethal injection at the request of the person). (2) Unconscious comprising (a) emergency (e.g. advanced directives concerning resuscitation of an otherwise healthy person in the event of cardiac failure) (b) not about to die (e.g. person in a persistent vegetative state). (3) Conscious and incompetent (e.g. a person with advanced Alzheimer's disease.). *Life's Dominion*, 183–190.
35. Dworkin, *Life's Dominion*, 239.
36. Ibid., 166.
37. See ibid., 224.
38. Ibid., 239.
39. See ibid., 221. "A person's dignity is normally connected to his capacity for self-respect."
40. See ibid., 70.

41. See ibid., 201–202. Dworkin distinguishes between experiential interests and critical interests. Experiential interests are things one finds pleasurable for their own sake, like watching a football match, or painful and unpleasant things that one would rather avoid, like going to the dentist. But, according to Dworkin, one would not say that a person lived a worse life because they had to go to the dentist. There is not (or should not) be any shame or regret in having to occasionally go to the dentist, regardless of how unpleasant it may be. Critical interests, by contrast, do carry this sort of weight for people; they believe that their lives would be worse off, and mistaken, if they did not recognise and satisfy these interests. These tend to be the kinds of things by which people would make critical judgements about what constitutes a good life. They are things that people should want, and hence there is an aspirational quality to them. Dworkin provides three examples: cultivating close friendships, having a good relationship with one's children, and a degree of success in one's work. They are the things that we do, not only because they are good at the moment, but because they say something about our character, about the "general style of life [we] think appropriate."
42. See ibid., 73–74: "It is not important that there be more people. But once a human life has begun, it is very important that it flourish and not be wasted."
43. See ibid., 236: "Dignity is the central aspect of the value we have been examining throughout this book: the intrinsic importance of human life."
44. See ibid., 11–14, 21–25, 28, 34, 69–71, 152–155, 237–241.
45. Ibid., 90.
46. See ibid., 90.
47. See ibid., 240.
48. See ibid., 234.
49. See ibid., 239.
50. Ibid., 205.
51. Ibid.
52. Ibid. 239.
53. Quill, "Death and Dignity," 691–694.
54. Dworkin, *Life's Dominion,* 205: "Of course, the ideal of integrity does not itself define a way to live: it presupposes substantive convictions."
55. See Ross, "Liberalism."
56. See, for example, Martha Nussbaum's treatment of shame associated with poverty and disability in liberal society in *Hiding from Humanity*, 286, 311, 318–319.

A Descriptive Category and a Normative Criterion

57. For example Quill, "Death and Dignity," highlights the fact that her own family felt it was important that they respect her choice: "We talked about what a remarkable person she had been. They seemed to have no doubts about the course she had chosen or about their cooperation …"
58. Farley, "A Feminist Version of Respect for Persons." See also Mitchell, *Morality: Religious and Secular*, 134.
59. This certainly seems to be why her case is recounted in books and articles, such as Dworkin's and Quill's, that advocate aid in dying and the respect and civil protection of personal choice in end-of-life decisions.
60. See Dworkin, *Life's Dominion*, 235–237. Cf. also Jackson, "A House Divided, Again: Sanctity vs. Dignity in the Induced Death Debates." What I call the Dignity We Have is similar to what Jackson calls sanctity of life, and what I call the Dignity We Acquire is similar to what Jackson calls personal dignity.
61. Cf. Vatican Council II, "Declaration on Religious Freedom (*Dignitatis Humanae*)."
62. See Pope John Paul II, "Familiaris Consortio," Apostolic Exhortation of Pope John Paul II to the Episcopate, to the Clergy and to the Faithful of the Whole Catholic Church on the Role of the Christian Family in the Modern World (November 22, 1981).

CHAPTER 5

GOD AND HUMAN DIGNITY

One of the criticisms raised in the introduction involved the relationship between the concept of human dignity and the belief in God. This is because, particularly among Judeo-Christian believers, the concept of human dignity is based on the idea that human beings are created in the image of God. So-called 'liberal' non-believers are therefore suspicious of the concept of human dignity because they see it as a cover for 'conservative' religious values. That may occasionally be true, but this should not be cause for dismissal of the concept of human dignity. Instead, the notions of human dignity that so-called liberals and conservatives alike claim to be using should both be subject to critique by a multidimensional understanding of human dignity like that put forward in this book.

I maintain, nevertheless, that such a proper multidimensional understanding of human dignity can easily be reconciled with a belief in God and the idea that human beings are created in the image of God, and still be accessible and relevant to non-believers. The key lies in how one interprets, theologically and anthropologically, what it means to be created in the image of God.

Throughout this book, in making the case for a multidimensional understanding of human dignity, I have largely avoided the discussion of God, and of creation in the image of God as the basis for human dignity, in order precisely to show that human dignity is a concept that is relevant for all human persons, believers and non-believers alike. Having shown that a case for the concept of human dignity can indeed be made without reference to God, I shall now show how the proposed vision of human dignity is nevertheless in accordance with a Catholic Christian theological perspective.

What follows are excerpts from a recent article in which I demonstrated how the Component Dimensions of Human Dignity model can be derived from the Second Vatican Council's Pastoral Constitution on the Church in the Modern World, *Gaudium et spes* (GS)[1] using a combination of a hermeneutic of suspicion and a hermeneutic of generosity. This entailed first breaking down what GS said in relation to human dignity using a hermeneutic of suspicion to point out potential conflicts and then reconstructing these using a hermeneutic of generosity. I shall limit myself here to demonstrating only the latter.[2]

GS has gone to great lengths to elaborate a complex and comprehensive understanding of human dignity that is expressly intended to function as a pivotal category in contemporary ethical discourse.[3] GS presents important developments in the Roman Catholic Church's thinking on the dignity of the human person.[4] What is particularly important to note for the purposes of this argument is that these developments were, in many ways, a response to "the methodological specialization of modern intellectual life [that] had increasingly led to competing conceptions of the human person."[5] Moreover, in its attempts to correct this confusion that these alleged ambiguities cause, "*Gaudium et spes* is the first conciliar text in the history of the Church that is addressed to all human beings."[6] Thus, since it is precisely such competing conceptions that lead to the ambiguity in the concept of the dignity of the human person that was criticised in Chapter 1 of this book, and since GS tries to address this problem in a way that speaks to all human beings, this document is a good place to look for a more complex, though nevertheless theologically grounded understanding of human dignity.[7]

5.1. The Existential Component Dimension
For the new social problems,[8] and spiritual and religious crises,[9] that human beings are faced with, GS proposes a solution based on the proposition that, "... man was created 'to the image of God,'[10] is capable of knowing and loving his Creator, and was appointed by Him as master of all earthly creatures ... ."[11] The use of the word "capable" provides the first insight into how GS sees human dignity as something that is Already and at the same time Not Yet. To say that human beings are created in the image of God means that the human person has the light of reason, the power of free choice, the ability to love and dominion over corporal things.[12] Thus, one can infer from this that the capacities of reason, free choice and love are inherent in the notion of human dignity in GS.[13] Therefore, this dignity one Already has can indeed be seen as a capacity, a potential.

In GS, dignity appears to have a Not Yet element, in the sense that it is something that is to be pursued and acquired. GS identifies the "root reason for human dignity" with the human person's "call to communion with God."[14] The human person has dignity because he "... would not exist were he not created by God's love and constantly preserved by it."[15] By being created in love, the human person is called to converse with the one who created him. This call is strongly evident in the biblical tradition—the call to a covenant relationship. What is also clear from the biblical tradition is that the human person is free to respond, or not, to this call. After all, "*Imago Dei* in man is the basis for human freedom."[16] This free response illustrates the Not Yet element of the Existential Component Dimension, namely that human beings acquire dignity by means of a positive response to God's call. According to GS, the human person "... cannot live *fully* according to truth unless he freely acknowledges that love and devotes himself to His Creator" (italics added).[17] Nevertheless, in the way that GS very subtly handles the question of atheism, the document acknowledges that this drive to fulfil one's potential, to seek the truth, or to find immortality as the case may be, is universal. In other words, though GS proposes a particular means to the acquisition of dignity,[18] it also points out that the drive to acquire it, even by what GS considers to be mistaken means, is universal.[19]

GS's claim that all people already have dignity as a result of the incarnation of the Son of God, can also be interpreted in a similar light.[20] In fact, this fits perfectly within the theological framework of the Already and the Not Yet. Though all human beings Already have dignity because the Son of God, through his incarnation, "… has united Himself in some fashion with every man,"[21] this is the precondition of our being able to fulfil our inherent potential, because, "Whoever follows after Christ, the perfect man, becomes himself more of a man."[22] Or, put differently, according to GS, it is by following Christ that you can 'become what you are.' Thus, at an existential level, the death and resurrection of Jesus Christ has made it possible for the Kingdom of God to come about, but it is a Kingdom that requires both human action, freely chosen, and God's grace, as human beings choose to become more like Jesus Christ, the perfect human being. Thus, according to professor of systematic theology at the Catholic University of Leuven Lieven Boeve, GS is a document that both acknowledges the modern striving for progress and emancipation—and values its desire to realise the fullness of humanity—and that, at the same time, points out modern ambiguities. As a correction it proposes that the ultimate fulfilment and completion of this striving can only be found in God.[23]

The next question, then, is how are human beings to go about fulfilling the dignity that inheres in their God-given capacities? How does the concept of human dignity relate to human moral behaviour?

5.2. The Behavioural Component Dimension

We have already seen that the way one acquires dignity has something to do with answering God's call to communion and with striving to imitate the example of Jesus Christ. What does that mean in concrete terms? I would propose that, in GS, the answer lies precisely in how one lives one's life in this world.[24] In other words, it is strongly associated with how we behave in moral terms. The idea that one acquires dignity via morally good behaviour is presented clearly in GS, 16 and 17. Key terms are italicised in the extracts below.

> 16. In the depths of his conscience, man detects a law which he does not impose upon himself, but which holds him to obedience. Always summoning him to love good and avoid evil, the voice of conscience when necessary speaks to his heart: do this, shun that. For man has in his heart a law written by God; *to obey it is the very dignity of man*; according to it he will be judged. ...
>
> 17. ... Man *achieves* such dignity when, emancipating himself from all captivity to passion, he pursues his *goal* in a spontaneous *choice of what is good*, and procures for himself through effective and skilful action, apt helps to that end.

Notice that it is not the law, but rather obedience to the law that is "the very dignity of man." Only through obeying one's conscience, the moral law of God in one's heart, by freely performing morally good action, is dignity achieved.[25] Dignity is thus both freedom and the correct use of that freedom.

Furthermore, from what has already been considered of GS it can be affirmed that dignity is a moral good, an end in itself, because it is the beginning and end of human existence. One cannot speak of human existence without speaking of dignity.

On one hand the moral good of the dignity one has is grounded in the fact that all human beings are created by a loving God and Already redeemed by His Son. If one loves God and responds to God's call, then this necessarily entails being morally good by loving all human beings, even those who do not recognise their dignity as a gift from a loving God, and who thereby put it in jeopardy through immoral behaviour; those "...

of our contemporaries [who] have never recognized this intimate and vital link with God, or have explicitly rejected it."[26]

On the other hand, dignity is a moral good because it is the active response to God's call. Here the emphasis is not on the moral good of the dignity of the human person in general, i.e., the inherent worth of all human persons, but on the moral good of the dignity that one acquires by responding to God, the dignity that is acquired by morally good behaviour in accordance with one's conscience.[27]

Thus, here too, at the behavioural level, dignity can be understood in terms of Already and Not Yet. It is Already a moral good. The human capacities that constitute human dignity should be protected and nurtured. But as a moral good is it also an end, both personal and social, that has Not Yet been realised and that is therefore pursued through morally good behaviour. The more morally good one is, the more one realises one's dignity. This brings us then to the next Component Dimension, namely the Cognitive Component Dimension. I have said that reason, conscience, and free will all constitute part of what it means to be human.[28] These can be grouped together under the idea that human beings are capable of conscious self-awareness. Thus, I shall next address GS's understanding of dignity at this level.

5.3. The Cognitive-Affective Component Dimension

The inherent worth of the human person lies in her being created out of love to the image of God. However, it must be asserted that in GS this means that a person has inherent worth because she is intelligent, free and has a conscience, or in other words, has the potential to acquire dignity by freely responding to the call of a loving God by obeying her conscience.[29]

However, it must likewise be affirmed that this inherent worth is not dependent on her realising any of these qualities. GS, 27 defends the idea of the inherent worth of a person regardless of her faults: "But it is necessary to distinguish between error, which always merits repudiation, and the person in error, who never loses the dignity of being a person even when he is flawed by false or inadequate religious notions." [30] In other words, even those who show no sign of acquiring dignity themselves Already have an inherent worth, a dignity that must be recognised as a moral good.

On the other hand, GS also links dignity with the idea of a sense of self-worth. I propose that this conscious self-appreciation is part of the Not Yet aspect of dignity, such that one becomes aware of one's potential, aware of one's being called by God (see for example GS, 16 mentioned above), and so sets out to pursue dignity by performing morally good behaviour, i.e., loving God and loving neighbour. One could say then that this sense of self-worth that has to be acquired can have two aspects, the first in relation to God and the second in relation to one's neighbour, or more broadly, one's society.

In the case of the first, the awareness that one is not only loved by the Creator of the universe, but that the incarnate God suffered so that one might never have to live in fear, replaces despair with hope and thus it must also replace the sense of worthlessness with a sense of self-worth.[31]

In the case of the second, a human person flourishes in a society in which their basic needs are met and they are able to contribute to the flourishing of others. GS, 9 states, "… it devolves on humanity to establish a political, social and economic order which will growingly serve man and help individuals as well as groups to affirm and develop the dignity proper to them." Consequently GS, 31 states that, "… a man can scarcely arrive at the needed sense of responsibility, unless his living conditions allow him to become conscious of his dignity, … ."[32]

This then leads to the Social Component Dimension.

5.4. The Social Component Dimension

"For by his innermost nature man is a social being, and unless he relates himself to others he can neither live nor develop his potential."[33] Co-operation among human beings is a key factor in the incredible technological progress that has been witnessed in the last two centuries. However, GS states that "... brotherly dialogue among men does not reach its perfection on the level of technical progress, but on the deeper level of interpersonal relationships. These *demand* a mutual respect for the full spiritual dignity of the person... . God, Who has fatherly concern for everyone, has willed that all men *should* constitute one family and *treat one another in a spirit of brotherhood,*"[34] (Italics added). By using the words "demand" and "should", GS, in almost identical wording to that of the 1948 United Nations' *Universal Declaration of Human Rights*, acknowledges that human beings do not yet always treat one another in a spirit of brotherhood. In this sense, even though human beings have dignity because they are created in the image of God, they have Not Yet acquired true dignity, i.e., the dignity that comes from respecting others' dignity. GS then cites the greatest commandment to support this: "Thou shalt love thy neighbor as thyself... . Love therefore is the fulfillment of the Law."[35]

In paragraphs 26, 27 and 31,[36] GS makes the link between the human person's inherent worth, a consequence of one's dignity as potential, and the rights necessary for living out this dignity. Without recognition of these basic rights and the performance of these duties, the human person's ability to realise her dignity is diminished. Thus, although one has dignity as a human person, one might not achieve the potential that this dignity affords one—by acquiring dignity in the sense of self-worth—if society doesn't recognise the inherent worth of that potential.

Ultimately, due to human failings and limitations, and the conditioning of our particular time and place,[37] GS maintains, in accordance with the eschatological tension of the Already and the Not Yet, that we shall always fall short of the ultimate acquisition of our dignity, even as we work towards it. Freedom is what has given us the power to think that we can seek and find our own solutions. But, our historicity means that no 'free' application of these capacities is entirely free, and hence will always be a limited and imperfect reflection of one's potential dignity. Nevertheless, the very fact that we pursue truth means that there is always hope.

> For after we have obeyed the Lord, and in His Spirit nurtured on earth the values of human dignity, brotherhood and freedom, and indeed all the good fruits of our nature and enterprise, we will find them again, but freed of stain, burnished and transfigured, when Christ hands over to the Father: 'a kingdom eternal and universal, a kingdom of truth and life, of holiness and grace, of justice, love and peace.' On this earth that Kingdom is already present in mystery. When the Lord returns it will be brought into full flower.[38]

ENDNOTES

1. Vatican Council II, "Pastoral Constitution of the Church in the Modern World (*Gaudium et spes*)."
2. Kirchhoffer, "Become What You Are."
3. See Eberstadt, "*Gaudium et Spes*,", 81–82. See also GS, 12.
4. See Dwyer, "Person, Dignity of;" see also Pope, "Natural Law in Catholic Social Teachings," 53–54, who identifies four key features: "a new openness to the modern world, a heightened attentiveness to historical context and development, a return to scripture and Christology, and a special emphasis on the dignity of the person."
5. Hollenbach, "Commentary on *Gaudium et Spes*," 277.
6. Hünerman, "The Final Weeks of the Council," 424.
7. I shall focus on Part I of *Gaudium et spes*. Part II is not addressed here because the analysis of Part I is sufficient for the purposes of this book. Part II focuses on more concrete problems and is therefore of less theoretical value in this research. Of course, *Gaudium et spes* is not the only Church document that makes mention of human dignity. A notable example would be the Declaration on Religious Freedom, *Dignitatis humanae* (1965). Nevertheless, despite its title, the latter's use of the notion of human dignity is primarily in support of the notion of religious freedom, whereas in *Gaudium et spes*, human dignity is the basis of a theological anthropology that is developed in order to provide orientation to the much broader discussion of the role of human beings and the Church in the modern world.
8. GS, 3.
9. GS, 4 and 7.
10. The link between the *imago Dei* and human dignity in GS is apparent from chapter V of the Theological Subcommission's preparatory document *De ordine morali christiano* published in the first volume of schemata and delivered to the council fathers in September 1962, which expressly links human dignity with the fact that man is made to the image of God. See Moeller, "History of the Constitution," 4–5.
11. GS, 12.
12. See Vatican Council II. Theological Subcommission, "De ordine morali christiano." The Latin states, "Humanae personae dignitas in eo sita est, quod homo ad imaginem et similitudinem Dei factus, et natura sua imme-

diate ad Deum ordinatus, rationis lumen, liberae electionis potestatem, amoris flammam, rerumque corporalium dominum a Deo accepit." The earlier preparatory document "De ordine morali" discussed by the Central Preparatory Commission in January 1962 put the chapter on dignity before the chapter on sin, thus making it chapter IV. Nevertheless, it contains similar language.
13. Incidentally, this association of the *imago Dei* with particular capacities also overcomes one of the (reductionist) criticisms of religiously-based notions of human dignity detailed in Chapter 1, namely, that since the claim that human dignity has a divine origin is a matter of faith and cannot be verified, human dignity itself should be called into question. These human capacities are observable, meaning that one can affirm human dignity regardless of one's religious beliefs.
14. GS, 19.
15. GS, 19.
16. Erhueh, *Vatican II: Image of God in Man,* 78. Erhueh traces the history and meaning of the term *Imago Dei* in GS. He includes an analysis of the use of the term in the various preparatory documents, including the "Vota et Consilia Episcoporum" and the so-called Seventy Schemata.
17. GS, 19. See also Ratzinger, "The Dignity of the Human Person," 146. "The faith that man is a partner speaking with God, called to enter into a community of love, created to see and love him, guarantees man a dignity which no one else can give him."
18. Cf. Vatican Council II, "Declaration on Religious Freedom (*Dignitatis Humanae*)." Henceforth referred to as DH. "Religious freedom, in turn, which men demand as necessary to fulfill their duty to worship God, has to do with immunity from coercion in civil society. Therefore it leaves untouched traditional Catholic doctrine on the moral duty of men and societies toward the true religion and toward the one Church of Christ" (par. 1).
19. See, for example, GS, 4, 10, 12, 13, and 18. Cf. DH, 2: "It is in accordance with their dignity as persons—that is, beings endowed with reason and free will and therefore privileged to bear personal responsibility—that all men should be at once impelled by nature and also bound by a moral obligation to seek the truth, especially religious truth. They are also bound to adhere to the truth, once it is known, and to order their whole lives in accord with the demands of truth."
20. See also Pope, "Natural Law," 54: "The doctrine of the incarnation generates a powerful sense of the worth of each person."

21. GS, 22.
22. GS, 41.
23. See Boeve, "De Crisis van Europa: Een Zaak van Geloof of Ongeloof?" 56.
24. For example, GS, 39 states, "... the expectation of a new earth must not weaken but rather stimulate our concern for cultivating this one. For here grows the body of a new human family, a body which even now is able to give some kind of foreshadowing of the new age."
25. Moreover, it would seem that dignity can be lost by not behaving in a morally good way. See GS, 16: "Conscience frequently errs from invincible ignorance without losing its dignity. The same cannot be said for a man who cares but little for truth and goodness, or for a conscience which by degrees grows practically sightless as a result of habitual sin." I would interpret this as saying that one's inherent dignity, like that of the violent criminal in Chapter 4.2, remains always intact, because the possibility always exists that one can fulfil that potential, for example with the help of God's grace. Nevertheless, the violent criminal has lost any acquired dignity by virtue of his habitual attacks on the dignity and life of others.
26. GS, 19. See also Vatican Council II, "Message to Humanity," 5. This statement, released nine days after the start of the Council, clearly names the dignity of the human person as a moral good to which Christians are called to direct their activities. Indeed, the Council Fathers appear to state that the dignity of the human person is one of the primary ends of the Council itself: "As we undertake our work, therefore, we would emphasize whatever concerns the dignity of man ... ."
27. See GS, 14: "... the very dignity of man postulates that man glorify God in his body and forbid it to serve the evil inclinations of his heart."
28. See also Verstraeten, "Mensenrechten en Menselijke Waardigheid," 222, who presents a similar interpretation of GS, 17 with regard to the relationship of freedom, reason and conscience to dignity.
29. For example, "For its part, authentic freedom is an exceptional sign of the divine image within man." GS, 17.
30. GS, 27.
31. Despite its strong emphasis on the requirement for faith in order to truly live out human dignity, GS does acknowledge the possibility that dignity can be achieved without it. "All this holds true not only for Christians, but for all men of good will in whose hearts grace works in an unseen way. For, since Christ died for all men, and since the ultimate vocation of man is in

fact one, and divine, we ought to believe that the Holy Spirit in a manner known only to God offers to every man the possibility of being associated with this paschal mystery." GS, 22. See also Moeller, "History", 50–51, 60 who mentions on several occasions that those tasked with drafting the texts went to great lengths to use language of universal appeal.
32. See also GS, 27: "... whatever insults human dignity, such as subhuman living conditions, arbitrary imprisonment, deportation, slavery, prostitution, the selling of women and children; as well as disgraceful working conditions, where men are treated as mere tools for profit, rather than as free and responsible persons; all these things and others of their like are infamies indeed. They poison human society, but they do more harm to those who practice them than those who suffer from the injury."
33. GS, 12. See also Hollenbach, "Commentary on *Gaudium et Spes*," 279, who argues that the "Council strongly emphasized the social nature of the person and stressed the implications of sociality for its understanding of justice. It challenged all individualistic notions of human dignity ... ."
34. GS, 23–24.
35. Rom 13:9–10. See GS, 24. In addition, "the fact that the human person, although or because he is a self-contained creature loved by God for his own sake, can only truly find himself by meeting and giving himself to others, has its deepest ground in the fact that his Creator himself subsists in three persons who are constituted by their mutual relationships." Semmelroth, "The Community of Mankind," 66.
36. E.g. GS, 26 states "... there is a growing awareness of the exalted dignity proper to the human person, since he stands above all things, and his rights and duties are universal and inviolable. Therefore, there must be made available to all men everything necessary for leading a life truly human, such as food, clothing, and shelter; the right to choose a state of life freely and to found a family, the right to education, to employment, to a good reputation, to respect, to appropriate information, to activity in accord with the upright norm of one's own conscience, to protection of privacy and rightful freedom, even in matters religious."
37. See GS, 4–8. See also Pope, "Natural Law ," 53–54; Dwyer, "Person, Dignity of."
38. GS, 39.

Chapter 6

Conclusion

Revisiting the Critique of Human Dignity

This book began with the statement of a primary thesis and an overview of the research claim being put forward. The primary thesis reads as follows: the dignity of the human person is a valuable, multidimensional concept for contemporary ethical discourse, because, properly understood, it can serve both as a descriptive category and a normative criterion. The concept, thus, provides the basis for a framework that can help to both understand and evaluate human moral behaviour.

This thesis and the accompanying detailed research claim constitute a response to recent criticisms that have called the value of the concept of human dignity into question for contemporary ethical discourse. Chapter 1 highlighted how the rise of 'dignity talk' in various contexts has given cause for this justified criticism of the concept of human dignity, a concept which is, unfortunately, often abused as a rhetorical weapon of moralistic diatribe.

Chapter 2 then sought to demonstrate that taking the critique in Chapter 1 seriously, and especially the problems regarding 'dignity talk' and the tendency towards moralism, does not necessarily have to entail a dismissal of the concept of human dignity from ethical discourse. On the contrary, provided one bases one's understanding of human dignity on (a) an appropriate understanding of ethics as hermeneutical, (b) a multidimensional understanding of the human person as a historically-situated, meaning-seeking and meaning-giving, corporeal subject in relationship, and (c) a multidimensional understanding of the moral event, then one can reconstruct a multidimensional understanding of human dignity that takes the criticisms seriously while simultaneously making a case for the continued value of the concept of human dignity for contemporary ethical discourse.

In this book, this multidimensional understanding of human dignity has taken the form of the proposed Component Dimensions of Human Dignity model developed in Chapter 3. The value of such a multidimensional understanding of human dignity as both a descriptive category and as a normative criterion was briefly demonstrated in Chapter 4. Of course, a great deal of work still needs to be done in applying this multidimensional understanding of human dignity to other areas of ethical discourse. Nevertheless, the two examples given in Chapter 4, though brief, do at least point to the potential of such a multidimensional understanding of human dignity as a useful hermeneutical tool to unpack the various existential and moral meanings involved in contemporary ethical issues. Moreover, such a multidimensional understanding of human dignity, underpinned by a hermeneutical ethics, helps to avoid the pitfalls of inhumane moralism and amoral relativism, while at the same time preserving the place of moral language.

This concluding chapter revisits the six main criticisms levelled at the contemporary use of the concept of human dignity that were summarised at the end of Chapter 1. The aim is to show how the multidimensional understanding of human dignity proposed in this book both takes these criticisms into account and constitutes a response that reinforces the concept of human dignity's value for ethical discourse rather than its vacuity.

Conclusion 311

6.1. Overcoming the Problem of 'Dignity Talk'
Section 1.7.1. said that an adequate defence of the concept of human dignity would have to be able to explain and offer a corrective to 'dignity talk'. 'Dignity Talk' is characterised by a clichéd appeal to the concept of human dignity to justify a rights claim or particular course of moral behaviour in a way that assumes that simply by making this appeal, the argument is won. The problem then is that opposing sides of an ethical debate might both end up using the concept of human dignity in this way without any explication of what they mean by human dignity, resulting in a deadlock. Therefore, an adequate defence of the concept of human dignity must be able to identify what is true and what is false in the understandings of the human dignity appealed to by the protagonists.

The Component Dimensions of Human Dignity model is constructed on the basis of a " both...and" approach. This means that it incorporates various bases of human dignity offered in 1.5 into an integrated, multi-dimensional whole that covers various aspects of human existence and experience along a temporal axis of the Already and the Not Yet.

As a result, as demonstrated in Chapter 4, it provides a useful lens through which one can identify those aspects most important to a particular person's understanding and use of the concept of human dignity in ethical discourse, and both how and why this understanding is at odds with other understandings. So, for example, in discussion with James Gilligan, it was able to identify the violent criminal's association of human dignity with a particular sense of self-worth based on fear. And, in discussion with Ronald Dworkin, it was able to identify the dying woman's association of human dignity with self-respect based on autonomous self-control. Moreover, where necessary, the model is then able to identify the inadequacies of such views to the extent that they do not take properly into account other aspects of human dignity. In so doing, the model invites a reassessment of the person's chosen moral behaviour based on these other aspects, most notably, in both cases, the idea captured in the Social Component Dimension, that one's own dignity depends on the dignity one affords others. The model thus serves a twofold purpose of, first, revealing what the person believes is really at stake, and then, second, also revealing what they may be overlooking in their moral decision-making process.

The combination of these two aspects means that, instead of two opposing parties simply repeatedly claiming that what the other party is doing is against human dignity, a hermeneutical enquiry into what they really mean, and what perhaps they should also take into account as ethically relevant and meaningful if they are to avoid an inappropriate reductionism, can begin to take place. This may or may not lead to the resolution of ethical conflicts, but it will at least make the protagonists aware of what is really at stake, and of the existential significance of their opponent's argument. I have shown that it is precisely with such a hermeneutical enquiry in mind that a proper multidimensional understanding of human dignity is particularly useful. Though this may not always overcome ' dignity talk' it is a step in the right direction, as it helps to return the focus to what is really at stake, namely the human longing to live an ethically meaningful and relevant life in relationship to the world and all of reality.

6.2. The Universal Claim *and* Particular Experience

Section 1.7.2 highlighted the fact that though numerous prominent documents state that all human beings already have dignity, this dignity is often not apparent in the particular experience of individuals. This in turn raises questions as to the alleged absolute inviolability of human dignity. If the latter is true, why is it apparently violated so often?

In Chapter 3, section 3.4.2, I explained how the Existential Component Dimension of Human Dignity with its Already and Not Yet Complementary Duality of The Dignity We Have and The Dignity We Acquire overcomes this criticism. By grounding the dignity that all human beings already have in the potential inherent in the human person as a meaning-seeking, historical, corporeal subject in relationship possessing numerous capacities, including, among others, the capacities to experience, judge, and engage in moral behaviour, it is possible to make a universal claim regarding human dignity despite the experience of its absence at times.

This universal claim is twofold, and is captured in the Already pole of the Behavioural Component Dimension. Human dignity is a moral good in two ways, first as an inherent potential, and second as the meaningful realisation of that potential. The latter is impossible without the former. But the former also places limits on the human person and his society, especially in light of historicity, that make the full universal realisation of the latter always Not Yet. Hence, the particular absence can be accounted for by the fact that dignity is also something that has to be acquired as the realisation of the potential affirmed as a universal good by the Already pole. This also accounts for the apparent relativity in both the experience of dignity and in the various behavioural strategies employed to acquire it. Nevertheless, as the Social Component Dimension reiterates, due to the relationship between the two senses of dignity as a moral good, whatever strategy one employs, one should strive, through one's moral behaviour in and through one's relationships, to work for the good of both the universal claim and its particular realisation as this promises to give one's life the meaning one seeks. In this way, though a degree of relativity in particular interpretations, experiences and behaviour may be inevitable, this does not mean that one has to accept moral relativism.

6.3. Human Dignity as Both the Ground and the End of Moral Behaviour

The criticism highlighted in 1.7.3 is similar to that in 1.7.2 just dealt with. This criticism is that there seems to be a confused use of dignity, especially in relation to rights discourse, whereby, on the one hand it is claimed that because human persons *have* dignity they have rights, while on the other it is claimed that human persons have rights in order that they can live with the dignity to which they aspire, or in other words, that human persons have a right to dignity.[1] This apparent contradiction was made evident in section 1.5, in which differing bases for human dignity were offered such that human dignity seemed to be either something that human beings already have or something to which they aspire.

Again in section 3.4.2, I demonstrated how the Complementary Duality of the Dignity We Have and the Dignity We Acquire takes this into account as already described in 6.2 above. Moreover, I maintain that the problem arises precisely when one tries to separate the two and treat the dignity one has as entirely distinct from the dignity one acquires.

If one only treats dignity as something that all human persons already have, then one might argue that dignity is the ground of human rights. However, at best one can then say that there is a deontological obligation to respect that dignity. In other words, one has to respect human rights because all human persons have dignity. This reasoning, however, radically reduces morality, since it removes any teleological incentives from the equation, which, as shown in the discussion on the multidimensionality of the moral event in 2.1.3.4 and 2.3.2.2, should not be done.

On the other hand, if one only treats dignity as some acquired sense of self-worth, then one could say that human dignity is the end of human rights or even claim that one has a right to dignity. However, I seriously question whether it is then even possible to formulate universal human rights, because one can only assert those rights that one believes are necessary for one's own sense of self-worth. Consider, for example, the violent criminal who insists on respect because he claims he has dignity, but who does not acknowledge any dignity in others.

The key to unravelling the problem, then, lies precisely in treating dignity as a 'both…and' concept, i.e., as both something that all human beings already have in the form of a potential, as well as something that all human being's desire as the full realisation of that potential. When speaking of human dignity as the *ground* of human rights one is talking of human dignity as an inherent *potential*. A potential always implies an end that would constitute the fulfilment of that potential, in this case the realisation of a sense of a meaningful life well lived. In other words, human dignity is the ground of human rights precisely because it is the end of human rights.

This becomes clearer when using another right as an example. Though rights are intended to guarantee certain basic goods to a person because these goods are good for a person, like life, autonomy, education, and so on, the very articulation of rights means that these goods are not always guaranteed. All rights articulations are, in other words, an attempt to concretely actualise goods that are otherwise only *potentially* present. The right to life, for example, is an attempt to guarantee that one can live out one's days free of the fear of randomly being killed by one's government. In reality, however, though one is alive today, one is only *potentially* alive tomorrow. One is alive, and one desires to be alive tomorrow. Because one is alive, one has rights. Because it is good for one to still be alive tomorrow, one also has a right to life.

The concept of human dignity functions as an umbrella term that contains within it many other goods, such as life, autonomy, and so on. Therefore, in a way similar to what has been said about life and the right to life, one can say that one has dignity, because one is alive, has a capacity to reason, and to act morally, and so on. At the same time, one desires the full realisation of this dignity tomorrow through the way one lives one's life. Because one has dignity as a human person, one has rights. Because it is good for one to realise the fullness of one's dignity as a sense of a meaningful life well lived tomorrow, one has a right to dignity.

The Behavioural Component Dimension helps to clarify this further. Human dignity is both the ground and end of moral behaviour, and hence of human rights, because human dignity is a moral good in two senses.

Because one seeks to realise the good of one's own dignity as self-worth (the first sense), one engages in what one believes to be morally good behaviour. But this supposedly morally good behaviour only truly moves towards realising one's own dignity if it is also objectively morally good such that it does not infringe on others' inherent worth (the second sense), and preferably enhances others' self-worth (see the Cognitive-Affective, and Social Component Dimensions). Thus, the realisation of the first sense (Self-Worth) depends on securing the second sense (Inherent Worth). The purpose of human rights is precisely to secure the second sense (i.e., the basic goods that constitute a necessary precondition for the healthy realisation of human dignity as self-worth) so that the realisation of the first sense (Self-Worth) becomes possible.

6.4. There Is Indeed Such a Thing as Human Dignity

Ruth Macklin[2] argued that human dignity is a useless concept, because ultimately what people really mean when they talk about dignity is simply respect for personal autonomy. I elaborated on this criticism in Chapter 1, especially in light of 1.5 which investigated the various bases of human dignity, by saying that it appears that when people appeal to human dignity they may in fact just mean something else, like life, autonomy, pride, etc. An adequate defence of dignity has to show that dignity has a meaning of its own, and that this meaning is relevant to ethics.

Though Macklin is right to say that sometimes dignity is used in ethical discourse when something else is meant (consider the strong link to autonomy in the case of the dying woman in 4.2), I have shown that, properly understood, human dignity refers to the multidimensional existential reality of the human person. Moreover, it is this multidimensionality that makes it so valuable to ethical discourse as a concept that can help us both to unpack the other meanings that people may associate with it, and to evaluate these. In this sense, the value of the concept of human dignity is precisely that it links together so many other concepts that are relevant and integral to human moral life such that when people use it in ethical discourse, instead of being the end of ethical discourse, the last decisive word, it actually constitutes the starting point of the real hermeneutical venture that ethics is supposed to be.[3]

6.5. The Concept of Human Dignity Can Still Be Based on Religious Doctrines and Be Accessible to Non-Believers

Bagaric and Allan, in particular, have argued that basing human dignity on religious beliefs, such as the idea that human beings are created in the image of God, is not really useful in a pluralised world. Moreover, harsher critics, like Steven Pinker,[4] have argued that human dignity is just a cover for a conservative 'theocon' agenda (see 1.6, and 1.7.5).

My approach in this book has intentionally avoided explicitly basing human dignity on religious beliefs. This was done in order to develop a multidimensional understanding that is valuable to and critical of all segments of the religious and ethical spectrum. Nevertheless, in Chapter 5, I have also shown, in light of a reading of *Gaudium et spes*, that the multidimensional understanding of human dignity described here is not in conflict with an adequate theologically based understanding of the human person created in the image of God. In other words, a proper religiously-grounded understanding of the human person should likewise be multidimensional and based on multidimensional understandings of the human person and the moral event.

In this way, the multidimensional understanding of human dignity proposed in this book is also able to act as a critique of inappropriate religious understandings of human dignity that mistakenly confuse human dignity with respect for God, as discussed in 1.6. Human persons do not have dignity because God made them; human persons have dignity because of what God made them to be. Therefore there is a distinct difference between asserting, as *Dignitatis Humanae* does, that there is a "... traditional Catholic doctrine on the moral duty of men and societies toward the true religion and toward the one Church of Christ" (par 1.) and asserting that "the right to religious freedom has its foundation in the very dignity of the human person" (par. 2). The former would not be possible without the latter. It is because of what one has been made to be (i.e. a person with dignity and all which that entails, such as freedom and conscience) that one is able to acknowledge in faith that one is made by

God and to love and respect God accordingly. Thus one cannot impose the religious aspects of this respect for God by coercion or trickery, for to do so would be to undermine the very human dignity that is a precondition of this respect for God. In other words, if, based on religious convictions, one wants to claim that human life is inviolable from conception to natural death, one must first show how this claim serves the realisation of a proper multidimensional understanding of human dignity and the flourishing of human life before one claims that not respecting this principle is an offence to God.

6.6. Human Dignity Is a Useful Descriptive Category and Normative Moral Criterion

Finally, the accusation that human dignity is a "vacuous" concept and hence of little use as a normative criterion has been shown to be wrong. It remains true that one-dimensional understandings of human dignity that seek to function purely as the normative basis for ethical arguments are problematic, as demonstrated in the discussion on 'dignity talk'. To that extent, at least, the critique is correct when it says that such usage may lead to a certain vacuity in the concept, the consequences of which are moralism and moral relativism (see 2.2.1, and 2.2.2, respectively). Nevertheless, I have demonstrated that the conclusion that human dignity is vacuous and hence of little use as a normative criterion is wrong, because such a conclusion is based on mistaken methodological assumptions regarding ethics as legalistic *techne*, an overemphasis on a hermeneutic of suspicion, and reductionist views of the human person and the moral event, such that human dignity is expected to function as a one-dimensional concept that can either mean this or mean that. I have argued that, on the contrary, in light of a hermeneutical ethics, a hermeneutic of generosity, and multidimensional understandings of the human person and the moral event, human dignity is not an 'either...or' but instead a 'both...and' concept. And that therein lies the richness and value of human dignity as a concept for ethical discourse. Indeed, this value exceeds that of simply being a normative criterion, because human dignity has also been

Conclusion

shown to be particularly useful as a descriptive category that facilitates the hermeneutical process of doing ethics by asking about the meanings involved in moral behaviour. Nevertheless, it has also been shown to have value as a normative criterion (see Chapter 4).

Now, it may be that the way in which the multidimensional understanding of human dignity developed here functions as a normative criterion is still not 'normative' with the kind of 'either…or' rigour that ethics as a legalist *techne* might prefer; it cannot be used to declare always and everywhere unequivocally whether something is right or wrong. But even if it could offer this kind of certainty, which I maintain no criterion absolutely can, it would undermine the very notion of a meaningful, well-lived, human life, something to which I believe all human persons aspire, and which underpins the very concept of human dignity itself.

Human dignity does not serve the law; the law serves human dignity. Law, like ethics, exists precisely because human persons long to realise a sense of a meaningful life well lived, and because they have to do so in a community of fellow travellers. Law exists to facilitate this journey and to make the highways safe from those who would seek to reach their destination at the expense of others.

More often than not, though, life is not black and white, and the moral choices we face are not unequivocal. Right and wrong is less often at stake than right and better. There is pre-moral good and bad in just about everything that we do. This is where law must needs give way to ethics. And it is for ethics that a proper understanding of the dignity of the human person, as, for example, presented here in the Component Dimensions of Human Dignity model, offers us a hermeneutical tool and a horizon of possibility. It helps us to distinguish the wood from the trees and to ask the right questions about the moral meanings that matter to us. It offers a vision of a world in which all human persons live out a fulfilling and meaningful existence in relationship to all that is, a life of dignity. And most importantly, it puts morality where it rightly belongs, not in books of law, but in the conscience of the human person searching for a meaningful, well-lived life in and through his or her relationships to others, the world, and God.

Finally, the model, by including the eschatological tension of the Already and the Not Yet, also serves a critical function, in that it stands as a caveat to the ideological certainties that human beings are so easily seduced into believing. It is a warning that reminds us that our humanity, though dignified, is nevertheless flawed, not only because it is always Already conditioned by a particular historical situatedness, but also because in the pursuit of the universal ideal of dignity, we are always in danger of being too sure that we have found the ultimate way to bring the Not Yet to fruition. Thus, it represents an 'eschatological proviso' that says that as we work to realise our own dignity and the dignity of others, we should do so humbly in the hope that the means we choose to reach our end are indeed worthy of the end we seek to attain. In the words of the prophet Micah, "He has told you, O mortal, what is good; and what does the Lord require of you but to do justice, and to love kindness, and to walk humbly with your God?" (6:8, NRSV).

ENDNOTES

1. It is also true that one could say that human rights are ends in themselves. This, nevertheless, still leaves one with the problem of how to adjudicate between competing rights claims. It is at this point that appeals are often made to human dignity with the consequent rise of 'dignity talk'. Therefore, how the concept of human dignity and human rights are related to one another is still important.
2. See Macklin, "Dignity is a Useless Concept."
3. See Jans, "Enjoying and Making Use of a Responsible Freedom," 108: "… the reference to human dignity is not a shortcut allowing to dispense from the handicraft of concrete ethics, but first and most the indication that there are indeed serious ethical questions facing us, questions that challenge us as concrete subjects to bring to bear on them our responsible freedom." See also Selling, "The Polarity of Ethical Discourse," who states, "… 'ethics' refers to the study of how persons make and carry out ethical decisions." And further on he states, "Ethicists don't tell people what to do or not to do. They provide information or awareness about the things that people might take into account in determining their own decision-making and behavior."
4. Pinker, "The Stupidity of Dignity."

Bibliography

Aquinas, Thomas. *Summa Theologiae,* vol. 16. Edited by Thomas Gilby O.P. Cambridge: Blackfriars, 1969.

Aristotle. *Politica.* Translated by Benjamin Jowett. In *The Basic Works of Aristotle,* ed. Richard McKeon, 1127–1324. New York: Random House, 1941.

Aristotle. *Physics.* Translated by Robin Waterfield. Oxford: Oxford University, 1996.

Aristotle. *The Metaphysics.* Translated by Hugh Lawson-Tancred. London: Penguin Classics, 1998.

Aristotle. *The Nicomachean Ethics.* Translated by J.A.K. Thomson, revised with notes and appendices by Hugh Tredennick. London: Penguin Classics, 1976; 2004.

Arnold, Robert M., and Stuart J. Youngner. "The Dead Donor Rule: Should We Stretch it, Bend it, or Abandon it?" *Kennedy Institute of Ethics Journal* 3, no. 2 (1993): 263–278.

Ashby, Warren. "Teleology and Deontology in Ethics." *Journal of Philosophy* 47, no. 26 (1950): 765–773.

Ausloos, Hans, and Bénédicte Lemmelijn. *De bijbel: een (g)oude(n) gids. Bijbelse antwoorden op menselijke vragen.* Leuven: Acco, 2005.

Ausloos, Hans, and Bénédicte Lemmelijn. *The Book of Life. Biblical Answers to Existential Questions.* Translated by David Kirchhoffer. Louvain Theological and Pastoral Monographs, 41. Leuven: Peeters; Cambridge: William B. Eerdmans, 2009.

Bagaric, Mirko, and James Allan. "The Vacuous Concept of Dignity." *Journal of Human Rights* 5 (2006): 257–270.

Baghramian, Maria. *Relativism.* The Problems of Philosophy. London: Routledge, 2004.

Baier, Annette C. "Moralism and Cruelty: Reflection on Hume and Kant." *Ethics* 103, no. 3 (1993): 436–437.

Baker-Fletcher, Garth. "Somebodyness and Self-Respect: Themes of Dignity in Martin Luther King and Malcolm X." *Union Seminary Quarterly Review* 48, no. 1–2 (1994): 7–18.

Baldick, Robert. *The Duel: A History of Duelling.* London: Hamlyn, 1970.

Barker, Gary, and Christine Ricardo. *Young Men and the Construction of Masculinity in Sub-Saharan Africa: Implications for HIV/AIDS, Conflict and Violence.* Social Development Papers: Conflict Prevention and Reconstruction, no. 26. Washington, DC: World Bank, 2005.

Baumeister, Roy F., Laura Smart, and Joseph M. Boden. "Relation of Threatened Egotism to Violence and Aggression: the Dark Side of High Self-Esteem." *Psychological Review* 103, no. 1 (1996): 5–33.

Bayertz, Kurt. "Human Dignity: Philosophical Origin and Scientific Erosion of an Idea." In *Sanctity of Life and Human Dignity,* edited by Kurt Bayertz, 73–90. Philosophy and Medicine, no. 52. Dordrecht: Kluwer Academic, 1996.

Bayertz, Kurt. "Introduction: Sanctity of Life and Human Dignity." In *Sanctity of Life and Human Dignity,* edited by Kurt Bayertz, xi–xix. Philosophy and Medicine, no. 52. Dordrecht: Kluwer Academic, 1996.

Beattie, Tina. *The New Atheists: The Twilight of Reason and the War on Religion.* London: Darton, Longman, and Todd, 2007.

Beauchamp, Tom L., and James F. Childress. *Principles of Biomedical Ethics,* 5th ed. New York: Oxford University, 2001.

Bedau, Hugo Adam. *Death is Different: Studies in the Morality, Politics and Law of Capital Punishment.* Hannover, MA: Northeastern University, 1987.

Benedict XVI. Address to the Members of the Pontifical Academy of Sciences. November 6, 2006. http://www.vatican.va/holy_father/benedict_xvi/index.htm.

Benedict XVI. Address to the Members of the "Pro Petri Sede" and "Etrennes Pontificales" Associations. October 30, 2006. http://www.vatican.va/holy_father/benedict_xvi/index.htm.

Benedict XVI. Address to the Participants in the Symposium on the Theme: "Stem Cells: What Future for Therapy?" Organized by the Pontifical Academy for Life. September 16, 2006. http://www.vatican.va/holy_father/benedict_xvi/index.htm.

Benedict XVI. Common Declaration by His Holiness Benedict XVI and His Beatitude Christodoulos, Archbishop of Athens and All Greece. December 14, 2006. http://www.vatican.va/holy_father/benedict_xvi/index.htm.

Benedict XVI. Letter to Card. Walter Kasper on the occasion of the Second Conference on Peace and Tolerance, organized by the Ecumenical Patriarchate of Constantinople in conjunction with the Appeal of Conscience Foundation. November 4, 2005. http://www.vatican.va/holy_father/benedict_xvi/index.htm.

Benedict XVI. Letter to H.E. Mr. Roh Moo-hyun, President of the Republic of Korea. February 15, 2007. http://www.vatican.va/holy_father/benedict_xvi/index.htm.

Benedict XVI. Letter to Jean-Louis Cardinal Tauran on the Occasion of the Colloquium organized by UNESCO in Paris. May 24, 2005. http://www.vatican.va/holy_father/benedict_xvi/index.htm.

Benedict XVI. Letter to the Italian Bishops on occasion of the 55th General Assembly held in Assisi. November 10, 2005. http://www.vatican.va/holy_father/benedict_xvi/index.htm.

Benedict XVI. "The Human Person, the Heart of Peace," Message for the Celebration of the World Day of Peace. January 1, 2007. http://www.vatican.va/holy_father/benedict_xvi/index.htm.

Bengtsson, Jan Olof. *The Worldview of Personalism: Origins and Early Development*. Oxford Theological Monographs. Oxford: Oxford University, 2006.

Bernardin, Joseph Cardinal. *The Consistent Ethic of Life*. Edited by Thomas G. Fuechtmann. Kansas City: Sheed & Ward, 1988.

Bernasconi, Robert. "Hermeneutics." In *Dictionary of Ethics, Theology and Society*, edited by Paul Barry Clarke and Andrew Linzey, 429–431. London: Routledge, 1996.

Beyleveld, Deryck, and Roger Brownsword. *Human Dignity in Bioethics and Biolaw*. Oxford: Oxford University, 2001.

Birnbacher, Dieter. *Analytische Einführung in die Ethik,* 2nd ed. Berlin: De Gruyter, 2007.

Birnbacher, Dieter. "Hilft der Personen Begriff bei der Lösung bioethischer Fragestellungen?" In *Menschenleben – Menschenwürde,* edited by Walter Schweidler, Herbert A. Neumann, and Eugen Brysch, 31–44. Berlin: LIT Verlag, 2003.

Boeve, Lieven. "De Crisis van Europa: Een Zaak van Geloof of Ongeloof?" *Bijdragen, International Journal in Philosophy and Theology* 67 (2006): 152–179.

Bostrom, Nick. "Dignity and Enhancement." In *Human Dignity and Bioethics: Essays Commissioned by the President's Council on Bioethics,* edited by President's Council on Bioethics, 173–206. Washington, DC: *n.p.*, 2008.

Bostrom, Nick. "In Defense of Posthuman Dignity." *Bioethics* 19, no. 3 (2005): 203–214.

Boyle, Jimmy. *A Sense of Freedom*. London: Pan, 1977.

Bradley, Francis Herbert. *Ethical Studies,* 2nd ed. Introduction by Richard Wollheim. Oxford: The Clarendon Press, 1927. Reissue, Oxford: Oxford University, 1988.

Brenner, M. Harvey. *Mental Illness and the Economy*. Cambridge, MA: Harvard University, 1973.

Brenner, M. Harvey. "Personal Stability and Economic Security." *Social Policy* 8, no. 1 (1977): 2–4. Referred to in James Gilligan, *Violence: Reflections on a National Epidemic,* 196. New York: Vintage Books, 1997.

Bretzke, James T. *Consecrated Phrases: a Latin Theological Dictionary,* 2nd ed. Collegeville, MN: Liturgical Press, 2003.

Broeckaert, Bert. "Ethical Issues at the End of Life: a very short introduction." In *Palliative Care Nursing: Principles and Evidence for Practice,* edited by Sheila Payne, Jayne Seymour, and Christine Ingleton, 385–401. Maidenhead: Open University Press, 2004.

Broeckaert, Bert, and Juan Manuel Núñez Olarte. "Sedation in Palliative Care: Facts and Concepts." In *The Ethics of Palliative Care: European Perspectives,* edited by Henk ten Have and David Clark, 166–180. Buckingham: Open University Press, 2002.

Broesterhuizen, Marcel. "Doofheid: beperking of kracht." *Tijdschrift voor Theologie* 43, no. 1 (2003): 53–77.

Browning, Don S. "Human Dignity, Human Complexity and Human Goods." In *God and Human Dignity,* edited by R. Kendall Soulen and Linda Woodhead, 299–316. Grand Rapids, MI: William B. Eerdmans, 2006.

Burggraeve, Roger. "Meaningful Living and Acting. An Ethical and Educational-Pastoral Model in Christian Perspective (Part I)." *Louvain Studies* 13 (1988): 3–26.

Burggraeve, Roger. "Meaningful Living and Acting. An Ethical and Educational-Pastoral Model in Christian Perspective (Part II)," *Louvain Studies* 13 (1988): 137–160.

Burggraeve, Roger, and Ilse Van Halst. *Al de Vragen van Ons Leven.* Tielt: Lannoo, 2005.

Burrow, Rufus, Jr. *Personalism: A Critical Introduction.* St. Louis, MO: Chalice Press, 1999.

Burrow, Rufus, Jr. *James H. Cone and Black Liberation Theology.* Jefferson: McFarland, 1994.

Bushman, Brad J., and Roy F. Baumeister. "Does Self-Love or Self-Hate Lead to Violence?" *Journal of Research in Personality* 36, no. 6 (2002): 543–545.

Bushman, Brad J., and Roy F. Baumeister. "Threatened Egotism, Narcissism, Self-Esteem, and Direct and Displaced Aggression: Does Self-Love or Self-Hate Lead to Violence?" *Journal of Personality and Social Psychology* 75, no. 1 (1998): 219–229.

Catechism of the Catholic Church. Nairobi: Paulines-Mambo Press, 1994.

Cavadino, Michael, and James Dignan. *The Penal System: An Introduction,* 4th ed. London: Sage, 2007.

Chaskalson, Arthur. "Human Dignity as a Constitutional Value." In *The Concept of Human Dignity in Human Rights Discourse*, edited by David Kretzmer and Eckart Klein, 133–144. The Hague: Kluwer, 2002.

Christie, Dolores L. *Last Rights: a Catholic Perspective on End-of-Life Decisions*. Oxford: Sheed and Ward, 2003.

Coppens, Charles. *A Brief Text-book of Moral Philosophy. n.p.*: Catholic School Book Company, 1895.

Cuddeback, Kateryna Fedoryka, and Paulina Taboada. "Introduction." In *Person, Society and Value: Towards a Personalist Concept of Health*, edited by Paulina Taboada, Kateryna Fedoryka Cuddeback, and Patricia Donohue-White, 1–18. Philosophy and Medicine, no. 72. Dordrecht: Kluwer Academic, 2002.

Curran, Charles E. "Absolute Moral Norms." In *Christian Ethics: An Introduction*, edited by Bernard Hoose, 72–83. London: Cassell, 1998.

Curran, Charles E. *Catholic Moral Theology in the United States: A History*. Washington, DC: Georgetown University, 2008.

Curran, Charles E., and Richard A. McCormick, eds. *Natural Law and Theology*. Readings in Moral Theology, no. 7. New York: Paulist Press, 1991.

Davis, F. Daniel. "Human Dignity and Respect for Persons: a Historical Perspective on Public Bioethics." In *Human Dignity and Bioethics: Essays Commissioned by the President's Council on Bioethics*, edited by President's Council on Bioethics, 19–36. Washington, DC: *n.p.*, 2008.

Dawkins, Richard. *The God Delusion*. New York: Houghton Mifflin Harcourt, 2006.

De Botton, Alain. *Status Anxiety*. London: Hamish Hamilton, 2004.

Demmer, Klaus. *Shaping the Moral Life: An Approach to Moral Theology*. Translated by Roberto Dell'Oro, edited by James F. Keenan. Washington DC: Georgetown University, 2000.

Dennett, Daniel C. *Darwin's Dangerous Idea: Evolution and the Meanings of Life*. New York: Simon and Schuster, 1995.

De Stexhe, Guillaume. "The Sense of Ethics in Human Existence." In *Matter of Breath: Foundations for Professional Ethics*, edited by Guillaume de Stexhe and Johan Verstraeten, 59–88. European Ethics Network Core Materials for the Development of Courses in Professional Ethics. Leuven: Peeters, 2000.

De Tavernier, Johan. "The Historical Roots of Personalism. From Renouvier's *Le Personnalisme*, Mounier's *Manifeste au service du personnalisme* and Maritain's *Humanisme intégral* to Janssens's *Personne et Société*." *Ethical Perspectives* 16, no. 3 (2009): 361-392.

Dewey, John. *Lectures on Ethics, 1900–1901*. Edited and with an introduction by Donald F. Koch. Carbondale, IL: Southern Illinois University, 1991; paperback edition, 2008.

Dicke, Klaus. "The Founding Function of Human Dignity in the Universal Declaration of Human Rights." In *The Concept of Human Dignity in Human Rights Discourse*, edited by David Kretzmer and Eckart Klein, 111–120. The Hague: Kluwer, 2002.

DiSanto, Ron. "The Threat of Commodity-Consciousness to Human Dignity." In *Made in God's Image: The Catholic Vision of Human Dignity*, edited by Regis Duffy and Angelus Gambatese, 54–82. New York: Paulist Press, 1999.

Drenth von Februar, Marjolijn. "A Better Life for All: Globalisation and Human Dignity." In *Globalisation and Human Dignity: Sources and Challenges in Catholic Social Thought*, edited by Wim van de Donk, Richard Steenvoorde, and Stefan Waanders, 17–71. Budel: Damon, 2004.

Dresser, Rebecca. "Human Dignity and the Seriously Ill Patient." In *Human Dignity and Bioethics: Essays Commissioned by the President's Council on Bioethics*, edited by President's Council on Bioethics, 505–512. Washington, DC: n.p., 2008.

Dreyfus, Hubert. "Beyond Hermeneutics: Interpretation in Late Heidegger and Recent Foucault." In *Hermeneutics: Questions and Prospects*, edited by Gary Shapiro and Alan Sica, 66–83. Amherst: University of Massachusetts, 1984; paperback edition, 1988.

Driver, Julia. *Ethics: The Fundamentals*. Oxford: Blackwell, 2007.

Duguid, Stephen. *Can Prisons Work? The Prisoner as Object and Subject in Modern Corrections.* Toronto: University of Toronto, 2000.

Dunn, James D.G. *The Theology of Paul the Apostle.* Grand Rapids, MI: Eerdmans, 1998; paperback edition, 2006.

Dworkin, Ronald. *Life's Dominion: An Argument about Abortion, Euthanasia and Individual Freedom.* New York: Knopf, 1993; New York: Vintage Books, 1994.

Dwyer, John C. "Person, Dignity of." In *The New Dictionary of Catholic Social Thought,* edited by Judith A. Dwyer, 724–737. Collegeville: The Liturgical Press, 1994.

Eberstadt, Mary. "Gaudium et Spes." In *A Century of Catholic Social Teaching,* edited by George Weigel and Robert Royal, 81–82. Washington, DC: Ethics and Public Policy Centre, 1991.

Eckert, Joern. "Legal Roots of Human Dignity in German Law." In *The Concept of Human Dignity in Human Rights Discourse,* edited by David Kretzmer and Eckart Klein, 41–54. The Hague: Kluwer, 2002.

Egonsson, Dan. *Dimensions of Dignity: The Moral Importance of Being Human.* Dordrecht: Kluwer, 1998.

Erhueh, Anthony O. *Vatican II: Image of God in Man.* Rome: Urbaniana University, 1987.

Fackenheim, Emil. "Nazi 'Ethic', Nazi Weltanschauung and the Holocaust: A Review Essay." *Jewish Quarterly Review* 83, no. 1–2 (1992): 167–172.

Farley, Margaret A. "A Feminist Version of Respect for Persons." *Journal of Feminist Studies in Religion* 9, no. 1–2 (1993): 183–198.

Fehr, Ernst, and Simon Gächter. "The Puzzle of Human Cooperation." *Nature* 421 (2003): 912.

Finnis, John. *Moral Absolutes: Tradition, Revision, and Truth.* Washington, DC: Catholic University of America, 1991.

Fleisher, Mark. "Lost Youth and the Futility of Deterrence." In *The Use of Punishment,* edited by Seán McConville, 89–115. Cullompton: Willan, 2003.

Fox, James Alan, and Marianne W. Zawitz. "Homicide Trends in the United States: 2002 Update." *Bureau of Justice Statistics Crime Brief* NCJ 204885 (November 2004).

Frankena, William K. *Ethics,* 2nd ed. Englewood Cliffs, NJ: Prentice Hall, 1973.

Frankena, William K. "McCormick and the Traditional Distinction." In *Doing Evil to Achieve Good,* edited by Richard A. McCormick and Paul Ramsey, 145–164. Chicago: Loyola University, 1978.

Frankfurt, Harry G. "Freedom of the Will and the Concept of a Person." *Journal of Philosophy* 68 (1971): 5–20.

Frankl, Victor E. *Man's Search for Meaning.* Boston: Beacon Press, 1959; revised paperback edition, New York: Pocket Books, 1985.

Fries, Heinrich. *Fundamental Theology.* Translated by Robert J. Daly. Washington, DC: Catholic University of America, 1996.

Fuchs, Esther. "Points of Resonance." In *On the Cutting Edge: The Study of Women in Biblical Worlds: Essays in Honor of Elisabeth Schüssler Fiorenza,* edited by Jane Schaberg, Alice Bach, and Esther Fuchs, 1–20. New York: Continuum, 2003.

Fuchs, Josef. *Human Values and Christian Morality.* Translated by M. H. Heelan, Maeve McRedmond, Erika Young, and Gerard Watson. Dublin: Gill and Macmillan, 1970.

Fukuyama, Francis. *Our Posthuman Future: Consequences of the Biotechnology Revolution.* London: Profile Books, 2002; paperback edition 2003.

Gadamer, Hans-Georg. "The Hermeneutics of Suspicion." In *Hermeneutics: Questions and Prospects*, edited by Gary Shapiro and Alan Sica, 54–65. Amhurst: University of Massachusetts, 1984; paperback edition, 1988.

Gadamer, Hans-Georg. *Truth and Method,* 2nd revised ed. Translation revised by Joel Weinsheimer and Donald G. Marshall. London: Continuum, 1989; 2004.

Gewirth, Alan. *Reason and Morality.* Chicago: University of Chicago, 1978.

Gilligan, James. *Preventing Violence*. Prospects for Tomorrow. New York: Thames and Hudson, 2001.

Gilligan, James. "Punishment and Violence: Is the Criminal Law Based on One Huge Mistake?" *Social Research* 67, no. 3 (2000): 745–772.

Gilligan, James. "Shame, Guilt and Violence." *Social Research* 70, no. 4 (2003): 1149–1180.

Gilligan, James. *Violence: Reflections on a National Epidemic*. New York: Putnam Books, 1996; New York: Vintage Books, 1997.

Glendon, Mary Ann. *Rights Talk: the Impoverishment of Political Discourse*. New York: Maxwell Macmillan International, 1993.

Graham, Mark E. *Josef Fuchs on Natural Law*. Washington, DC: Georgetown University, 2002.

Grisez, Germain, and Russell Shaw. *Fulfillment in Christ: A Summary of Christian Moral Principles*. Notre Dame, IN: University of Notre Dame, 1991.

Gula, Richard M. *Reason Informed by Faith: Foundations of Catholic Morality*. Mahwah, NJ: Paulist Press, 1989.

Gutiérrez, Gustavo. *A Theology of Liberation: History, Politics and Salvation*. Revised edition. New York: Maryknoll, 1988.

Haas, Peter J. "Doing Ethics in an Age of Science." In *Good and Evil After Auschwitz: Ethical Implications for Today,* edited by Jack Bemporad, John T. Pawlikowski, and Joseph Sievers, 109–118. Hoboken, NJ: Ktav Publishing, 2000.

Haas, Peter J. *Morality After Auschwitz: The Radical Challenge of the Nazi Ethic*. Philadelphia: Fortress, 1988.

Hall, Richard A. Spurgeon. *The Ethical Foundations of Criminal Justice*. Boca Raton, FL: CRC Press, 2000.

Hamel, Ronald P., and James J. Walter, eds. *Artificial Nutrition and Hydration and the Permanently Unconscious Patient: The Catholic Debate*. Washington DC: Georgetown University, 2007.

Harris, Sam. *The End of Faith: Religion, Terror, and the Future of Reason*. New York: W.W. Norton and Co., 2004.

Bibliography 333

Heidegger, Martin. *Gelassenheit*. Pfullingen: Neske, 1959.

Heidegger, Martin. *Being and Time*. Oxford: Blackwell, 1962. Reprint, 2005.

Hitchens, Christopher. *God is Not Great: The Case Against Religion*. London: Atlantic Books, 2007.

Hollenbach, David. "Commentary on *Gaudium et Spes*." In *Modern Catholic Social Teaching: Commentaries and Interpretations*, edited by Kenneth R. Himes, 266–291. Washington, DC: Georgetown University, 2004.

Hoose, Bernard. *Proportionalism: The American Debate and Its European Roots*. Washington, DC: Georgetown University, 1987.

Hughes, Gerard J. "Our Human Vocation (Paragraphs 1691–2051)." In *Commentary on the Catechism of the Catholic Church*, edited by Michael J. Walsh, 336–356. London: Geoffrey Chapman, 1994.

Human Rights Watch. *Double Jeopardy: CIA Renditions to Jordan*. New York: Human Rights Watch, 2008.

Hünerman, Peter. "The Final Weeks of the Council." In *History of Vatican II*, vol. V, edited by Giuseppe Alberigo, English version edited by Joseph A. Komonchak, translated by Matthew J. O'Connell, 363–483. Maryknoll and Leuven: Orbis and Peeters, 2006.

International Criminal Court. *Elements of Crimes*. The Hague: International Criminal Court, 2011.

Irwin, Terence. Glossary in *Nicomachean Ethics,* by Aristotle. Translated with introduction, notes, and glossary by Terence Irwin, 2nd ed, 315–354. Indianapolis: Hackett Publishing, 1999.

Jackson, Timothy P. "A House Divided, Again: Sanctity vs. Dignity in the Induced Death Debates." In *In Defense of Human Dignity: Essays for Our Times,* edited by Robert P. Kraynak and Glenn Tinder, 139–163. Notre Dame: Notre Dame, 2003.

Jans, Jan. "Enjoying and Making Use of a Responsible Freedom: Background and Substantiation of *Human Dignity* in the Second Vatican Council." In *Sustaining Humanity beyond Humanism / Humanität über den Humanismus hinaus erhalten*, 39. Jahrestagung in Bruxelles,

Belgien, 28 August–1 September 2002, 101–111. Aarhus: Societas Ethica, 2003.

Jans, Jan. "Personalism: The Foundations of an Ethics of Responsibility." *Ethical Perspectives* 3, no. 3 (1996): 148–156.

Janssens, Louis. "Artificial Insemination: Ethical Considerations." *Louvain Studies* 8 (1980): 3–29.

Janssens, Louis. "Norms and Priorities in a Love Ethics." *Louvain Studies* 6 (1977): 207–238.

Janssens, Louis. "Ontic Evil and Moral Evil." *Louvain Studies* 4 (1972): 115–156.

Janssens, Louis. "Personalism in Moral Theology." In *Moral Theology: Challenges for the Future: Essays in Honor of Richard A. McCormick*, edited by Charles E. Curran, 94–107. New York: Paulist Press, 1990.

Janssens, Louis. "Personalist Morals." *Louvain Studies* 3 (1970): 5-16.

Jasper, David. *A Short Introduction to Hermeneutics*. Louisville, KY: Westminster John Knox Press, 2004.

Jeannot, Thomas M. "A Postsecular Exchange: Jacques Maritain, John Dewey, and Karl Marx." In *Philosophical Theory and the Universal Declaration of Human Rights*, edited by William Sweet, 83–98. Ottawa: University of Ottawa, 2003.

Jewkes, Rachel, and Naeema Abrahams. "The Epidemiology of Rape and Sexual Coercion in South Africa: an Overview." *Social Science and Medicine* 55 (2002): 1231–1244.

John Paul II. "Familiaris Consortio," Apostolic Exhortation of Pope John Paul II to the Episcopate, to the Clergy and to the Faithful of the Whole Catholic Church on the Role of the Christian Family in the Modern World. November 22, 1981. http://www.vatican.va/holy_father/john_paul_ii/apost_exhortations.

Johnson, Dominic D.P., Pavel Stopka, and Stephen Knights. "The Puzzle of Human Cooperation." *Nature* 421 (2003): 911–912.

Kagan, Shelly. *Normative Ethics*. Dimensions of Philosophy Series. Boulder: Westview Press, 1998.

Kant, Immanuel. *Groundwork of the Metaphysics of Morals*. Translated and analysed by H. J. Paton. New York: Harper Torchbooks, 1964.

Kant, Immanuel. *Grounding for the Metaphysics of Morals*. Translated by James W. Ellington, 3rd ed. Indianapolis: Hackett Publishing, 1993.

Kass, Leon R. "Defending Human Dignity." In *Human Dignity and Bioethics: Essays Commissioned by the President's Council on Bioethics*, edited by President's Council on Bioethics, 297–331. Washington, DC: *n.p.*, 2008.

Kearney, Richard. "Between Tradition and Utopia: The Hermeneutical Problem of Myth." In *On Paul Ricœur: Narrative and Interpretation*, edited by David Wood, 55–73. London: Routledge, 1991.

Kearney, Richard. *On Paul Ricœur: The Owl of Minerva*. Aldershot: Ashgate, 2004.

Keenan, James F. "Roger Burggraeve's Ethics of Growth in Context." In *Responsibility, God and Society: Theological Ethics in Dialogue. Festschrift Roger Burggraeve,* edited by Johan De Tavernier, Joseph A. Selling, Johan Verstraeten, and Paul Schotsmans, 287–304. BETL, no. 217. Leuven: Peeters, 2008.

Keenan, James F. "Towards an Inclusive Vision for Moral Theology Part II: An Agenda for the Future." *Pacifica* 13 (2000): 67–83.

Kenny, Anthony. *Ancient Philosophy*. A New History of Western Philosophy, vol. 1. Oxford: Oxford University, 2004; paperback edition, 2006.

Kirchhoffer, David G. "Become What You Are: On the Value of the Concept of Human Dignity as an Ethical Criterion in Light of Contemporary Critiques" *Bijdragen, International Journal of Philosophy and Theology* 70, no. 1 (2009): 45–66.

Kirchhoffer, David G. "Benedict XVI, Human Dignity, and Absolute Moral Norms." *New Blackfriars* 91, no. 1035 (2010): 586-608.

Kirchhoffer, David G. "Pope Benedict XVI on the Dignity of the Human Person: A Blessing or a Curse for the European Project?" *Bulletin ET* 18, no. 1–2 (2007): 155–169.

Kirchhoffer, David G. "Sacrament and Being: On Overcoming Ontotheology in Sacramental Theology." *Questions Liturgiques/Studies in Liturgy,* 88, no. 2 (2007): 143–156.

Kirchhoffer, David G. "The Good, the Bad and Those Who Think They Are: An investigation of the theology and science of Charity." *St Augustine Papers* 4, no. 2 (2003): 1–17.

Knauer, Peter. "The Hermeneutic Function of the Principle of Double Effect." *Natural Law Forum* 12 (1967): 132–162.

Kohler, Gernot, and Norman Alcock. "An Empirical Table of Structural Violence." *Journal of Peace Research* 13, no. 4 (1976): 343–356. Referred to in James Gilligan, *Violence: Reflections on a National Epidemic,* 196. New York: Vintage Books, 1997.

Kopelman, Loretta M. "If HIV/AIDS is Punishment, Who is Bad?" *Journal of Medicine and Philosophy* 27, no. 2 (2002): 231–243.

Kopfensteiner, Thomas R. "The Theory of the Fundamental Option." In *Christian Ethics: An Introduction,* edited by Bernard Hoose, 123–134. London: Cassell, 1998.

Labouvie-Vief, Gisela. "Dynamic Integration: Affect, Cognition, and the Self in Adulthood." *Current Directions in Psychological Science* 12, no. 6 (2003): 201–206.

Leatherman, Thomas L. "Poverty and Violence, Hunger and Health: A Political Ecology of Armed Conflict." In *Globalization, Health and the Environment,* edited by Greg Guest, 55–80. Lanham, MD: Altamira Press, 2005.

Lee, Bandy, and James Gilligan. "The Resolve to Stop the Violence Project: transforming an in-house culture of violence through a jail-based programme." *Journal of Public Health* 27, no. 2 (2005): 149–155.

Lewis, Michael, Jeannette M. Haviland-Jones, and Lisa Feldman Barret, eds. *Handbook of Emotions*. 3rd ed., New York: Guilford Press, 2008.

Linker, Damon. *The Theocons: Secular America under Siege*. New York: Doubleday, 2006.

Livingston, James C., and Francis Schüssler Fiorenza with Sarah Coakley and James H. Evans, Jr. *Modern Christian Thought: The Twentieth Century.* 2nd ed. Minneapolis: Fortress Press, 2006.

Loose, Donald, and Stefan Waanders, eds. *Work and Human Dignity in the context of Globalisation.* Budel: Damon, 2007.

Machiavelli, Niccolò. *The Prince.* In *Machiavelli: The Chief Works and Others,* vol. 1. Translated by Allan H. Gilbert. Durham, NC: Duke University, 1959; 1999.

MacIntyre, Alasdair. *After Virtue: A Study in Moral Theory,* 2nd ed. London: Duckworth, 1985.

MacIntyre, Alasdair. *Dependent Rational Animals: Why Human Beings Need the Virtues.* Peru, IL: Open Court, 1999; paperback edition, 2002.

Macklin, Ruth. "Dignity is a Useless Concept." *BMJ* 327 (20 December 2003): 1419–1420.

Magai, Carol. "Long-Lived Emotions: A Life Course Perspective on Emotional Development." In *Handbook of Emotions,* 3rd ed., edited by Michael Lewis, Jeannette M. Haviland-Jones, and Lisa Feldman Barret, 376–392. New York: Guilford Press, 2008.

Mansfield, Harvey C. *Manliness.* New Haven, CT: Yale University, 2006.

Marx, Reinhard. "Sozialethik als hermeneutische Ethik— Bedenkenswerte Aspecte." *Jahrbuch für Christliche Sozialwissenschaften* 43 (2002): 241–247.

Maxfield, Michael G., and Cathy S. Widom. "The Cycle of Violence: Revisited Six Years Later." *Archives of Pediatrics and Adolescent Medicine* 150, no. 4 (1996): 390–395.

May, William E. *An Introduction to Moral Theology,* 2nd ed. Huntington, IN: Our Sunday Visitor, 2003.

McCord, Colin, and Harold P. Freeman. "Excess mortality in Harlem." *New England Journal of Medicine* 322, no. 3 (1990): 173–177.

McCormick, Richard A. *Notes on Moral Theology: 1981 through 1984.* Lanham, MD: University Press of America, 1984.

Meeks, M. Douglas. "The Economy of Grace: Human Dignity in the Market System." In *God and Human Dignity,* edited by R. Kendall

Soulen and Linda Woodhead, 196–214. Grand Rapids, MI: William B. Eerdmans, 2006.

Metz, Johann Baptist. "Religion and Society in the Light of a Political Theology." *Harvard Theological Review* 61, no. 4 (1968): 507–523.

Metz, Johann Baptist. *Zur Theologie der Welt*. Mainz: Matthias Grünewald Verlag; Munich: Chr. Kaiser Verlag, 1969.

Meyer, Michael J. "Dignity as a (Modern) Virtue." In *The Concept of Human Dignity in Human Rights Discourse*, edited by David Kretzmer and Eckart Klein, 195–208. The Hague: Kluwer, 2002.

Mich, Marvin L. "Commentary on Mater et magistra." In *Modern Catholic Social Teaching: Commentaries and Interpretations*, edited by Kenneth R. Himes, 191–216. Washington, DC: Georgetown University, 2004.

Mieth, Dietmar. "Das Proprium Christianum und das Menschenwürdeargument in der Bioethik," *Theologische Quartalsschrift* 180 (2000): 252–271.

Mieth, Dietmar. *Moral und Erfahrung: Beiträge zur theologisch-ethischen Hermeneutik*. Studien zur Theologischen Ethik, no. 2. Freiburg–Vienna: Universitätsverlag Freiburg and Verlag Herder, 1977.

Mieth, Dietmar. *Moral und Erfahrung II: Entfaltung einer theologisch-ethischen Hermeneutik*. Studien zur Theologischen Ethik, no. 76. Freiburg–Vienna: Universitätsverlag Freiburg and Verlag Herder, 1998.

Mieth, Dietmar. "Sozialethik als hermeneutische Ethik." *Jahrbuch für Christliche Sozialwissenschaften*, 43 (2002): 217–240.

Miles, Margaret R. "Hermeneutics of Generosity and Suspicion: Pluralism and Theological Education." *Theological Education* 23, Suppl. (1987): 34–52.

Mill, John Stuart. *On Liberty*. In *Collected Works of John Stuart Mill*, vol XVIII. Edited by J.M. Robertson. Toronto and London: University of Toronto Press and Routledge & Kegan Paul, 1977.

Miller, Arthur. "Tragedy and the Common Man." *New York Times*, February 27, 1949.

Mitchell, Basil. *Morality: Religious and Secular*. Oxford: Clarendon Press, 1980.

Moeller, Charles. "History of the Constitution." In *Commentary on the Documents of Vatican II*. Vol. V, *Pastoral Constitution on the Church in the Modern World*, edited by Herbert Vorgrimler, 1–76. New York and London: Herder and Herder/Burns & Oates, 1969.

Muelder, Walter G. Foreword to *Personalism: A Critical Introduction*, by Rufus Burrow, Jr. St. Louis, MO: Chalice Press, 1999.

Munro, Bradley R. "The Universal Declaration of Human Rights, Maritain, and the Universality of Human Rights." In *Philosophical Theory and the Universal Declaration of Human Rights*, edited by William Sweet, 109–126. Ottawa: University of Ottawa, 2003.

Murray, Charles. *In Pursuit: Of Happiness and Good Government*. New York: Simon and Schuster, 1988.

National Center for Health Statistics. *Health, United States, 2004 with Chartbook on Trends in the Health of Americans.* Hyattsville, MD: U.S. Department of Health and Human Services, 2004.

Niebuhr, Reinhold. *The Nature and Destiny of Man: A Christian Interpretation*. One Volume Edition. New York: Charles Scribner's Sons, 1955.

Nielsen, Torsten O. "Guidelines for legalized euthanasia in Canada: A proposal." *Annals of the Royal College of Physicians and Surgeons of Canada* 31, no. 7 (1998): 314–318.

Nordenfelt, Lennart. "The Varieties of Dignity." *Health Care Analysis* 12, no. 2 (2004): 69–81.

Nussbaum, Martha C. *Frontiers of Justice: Disability, Nationality, Species Membership*. Cambridge, MA: Harvard University, 2006.

Nussbaum, Martha C. *Hiding from Humanity: Disgust, Shame, and the Law*. Princeton: Princeton University, 2004.

Nussbaum, Martha C. "Human Dignity and Political Entitlements." In *Human Dignity and Bioethics: Essays Commissioned by the President's Council on Bioethics*, edited by President's Council on Bioethics, 351–380. Washington, DC: *n.p.*, 2008.

Nussbaum, Martha C. *Women and Human Development: The Capabilities Approach*. Cambridge: Cambridge University, 2000.

Otten, Mac W., Jr., Steven M. Teutsch, David F. Williamson, and James S. Marks. "The effect of known risk factors on the excess mortality of black adults in the United States." *Journal of the American Medical Association* 263, no. 6 (1990): 845–850.

Palmer, Richard E. "On the Transcendability of Hermeneutics (A Response to Dreyfus)." In *Hermeneutics: Questions and Prospects*, edited by Gary Shapiro and Alan Sica, 84–95. Amherst: University of Massachusetts, 1984; paperback edition, 1988.

Palmer, Stuart. *A Study of Murder*. New York: Crowell, 1960.

Phan, Peter C. "Roman Catholic Theology." In *Oxford Handbook of Eschatology*, edited by Jerry L. Walls, 215–232. Oxford: Oxford University, 2008.

Pinker, Steven. "The Stupidity of Dignity." *The New Republic*, May 28, 2008. http://www.tnr.com/article/the-stupidity-dignity.

Pitt-Rivers, Julian. "Honor." In *International Encyclopaedia of Social Science*, edited by David L. Sills, 503–511. London: Macmillan, 1968.

Polkinghorne, John. "Anthropology in an Evolutionary Context." In *God and Human Dignity*, edited by R. Kendall Soulen and Linda Woodhead, 89–103. Grand Rapids, MI: William B. Eerdmans, 2006.

Pollefeyt, Didier. "The Kafkaesque World of the Holocaust: Paradigmatic Shifts in the Ethical Interpretation of the Nazi Genocide." In *Ethics After the Holocaust: Perspectives Critiques and Responses*, edited by John K. Roth, 210–242. St Paul, MN: Paragon House, 1999.

Pollefeyt, Didier. "The Morality of Auschwitz? A Critical Confrontation with Peter J. Haas's Ethical Interpretation of the Holocaust." In *Good and Evil After Auschwitz: Ethical Implications for Today*, edited by Jack Bemporad, John T. Pawlikowski, and Joseph Sievers, 119–138. Hoboken, NJ: Ktav Publishing, 2000.

Pope, Stephen J. *Human Evolution and Christian Ethics*. New Studies in Christian Ethics, no. 28. Cambridge: Cambridge University, 2007.

Pope, Stephen J. "Natural Law in Catholic Social Teachings." In *Modern Catholic Social Teaching: Commentaries and Interpretations,* edited by Kenneth R. Himes, 41–71. Washington, DC: Georgetown University, 2004.

Pope, Stephen J. *The Evolution of Altruism and the Ordering of Love.* Moral Traditions and Moral Arguments. Washington, DC: Georgetown University, 1994.

President's Council on Bioethics. *Human Dignity and Bioethics: Essays Commissioned by the President's Council on Bioethics.* Washington, DC: *n.p.*, 2008.

President's Council on Bioethics. "Session 5: Human Dignity and Bioethics: Essays Commissioned by the President's Council of Bioethics," 7 March 2008. Meeting Transcripts. Accessed 7 June 2012. http://bioethics.georgetown.edu/pcbe/transcripts/march08/session5.html.

Pullman, Daryl. "Human Dignity and the Ethics and Aesthetics of Pain and Suffering." *Theoretical Medicine* 23 (2002): 75–94.

Quill, Timothy E. "Death and Dignity: A Case of Individualized Decision Making." *New England Journal of Medicine* 324, no. 10 (1991): 691–694.

Rahner, Karl. *Foundations of Christian Faith.* Translated by William V. Dych. New York: Crossroad, 1989.

Rahner, Karl. "Theology of Freedom." In *Theological Investigations,* vol. 6, translated by Karl-H. Kruger and Boniface Kruger, 178–196. New York: Seabury Press, 1969.

Ratzinger, Joseph. "The Dignity of the Human Person." In *Commentary on the Documents of Vatican II,* vol. V, *Pastoral Constitution on the Church in the Modern World,* edited by Herbert Vorgrimler, 115–163. New York and London: Herder and Herder/Burns & Oates, 1969.

Ricœur, Paul. *Freud and Philosophy: An Essay on Interpretation.* The Terry Lectures. Translated by Denis Savage. New Haven: Yale University, 1970.

Ricœur, Paul. *Hermeneutics and the Human Sciences.* Edited and translated by John B. Thompson. Cambridge: Cambridge University, 1981.

Ricœur, Paul. *Oneself as Another.* Translated by Kathleen Blamey. Chicago: Chicago University, 1992.

Ricœur, Paul. "The Critique of Religion." Translated by R. Bradley DeFord. *Union Seminary Quarterly Review* 28, 3 (1973): 205–212.

Ricœur, Paul. "The Language of Faith." Translated by R. Bradley DeFord. *Union Seminary Quarterly Review* 28, no. 3 (1973): 212–224.

Ricœur, Paul. *Time and Narrative,* vol. 1. Translated by Kathleen Mclaughlin and David Pellauer. Chicago: University of Chicago, 1984.

Ricœur, Paul. "Two Essays by Paul Ricœur." Translated by R. Bradley DeFord. *Union Seminary Quarterly Review* 28, no. 3 (1973): 203–204.

Robinson, Geoffrey. *Confronting Power and Sex in the Catholic Church: Reclaiming the Spirit of Jesus.* Collegeville, MN: Liturgical Press, 2007.

Ross, Dorothy. "Liberalism." In *A Companion to American Thought,* edited by Richard Wightman Fox and James T. Kloppenburg, 397–400. Malden, MA: Blackwell, 1995; paperback edition, 1998.

Rowland, Christopher, ed. *The Cambridge Companion to Liberation Theology,* 2nd ed. Cambridge: Cambridge University, 2007.

Rubenstein, Richard L. *The Cunning of History: The Holocaust and the American Future,* 2nd ed. New York: Perennial Library, 1978.

Schockenhoff, Eberhard. *Natural Law and Human Dignity: Universal Ethics in an Historical World.* Translated by Brian McNeil. Washington, DC: Catholic University of America, 2003.

Schulman, Adam. "Bioethics and the Question of Human Dignity." In *Human Dignity and Bioethics: Essays Commissioned by the President's Council on Bioethics,* edited by President's Council on Bioethics, 3–18. Washington, DC: *n.p.,* 2008.

Schüssler Fiorenza, Elisabeth. *Sharing Her Word: Feminist Biblical Interpretation in Context.* Edinburgh: T&T Clark, 1998.

Schüssler Fiorenza, Elisabeth. *But She Said*. Boston: Beacon Press, 1992.

Schwöbel, Christoph. "Recovering Human Dignity." In *God and Human Dignity*, edited by R. Kendall Soulen and Linda Woodhead, 44–58. Grand Rapids, MI: William B. Eerdmans, 2006.

Segundo, Juan Luis. *The Liberation of Theology*. Maryknoll: Orbis, 1976.

Selling, Joseph A. "(In Search of) A Fundamental Basis for Ethical Reflection." *Ethical Perspectives* 1, no. 1 (1994): 13–21.

Selling, Joseph A. "The Context and the Arguments of Veritatis Splendor." In *The Splendor of Accuracy: an Examination of the Assertions Made by Veritatis Splendor*, edited by Joseph A. Selling and Jan Jans, 11–70. Kampen: Kok Pharos, 1994.

Selling, Joseph A. "The Human Person." In *Christian Ethics: An Introduction*, edited by Bernard Hoose, 95–109. London: Cassell, 1998.

Selling, Joseph A. "The Polarity of Ethical Discourse." *Australian Ejournal of Theology* 2 (2004): 1–7. http://aejt.com.au/__data/assets/pdf_file/0003/395670/AEJT_2.4_Selling_Polarity.pdf.

Selling, Joseph A., and Jan Jans, eds. *The Splendor of Accuracy: an Examination of the Assertions Made by Veritatis Splendor*. Kampen: Kok Pharos, 1994.

Semmelroth, Otto. "The Community of Mankind." In *Commentary on the Documents of Vatican II,* vol. V, *Pastoral Constitution on the Church in the Modern World,* edited by Herbert Vorgrimler, 164–181. New York and London: Herder and Herder/Burns & Oates, 1969.

Shell, Susan M. "Kant on Human Dignity." In *In Defense of Human Dignity: Essays for Our Times,* edited by Robert P. Kraynak and Glenn Tinder, 53–80. Notre Dame: Notre Dame, 2003.

Shklar, Judith N. *Legalism: Law, Morals, and Political Trials*. Cambridge, MA: Harvard University, 1964.

Siegel, Larry J. *Criminology,* 10th ed. Belmont, CA: Thomson, 2006.

Singer, Peter. "All Animals are Equal." In *Applied Ethics,* edited by Peter Singer, 215–228. Oxford Readings in Philosophy. Oxford: Oxford University, 1986.

Singer, Peter. *Practical Ethics,* 2nd ed. Cambridge: Cambridge University, 1993.

Solomon, Robert C. "The Philosophy of Emotions." In *Handbook of Emotions,* 3rd ed., edited by Michael Lewis, Jeannette M. Haviland-Jones, and Lisa Feldman Barret, 3–16. New York: Guilford Press, 2008.

Soulen, R. Kendall, and Linda Woodhead. "Introduction: Contextualising Human Dignity." In *God and Human Dignity,* edited by R. Kendall Soulen and Linda Woodhead, 1–24. Grand Rapids, MI: William B. Eerdmans, 2006.

Spaemann, Robert. "Sind Alle Menschen Personen? Über neue philosophische Rechtfertigungen der Lebensvernichtung." In *Tüchtig oder tot? Die Entsorgung des Leidens,* edited by Jürgen-Peter Stössel, 133–147. Freiburg: Herder, 1991.

Stewart, Ian. *Does God Play Dice? The New Mathematics of Chaos,* 2nd ed. Oxford: Blackwell, 1997; reprint 2002.

Stone, Bryan P. *Effective Faith: A Critical Study of the Christology of Juan Luis Segundo.* Lanham: University Press of America, 1994.

Sulmasy, Daniel P. "Dignity and Bioethics: History, Theory, and Selected Applications." In *Human Dignity and Bioethics: Essays Commissioned by the President's Council on Bioethics,* edited by President's Council on Bioethics, 469–501. Washington, DC: *n.p.,* 2008. Taylor, Charles. *Sources of the Self: The Making of Modern Identity.* Cambridge: Cambridge University, 1989.

Taylor, Craig. "Moralism and Morally Accountable Beings." *Journal of Applied Philosophy* 22, no. 2 (2005): 153–160.

Thompson, John B. Editor's introduction to *Hermeneutics and the Human Sciences,* by Paul Ricœur, edited and translated by John B. Thompson. Cambridge: Cambridge University, 1981.

Tillich, Paul. *Systematic Theology,* vol. 2. Chicago: University of Chicago, 1957; paperback edition, 1975.

Tinder, Glenn. "Against Fate: An Essay on Personal Dignity." In *In Defense of Human Dignity: Essays for Our Times,* edited by Robert P. Kraynak and Glenn Tinder, 11–51. Notre Dame: Notre Dame, 2003.

Todorov, Tzvetan. *Hope and Memory: Reflections on the Twentieth Century.* London: Atlantic Books, 2003.

Toulmin, Stephen. "How Medicine Saved the Life of Ethics," *Perspectives in Biology and Medicine* 25, no. 4 (1982): 736–750.

Tracy, David. *Plurality and Ambiguity: Hermeneutics, Religion, Hope.* San Francisco: HarperSanFrancisco, 1987; reprint, Chicago: University of Chicago, 1994.

Tredennick, Hugh. "Appendix 6: Substance and Change," in *The Nicomachean Ethics,* by Aristotle. Translated by J.A.K. Thomson, revised with notes and appendices by Hugh Tredennick, 296–299. London: Penguin Classics, 1976; 2004.

Tutu, Desmond. *No Future Without Forgiveness.* New York: Doubleday, 1999.

United Nations. *Charter of the United Nations.* 1945.

United Nations. *Convention against Torture and Other Cruel, Inhuman, Degrading Treatment or Punishment.* 1984.

United Nations. *Convention on the Elimination of All Forms of Discrimination Against Women.* 1979.

United Nations. *Convention on the Rights of the Child.* 1989.

United Nations. *International Covenant on Civil and Political Rights.* 1966.

United Nations. *International Covenant on Economic, Social and Cultural Rights.* 1966.

United Nations. *Universal Declaration of Human Rights.* 1948.

United Nations' Office of the High Commissioner for Human Rights. *Geneva Convention relative to the Treatment of Prisoners of War.* 1949.

United Nations'Office of the High Commissioner for Human Rights. "Ratification and Reservations." Accessed 30 May 2008. http://www2.ohchr.org/english/bodies/ratification/ index.htm.

U.S. President. "Message to the House of Representatives Returning Without Approval the 'Intelligence Authorization Act for Fiscal Year 2008', March 8, 2008." *Weekly Compilation of Presidential Documents* 44, 10 (March 17, 2008): 346–347.

U.S. President. "Remarks on the War on Terror, September 6, 2006." *Weekly Compilation of Presidential Documents* 42, 36 (September 11, 2006): 1569–1575.

Van Deurzen, Emmy, and Raymond Kenward. *Dictionary of Existential Psychotherapy and Counselling*. London: Sage, 2005.

Van Tongeren, Paul. "Ethics, Tradition and Hermeneutics." In *Matter of Breath: Foundations for Professional Ethics,* edited by Guillaume de Stexhe and Johan Verstraeten, 119–32. European Ethics Network Core Materials for the Development of Courses in Professional Ethics. Leuven: Peeters, 2000.

Van Tongeren, Paul. "The Relation of Narrativity and Hermeneutics to an Adequate Practical Ethics." *Ethical Perspectives* 1, no. 2 (1994): 57–70.

Van Tongeren, Paul, Gerd Schank, and Herman Siemens, eds. *Nietzsche Wörterbuch,* Band 1. Berlin: Walter de Gruyter, 2004.

Vatican Council II. "Declaration on Religious Freedom (*Dignitatis Humanae*)." December 7, 1965. In *The Documents of Vatican II,* edited by Walter M. Abbot and translation edited by Joseph Gallagher, 675–696. London: Geoffrey Chapman, 1966.

Vatican Council II. "Message to Humanity." October 20, 1962. In *The Documents of Vatican II,* edited by Walter M. Abbot and Joseph Gallagher, 3–7. London: Geoffrey Chapman, 1966.

Vatican Council II. "Pastoral Constitution of the Church in the Modern World (*Gaudium et Spes*)." December 7, 1965. In *The Documents of Vatican II,* edited by Walter M. Abbot and translation edited by Joseph Gallagher, 199–308. London: Geoffrey Chapman, 1966.

Vatican Council II. Theological Subcommission. "De ordine morali." In *Acta et Documenta Concilio Oecumenico Vaticano II Apparando,* series 2, volume 3, part 1, 24–53. Vatican City: Typis Polyglottis Vaticanus, 1969.

Vatican Council II. Theological Subcommission. "De ordine morali christiano." In *Schemata Constitutionum et Decretorum de Quibus Disceptabitur in Concilii Sessionibus,* Series I, 73–96. Vatican City: Typis Polyglottis Vaticanus, 1962.

Verstraeten, Johan. "An Ethical Agenda for Europe: Fundamental Problems on Practical Ethics in a Christian Perspective." *Ethical Perspectives* 1, no. 1 (1994): 3–12.

Verstraeten, Johan. "Globalisation and the Dignity of the Poor." In *Globalisation and Human Dignity: Sources and Challenges in Catholic Social Thought,* edited by Wim van de Donk, Richard Steenvoorde, and Stefan Waanders, 96–111. Budel: Damon, 2004.

Verstraeten, Johan. "Mensenrechten en Menselijke Waardigheid: Katholiek Sociaal Denken als Inspiratiebron." In *Mens van God, God van mensen: Leuvense theologen in gesprek met kardinaal Godfried Danneels,* edited by Mathijs Lamberigts and Leo Kenis, 217–230. Antwerp: Halewijn, 2005.

Verstraeten, Johan. "Catholic Social Thought as Discernment." In *Scrutinizing the Signs of the Times in the Light of the Gospel,* edited by Johan Verstraeten, 1–14. BETL, no. 208. Leuven: Leuven University Press and Peeters, 2007.

Vervenne, Marc. "'Satanic Verses'? Violence and War in the Bible." In *Swords into Plowshares: Theological Reflections on Peace,* edited by Roger Burggraeve and Marc Vervenne, 65–126. Louvain Theological & Pastoral Monographs, no. 8. Leuven: Peeters, 1991.

Victorian Law Reform Commission. *Workplace Privacy: Issues Paper.* Melbourne: Victorian Law Reform Commission, 2002.

Vidmar, Neil. "Retributive Justice: Its Social Context." In *The Justice Motive in Everyday Life,* edited by Michael Ross and Dale T. Miller, 291–313. Cambridge: Cambridge University, 2002.

Wallach, Michael A., and Lise Wallach. *Rethinking Goodness*. SUNY Series in Ethical Theory. Albany, NY: State University of New York, 1990.

Watts, Fraser. "Human Dignity: Concepts and Experiences." In *God and Human Dignity*, edited by R. Kendall Soulen and Linda Woodhead, 247–262. Grand Rapids, MI: William B. Eerdmans, 2006.

Wayman, Frank W., and Paul F. Diehl. "Realism Reconsidered: The Realpolitik Framework and Its Basic Propositions." In *Reconstructing Realpolitik,* edited by Frank W. Wayman and Paul F. Diehl, 3–28. Ann Arbor: University of Michigan, 1994.

Weber-Hassemer, Kristiane, "'Menschenwürde' im Bioethischen Diskurs." In *Die Würde des Menschens ist antastbar?,* edited by Irmgard Rode, Heinz Kammeier, and Matthias Leipert, 23–38. Schriftenreihe des Instituts für Konfliktforschung, no. 28. Münster: LIT Verlag, 2005.

Weisstub, David N., and David C. Thomasma. "Human Dignity, Vulnerability, Personhood." In *Personhood and Health Care,* edited by David C. Thomasma, David N. Weisstub, and Christian Hervé, 317–332. Dordrecht: Kluwer Academic Publishers, 2001.

Weitekamp, Elmar G.M., and Hans-Jürgen Kerner, eds. *Restorative Justice: Theoretical Foundations*. Cullompton: Willan, 2002.

Weitz, Rose. "Living with the Stigma of AIDS." *Qualitative Sociology* 13, 1 (1990): 23–38.

Welker, Michael. "Theological Anthropology versus Anthropological Reductionism." In *God and Human Dignity*, edited by R. Kendall Soulen and Linda Woodhead, 317–330. Grand Rapids, MI: William B. Eerdmans, 2006.

Wellmann, Carl. *The Proliferation of Rights: Moral Progress or Empty Rhetoric*. Boulder: Westview Press, 1999.

Wertheimer, Max. "Gestalt Theory: an address before the Kant Society, Berlin, 17th December 1924." In *A Source Book of Gestalt Psychology*, edited and translated by Willis D. Ellis, 1–11. *n.p.*: Kegan Paul, Trench, Trubner and Co., 1938; reprint Abingdon: Routledge, 2001.

Westberg, Daniel. "Good and Evil in Human Acts (Ia IIae, qq. 18–21)." In *The Ethics of Aquinas,* edited by Stephen J. Pope, 90–102. Washington, DC: Georgetown University, 2002.

Wils, Jean-Pierre. *Handlungen und Bedeutungen: Reflexionen über eine hermeneutische Ethik.* Studien zur theologischen Ethik, no. 92. Freiburg, Switzerland: Universitätsverlag and Verlag Herder, 2001.

Wils, Jean-Pierre. "The End of 'Human Dignity' in Ethics?" Translated by Gordon Wood. Concilium 203, special column (1989): 39–54.

Wister, Robert J. "Fragile Outcasts: Historical Reflections on Ministry to People with AIDS." In *Made in God's Image: The Catholic Vision of Human Dignity,* edited by Regis Duffy and Angelus Gambatese, 136–157. New York: Paulist Press, 1999.

Witte, John, Jr. "Between Sanctity and Depravity: Human Dignity in Protestant Perspective." In *In Defense of Human Dignity: Essays for Our Times,* edited by Robert P. Kraynak and Glenn Tinder, 119–134. Notre Dame: Notre Dame, 2003.

Yaghjian, Lucretia B. *Writing Theology Well: A Rhetoric for Theological and Biblical Writers.* New York: Continuum, 2006.

Youngner, Stuart J., and Robert M. Arnold. "Philosophical debates about the definition of death: who cares?" *Journal of Medicine and Philosophy* 26, no. 5 (2001): 527–537.

Youngner, Stuart J., Robert M. Arnold, and Michael A. DeVita, "When is 'dead'?" *Hastings Center Report* 29, no. 6 (1999): 14–21.

Zwart, Hub A.E. "The Moral Significance of our Biological Nature." *Ethical Perspectives* 1, no. 2 (1994): 71–76.

INDEX

Aquinas, Thomas, 220
Aristotle, 128, 167, 223–226
Australia, 67–68, 105
autonomy, 10, 17, 33, 55–56, 59,
   63, 80, 83–84, 87, 93–94, 98,
   100–101, 106–107, 126–127,
   132, 136, 141, 143, 148,
   150, 163, 228, 231–232,
   236, 238–241, 243, 267–268,
   272–279, 281–282, 311,
   315–316

Bayertz, Kurt, 83
Belgium, 51, 62, 143
Benedict XVI, Pope, 78, 229
Bernardin, Joseph Cardinal, 76
Beyleveld, Deryck, 55, 84, 239
Bostrom, Nick, 97, 232, 240
Brownsword, Roger, 55, 84, 239

capacity, 12, 19–20, 22, 25, 76, 79,
   82–87, 92–95, 97–100, 104, 137,
   139, 150, 169, 171, 174, 177,
   217, 219, 225–227, 230–235,
   239–245, 259, 267–269,
   275–276, 278–279, 297–298,
   300, 302, 312, 315
Christian, 15, 28, 33, 48, 76–78,
   84–85, 102–103, 107–108, 126,
   137–138, 144–145, 147, 151,
   153, 174–175, 181, 187, 215,
   295–296
conscience, 50, 64, 71, 75, 98–99,
   237, 270–271, 299–300, 317,
   319

corporeal, 10, 19–21, 23, 172, 207,
   214, 216, 220, 222, 231, 243,
   245, 263, 279, 310, 312

Dawkins, Richard, 153
death penalty, 5, 11, 49, 61–66, 79,
   88–89, 93, 145–146, 148, 153,
   178, 181, 229, 259, 268–270,
   272, 276–277, 280–281, 298,
   318
deconstruction, 34, 133–134, 136
Demmer, Klaus, 98, 237
desire, 10–18, 23, 61, 67–68,
   106, 127, 132, 138, 147,
   167, 170–172, 177–181,
   188, 207, 215, 217–219, 221,
   226, 236–237, 242–246, 263,
   267–268, 271, 275–276, 282,
   298, 314–315
Dewey, John, 241
Dignitatis Humanae, 53, 99, 237,
   317
dignity talk, 1–3, 6, 8–12, 14–26,
   28–36, 47–109, 123–127,
   129–137, 140–144, 146–151,
   156–158, 162–165, 167–169,
   177, 180, 183, 187–189,
   205–206, 208–214, 222–246,
   255–267, 269–283, 295–303,
   309–320
Dworkin, Ronald, 35, 83, 94, 257,
   266, 311

Egonsson, Dan, 81, 229
emotions, 82, 217–219, 231, 235

eschatological proviso, 15–17, 25, 165, 187–189, 207, 222, 280–281, 320
ethicist, 57, 128, 130, 160, 164–165, 167–168, 207, 255, 278
ethics, 1–2, 4, 6–8, 15–17, 23, 26, 30–35, 49, 56–58, 60, 73, 77–78, 84–85, 93–94, 96, 107–109, 124–131, 134, 136–138, 141, 143–145, 147, 149–150, 157–158, 160–161, 163–168, 172–173, 183–188, 206–207, 209–213, 228, 255–256, 262, 271, 274–275, 310, 316, 318–319
descriptive ethics, 1–2, 4, 6–11, 13, 15–18, 23, 26, 30–35, 49, 56–58, 60, 73, 77–78, 84–85, 93–94, 96, 107–109, 124–131, 134, 136–138, 141, 143–145, 147, 149–150, 157–158, 160–161, 163–168, 172–173, 180, 183–188, 205–213, 228, 246, 255–260, 262, 264, 266, 271–272, 274–275, 309–310, 316, 318–319
hermeneutical ethics, 1–2, 4, 6–8, 15–17, 23, 26, 29–35, 49, 56–58, 60, 73, 77–78, 84–85, 93–94, 96, 107–109, 124–131, 134, 136–138, 141, 143–145, 147, 149–150, 155, 157–158, 160–161, 163–169, 172–173, 183–188, 206–207, 209–213, 228, 255–256, 262, 271, 274–275, 278, 310, 312, 316, 318–319

normative ethics, 1–2, 4, 6–18, 22–24, 26, 28, 30–35, 48–49, 56–58, 60, 72–73, 77–78, 84–85, 93–94, 96, 107–109, 124–131, 134, 136–138, 141, 143–145, 147–150, 155, 157–158, 160–161, 163–168, 172–173, 180, 183–188, 205–213, 228, 244–246, 255–259, 262, 265–266, 271, 274–275, 279–280, 282, 309–310, 316, 318–319
European Union, 51, 68
euthanasia, 5, 10, 13, 33, 35, 60–63, 65, 75, 79–81, 86–87, 93, 101, 145–146, 148, 182, 208, 230, 239–242, 257, 261, 266–267, 269–271, 273, 276, 279–281, 314, 316
existential, 15, 19–20, 25, 86, 93–94, 125, 143, 183–184, 213–218, 221–226, 229, 231–234, 242, 245, 256–257, 263, 278, 297–298, 310, 312, 316

Farley, Margaret, 84, 86, 231, 276
fear, 156, 173, 175, 217, 246, 259–261, 264, 282, 301, 311, 315
feminist, 27, 84, 155
freedom, 50–51, 53, 61–62, 64, 79, 83, 85, 98–99, 103, 126, 130, 137, 170–172, 177–179, 184, 187, 224, 231, 236, 244, 266–267, 270–271, 274, 278, 282, 297, 299, 302–303, 317

ontological freedom, 50–51,
53, 61–62, 64, 73–74, 76,
78–79, 82–83, 85–87, 90,
98–99, 103–104, 126, 130, 137,
139–141, 149, 163, 170–172,
177–179, 184, 187, 224, 227,
230–232, 236, 244, 266–267,
270–271, 274, 278, 282, 297,
299, 302–303, 317
categorical freedom, 50–51, 53,
61–62, 64, 67, 79, 83, 85,
98–99, 103, 126, 130, 137, 159,
170–172, 176–180, 184, 187,
224, 231, 236, 241, 243–244,
266–267, 270–271, 274, 278,
282, 297, 299, 302–303, 317
Fukuyama, Francis, 81, 97, 229
fundamental option, 170–183,
186–188, 219, 221–222,
235–238, 244

Gadamer, Hans-Georg, 28, 135
Gaudium et Spes, 35, 52–53, 64, 74,
76, 226, 296, 317
Geneva Convention, 70, 217
Germany, 51
Gestalt, 137, 139
Ghandi, Mahatma
gift, 76, 78–80, 101, 103, 148, 163,
175–176, 187, 229, 299
Gilligan, James, 35, 88, 150, 162,
236, 246, 257–258, 260, 311
God, 15, 28, 33–36, 48, 53, 74–78,
80–82, 85, 92, 98–99, 101–104,
107–108, 137–138, 142, 148,
153, 163, 174–175, 181, 187,
215, 229, 295–302, 317–318,
320

hermeneutics, 1, 26–31, 34,
47–49, 73, 87, 100, 104–105,
109, 124, 130–131, 133–137,
140, 143–144, 149, 155, 157,
163–169, 172–173, 183–187,
206–207, 209–213, 228,
256, 278, 296, 310, 312, 316,
318–319
historicity, 11, 15, 20–21, 23, 146,
148, 172, 176, 178–180, 184,
188, 219, 221, 223, 226, 240,
244, 280, 283, 302, 313
honour, 63, 74, 89, 91, 94, 259, 261,
265, 270
human dignity, 1–3, 6, 10, 17, 26,
32, 205, 309
as descriptive category, 2, 6, 8–10,
17–18, 30, 35, 109, 129–130,
157, 164, 168, 180, 205, 208,
246, 255, 257–258, 260, 272,
309–310, 318–319
as normative criterion, 2, 6, 8–10,
14, 16–18, 24, 28, 33, 35, 48,
108–109, 125, 129, 147–148,
157, 180, 205, 207–208,
244–245, 255–258, 262, 275,
282, 309–310, 318–319
and multidimensionality, 1–4, 6,
8–12, 14–26, 28–36, 47–109,
123–127, 129–137, 140–144,
146–151, 156–158, 162–165,
167–169, 177, 180, 183,
187–189, 205–214, 222–246,
255–267, 269–283, 295–303,
309–320
component dimensions of, 3, 17–18,
25–26, 31, 34–35, 205, 208, 211,
234, 246, 257, 262, 278, 280,
296, 310–311, 319

human rights, 33, 48, 50–52, 54–55, 63–65, 69, 71–72, 74, 77, 86, 103, 105–106, 125, 127, 162, 226, 229, 238, 245, 302, 314–316

informed consent, 57
insight, 61, 90, 130, 164, 166, 168, 207, 210, 218, 232, 256, 260, 297

Janssens, Louis, 143–144, 169, 181, 213–214, 231, 243

Kant, Immanuel, 67–68, 84, 238
King, Martin Luther, 65, 96, 143, 240

legalism, 31, 124–129, 136, 141, 144, 147, 149, 157, 163–165, 177, 184, 206, 228, 318–319
love, 64, 84–87, 89, 91, 129, 134–135, 137, 142, 173, 181, 186–187, 217, 231, 258–259, 276, 297, 299–300, 302–303, 318, 320

Macklin, Ruth, 56–57, 93, 101–102, 107, 132, 141, 228, 241, 316
method, 1, 26–27, 29, 32–34, 36, 100, 108–109, 123–124, 126, 131–132, 134–137, 139–140, 142, 148–149, 155, 162–165, 184, 206, 208–209, 211–212, 226, 228, 296, 318
Meyer, Michael J., 96, 240
Mieth, Dietmar, 130, 166
Miles, Margaret R., 27

moral, 1–9, 12–18, 21–26, 28, 30–32, 34–35, 48, 54–56, 59–60, 67–68, 71, 73, 77, 80–82, 84, 86, 91, 93–100, 106–108, 124–130, 137, 141–142, 144–150, 152–169, 172–174, 176–189, 205–207, 209, 211–213, 216, 219–221, 224–225, 228, 233–234, 238–246, 255–258, 260–267, 269, 272–277, 279–280, 282–283, 298–301, 309–319
moral event, 1, 3–9, 12–15, 17–18, 22, 30–31, 108, 124, 137, 141, 144–149, 163–165, 169, 180, 183–185, 187, 206–207, 209, 211–213, 220–221, 228, 240, 256, 280, 310, 314, 317–318
moral good, 4–5, 8, 12–15, 17, 21–22, 24–26, 67–68, 80, 106, 156, 162, 238, 240–246, 257, 261–265, 273–277, 280, 282, 299–301, 313, 315, 319
moral relativity, 23, 72, 162–163, 184, 187, 275, 313
moral relativism, 23, 150, 157–163, 165, 183–187, 206–207, 212, 230, 255, 257, 275, 282–283, 310, 313, 318
moralism, 15–17, 23, 150, 152–158, 160–163, 165, 184–185, 187, 189, 206–207, 212, 230, 255, 257, 262, 274, 309–310, 318

narrative, 78, 94, 160–161, 167, 233, 237, 270, 279
Netherlands, 62

Index

norms, 4, 6–7, 9, 13, 21–23, 29, 54, 84, 88, 100, 144–147, 158, 167, 173, 176, 180–182, 184–189, 207, 218–219, 221, 244, 255, 259, 275, 280
Nordenfelt, Lennart, 93
Nussbaum, Martha, 85, 91, 231, 242

objective, 4, 7, 9, 13, 19, 23–24, 28, 67, 83, 125, 135, 160–161, 174, 241, 243, 256, 267, 275
ontological, 73–74, 76, 78, 82, 86–87, 90, 104, 139–141, 149, 163, 170–172, 177, 179, 227, 230–232, 236, 244

person, 2, 4, 10–11, 16–21, 24–25, 32, 50, 76, 87, 144, 149, 173–174, 177–179, 205, 207–208, 210, 212–213, 217, 222–223, 227–228, 240, 242–243, 245, 255–256, 263, 268, 279–280, 282, 295–296, 300, 309, 312–314, 316–319
  adequately considered, 1–5, 7–25, 30–36, 49–54, 59, 61, 64, 66–68, 70–71, 73–80, 82–83, 86–96, 98–99, 101, 103–104, 107–108, 124, 126, 132, 136–138, 141, 143–144, 146, 148–152, 154, 156–157, 163–165, 167–189, 205–207, 209, 211–240, 242–245, 256–258, 260–261, 265–270, 272–274, 276–277, 279–280, 283, 296–297, 300–302, 309–313, 315–319
Pinker, Steven, 30, 58, 78, 95, 97, 101, 317
Pope, Stephen J., 77, 85, 137, 151, 229, 231

potential, 12, 19–21, 23–26, 72, 85, 100, 103, 126, 133, 216, 223–227, 231–235, 242, 245, 263–266, 276, 296–298, 300–303, 310, 312–314
President's Council on Bioethics, 57, 78, 85, 95, 101
pride, 9, 16, 21, 63, 65, 88–92, 94, 107, 137, 145, 218, 236, 258–261, 263, 316
Pullman, Daryl, 94

Quill, Timothy, 92, 271

Reductionism, 29–31, 106, 124, 136–144, 149, 155, 157, 163–164, 166, 169, 177, 206, 228, 230, 312, 318
relativism, 23, 150, 157–163, 165, 183–187, 206–207, 212, 230, 255, 257, 275, 282–283, 310, 313, 318
relativity, 23, 72, 162–163, 184, 187, 275, 313
respect, 21, 24, 33, 52, 54–57, 59, 61–63, 67–68, 70, 79–80, 83–86, 88–96, 98, 101, 103–105, 107, 132, 151, 179, 184, 227, 229, 236–237, 239, 245–246, 258–259, 261–262, 264, 267–270, 272–277, 279, 281, 302, 311, 314, 316–318
Ricœur, Paul, 28, 130

self-worth, 10–17, 20–26, 89–93, 95, 98, 150, 177–178, 181–184, 207, 215–218, 221, 226, 233–237, 239, 242–246, 259, 262–266, 275–277, 280, 301–302, 311, 314–316

shame, 75, 89–93, 151, 218, 258–259, 261, 263, 280
South Africa, 52, 64–67, 147
species, 81–82, 87, 138, 142, 150, 229, 231–232
stem cell, 56–57, 65, 75
subjective, 4, 8, 89–90, 159, 161, 174, 178, 184, 241, 243, 245, 256–257, 261–262, 273, 275, 282

Taylor, Charles, 90, 96, 236, 240
techne, 31, 124–125, 127–129, 136–137, 144, 147, 149, 163–166, 177, 184, 206, 210, 228, 318–319
terrorism
theocon, 59, 317
theology, 14–15, 27, 29, 35, 83, 98, 103, 108, 126, 130, 138, 140, 144, 175–176, 187–188, 207, 220, 296, 298
theoria, 165–166

time, 4, 6, 10, 12–14, 17, 34, 52, 70–71, 94–95, 106, 123, 141, 145–148, 159, 165, 176–180, 187–188, 207, 209–212, 215, 218–219, 221–226, 233, 235–236, 239, 241–243, 245–246, 256–257, 259, 266, 271–272, 276, 278, 281, 297–298, 300, 302, 310, 312, 315
torture, 50, 69–71, 129
tragedy, 145–146, 179, 183
transhumanism, 97, 232

United Nations, 49–51, 77, 302
United States of America, 52, 57, 61, 69, 150, 272
Universal Declaration of Human Rights, 50, 64, 71–72, 74, 77, 226, 229, 302

Van Tongeren, Paul, 127, 165
Vatican Council II, 52, 98–99, 296
Violence, 35, 49, 63–64, 66, 70, 75, 88–90, 147, 150, 152–156, 161, 173, 181, 186, 208, 237, 257–260

Watts, Fraser, 96, 237

www.ingramcontent.com/pod-product-compliance
Lightning Source LLC
Chambersburg PA
CBHW021959160426
43197CB00007B/184